Teaching Children with
Learning and Behavior Problems

Teaching Children with Learning and Behavior Problems

second edition

Donald D. Hammill   •   Nettie R. Bartel
AUSTIN, TEXAS   TEMPLE UNIVERSITY

ALLYN AND BACON, INC.
BOSTON · LONDON · SYDNEY

Library of Congress Cataloging in Publication Data:

Hammill, Donald D.
  Teaching children with learning and behavior problems.

  Bibliography: p.
  1. Problem children—Education.   I. Bartel,
Nettie R., joint author.   II. Title.   [DNLM:
1. Child behavior disorders.   2. Education, Special.
3. Learning disorders.   LC 4661 H224t]
LC4661.H285   371.9   74–10910

ISBN 0–205–06017–X (paperbound)
ISBN 0–205–06018–8 (hardbound)

Contents

Preface

All teachers, whether they teach regular or exceptional children, frequently encounter youngsters at the preschool or elementary levels who are not responsive to instruction or who are disruptive in class. These children may evidence problems in reading, arithmetic, or other school subjects, in social adjustment or motivation, or in basic readiness skills such as language and perception. Most of these pupils are probably the victims of poor teaching, insufficient readiness experience, and/or inadequate motivation. No children are immune to the debilitating effects of these three factors; bright or retarded, sound or crippled, stable or difficult children can be affected at one time or another.

Over the years the schools have evolved numerous alternatives for handling below-average learners. Psychological services, special education classes, and remedial programs have been provided. However, with this proliferation of specialized educational services, teachers have become increasingly dependent upon noninstructional personnel to assist them in teaching children with school-related problems. Thus educational assessment has become the responsibility of the school psychologist; slow learners are shunted off to the "retarded" class; poor readers are referred to the remedial reading specialist; speech articulation cases are sent to the speech therapist; and troublesome children eventually are placed in classes for the "emotionally disturbed." The great majority of difficult pupils, however, remain in the regular class under the supervision of the teacher, who is expected to meet their individual needs.

It is quite clear today that many children presently enrolled in special education classes will be integrated into regular classes within the next few years. The trend of isolating problem children, which has been so prevalent during the past few decades, is being reversed as educators recognize that special class placements bring few benefits to mildly handicapped children. Educators and others find the special-class solution philosophically objectionable in the 1970s. These children are not likely to be returned to the educational mainstream without some provisions made on their behalf. These provisions will likely take the forms of resource rooms, consultants, tutors, and itinerant programs.

Teachers are presently responsible for the achievement of many children who are difficult to teach. In the future they will probably be responsible for more, not fewer of these children. However, many teachers lack the necessary information that would enable them to cope with these children. Many elementary and early childhood education teacher-training programs fail to sufficiently familiarize their students with basic assessment procedures, diagnostic and prescriptive teacher techniques, and remedial materials and methods. Yet knowledge of a wide variety of remedial and developmental instructional approaches and activities is necessary to accommodate the disparate educational needs of nonachieving pupils.

With these ideas in mind, we have written this book for teachers. Our intention was (1) to succinctly review the roles and duties of teachers in the management of children with school-related problems; (2) to provide teachers with a series of discussions which focus upon these school-related difficulties (for example, reading, spelling, arithmetic, language, perception, handwriting, and behavior); (3) to provide in each of these discussions basic information regarding appropriate assessment techniques and instructional methods; and finally (4) to provide teachers with a list of specific materials, sources, and teacher evaluations of their merit.

It was not our intention to present and discuss all the possible evaluation devices and instructional methods that are available to teachers today. This would have been a monumental effort, and one which we had neither the energy nor the experience to undertake. Instead, we have shared with the reader those educational approaches and ideas with which we have had some direct personal experience. We have also included several new programs which appear to be promising, although we have not used them.

We are not necessarily endorsing the materials or methods described here; rather, we have tried to provide information on representative techniques to enable teachers to choose appropriate materials for their pupils. Teachers are urged to evaluate the effectiveness of their selections in their own classrooms, as research on the efficacy of most programs is nonexistent.

D. D. H.

N. R. B.

Meeting the Special Needs of Children

Donald D. Hammill • Nettie R. Bartel

Most experienced teachers are able to recognize children who seem bright but who fail to make expected gains in a particular skill after repeated exposure to training. If the skill is reading, the teacher may notice that the child reads silently with comprehension at the appropriate age level, but does poorly in reading aloud. Another child may become confused when directions are given orally, while he exhibits comparative superiority in reading and writing. A third youngster may have adequate listening and speech skills, but manifest problems when he engages in fine and gross visual–motor activities.

Some pupils evidence discrepancies of varying degrees between their estimated intellectual ability and their actual performance; others show marked divergence between the skills in which they excel and those in which they are inadequate or marginal; and others are merely slow in acquiring necessary school behaviors. To a large extent, these problems involve the understanding or the use of spoken or written language and are manifested in difficulty with reading, thinking, talking, listening, writing, spelling, or arithmetic. They may also extend to perceptual–motor disorganization and behavior problems. The problems range from mild to intense and are occasionally associated with blindness, deafness, psychosis, and/or severe mental defect. For the most part, however, the difficulties are found in mild to moderate degree in children who are otherwise "normal."

In the past, school personnel have been quick to confuse a child's school problem with a diagnostic label. Children who performed inadequately in the classroom tended to be labeled "retarded," "disturbed," "learning disabled," or "deprived," when their problems in fact were reading, writing, or mathematics. While it is recognized that children exist for whom these labels are probably appropriate, teachers should be cautioned that labels have been applied to children in a rather indiscriminate fashion and that an uncounted number of pupils have been misdiagnosed and misplaced. Such terms have little utility for the classroom teacher who must devise instructional techniques that are effective for individual children, especially children with mild to moderate problems.

In practice, an educational program must be prepared by a teacher in response to an individual child's educational needs and behaviors, not in response to a diagnostic label or definition the child may or may not satisfy. The nature of the program that is prepared will reflect in large part the teacher's (and the school's) philosophy and attitudes regarding a number of educational matters. We direct the remainder of this chapter to a delineation of these factors and to a discussion of the issues that relate to them.

We have found it helpful to organize our thinking about these educationally important factors in terms of an instructional model, which is presented in Figure 1–1. While in practice the elements of the model are quite interrelated, for discussion purposes we have separated them arbitrarily into three basic parts: (1) the assumptions that influence instruction, (2) the components that are involved in instruction, and (3) the cycle that is used to implement instructional programs.

ASSUMPTIONS INFLUENCING INSTRUCTION

The program that the teacher elects for each child will necessarily reflect her assumptions and beliefs about the purpose of education, the nature of learning, and the role of the child, the teacher, and even of society in the schooling process. These assumptions are rarely made explicit as far as teachers are concerned; yet they govern almost all the decisions that a teacher makes. These assumptions include the answers (implicit or explicit) to such questions as: What are the schools for? What is this particular child supposed to get out of school? How is this child supposed to fit into society ultimately? What is the nature of the world and of the role of the child and the teacher within it? Let us briefly turn to this last question first.

A perusal of the many approaches to educating the child with learning and behavioral problems presented in this book will quickly lead the reader to the conclusion that the last question posed in the previous paragraph has not been answered. The various approaches are quite obviously based on differing, even inconsistent, assumptions about the nature of the world, and of the child and the teacher within it. For example, among the approaches reviewed, one will see evidence of a world view that is highly mechanistic and predictable. For such a perspective, the machine is the most appropriate metaphor. Here the child is seen as a relatively passive component in a

Figure 1–1. *Instructional Sequence Model.* [Adapted from N. R. Bartel, D. N. Bryen, and H. W. Bartel, Approaches for alternative programming. In E. L. Meyen, G. A. Vergason, and R. J. Whelan (eds.), *Alternatives for Teaching Exceptional Children* (Denver, Colo.: Love, 1975).]

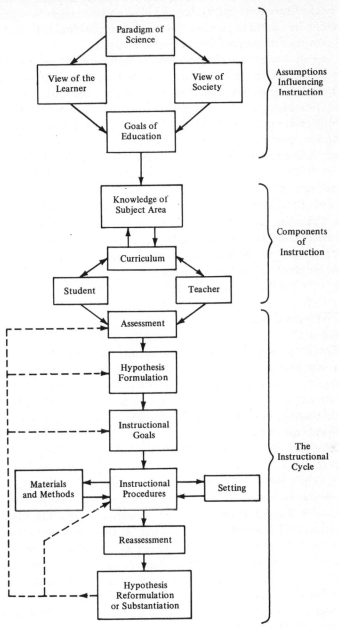

setting which is arranged so that events (instructional happenings) impinge on him in such a way that fully predictable outcomes will come about. The teacher serves as the master technician who engineers the learning environment in such a way that the most desirable results will occur. The act of learning then is something that happens to the child as a result of the application of predetermined forces. It follows that the ideal curriculum for such a viewpoint is "teacher-proof." That is, the program is packaged in such a way pedagogically and substantively that the teacher cannot interfere with the learning process. Similarly, the program is designed so that the probabilities are great that the child will emit the desired responses, and only the desired responses.

The contrasting position is that the essence of the world is not static and controllable, but on the contrary, is in continuous transition from one state to another by means of progressive differentiation. This leads one to think of students, even students with learning and behavioral problems, as active individuals who not only make predetermined "correct" responses, but who also interact with, and change, their learning environment. Thus, learning is not merely the quantitative accumulation of objective facts but is an active cognitive construction and transformation of reality.

That these issues have not been resolved in the education of children with learning problems is evident in the competing curricula that is present everywhere. On the one hand, one sees a widespread use of programmed materials, which promise precision, ease of measurement, and ready accountability. Clearly, the implicit assumption is that the curriculum developer has access to society's knowledge store and has arranged this knowledge in appropriate bits and sequences to which the learner needs only to be exposed following prescribed procedures. The behavior of both the teacher and the child are predictable. Seen from this orientation, the effective teacher is one who is able to move the child quickly through the prescribed components of the curriculum with minimal obtrusion stemming from teacher or child idiosyncrasies.

On the other hand, the aternative world view is noted for its open-endedness and unpredictability. Here curriculum designers and implementers frequently follow some variation of the Piagetian notion of assimilation and accommodation. That is, they acknowledge that the learner is shaped repeatedly by the realities of the world and that he returns the favor by continuously moving to reshape those world realities. To them, education is not getting children to make predictable responses, but is seeing to it that they are progressively being changed by and changing their environment. Clearly, these underlying assumptions have major implications for the choices that a teacher makes in instructional planning and implementation.

COMPONENTS OF INSTRUCTION

The choices that the teacher must make are further complicated by additional decisions that must be made concerning the components of instruction themselves. As can be seen in Figure 1–1, the teacher's job is to bring the child and the learning task into some kind of proximity with each other. However, even this seemingly simple responsibility turns out to be complicated.

It has long been taken for granted in educational circles that pupils and curricular materials cannot be randomly matched to each other. That is, if one is teaching social studies to a group of second graders, one cannot simply walk down to the school library and pull any text from the social studies section of the shelves and assume that it will meet the learner's needs. There is general agreement that the teacher should consider such factors as the age of the children, their overall developmental level, and their interests in selecting materials. Conversely, just because a teacher is fond of a particular reading series or spelling book does not mean that it can be used effectively with the group of children being instructed.

This brings us to a most interesting question and one that will surface repeatedly throughout this book. Just what are the child's characteristics that a teacher should take into account in selecting instructional materials? Conversely, just what are the curricular characteristics that a teacher must reckon with in determining their potential effectiveness with children? A perusal of the educational research literature quickly leads one to conclude that each of an almost infinite array of characteristics—ranging from whether the child went through a creeping stage or not to whether the child's father lives in the home—has been thought by someone to be a significant child variable that should be taken into account by the teacher. By no means does everyone agree on what to look for. Obviously, if the teacher is ever going to have any time to do any teaching, she must select from an almost endless range of pupil behaviors those that have sufficient implications for instruction to be worth noting and reporting.

A similar situation pertains as far as variability among curricular approaches is concerned. Thus, to use an example from beginning reading, serious claims have been made that picture words, words using a unique alphabet, or words printed in different colors, to name a few, should be considered by the classroom teacher for teaching reading to certain children. Is the teacher to assume that letter color aptitude, for example, is a significant child characteristic that should be measured and related to the use of color in the curriculum?

When one considers the possible permutations in the infinite range of potential child characteristics that could be measured and matched to an almost infinite range of curriculum characteristics, the problem becomes staggering indeed. This book represents an effort to reduce the teacher's task to more manageable proportions. First of all, we have tried to indicate the most promising aspects of the child's functioning to consider in instructional planning. We have drawn heavily for this from developmental psychology, particularly the work of Piaget, Bruner, and Gagné.

On the curriculum side, some observations are also in order. We note that curricula may be said to spread themselves on a continuum ranging from (1) the wholistic, open-ended approaches that rely heavily on the child's ability to learn inductively and incidentally to (2), at the other end of the continuum, approaches that are narrow in focus—specific and prescribed. We recognize that as one would expect from the brief discussion above on variations in world view, this question, being a derivative of the larger question noted above, is also unresolved.

It is probably fair to say that many of the newer approaches which have been found to be most successful with children who have learning and behavioral problems find themselves at the prescriptive end of the scale, and the reader will find such approaches heavily represented in the chapters of this book. One could probably make a case that the boys and girls for whom this book is written are precisely those for whom the more widely used unstructured wholistic educational approaches have been unsuccessful. That is, they are the youngsters who have failed to learn intuitively, inductively, and incidentally. The generalizations, concepts, cognitive structures, and facts that other children seem to pick up without any specific instruction have, for some reason, not been acquired by these children. It is for that reason that we have included throughout the book so many references to prescriptive teaching approaches. In doing so, however, we caution the reader that to date no instructional system or program has been devised which can anticipate all the learning possibilities that occur in the classroom. No program can preplan every possible utterance or action of the teacher or pupil.

Even while using one of the many structured approaches described in the subsequent pages, we urge teachers to look for those unique teaching/learning interactions which cannot be fully planned in advance. Furthermore, we caution teachers against making the presumption that the only significant learning is that which the teacher has decided on ahead of time and against the further presumption that everything that is important can be reduced to a paper-and-pencil test or lesson. The highly structured approaches have been at their best in teasing out the subelements of such complicated tasks as decoding words and sentences and arithmetic computation. They have been much less successful in helping teachers develop ways of teaching and measuring reading comprehension and arithmetic understanding. The problem that faces the classroom teacher, however, is that she cannot sit still, letting time go by, while the theoreticians and the experts decide whether, for example, the reading act is a unitary phenomenon or whether it can be validly broken into subelements.

The seeming inability of many children to master content that is presented in the traditional way has led to numerous efforts at presenting the content in a different format or medium or in the same content but in different-sized chunks. This breaking down of a body of content into its component parts or steps has become known as "task analysis," "learning hierarchies," or the "diagnostic approach." In each instance, the specific step presented to the child is based on what he has previously mastered and is "tailored" in such a way that the child has a high likelihood of mastering the task. Although the specifics of the procedures recommended by the various proponents of task analysis vary, several general commonalities characterize the approach. All advocates of task analysis recommend the differentiation of tasks into micro units or subordinate subskills or lower-level topics which the learner can master one step at a time. Only when the child has demonstrated success on one task is the next task in the hierarchy presented to him. The teacher does not have to undertake a complete task analysis for every bit of classroom instruction. Most curricular guides, if well organized and well differentiated, can be used as rough task analytic outlines. In fact, a good scope-and-sequence chart can serve many of the functions of a task analysis.

Having reviewed in some detail the assumptions influencing instruction and the components of instruction, we turn next to a consideration of the sequential nature of the instructional process itself.

THE INSTRUCTIONAL CYCLE
(THE INDIVIDUALIZED EDUCATIONAL PLAN)

The various stages of the instructional cycle coincide to a great extent with what has become known as the Individual Educational Plan (IEP). The IEP is a requirement of the new federal law, Education of All Handicapped Children Act (P.L. 94–142), which mandates that every handicapped child must have an individually planned and implemented educational program. While, legally speaking, the IEP is required only of handicapped children, we assert that it is equally appropriate for every child, handicapped or not, who has been singled out to receive special instruction or services. The elements of the IEP include: the assessment of the child, the formulation of long-range goals and short-term objectives, a description of the proposed educational intervention with specification of type and duration of each aspect of instruction, and an evaluation of the effort. These elements are closely related to the steps specified in the instructional cycle of our model (Figure 1–1). Because the IEP will be required of all handicapped children, no matter what their educational setting, and because the IEP concept is implicit in subsequent chapters of this book, we offer the following as a general overview, which is adaptable to each of the subsequent chapter contents.

Assessment

Before an instructional plan can be developed, the teacher must have a picture of the child's overall functioning and of his specific abilities and problem areas. In general, the teacher will find that norm-referenced standardized tests, readily available from commercial publishers, are quite helpful in establishing a summary statement of the child's status; for more specific, directly instructionally relevant information, more informal techniques will be most helpful. Because of the important differences in the functions of norm-referenced and informal assessment, we present separate descriptions in the following section.

Norm-referenced assessment. The norm-referenced evaluation, a part of the total diagnostic effort, (1) is characterized by the use of standardized tests, (2) often requires some degree of training for proper administration, and (3) may be undertaken in the classroom by the teacher or in settings other than the classroom by personnel employed for the expressed purpose of testing children. The information acquired is of a decidedly quantitative nature and tends to compare a specific child's performance with national or regional normative data. The results, therefore, are often reported in terms of quotients, scaled scores, grade equivalents, or percentiles. In general, such evaluation attempts to assess many areas of mental function, including intelligence, language development, academic achievement, speech development, perceptual–motor skills, and social and emotional development.

The number of standardized testing instruments which the teacher may select are almost limitless. A comprehensive resource is Buros (1972), *The Seventh Mental Measurements Yearbook,* in which most of the commonly used tests are reviewed. If the teacher needs a quick critical evaluation of an instrument, he should consult Hoepfner, Strickland, Stangel, Jansen, and Patalino (1970). In their book, *Elementary School Test Evaluations,* tests relating to language arts, social studies, social skills, perception, mathematics, intelligence, and perception, among other abilities, are rated "poor," "fair," or "good" on such factors as test validity, format, norm adequacy, and administration time.

Regrettably, not all of the available tests have been carefully constructed, so the teacher must choose among them with care. It is essential that the teacher have a clear idea of what she wants to measure and be able to specify it precisely. It is not enough to express an interest in obtaining a test of reading. Instead, the teacher must specify the kind of reading to be measured—silent, oral, word-call, word-recognition, or comprehension.

Once the type of reading skill to be tested has been decided upon, the teacher must review the tests that are applicable. The major concern now shifts to realiability. If the teacher intends to utilize the test information for diagnosing problems in individual pupils, the test employed must have a sufficiently high reliability coefficient; it must exceed .80 (Anastasi, 1968), although some authorities prefer .90 or better (Guilford, 1956a). Tests whose reliabilities do not reach this level are of dubious diagnostic value to the teacher. If, however, the teacher is involved in conducting research, where the performance of groups rather than of individuals is of primary interest, tests of lower reliability are suitable. For teachers who would like to know more about the concepts of reliability and validity and their role in the classroom, the book by Garrett (1965), *Testing for Teachers*, or any other introductory measurement textbook is recommended.

The advantages of norm-referenced tests lie in their objectivity. They are standardized; their reliabilities and validaties are known; and they have national reputations. Their grade-equivalent figure or percentile score provides a capsule description of the child's overall skills, providing useful information if the child has just been assigned to a new classroom, if the teacher is attempting to summarize his achievement or note his year-to-year overall growth, or if the teacher is trying to decide whether the child is in need of more intensive and detailed informal evaluation.

The disadvantages of most standardized tests should, however, be kept firmly in mind. The results of a sound-blending test may enable the teacher to identify particular children with problems in that area, but they do not indicate the specific blends in need of development. Problem children vary widely in day-to-day performance; tests administered on any given day can reflect pupil fatigue, attitude, or temperament, rather than specific skill in a subject.

Many tests and scales are described in this book which are not recommended for teacher use. Usually, the reason is the test's low reliability or lack of demonstrated school value. They are included because, whether good or inadequate, these tests are employed extensively in schools, and therefore discussion of them is necessary to point out their shortcomings and specify possible situations in which they might be used.

Informal assessment. The informal evaluation should be undertaken by an educationally oriented person, usually an educational diagnostician or a teacher. Informal evaluation is used to detect areas of weakness and strength; to verify, probe, or discard the conclusions and recommendations based on the formal evaluation; to deduce the child's particular instructional or behavioral needs; and to formulate a remedial program for him. This is accomplished through an ongoing process of teaching the child and analyzing his responses to various instructional tasks. For example, the teacher may wish to determine if the child "knows his colors." To our knowledge, there are no norm-referenced tests that yield this information; therefore, the teacher must discover the child's competency on his own by probing for answers to the following questions.

1. Can he match the basic colors (place red chips together, blue chips together, and so forth)? If not, what colors does he have difficulty in matching?
2. If asked to point to the red chip, then to the blue chip, and so forth, can he select the correct chip from among others of different colors?
3. If the teacher points to the red chip, then to the blue chip, and so forth and says "What color is this?" does the child answer correctly?

These three questions all relate to the general question of whether or not the child can recognize colors, but they also provide different kinds of information about the level of his knowledge, the particular colors he does not know, and how to begin to teach him. First he learns to discriminate among the colors, then he learns the labels (receptive language), and finally he uses the labels in speech (expressive language).

The testing process just described is called analytic, diagnostic, or prescriptive teaching. For the teacher, it is by far the most profitable assessment procedure, but it too has hazards that should be pointed out. First, the method is only as good as the competency of the teacher; second, the teacher's experience often is a poor substitute for normative data; and third, the reliability of the teacher as an observer is always unknown. However, the effectiveness of a teacher is invariably dependent on her capacity to provide individualization of instruction for her pupils (i.e., individual planning, not necessarily tutoring on a one-to-one basis). To individualize instruction the teacher must engage in diagnostic teaching.

Several educators specialize in this approach (Johnson and Myklebust, 1967; Johnson, 1967; R. M. Smith, 1968, 1969; Valett, 1967; Reger, Schroeder, and Uschold, 1968; Peters, 1965; Stephens, 1970). Their approaches include a careful diagnosis of the tasks that the child can and cannot accomplish, followed by a remediation that is tailored to the individual child's strengths and weaknesses. Constant monitoring of the child's progress is necessary to ensure that the remediation efforts remain relevant.

A carefully conceived description of how instructional decisions based on diagnostic information are actually made has recently been offered by Drew, Freston, and Logan (1972). Speaking from a perspective of what they call "a combined evaluative approach," Drew et al. portray the teacher's role as heavily oriented toward criterion-referenced evaluation. Criterion-referenced evaluation implies that the teacher will assess a youngster's skills primarily in terms of the actual operations the child can or cannot perform, rather than in terms of how he stands relative to some norm or relative standard (such as that utilized in formal assessment). For example, the child is described as having mastered the sounds of all the vowels and consonants, including blends, except for "str," "thr," and "scr," instead of designating him as one who reads orally at a grade equivalent of 2.2. The most enthusiastic supporters of criterion-referenced evaluation are teachers; this is not surprising in view of the fact that this approach yields information that is very directly usable by the teacher in planning remediation activities. Knowing that a child has not yet mastered the blends "str," "thr," and "scr" is more helpful for making day-to-day instructional decisions than knowing that he reads at a grade equivalent of 2.2.

Setting Long-Range Goals and Short-Term Objectives

Once the teacher has completed the analysis of a child's performance and has identified those areas of his functioning that need strengthening, goals and objectives for that child can be developed. As noted previously, the specific goals that are established will be heavily affected by the teacher's assumptions concerning the nature of the child and by her beliefs about the overall goals of education. Thus, the teacher who states in the IEP that a long-range goal is for the child to become familiar with certain classic English poems is manifesting a belief that the job of the schools is to transmit culture. Similarly, the teacher who states that a long-range goal is for the child to attain a fifth-grade reading comprehension level is expressing her belief that a purpose of education is to help the child develop functional adult competencies. A third type of goal might be even more open-ended, in that the child might be expected to become a more creative citizen or in some way to positively affect his environment.

Short-range objectives are also required in the IEP and should be derivatives of the long-range goals. Objectives serve an important communication function in that, if well expressed, they convey a picture of the behaviors the child will perform after instruction is completed. Several additional criteria characterize well-written objectives. For example, the desired behavior should be stated in terms that are objective and measurable; furthermore, the conditions under which the student is supposed to perform should be described. Additional information about objectives that relate to the various areas of pupil performance are addressed in the chapters that follow.

Instructional Materials, Procedures, and Settings

Once the objectives have been specified, the teacher is faced with the task of selecting appropriate instructional materials and methods. In addition, an educational setting that enhances the child's likelihood of meeting the objectives must be selected. These two considerations are addressed next.

Materials and procedures. The selection and implementation of the most effective materials for a given child is based directly on the observed abilities and problems that the child manifests. For example, in the arithmetic area, a child's initial profile might appear as show in Figure 1–2. The child's profile in this graph would be interpreted to indicate that the child is having a great deal of difficulty in multiplication (he has not yet been exposed to division), and a further weakness is apparent in his understanding of place value.

The next task for the teacher is to further explore the child's trouble in multiplication and place value. To consider the multiplication example only, the teacher might probe as reflected in Figure 1–3.

In the second level of this graph, immediately below the child's characteristics, the profile of a multiplication program is sketched that should be maximally effective with the child. Note, for example, that the program is very strong in presenting multiplication as an array of rows and columns (precisely where the child is weakest), pays little attention to multiplication as repeated addition (which the child has already mastered), and emphasizes the role of zero and multiplying by multiples of 10 (both areas where the child is very weak).

Figure 1–2. *Graph of Arithmetic Ability*

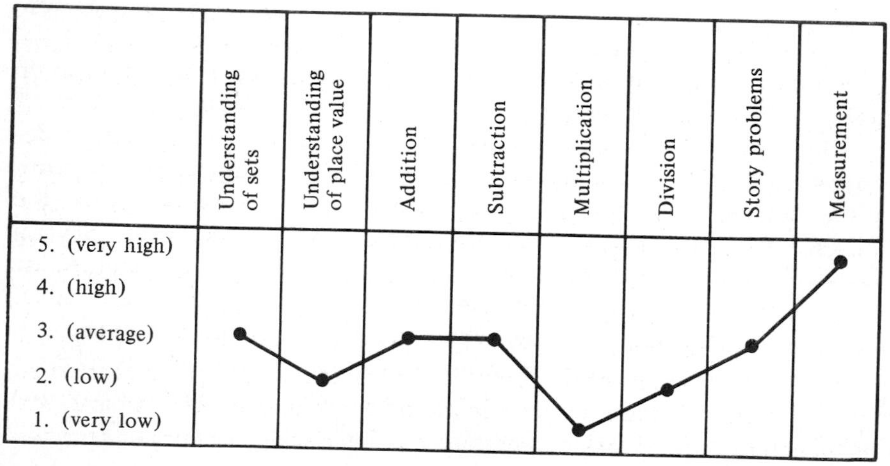

Figure 1–3. *Graph of Multiplication Ability*

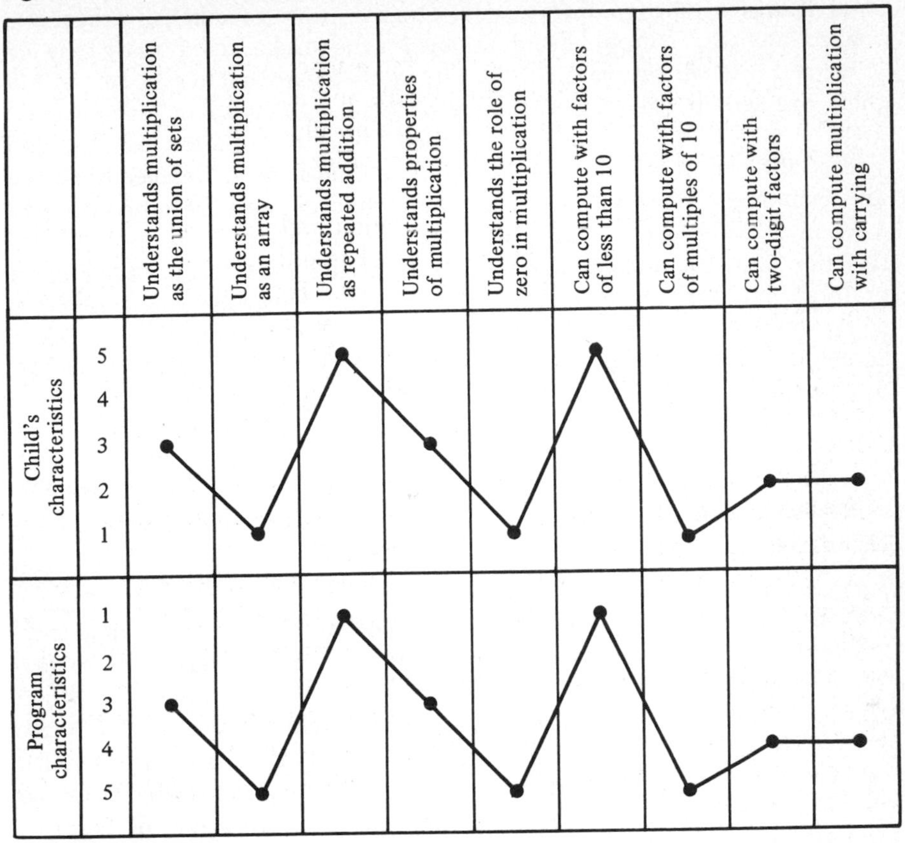

		Understands multiplication as the union of sets	Understands multiplication as an array	Understands multiplication as repeated addition	Understands properties of multiplication	Understands the role of zero in multiplication	Can compute with factors of less than 10	Can compute with factors of multiples of 10	Can compute with two-digit factors	Can compute multiplication with carrying
Child's characteristics	5 4 3 2 1	3	1	5	3	1	5	1	2	2
Program characteristics	1 2 3 4 5	3	5	1	3	5	1	5	4	4

It is not expected that the teacher will find ready-made programs for every profile of abilities and disabilities that might be discovered in her classroom. The teacher will have to adapt, modify, and improvise. Sometimes the two profiles—child characteristics and program characteristics—will not fit well. In that case, it is still important for the teacher to sketch the interface, so that she will be cognizant of potential problems and be able to anticipate program failures. There will be cases in which the teacher is at a loss as to how to plan a program that fits a particular child's needs. In those cases, she should plot the child's profile in the area of difficulty and consult with the nearest regional Instructional Materials Center and possibly acquire the appropriate materials there. A perusal of the many approaches suggested in the subsequent chapters of this book for arithmetic, reading, language, spelling, and writing should also provide ideas for the teacher who is faced with the difficult but crucial task of matching child variables to program variables.

It is not suggested that every time a teacher wants to make an instructional decision, she go through the lengthy, time-consuming procedures spelled out here. It would be impossible for the teacher to have any time left to teach if that were the case. However, we are aware that in every classroom there are certain children who have particular difficulty in given subject areas. With these children, previous efforts at remediation usually have yielded little improvement. Ultimately, the time spent in detailed diagnosis and planning is time well spent for these children, and the pinpointing of areas of difficulty is well worth the extra effort involved. To some extent the selection of instructional materials reflects an individual teacher's subjective preferences in style, format, and response mode. However, an awareness of certain guidelines can facilitate intelligent curricular decision making. These guidelines have to do with three basic aspects involving material selection: design, method, and practicality.

Design. Curriculum design is concerned with the overall organization of the school experiences of a child. Specific questions that might be posed as questions of design are:

1. Is the material organized into subject areas such as reading, arithmetic, and social studies, or is it organized in terms of "experiences" or "units" that cut across traditional subjects? Which approach makes the most sense for the child under consideration?

2. If organized in terms of subject areas, is the material ordered in heirarchical, sequential steps? Are the sequences related to known facts in child development (e.g., the Piagetian stages of cognitive development)? Is the order of sequences logically related to such order as exists within the subject area itself—that is, in arithmetic, multiplication should be taught before division because multiplication skills are required in the operations of division? Ideally, instructional materials should incorporate both what is known about child development and what is known about the structure of the discipline itself.

3. What criterion is required for the student to proceed from one step to the next? Is mastery of a preceding task a prerequisite to going on to a subsequent task? Is some kind of prerequisite external "readiness scores" required before entry into the program or before going on to new units? If so, do these readiness scores bear a manifest relationship to the material they are supposed to make the child ready for? In general, the closer the readiness task is to the actual required skill, the more effective its prediction. For example, ability to walk a balance beam has much less "face validity"

as a reading readiness predictor than, say, being able to distinguish "d" from "b."

4. A further consideration underlying the design of materials has to do with its rationale. Is there implicit or explicit evidence that sound teaching and/or learning principles were involved? For example, have the authors and producers accounted for motivational factors? Is there any utilization of reinforcement (tangible rewards, social approval, or immediate feedback to the child)? Are basic skills incorporated as a basis for further learning? Is there any research evidence on soundness of the rationale (i.e., are there basic or applied studies supporting the approach)?

A well-designed program has clearly defined objectives for each program component. In any given lesson, the teacher should be able to state unequivocally what the purpose of the lesson is. How clear are the objectives for the materials under consideration? Are the objectives precise enough for the teacher to ascertain whether they have been reached or not? Are the objectives appropriate for the age and grade of the child? Are the objectives compatible with the learning experiences of the child in other subject areas (e.g., do they permit coordination between social studies and reading)?

Method. Questions of method are variations of the question, what do the teacher and the pupils have to do to successfully use the materials? One set of these questions concerns the "who" of the instructional process. Can the children be instructed as one large group? If not, are provisions made for occupying the other members of the class productively? Can the material be adapted for either a tutoring, small-group, or large-group situation? Must the teacher be actively involved in all phases of the instruction, or can the youngsters work on their own some or all of the time? To use the materials, what does the teacher have to do or say? Are the instructions too complicated? Is it physically possible for the teacher to do what is required (e.g., position figures on the flannelboard while reading verbatim instructions, and at the same time walk up and down the aisles to check each child's response)? Is there a balance between teacher-doing and pupil-doing, and between teacher-talk and pupil-talk? Are a variety of responses elicited from the pupils (e.g., oral and written responses, manipulation, painting, demonstrating)? Are several sensory modalities, either simply or in combination, involved? Is there undue penalty for a child who is deficient in one response (e.g., the child who cannot use his hands or has difficulty in oral expression)? Are the required responses related to the desired learning? For example, if the desired outcome is silent reading comprehension, is the child required to read silently and tested on his mastery, or is he merely required to "word-call" orally?

Is the material sufficiently flexible to make possible adaptations that facilitate learning? For example, can the child who has a visual problem still learn through auditory or tactile means? Is there a way that children can serve as each other's tutors, to relieve pressure on the teacher? Can the material readily be broken into smaller steps, or supplemented with other materials, for those children who have difficulty?

Can the material be individualized, both in terms of rate of presentation and in terms of intensity? That is, can the rapid learner move through the material quickly, and the slow learner more deliberately? Are there provisions for the child who is making virtually no incorrect responses to skip unnecessary examples or pages? Conversely, does the material incorporate an opportunity for the child who is making many errors to relearn the material, perhaps through a different format or presentation?

What flexibility is present in the materials with respect to switching to another approach if that should appear desirable? Some programs are so unique that switching to another is impractical because of the material's limited ability to generalize to other areas. For example, if a teacher decided to use a reading program with a unique orthography, he must be aware of the fact that this is a long-term decision, and difficult to change. One cannot switch orthographies every few months without seriously hampering a child's growth in reading. Similarly, certain programmed programs in reading and arithmetic are so unique that there are really no alternatives to which the child may reasonably be switched if it becomes necessary to do so for reasons of program failure or because of a move on the part of the child.

Practicality. Finally, there are some practical considerations that need to be taken into account in instructional material selection. First, how attractive is the material? Would a youngster want to use it because of its appeal, effective use of color, format, motivational devices, attractive visual arrangement, uniqueness, or variation in presentation made? Are the materials practical and durable? Is the price reasonable? Are there any hazardous elements present? Can the material be used independently, or does it require close supervision? Is the quality of drawings or photographs adequate? Can the materials be brought out, used, and reassembled for storage in a reasonable length of time? Are the materials reusable, or must new kits, sets, or workbooks be purchased for each additional student? Is use of the materials or the grading of the students' responses unnecessarily boring or laborious for the teacher?

The teacher will quickly find that no one program, no matter how excellent, will work with all children, and some programs will not work with any children. For this reason, a teacher needs to have access to many approaches, involving a variety of different formats, strategies, and modalities. Based on her knowledge of the needs of a particular child, the teacher is then able to make intelligent decisions regarding the how, what, and when of instruction. This knowledge is particularly imperative, since few companies see any need or obligation to demonstrate that their products do, in fact, work, before offering them to the public. The materials are beautifully packaged, widely advertised, and sold in staggeringly large quantities, usually long before there is evidence to support their value. Efficacy research follows the availability of commercial materials by 3 to 5 years, if ever. Therefore, teachers almost always are required to use unvalidated programs. There exists no "consumer's report" for teachers, no book that can be consulted to point out shortcomings, limitations, or strengths of the various materials. It is strictly a "buyer, beware" market.

However, many of the teaching methods commonly used in the schools have existed for years and a body of research has accumulated about many of them. The teacher, therefore, is well advised to undertake a library investigation of the particular method he wants to implement to see what success others have had with the program. *Educational Index, Dissertation Abstracts, Mental Retardation Abstracts,* and *Special Education Abstracts* are profitable initial sources of information. Many companies have assembled data on their programs and will provide it upon request; of course, do not expect to find anything critical from this source.

Although research on a particular method may not exist, use of that method should not necessarily be avoided. The teacher could use it on an experimental basis. For example, the teacher can test pupils in arithmetic, implement the unvalidated program for several months, and then retest the pupils to see if the program was indeed profitable. If the pupil performance could be compared to that of a control group, the results of the study would be made considerably more creditable.

Because of our recognition of the importance of this topic to good educational practice, we have devoted a major part of each of the following chapters to descriptions of widely used programs, methods, and materials. Where information is available regarding the effectiveness of the approaches that are described, it too is presented. In addition, an entire chapter dealing specifically with selecting and analyzing methods has been included in the book.

The educational setting. It should be stressed again that this book does not purport to deal with the management difficulties of profoundly retarded, psychotic, autistic, aphasic, dyslexic, or severely sensory-impaired children, although the techniques presented can be adapted to ameliorate their school-related problems. For these children, the instructional setting is likely to continue to be the special class or large or small residential facility. Actually, the number of children for whom such placements are appropriate is quite small. The overwhelming majority of children who evidence problems are in need of remedial education designed to enable them to function in the regular class as soon as possible. There are several models that can be employed in the schools to provide pupils with needed services.

The regular classroom. Most children who develop difficulties in school can be successfully managed by their regular teacher; their problems tend to be of a mild and easily corrected variety. The regular classroom is by far the most desirable setting for children to receive remedial help, and the classroom teacher is usually the best person to direct the remedial lessons. In this way, the child remains with his peers and does not have to suffer the indignity of leaving the room to obtain corrective help elsewhere. However, often the teacher–pupil ratio is too high, the teacher lacks the experience, or the pupil's problem is too obdurate to be amelioriated in the regular classroom setting. Alternatives must then be sought.

The special class. The most frequently employed alternative for dealing with children with behavioral and/or educational problems has been the self-contained special class. Many arguments set forth in defense of this placement are apparently reasonable. It is often argued that children placed in these classes receive the benefits of specially trained teachers, special materials and methods, smaller classes, and individualized instruction. In fact, this is rarely the case. Until only recently, untrained teachers were the rule rather than the exception; although the class enrollments were smaller than regular classes, there did not seem to be any more individualization of instruction; and the teachers seemed to use much the same approach toward classroom management and selection of materials that was used in the regular class.

Research has accumulated which indicates that children placed in special classes achieve in schoolwork no better than, and often not as well as, similar children left in the regular class. Findings regarding the effects of such placements on self-concept and adjustment are equivocal at the present time.

Special classes exist in assorted types and are restricted to children diagnosed as having a specific condition, such as mental retardation, emotional disturbance, or learning disability. For the most part, children placed in these settings are more similar to typical children than they are different from them. Although they may be poor readers or difficult to cope with, there is little justification for subjecting them to such a drastic measure as isolation from the regular class.

Because of the added stigma that inherently goes with placement in a self-contained class, the segregation of the child from his age-mates, and the doubtful benefits to be derived, this alternative should be used with considerable caution and viewed as a last resort. For readers who are interested in additional references concerning the use of the special class for handling children with learning or behavior problems, the work of Dunn (1968), Christopolos and Renz (1969), Lilly (1970), and Iano (1972) is strongly recommended.

The special school. The special school for children with various learning problems is the natural extension of the self-contained class. Here the child is not only segregated from his peers but removed from the regular school premises completely. He may attend the special school and return home after classes or he may be in residence at the school. The advantage of such a placement is the child's immersion in a total remedial program. In addition to the expense involved, the pro and con arguments are basically the same as those advanced regarding the special class. This placement should be viewed as a last possible alternative for children who cannot be accommodated to any other setting.

The resource room. The resource room is a promising alternative to self-contained facilities. This model permits the pupil to receive instruction individually or in groups in a special room outfitted for that purpose. The emphasis is on teaching specific skills that the pupil needs. At the end of his lesson, he returns to the regular classroom and continues his education there. In this way, he is based in the regular class with his age-mates and leaves only for periods of time during the school day. There are several variations of the resource room model that deserve some mention.

1. *The categorical resource room.* These rooms are operated in the same way as the resource rooms; however, to qualify for placement the pupil must satisfy a designated special education category or definition, such as retarded, disturbed, or learning disabled. Readers who are interested in implementing this variation of the resource room model are referred to the work of Glavin, Quay, Annesley, and Werry (1971), who successfully used the resource rooms with emotionally disturbed children; Sabatino (1971) with learning disabled children; and Barksdale and Atkinson (1971) with mentally retarded children.

2. *The noncategorical resource room.* This variation is highly recommended. Children who are referred to the resource room are not labeled by category, and programs are designed for them on a basis of instructional, emotional, and behavioral need. Even "gifted" youngsters can be accommodated. In addition to the fact that the children involved remain in the regular classroom for most of the day, there are distinct advantages to this alternative. They include: (a) handicapped children do not have to be bused to the nearest school where there is an appropriate categorical class;

(b) the number of children who can be seen daily is at least two-and-a-half times the number seen in the self-contained class; (c) the room serves all children in the school and is not limited to special-education-type children; and (d) the close communication between resource room and regular teacher allows for cooperative handling of the child and his problem. Readers interested in the dynamics of setting up a noncategorical resource room are referred to *The Resource Room: Rationale and Implementation* (Hammill and Wiederholt, 1972a).

3. *The itinerant program.* The problems handled by this program may be either disability based or noncategorical. The program is constructed around mobile resource rooms and the teacher is not "housed" in any one school. Its advantage lies in its mobility, but it has serious limitations. They include: (a) since the teacher is not attached to a particular school, it is difficult for her to become fully accepted in any of the schools in which she operates; (b) much teacher time is spent in transit; and (c) transportation of materials is a chronic problem.

Readers who desire a rather comprehensive account of the operation of resource programs are referred to *The Resource Teacher: A Guide to Effective Practices* by Wiederholt, Hammill, and Brown (1978). In this volume, the authors have described in detail the types of resource programs that can be implemented in the schools; have defined the role of the resource teacher relative to assessment, instruction, and consultation; and have outlined the procedures to be followed in setting up a program. In addition, they have reviewed the kinds of activities in which the teacher should engage to help children improve in reading, math, spoken language, spelling, handwriting, written expression, and behavior.

Reassessment and Hypothesis Reformulation

In the instruction model (Figure 1–1), the last stage pertains to the evaluation of pupil progress and its use in reformulating educational goals and objectives and/or in revising instructional procedures. This activity is also an important part of the IEP. The program evaluation should be continuous (i.e., occurring periodically throughout the year), and the findings should be incorporated immediately into instructional action by accelerating, attenuating, modifying, or even discontinuing the child's program. It should be clear to teachers and parents alike that maximum accountability can be derived only from an evaluation plan that provides ongoing feedback. It is not in the interests of the child to be evaluated only at the end of the year, when it is too late to do anything about it if objectives have not been met.

Naturally, the evaluation plan should be developed in such a way that it permits the answering of the question: Were the long-term goals and short-term objectives for this child actually achieved? Because at the present time there exists no comprehensive test package that adequately tests children in all areas of functioning, the plan will have to have several dimensions, including the use of both norm-referenced and informal assessment techniques. Also, direct observation of the child's performance may be used. If the objectives are precisely stated in such terms as "The child will be able to correctly read aloud the ten first words of the Dolch Sight List with 90 percent accuracy in 3 minutes," the objective itself becomes the evaluation plan. There should be little question as to whether or not the child has achieved this particular objective; it can be easily established by direct observation.

It should be clear that the various elements of our instructional model, and of the IEP as well, are interrelated intimately and dependent on each other for consistency and for effectiveness. This is the case because each aspect of the teaching–learning process directly affects, and is affected by, every other aspect. The cyclical, interrelated nature of the elements is implicit in the model.

Teaching Children with Reading Problems

2

John E. Boyd • Nettie R. Bartel

In every typical class in every typical school there are a few atypical children who experience difficulty in learning to read and thereby consume a disproportionate amount of the teacher's time and effort. The teacher may overlook forgetfulness, general awkwardness, shyness, and even a short attention span; but poor reading cannot be ignored. This is because some reading skill is involved in virtually every school subject. If the child cannot read adequately, his entire school experience will suffer. This concern about reading is shared by educators, by parents, and by the public in general.

Even though a tremendous amount of effort has been directed toward developing better assessment and remediation techniques in reading, and toward increasing the number of psychologists, guidance counselors, and reading specialists in the schools, as yet there are not enough specialists. Therefore, the teacher must deal on a daily basis with children who have reading problems, while satisfying the needs of the rest of the students in the class. It is to help her in this effort that the four sections of this chapter were prepared. The first section deals with the nature of reading; some of the common reading problems that are found in the classroom are described in the second part. The third section presents a variety of assessment strategies that can be used to determine the appropriate instructional level of individuals, as well as specific areas of weakness in reading. The final section explains various approaches to the teaching of reading, describes some materials that can be used in the ongoing reading program, and offers specific examples of methods to overcome reading weaknesses.

The information presented in this chapter should be regarded as a starting point. The teacher should take this initial information and, using her own experiences, resources, and knowledge, continue to develop and refine materials that will best suit her own teaching situation. The teacher must be aware that unanticipated needs will arise that must be met. By careful planning and organization, the teacher can build a file of materials, both commercial and teacher-made, that will be readily available for use when the need arises. Just as children grow in their development of reading skill, teachers must grow in their acquisition of the skills in teaching reading and in their knowledge of the subject.

THE NATURE OF READING

The individual who would attempt to improve reading skills in children must first understand what reading is. Such an understanding is not easily acquired, for "the process of learning to read is not very well understood. Researchers do not yet know enough about the developed skills of the fluent reader, the end product of the instructional process, let alone the process of acquiring these skills" (F. Smith, 1971, p. vii). Dechant (1964) stated that "there are as many definitions or descriptions of reading as there are reading experts" (p. 15). To some authors reading is responding orally to printed symbols (i.e., word calling). This definition does not acknowledge that obtaining meaning is part of the reading process. Other definitions include both the ability to correctly pronounce words and to gain the meaning that is being conveyed. For the purpose of this chapter, reading is regarded as the meaningful interpretation of printed symbols in light of the reader's own background of experience and, as such, is regarded as an ability to attach meanings to words, phrases, sentences, and longer selections.

Y. M. Goodman (1970) has described reading as a "psycholinguistic guessing game." What Goodman has in mind is that in the reading act, the reader makes successive sets of hypotheses and that he uses semantic, syntactic, and graphic cues to confirm or disconfirm these hypotheses or guesses. For example, let us suppose that a second grader, Tommy, is confronted with the following paragraph to read:

Little Fox and His Friends

Once there was a little fox who didn't like the dark. One morning, before the sun came up, Little Fox woke up all alone. His mother had gone hunting in the forest.

Simply by reading, or by being told what the story is about, the child can develop some expectancies about the content. He can, for example, expect to read about other animals. He can expect that the story will have words that refer to life in the forest. Particularly, if the teacher introduces the story carefully, if a Directed Reading Activity format (to be discussed later in the chapter) is used, the child will have some questions, expectancies, or hypotheses cued for him.

However, the child has other information available to him. By second grade, he has had a lot of experience with his language (presumably English). This experience can help him as he begins to read the paragraph. If he has been exposed to stories such as fairy tales, he will know that the word right after the first word "Once" will probably be "upon" (for "Once upon a time . . .") or "there" (for "Once there was . . ."). Now, although the word "there" in isolation is frequently difficult for second-graders, the cognitively and linguistically active child can be enormously helped in the reading task by, in this case, his prior knowledge of the way stories often begin and by his knowledge of the syntax of the English language.

The next word that may give the child difficulty is "didn't." The main cues that the child can use here are syntactic and visual. By the second grade, the child's knowledge of English is such that he knows when he hears a sentence such as "Once there was a fox who . . ." that the next word will tell something about what the fox did or did not do. This knowledge, coupled with the child's understanding of the acoustic sound of /d/, the initial letter, may provide enough information for him to "guess" or "hypothesize" the correct word. If he guesses correctly, without too long a hesitation to break his train of thought, the next word, "like," will probably be easy for him. If he had to pause to ponder over "didn't," "like" will be more difficult, because he does not have the string of words "Once there was a little fox who didn't . . ." to help him figure out "like." We could continue our hypothetical analysis, showing how a wrong guess slows the child down and interferes with the cues of meaning and syntax.

According to Goodman, the best readers are those who can "guess" correctly most of the time, with a minimum use of cues. F. Smith (1971) has shown the significance of interaction and balance among the various types of cues—context, syntax, and visual. Smith makes the point that there are a very large number of cues potentially available to the reader—if he had to use all of them, the reading act would be very slow indeed. However, since the cues are so redundant, the good reader selects and uses only a few. The effective use of context cues or of syntactic cues takes some of the interpretative load off the graphic cues so that even if the beginning reader is not completely sure of all the distinctive features of a given letter or word, he needs only a little extra help to figure out the word. If he is uncertain, however, in each of the areas that could potentially help him—context or semantics, syntax, and graphic—he will slow down in his reading; and because of normal memory limitations, semantic and syntactic cues will fade rapidly. While it is true that semantic and syntactic information can help with the visual, it is also true that unless some visual cues are interpretable by the child, the child quickly loses the semantic and syntactical help that he had going for himself.

It does not take a great deal of imagination to see the potential reading problems that would be encountered by a child who was unfamiliar with the distinguishing features of the letters of the alphabet and who also was unsure of the content which he was supposed to read. When this situation is compounded with unfamiliarity with Standard English syntax, as is the case with many boys and girls growing up in the inner cities of our nation, it is not difficult to see why so many children have reading problems. Such children are indeed triply handicapped, in that they cannot "trade" one type of information—semantic, syntactic, or graphic—for another the way proficient readers do. It is ironic, indeed, that the process that will ultimately make it possible for the child to gain a knowledge of the world—reading—is in its initial stages itself heavily dependent on such knowledge.

Teachers who are not sure about the need to provide additional informational "prompting" for beginning readers are urged to consider their own reading behavior when confronted with reading material that is unfamiliar and perhaps highly technical. In such a situation, all of us slow down in rate; we go back over the material; we skip over words, hoping we can make some sense out of them on the basis of the rest of the passage. One way or the other we try to narrow down what the author is saying, to answer the questions in our minds. As Smith (1971) put it: "All information acquisition in reading, from the identification of individual letters or words to the comprehension of entire passages, can be regarded as the reduction of uncertainty" (p. 12).

Given that the child uses any information available to him to help him develop hypotheses about his reading, how does he, in fact, attempt to identify unknown words for which he has no syntactic or semantic cues? No one knows for sure what happens in the mind of a child as he attempts to identify such a word. However, a number of explanations have been proposed. The most widely known of these are those developed by Gibson (1965, 1970), Venezky and Calfee (1970), and F. Smith (1971). All these persons suggest that the child does not apply a set of decoding rules to identify unknown words. For anything except the shortest words, such a procedure would be too time-consuming for an efficient reader. Rather, they suggest that readers mediate the identification of unfamiliar words by comparing the unknown word to known words or word parts. They do not agree on the form that such words or word parts (stored in the memory) take. There is general agreement that when a child is confronted with a new word, he searches through his memory store and compares the unknown to the known. The unknown word that cannot be recognized as a whole is segmented in some way. These word segments, or word wholes, are compared to the reader's memory of known words or word segments. Next, a recombining process takes place, resulting in a word for which the reader has an acoustic or semantic category. Some kind of transfer takes place in comparing the unknown to the known.

Gibson and Smith also believe that readers generate their own rules by comparing and contrasting features, and receiving feedback as to the correctness of the responses. This feedback may be generated by the self, as in the case in which a reader "tries out" a word to see if it fits into an acoustic or semantic category (Cunningham, 1975–1976). Samuels, Begy, and Chen (1975–1976) found that good readers are better able to generate a target word given context and fragments, such as the first letter of the target word. They also found that readers who read at, rather than below, grade level were able to recognize words more quickly, even though all subjects had been pretested, and all could read all the words.

These findings led Samuels et al. to interpret their results as supportive of a "hypothesis/test" theory of word identification. Similar to F. Smith (1971), Samuels et al.'s model reflects a cognitive view of word processing which holds that the identification of words is an active, constructive act in which the output is greater than, and different from, the input. That is, the reader does not merely "transcribe" the written word into spoken form, but he brings something quite apart from the printed page to the word identification act. That "something" is his own knowledge, ideas, experiences, and hypotheses. A good reader uses semantic, syntactic, and visual cues to recognize words and sentences and to get the "sense" of the passage. Word identification is constructive and integrative, with the reader melding together bits of visual, syntactic, and context information to derive meaning. In the fluent reader, the process is enormously efficient; the reader uses just enough visual cues to "fill in," that is, to confirm or disconfirm the ideas that he is developing about the passage.

There are today virtually no reading authorities who seriously contend that the reading act is passive, rather than active (Williams, 1973). There is apparent consistency in the position that reading is a complex cognitive skill, the goal of which is obtaining information. However, if one examines textbooks on the teaching of reading, one finds that there is much more space devoted to topics such as "phoneme–grapheme correspondence" than to consideration of the teaching of complex information processing and comprehension skills. The methodology of teaching reading has simply not kept up with the changing viewpoint concerning the cognitive, constructive aspects of the reading act. This chapter is evidence of that very point. Currently, there are many more ways available to the teacher who wishes to assess a child's word attack skills than there are to the teacher who is interested in measuring a child's comprehension skills in anything other than the grossest fashion. The typical scope-and-sequence chart accompanying many reading series invariably shows much greater differentiation of the "decoding" skills as opposed to the "understanding" skills. The scope-and-sequence chart shown as Table 2–2 (p. 43), which is adapted from a well-known text on reading and learning disabilities (Kaluger and Kolson, 1969), exemplifies this point very well. While there are several taxonomies of comprehension skills available (an excellent one is presented in the next section), there are few published accounts on how to translate these aspects of comprehension into teaching procedures.

The simple view of the reading process that was fashionable in some circles in the 1960s and which underlies a number of reading programs has a good deal of initial appeal. Teaching only observable, easily measured reading skills makes it easy to specify precisely what the child can and cannot do. Objectives can be clearly stated, and it can be determined whether they have or have not been met. Such a clearly defined, observable, and easily measured set of skills is clearly appealing to the teacher of a child who has a reading problem. Unfortunately, there is much more to the reading act than learning to say "cat" when presented with the letters c-a-t. Accordingly, it is to comprehension that we turn next.

In recent years, publishers have literally flooded the market with supplementary practice books, audiovisual materials, games, and other materials which are supposed to improve a child's reading ability. Many (some?) of these are no doubt useful; others are of dubious value; many "innovative" programs are actually old techniques in new packages. For the most part, these published materials emphasize word recognition and word-call skills; and as a result, the reading instruction in too many schools is devoted almost totally to phonics-type exercises with a few literal comprehension questions "thrown in for good measure." This is indeed unfortunate, for reading is much more than just word calling. As early as 1917, Thorndike observed that "reading is thinking." As such, the ability to comprehend printed matter is of primary importance in the reading act. However, comprehension cannot be regarded as a single, unitary skill. There are at least three broad areas of comprehension:

1. Literal—understanding the primary, direct (i.e., literal) meaning of words, sentences, or passages.
2. Inferential—understanding the deeper meanings that are not literally stated in the passage.
3. Critical—passing judgment on the quality, worth, accuracy, and truth of the passage.

Barrett has differentiated comprehension skills even further in *Taxonomy of Cognitive and Affective Dimensions of Reading Comprehension* (see Clymer, 1968). The basic, paraphrased outline of the taxonomy follows.

1.0. *Literal comprehension.* Literal comprehension focuses on ideas and information that are *explicitly* stated in the selection.

    1.1. *Recognition* requires the student to locate or identify ideas or information explicitly stated in the reading selection.

        1.11. Recognition of details

        1.12. Recognition of main ideas

        1.13. Recognition of a sequence

        1.14. Recognition of comparisons

        1.15. Recognition of cause-and-effect relationship

        1.16. Recognition of character traits

    1.2. *Recall of details.* Recall requires the student to produce from memory ideas and information explictly stated in the reading selection.

        1.21. Recall of details

        1.22. Recall of main ideas

        1.23. Recall of a sequence

        1.24. Recall of comparisons

        1.25. Recall of cause-and-effect relationship

        1.26. Recall of character traits

2.0. *Reorganization.* Reorganization requires the student to analyze, synthesize, and/or organize ideas or information explicitly stated in the selection.

    2.1. Classifying

    2.2. Outlining

    2.3. Summarizing

    2.4. Synthesizing

3.0. *Inferential comprehension.* Inferential comprehension is demonstrated by the student when he uses the ideas and information explicitly stated in the selection, his intuition, and his personal experiences as a basis for conjectures and hypotheses.

    3.1. Inferring supporting details

    3.2. Inferring main ideas

    3.3. Inferring sequence

    3.4. Inferring comparisons

    3.5. Inferring cause-and-effect relationships

    3.6. Inferring character traits

    3.7. Predicting outcomes

    3.8. Interpreting figurative language

4.0. *Evaluation.* The purposes for reading and teacher's questions, in this instance, require responses by the student which indicate that he has made an evaluative judgment by comparing ideas presented in the selection with external criteria provided by the teacher or other sources or with internal criteria provided by the student himself.

    4.1.   Judgment of reality or fantasy

    4.2.   Judgment of fact or opinion

    4.3.   Judgment of adequacy and validity

    4.4.   Judgment of appropriateness

    4.5.   Judgement of worth, desirability, and acceptability

5.0.   *Appreciation.*   Appreciation involves all the previously cited cognitive dimensions of reading, for it deals with the psychological and aesthetic impact of the selection on the reader.

    5.1.   Emotional response to the content

    5.2.   Identification with characters or incidents

    5.3.   Reaction to the author's use of language

    5.4.   Imagery

TYPES OF READING PROBLEMS

Ideally, a child should be reading at a level commensurate with his mental age, *not* his chronological age or grade placement. Unfortunately, there are many children who for one reason or another do not read at their mental age level. Children with reading problems are often labeled with terms such as "corrective," "retarded," or "remedial." Sometimes more complicated and threatening labels are attached—"strephosymbolic," "dyslexic," "brain injured," and so on. The list could go on *ad nauseum*. However, it does the teacher little good to become acquainted with medical or psychological terminology, since the terminology alone is of no assistance in helping the child with a reading problem. In fact, most of the reading problems found in a classroom are not those of a highly clinical nature; rather, they have a relatively obvious cause.

Occasionally, the terms "developmental," "corrective," and "remedial" are used in connection with poor readers. It should be pointed out that these words have no precise (i.e., not generally accepted) meaning among professionals working in the field. For example, "developmental" may refer to a class (or to a child) in which the students are taught using regular class methods; sometimes the use of the term is limited to pupils who are performing at a level commensurate with their ability; sometimes it is used also with pupils who are working far behind expectancy but where regular class methods are being used. A "corrective" class may be one in which the children are functioning below expectancy but do not appear to have any associated learning problems (e.g., brain damage, specific learning disabilities, etc.); it may also refer to any student who is 1 to 2 years behind expectancy regardless of the presence or absence of any associated learning problems. To some professionals, "remedial" students have associated learning problems; to others, the term is applied to all pupils who are more than 2 years behind expectancy in reading. Because of this confusion, we rarely use any of these terms; but if these terms are used in their schools for any purpose, we do recommend that teachers become familiar with their local definitions.

Some children may experience temporary lags in reading development due to external causes and a few may have serious word-learning problems. A child may fall behind in reading due to an extended absence from school, to a temporary failure in vision (which can be corrected by appropriately prescribed glasses), to a temporary failure in hearing (e.g., a tonsilectomy sometimes causes a temporary loss of hearing), to a constant change in schools, to a radical change in the reading program (e.g., from a basal approach to an augmented alphabet approach such as i/t/a), or to poor teaching. In such cases, nothing is wrong with the child's central nervous system; he is not mentally retarded, nor is he emotionally disturbed. If appropriate steps are taken through the careful assessment of his needs and proper instruction is provided, the difficulty can usually be overcome by using appropriate materials designed for the child's instructional level. Most of these problems can be handled in the ongoing classroom situation.

A few children evidence severe reading problems and experience great difficulty in attaching meaning to word or wordlike symbols when taught by the usual visual–auditory techniques. Often these children need specialized word-learning techniques similar to those presented in the Examples of Specific Remedial Techniques in Reading section of this chapter (p. 92).

ASSESSING READING PROBLEMS

The classroom teacher must not only know the level at which to initiate instruction but also as much as possible about the strengths and weaknesses of individual pupils. If a child's overall instructional level in reading is third grade, it does not necessarily mean that he must be taught all skills found at the third-grade level. He may have mastered a number of skills very well but is impeded from further advancement due to a few particular areas of weakness. If the teacher can determine these specific areas and deal with them, the child will advance more quickly than if he has to spend time reviewing skills in which he is already competent.

There are a number of ways to determine the appropriate instructional level for each child. Naturally, some kind of assessment process must be employed. This process can range from teacher judgment to complete reliance on standardized tests; neither of these, by themselves, can be regarded as adequate. Standardized tests can be used to estimate the range of reading abilities within a specific group. Generally, only two subtests, vocabulary (word meaning) and comprehension (factual understanding), are included on these tests. However, there are many aspects of reading that these tests do not measure. Standardized tests give no clues to the individual student's reading process; for example, two students may arrive at the same grade equivalency by different thinking processes. A classroom teacher should study individual reading profiles, look at test scores, read anecdotal records, and discuss a specific child with the previous year's teacher. All of these procedures have some limitations. The records may be inadequate or inaccessible, and last year's teacher may be biased or no longer available. In some situations, a referral can be made to a specialist; but what does the teacher do until the evaluation is completed, a conference is held, and materials are gathered?

Samples of some informal assessment devices that teachers can use to estimate the level of instruction and detect specific shortcomings are presented in this section. These procedures can be used in the classroom and require no special training for administration and interpretation. The instruments are easily constructed from accessible classroom materials; the child is not placed in a formal testing situation, which often arouses tension and influences results; and the tests can be constructed for his particula achievement level, no matter what grade he is in. It is possible for teachers to develop their own tests; however, as they may not have the time to do this, some general screening devices are presented.

A discussion of assessment must be introduced with a word of caution. Overtesting can be as undesirable as no testing at all. A full clinical evaluation of a child's reading problems may take as long as 2 full days to complete. Yet, very few children need this kind of detailed work. A few teachers who have been exposed to some formal training in the evaluation of reading, as in a graduate course, become overzealous and feel that every child needs to be given an Informal Reading Inventory (see p. 53), an interest inventory, an attitude scale, an associative learning test, a test of memory span, and so on. Actually, all this testing can consume too many hours that could better be devoted to instruction. A good rule to follow is to test minimally to find out where to initiate instruction and to identify areas of strength and weakness. Then, through diagnostic teaching, the teacher can continue to uncover the student's needs and to meet them with appropriate instruction as they arise.

Checklist of Reading Difficulties

The teacher should become familiar with the more common symptoms of reading difficulty. Ideally, he should keep a record on each child and review it frequently. If this is not possible or practical, then it is suggested that the teacher keep a copy of a checklist on her desk and note observable symptoms of various students. This information can be invaluable, not only for the teacher, but also for any other professional to whom the child may be referred. Once the observable symptoms have been noted, the next step is to decide upon an appropriate intervention. For example, if a child holds his book very close to his eyes when he reads, should he be referred to a specialist in vision? Should he be given less difficult materials? Should he undergo a behavior-modification plan? Should he be given extra practice in word-attack skills? What happens when he is asked to read less difficult material? Does the problem still persist? Similar questions can be raised about any observable symptom. An example of a teacher-constructed checklist is provided in Figure 2–1.

Screening Devices

Although today "round robin" reading is generally condemned as a teaching method, the procedure does enable the teacher to quickly identify those children who need immediate attention. Each child is asked to read a short passage from a book to determine whether he can pronounce the words successfully. If he has trouble with more than five running words out of every hundred, reads in a word-by-word manner, reads too slowly, or exhibits other difficulties, it is likely that the material is too difficult for him.

The oral reading should be carried out in a nonthreatening manner and the more severe cases of reading failure should be noted by the teacher without drawing embarrassing attention to the child. This can be accomplished in a small-group situation by having the lesson prefaced by the teacher saying, "This is a new reading book; this morning I want to find out if it is the right book for this group." If this approach is not deemed advisable, then the teacher can call on each child to read on an individual basis while the rest of the group is engaged in some other activity. Once the more severe cases have been identified, the teacher can begin to explore them further in order to pinpoint specific weaknesses in both word calling and comprehension.

Word-Recognition Tests

In general, word-recognition tests serve three purposes. First, they serve as a sample of the child's sight vocabulary; second, they give clues to the word-

Figure 2–1. *Teacher-Constructed Checklist of Reading Difficulties*

Teacher _____

School _____

Grade _____

Student _____   Date _____

I.   General

_____ points to each word with finger

_____ uses thumb as a guide

_____ appears tense in reading situation

_____ is easily distracted

_____ moves head as he reads

_____ holds book too close

_____ holds book too far away

_____ tries to avoid reading

_____ is unable to sit still

_____ covers one eye when reading

II.   Oral Reading

_____ reads in a slow word-by-word manner

_____ reads very rapidly and ignores punctuation

_____ has difficulty in pronouncing many words

_____ adds words

_____ omits words

_____ spells out words that he doesn't know

_____ guesses at unknown words

_____ reverses words

_____ reverses letters within words

Oral Reading (*continued*)

_____ stops at the end of each line

_____ repeats words

_____ repeats phrases

_____ repeats lines

_____ reads in a loud voice

_____ reads the pictures instead of the words

III.   Comprehension

_____ cannot recall basic facts

_____ uses background of experience rather than reading material to answer questions

_____ cannot make inferences

_____ cannot draw conclusions

_____ cannot answer questions pertaining to vocabulary

_____ makes guesses

_____ gives answers in great detail

IV.   Other Observations

_____

_____

_____

_____

_____

_____

attack skills that the child uses as he tries to work out unfamiliar words; and, third, they give some indication of where to initiate reading instruction with the child. The words for sample lists below have been taken from basal reader glossaries, the Durrell List, the Thorndike List, and other word lists. Word-recognition tests are easily constructed and administered. It must be remembered that they only measure a child's sight vocabulary and his word-attack skills. This kind of test does not measure meaning or comprehension. Therefore, word-recognition tests, if used alone, may place the child above his true instructional level. This is because many children can "read" a passage glibly and then not be able to recall the most obvious literal information included in the text. "Oh, I read it; I didn't know that I was supposed to remember anything," has been said by more than one student to a puzzled teacher who cannot understand how a child can word-call so well but not understand or retain any of the author's thoughts expressed in the passage.

San Diego Quick Assessment. This device is a graded word list formed by selecting words from basal reader glossaries and from the Thorndike Word List. The graded word list has two uses: (a) to determine a reading level, and (b) to detect errors in word analysis. The information can be used to group students for corrective purposes or to select appropriate reading materials for those students. To administer this device, the teacher should:

1. Type out each list of ten words on an index card in primary type.
2. Begin with the card that is at least 2 years below the student's grade-level assignment.
3. Ask the student to read the words aloud; if he misreads any on the initial list, drop to easier lists until he makes no errors.
4. Encourage the student to attempt to "sound out" words with which he is having difficulty. In this way, the teacher can get some idea of the attack skills that he is employing.
5. Have the student read from increasingly difficult lists until he misses at least three words.

The level at which a student misses no more than one out of ten words is his independent reading level. Two errors on a list indicate his instructional level. Three or more errors identify the level at which reading material will be too difficult for him.

These lists[1] are available up to the eleventh grade, but for practical purposes, only the lists for the first six grades are presented here. For the remainder, consult LaPray and Ross (1969).

1. From M. LaPray and R. Ross, The graded word list: A quick gauge of reading ability. *Journal of Reading*, 1969, 12. Reprinted with permission of M. LaPray and the International Reading Association.

Preprimer	*Primer*	*Grade 1*	*Grade 2*
see	you	road	our
play	come	live	please
me	not	thank	myself
at	with	when	town
run	jump	bigger	early
go	help	how	send
and	is	always	wide
look	work	night	believe
can	are	spring	quietly
here	this	today	carefully

Grade 3	*Grade 4*	*Grade 5*	*Grade 6*
city	decided	scanty	bridge
middle	served	certainly	commercial
moment	amazed	develop	abolish
frightened	silent	considered	trucker
exclaimed	wrecked	discussed	apparatus
several	improved	behaved	elementary
lonely	certainly	splendid	comment
drew	entered	acquainted	necessity
since	realized	escaped	gallery
straight	interrupted	grim	relatively

Queens College Educational Clinic: Sample Word List (Harris, 1970). The following word lists were taken from two sources: the words for the preprimer, primer, first-, second-, and third-grade lists were taken from Stone (1950)[2] and the fourth- and fifth-grade lists were taken from Durrell (1956).[3] The lists are used successfully in helping to assess specific weaknesses in word-calling and word-attack skills.

Preprimer	*Primer*	*1st reader*
on	all	another
big	cake	cry
run	how	hopped
dog	from	gate
up	into	snow
look	story	next
to	that	bunny
me	wanted	thought
it	playing	well
good	milk	running

2. Reprinted from *Progress in Primary Reading* by Clarence R. Stone, © 1950, with permission of McGraw-Hill, Inc.
3. Donald D. Durrell, *Improving Reading Instruction*, 2nd ed. (New York: Harcourt Brace Jovanovich, Inc., 1956). Used with permission of the author and publisher.

Grade 2	Grade 3	Grade 4	Grade 5
clang	cheek	addition	accomplish
fruit	reason	blizzard	commotion
quick	plain	compound	decorate
teach	freeze	embrace	essential
sound	knife	groove	marvelous
music	inch	introduce	grateful
often	moment	magic	population
straight	president	nonsense	remarkable
dark	shovel	permanent	suggestion
cannot	whale	scratch	territory

By carefully recording the student's responses, the teacher can assess weaknesses in his word-attack skills. Of course, *every* error should not be treated as a significant problem. However, by administering several levels, patterns usually emerge. For example, if a child in fifth or sixth grade misses many words at the preprimer or primer levels, he probably has not established a basic sight vocabulary. At levels beyond this, the child may miss initial consonants, final consonants, endings, or make other errors. A list of some of the common word-attack errors follows.[4]

	Problem	Example
1.	Omission of letters in a word	The child reads "here" for "where" The child reads "away" for "always"
2.	Whole-word reversals	The child reads "was" for "saw" The child reads "no" for "on" The child reads "pot" for "top"
3.	Letter confusion	The child reads "ban" for "pan" The child reads "dut" for "put" The child reads "dug" for "bug"
4.	Substitutions	The child reads "what" for "that" The child reads "aways" for "always"
5.	Added or omitted endings	The child reads "fastest" for "fast" The child reads "hard" for "harder"
6.	Initial sounds	The child reads "fish" for "wish" The child reads "bone" for "gone"
7.	Confused ending sounds	The child reads "cane" for "can" The child reads "looks" for "looking"
8.	Medial vowel	The child reads "run" for "ran" The child reads "rat" for "rot"
9.	Medial syllable omission	The child reads "visting" for "visiting" The child reads "artcle" for "article"

4. From A. J. Harris, *How to Increase Reading Ability*, 5th ed. (New York: David McKay Company, Inc., 1970), p. 178. Used with permission of the author and publisher.

The following example shows an analysis of a child's responses on the San Diego Quick Assessment:

Name: *Charles White*	Date *5/7/72*	Grade *3*
Second	**Third**	**Fourth**
100%	middle — *muddle*	served — *several*
✓	frightened — *fighted*	wrecked — *wuh-rek-ed*
	exclaimed — *exclamed*	improved — *improve*
	drew — *draw*	certainly — *ker-tan-ly*
	since — *science*	entered — *enter*
	realized — *realize*	interrupted — *interested*

The analysis of results is as follows: Charles has difficulty with medial vowel sounds (mud/mid, clam/claim, draw/drew); with medial parts (fighted/frightened, interested/interrupted, several/served); and endings (realize/realized, enter/entered). It should be ascertained whether Charles uses a dialect in which word endings are reduced or omitted. If this is the case, he should not be treated as having reading problems with endings.

Suggestions for remediation are several: individually review the short vowel sounds using known one-syllable words. Have Charles underline the short vowel. Review syllabication principles to show him how the medial vowel principle is used in longer words. Words with the *ai* diagraph should also be reviewed. Reinforcement of these skills can be done through the use of practice materials such as the *Barnell Loft Specific Series, Books A and B, Phonics We Use,* or teacher-made material. Exercises to call attention to word endings should be secured or developed.

The same kind of analysis can be done using the *Queen's College Educational Clinic Sample Graded Word List.*

Name: *Mary Johnson*	Date *5/8/72*	Grade *3*
Grade 2	**Grade 3**	**Grade 4**
100%	cheek — *check*	addition — *add-shun*
✓	plan — *plain*	groove — *grove*
	shovel — *shoved*	introduce — *in-ter-dick*

The analysis of results and remediation are as follows: Mary has difficulty with vowel sounds (*ee, ai, oo*). Appropriate skill work designed to overcome problems with vowel diagraphs should be secured. She also missed the endings on two words (shovel, introduce). This may be corrected through work in syllabication when she sees the syllable as one part of the word. In exercises of this type it would be well to have her underline the last syllable of words to call attention to them.

Teacher-constructed informal word-recognition tests. In her own reading program, the classroom teacher can sample the child's sight vocabulary and word-analysis skills with the material that the child will be using by preparing a typed list of twenty to twenty-five words from the word lists or glossaries found in most basal readers. The words can be chosen at random or by dividing the total number of words by 20 or 25 and taking every *n*th word; for example, if there are 375 words in the word list, divide 375 by 25. Since the answer is 15, take every fifteenth word from the list. This can later be refined to measure a number of phonic skills. (Do not overload the list with compound words, words of two syllables, or have a large group of words at any one level that follow the same phonic or structural pattern.)

The words can be printed on oaktag in individual lists. The lists can be presented in a number of ways. They can be read orally from the list by the student. The words can be flashed in a manual tachistoscopic manner by using two 3- by 5-inch index cards, or a slot can be cut in an index card wide enough to show one word at a time. The flash technique quickly exposes each word, but requires some practice on the part of the person presenting it. To flash a word, the two index cards are held together immediately above the first word on the list. The lower card is moved down to expose the word and the upper card is moved down to close the opening between them. The complete series of motions is carried out quickly with about a 1-second exposure, and the child sees the word only briefly. If the child responds correctly on the flash presentation, the examiner goes on to the next word. If, however, the child gives an incorrect response, the process is repeated untimed, the word is reexposed. No clues are given, but the child has an opportunity to reexamine the word and apply whatever analysis skills he has at his command to help him deduce the word. By carefully recording the child's responses in this untimed presentation, the teacher can get some idea of the child's word-attack skills as a basis for further instruction. Betts (1956) recommends that a child should achieve a flash score of approximately 95 percent at a given reading level before he is ready for the next level. The following is an example of a teacher-constructed word-recognition test for the sixth level of a basal series (Figure 2–2). In this case, the scores indicate that this level is too difficult for this student.

Analysis of the Child's Word-Attack Skills

To provide a more detailed analysis of the types of word-attack skills possessed by a child, a teacher may utilize one of two strategies. A commercially prepared test, which assesses the child's phonetic and structural analysis skills, may be given. A number of such tests are summarized in Table 2–1.

Figure 2–2. *Example of Informal Word-Recognition Test.* [From *Wings to Adventure* of The Ginn Basic Readers, 100 Edition, by David Russell and others. © Copyright, 1966, by Ginn and Company. Used with permission.]

Student List	Teacher's Record Sheet	Flash	Untimed
1. entry	1. entry	+	
2. wealth	2. wealth	−	*we ilth*
3. horrified	3. horrified	−	*horrible*
4. parcels	4. parcels	−	*park-els*
5. arrested	5. arrested	−	*rested*
6. yams	6. yams	−	*jam*
7. siren	7. siren	−	*sir en*
8. slice	8. slice	+	
9. trickle	9. trickle	−	*trick*
10. fragments	10. fragments	+	
11. gallant	11. gallant	−	*gallon*
12. sledge	12. sledge	−	*hedge*
13. gashes	13. gashes	+	
14. stealthily	14. stealthily	−	*stealy*
15. evidently	15. evidently	−	*evidence*
16. crackled	16. crackled	−	*cracked*
17. luxury	17. luxury	+	
18. available	18. available	+	
19. methods	19. methods	+	
20. expressions	20. expressions	−	*express*
	% correct = 35%		35%

Table 2-1. *Word-Analysis Tests*

Test	Publisher	Grades	Forms	Time	Measures	Administrator	Variability	Reliability
Botel Reading Inventory	Follett Publishing Co.	Grades 1–12	Two	90 minutes	Word opposites; word recognition; phonics	Classroom teacher		
DOLCH Word List	General Learning Press, 250 James St., Morristown, N.J. 07960	Grades 1–3	One	No time limit	Word recognition	Classroom teacher	No data available	No data available
SLOSSON Oral Reading Test	Slosson's Educational Publications, 140 Pine St., East Aurora, N.Y. 14052	Grades 1–12	One	10–15 minutes	Word recognition	Classroom teacher		

WRAT Subtest (Reading and Spelling)	Guidance Association, 1626 Gilpin Ave., Wilmington, Del. 19806	K–adult	One	20–30 minutes	Word recognition; spelling; mathematics	Classroom teacher		Reading and spelling, .92 to .98; arithmetic, .85 to .92
PIAT (Peabody Individual Achievement Test)	American Guidance Service	Grades K–12+	One	30–40 minutes	General information: reading recognition; letter names; letter sounds; visual discrimination of letters and words; mathematics; spelling; reading comprehension; comprehension of sentences	Classroom teacher	No validity coefficient available	Reading recognition .89; reading comprehension, —.64; test is least reliable with kindergarten
Doren Diagnostic (Group or Individual)	Educational Test Bureau, 720 Washington Ave., S.E. Minneapolis, Minn. 55414	Primary and intermediate grades	One	1–3 hours; may be given in sections	Letter recognition; beginning sounds; whole-word recognition; words within words; speech consonants; ending sounds; blending; rhyming; vowels; sight words; discriminate guessing	Classroom teacher	1.–.77 2.–.88 3.–.83 4.–.92	.53 to .88; median, .79

If an individual teacher wants additional information for in-depth probing, or if commercially prepared tests are not available or appropriate for the word-attack skills in question, the teacher may prepare her own test. A good scope-and-sequence chart outlining the major skill areas in the recommended order of presentation may be used as the framework for building the test. Typically, teachers find that word-attack tests are most informative if they are individually tailored for a specific child's difficulties. For example, if a commercially prepared word-attack test indicates that a child is having trouble with initial consonant blends, the teacher should proceed as follows. Consult a scope-and-sequence chart to establish whether the child is at about the place in the program where the blends are usually taught. On the chart we have provided (Table 2–2), the initial blends *st, pl, bl, br, tr, dr, gr,* and *fr* appear as skills to be taught near the end of first grade. The blends *cr, sn, sl, pr,* and *cl* are not taught until the beginning of second grade; the blends *thr, gl, squ, apr,* and *str* are typically taught in the latter half of grade two. So, depending on where the child is in the program, the teacher will construct a test with the appropriate items. The skill should be tested in a variety of ways—including the ability to discriminate one blend from another, e.g., between the spoken words /brown/ and /frown/. The child might be presented with pictures of such items as "clown" and "crown" and be asked to point to the one for which the teacher says the name. Or the child can be asked to circle all the pictures on a page that start with "pl." Other ideas for format can be found in workbook pages and in the Suggested Exercises sections of a good basal reading series. Note that the activities for testing the child are very similar to the activities for teaching him. In fact, the teacher should think of each day's instruction as a test/teach/test sequence, with each element of instruction being based specifically on the prior "test" results. This cyclical test/teach/test paradigm is especially adaptable to instruction in word-attack skills.

Informal Estimates of Comprehension

Once an instructional level in word recognition has been estimated, the teacher may want to determine the child's reading in context and his comprehension skills. The directions for developing an informal test to tap these areas are presented in some detail in the following outline. The teacher should use her own judgment as to how much of this test she feels she needs to administer. For some children, it may be necessary to administer only one or two levels to ascertain if the child's comprehension level is equal to his skills in word recognition. In other cases, the teacher may desire a more comprehensive prove of the student's skills.

Table 2–2. *Typical Scope-and-Sequence of Reading Skills Usually Taught at the Elementary Level*

First Grade

	Word-Study Skills	Comprehension Skills

Preprimer Stage	A. Word meaning and concept building
	B. Picture clues
	C. Visual discrimination
	  1. Left-to-right progression
	  2. Word configuration
	  3. Capital and lowercase letter forms
	D. Auditory perception
	  1. Initial consonants—$b, c, d, f, g, h, l, m, p, r, s, t, w$
	  2. Rhyming elements
	E. Structural analysis—ex. plural nouns: adding s
		A. Associating text and pictures
		B. Following oral directions
		C. Main idea
		D. Details
		E. Sequence
		F. Drawing conclusions
		G. Seeing relationships

Primer Stage	Review, reteach, or teach all skills that child has not mastered
	
	Expand vocabulary
	A. Context clues
	B. Phonetic analysis
	  1. Initial consonants
	  2. Rhymes
	  3. Learning letter names—n, l, p, d, g, r, c
	C. Structural analysis
		A. All those at preprimer level
		B. Forming judgments
		C. Making inferences
		D. Classifying

First Reader	A. All previous skills
	B. Phonetic analysis
	  1. Final analysis—n, d, k, m, t, p
	  2. Initial blends—$st, pl, bl, br, tr, dr, gr, fr$
	C. Structural analysis
	  1. Verb forms
	    a. Adding *ed*
	    b. Adding *ing*
	  2. Compound words
		A. All previously taught skills
		B. Recalling story facts
		C. Predicting outcome
		D. Following printed directions

Table 2–2. *Typical Scope-and-Sequence of Reading Skills Usually Taught at the Elementary Level (continued)*

Second Grade

Book One

Word-Study Skills	Comprehension Skills

A. Review and practice all first-grade skills
B. Phonetic analysis
  1. Rhyming words visually
  2. Consonants
    a. Initial—*j*
    b. Final—*x, r, l*
    c. Blends—*cr, sn, sl, pr, cl*
    d. Digraphs—*ai, oa*
C. Structural analysis
  1. Plural of nouns—adding *s* and *es*
  2. Variant forms of verbs
    a. Adding *es, ing*
    b. Doubling consonants before adding *ing* or *ed*
	A. All previously taught skills
	B. Making generalizations
	C. Seeing relationships
	D. Interpreting pictures

Book Two

Word-Study Skills	Comprehension Skills

A. All previously taught skills
B. Recognize words in alphabetical order
C. Phonetic analysis
  1. Consonant blends—*thr, gl, squ, apr, str*
  2. Phonograms—auditory and visual concepts of *ar, er, ir, ow, ick, ew, own, uck, ed, ex, ouse, ark, oat, ound*
  3. Vowel differences
    a. Vowels lengthened by final *e*
    b. Long and short sounds of *y*
    c. Digraphs—*ee, ea*
    d. Dipthongs—different sounds of *ow*
D. Structural analysis
  1. Contractions—*it's, I'm, I'll, that's, let's, don't, didn't, isn't*
  2. Variant forms of verbs—dropping *e* before adding *ing*
  3. Plural forms of nouns—changing *y* to *ies*
	A. Practice and use of all previously taught skills
	B. Making inferences
	C. Seeing cause-and-effect relationships

A. All previously learned skills
B. Word meaning
  1. Opposites
  2. Adding *ore, est* to change form and meaning of words
  3. Words with multiple meanings
C. Phonetic analysis
  1. Consonants
    a. Hard and soft sounds—*c, g*
    b. Recognizing consonants
    c. Digraphs
      (1) *ck*
      (2) Vowels
        (a) Silent vowels
        (b) Digraphs—*ai, ea, ou, ee, ay, ui*
    d. Structural analysis
      (1) Contractions—*who's, we're, you're, aren't, that's, I'm, couldn't*
      (2) Possessive words
      (3) Suffixes—*en, est, ly*
      (4) Variant forms of verbs
        (a) Changing final *y* to *i* before adding *ed*
        (b) Dropping *e* before adding *ing*
    e. Alphabetizing—first letter
    f. Syllabication—up to three-syllable words

A. All skills previously learned
B. Detecting mood of situation
C. Relating story facts to own experiences
D. Reading pictorial maps
E. Skimming

A. All previously learned skills
B. Word meaning
  1. Homonyms
    a. *dew, do*
    b. *sea, see*
    c. *whole, hole*
    d. *made, maid*
    e. *blew, blue*
    f. *ewe, you*
    g. *forth, fourth*
    h. *thrown, throne*

A. All previously learned skills
B. Problem solving

(*continued*)

Table 2–2. *Typical Scope-and-Sequence of Reading Skills Usually Taught at the Elementary Level (continued)*

Word-Study Skills	Comprehension Skills
Book Two	

Word-Study Skills:

2. Synonyms
   a. *throw, pitch*
   b. *quiet, still*
   c. *speak, say*
   d. *lift, raise*
   e. *tug, pull*
   f. *large, big*
   g. *swiftly, fast*
   h. *believe, think*
   i. *smart, clever*
   j. *come, arrive*
   k. *daybreak, dawn*
   l. *fastened, tied*
C. Phonetic analysis
   1. Consonants—hard and soft sounds of *g, c*
      a. *c* usually has a soft sound when it comes before *e* or *i*
      b. *g* usually has a soft sound when it comes before *e* or *i*
   2. Vowels
      a. Dipthongs—*ou, ow, or, oy, aw, au*
      b. Sounds of vowels followed by *r*
D. Structural analysis
   1. Plurals—change *f* to *v* when adding *es*
   2. Contractions—*doesn't, you'll, they're*
   3. Suffixes
      a. Recognizing as syllables
      b. Adding *ly* and *ily*
      c. Positive comparative and superlative forms of adjectives
   4. Prefixes—*un* changes meaning of words to the opposite
E. Alphabetizing—using second letter
F. Syllabication
   1. Between double consonants
   2. Prefixes and suffixes as syllables
G. Accent—finding syllables said more heavily

(continued)

1. All previously learned skills
2. Reading for comprehension
3. Finding the main ideas
4. Finding details
5. Organizing and summarizing
6. Recalling story facts
7. Recognizing sequence
8. Reading for information
9. Creative reading
   a. Classifying
   b. Detecting the mood of a situation
   c. Drawing conclusions
   d. Forming judgments
   e. Making inferences
   f. Predicting outcomes
   g. Seeing cause-and-effect relationships
   h. Problem solving
10. Following printed directions
11. Skimming

Word meaning:
A. Antonyms
B. Synonyms
C. Homonyms
D. Figures of speech
E. Sensory appeals in words

Word analysis:
A. Phonetic analysis
   1. Consonants
      a. Silent
      b. Two sounds of s
      c. Hard and soft sounds of c and g
      d. Diacritical marks
         (1) Long sound of vowels
         (2) Short sound of vowels
         (3) *a* as in *care*
         (4) *a* as in *bars*
         (5) *u* as in *burn*
         (6) *a* as in *ask*
         (7) *e* as in *wet*
         (8) *e* as in *letter*
         (9) *oo* as in *moon*
         (10) *oo* as in *foot*
      e. Applying vowel principles
         (1) Vowel in the middle of a word or syllable is usually *short*
         (2) Vowel coming at the end of a one-syllable word is usually *long*
         (3) When a one-syllable word ends in *e*, the medial vowel in that word is usually *long*
         (4) When two vowels come together, the first vowel is usually *long* and the second vowel is *silent*
B. Structural analysis
   1. Hyphenated words—*good-by, thirty-one, rain-maker*
   2. Finding root words in word variants

Table 2–2. *Typical Scope-and-Sequence of Reading Skills Usually Taught at the Elementary Level (continued)*

Word-Study Skills

3. Prefixes—*dis, re, un, im*
4. Suffixes—*ly, ness, ment, ful, ish, less*
5. Syllabication
   a. When a vowel sound is followed by one consonant, that consonant usually begins the next syllable
   b. When a vowel sound in a word is followed by two consonants, this word is usually divided between the two consonants
   c. Prefixes and suffixes are usually syllables
   d. Compound words are usually divided between the word parts
   e. In two-syllable words ending in *le* preceded by a consonant, the consonant joins the *le* and begins the final syllable
6. Accent

Comprehension Skills

Word-study skills

1. Antonyms—review and give practice in using context clues
2. Expand vocabulary
3. Review figures of speech and introduce new ones to enrich vocabulary
4. Homonyms—review and introduce new ones
5. Synonyms—review and introduce new ones to expand vocabulary
6. Use of dictionary and glossary
   a. Guide words
   b. Accent marks
   c. Diacritical marks
      1. Review $\bar{a}, \ddot{a}, \hat{u}, \breve{a}, oo, oo, \ddot{e}e$
      2. Review long and short vowels
   3. Introduce schwa, half-long *o*
   4. Introduce italic *u, i, a, e*
   5. Introduce ' in omitted vowel
   6. Respellings

Comprehension and study skills

Continue development in the following areas:

A. Main idea
B. Sequence
C. Reading for details
D. Appreciating literary style
E. Drawing conclusions
F. Enriching information
G. Evaluating information
H. Forming opinions and generalizing
I. Interpreting ideas
J. Using alphabetical arrangement
K. Using dictionary or glossary skills
L. Interpreting maps and pictures
M. Skimming for purpose
N. Classifying ideas
O. Following directions
P. Outlining

Locating and using information (study skills)

7. Phonetic analysis
   a. Review consonant sounds
   b. Review pronounciation of diacritical marks
   c. Review phonograms
8. Structural analysis
   a. Compound words
   b. Words of similar configuration
   c. Prefixes
      1. Review *un-, im-, dis-, re-*
      2. Introduce *in-, anti-, inter-, mis-*
   d. Suffixes
      1. Review *-en, -ment, -less, -ish, -ly, -ful, -y, -ed*
      2. Introduce *-sp, -or, -ours, -ness, -ward, -hood, -action, -al*
   e. Principles of syllabication
      1. Review rules already taught
      2. Consonant blends and digraphs are treated as singular sounds, and usually are not divided (*ma-chine*)
   f. Application of word analysis in attacking words outside the basic vocabulary

Q. Summarizing
R. Reading for accurate detail
S. Skimming

Introduce and teach:

A. Discrimination between fact and fiction
B. Perceiving related ideas
C. Strengthening power of recall
D. Using encyclopedias, atlas, almanac, and other references
E. Using charts and graphs
F. Using index and pronounciation keys
G. Reading to answer questions and for enjoyment of literary style

Word meaning:

A. Antonyms—review and give practice in
B. Homonyms—develop ability to use correctly
C. Classify words of related meaning
D. Enrich word meaning
E. Review use of synonyms
F. Use context clues in attacking new words
G. Expand vocabulary
H. Become aware of expressions that

Continue development in the following areas:

A. Main ideas
B. Sequence
C. Reading for details
D. Appreciating literary style
E. Drawing conclusions
   1. Predicting outcomes
   2. Forming judgments
   3. Seeing relationships
F. Extending and enriching information

Review skills in the following:

1. Alphabetical arrangement
2. Use of dictionary and glossary
3. Use of encyclopedia, almanac, and other references
4. Interpreting maps and pictures
5. Skimming for a purpose
6. Classifying ideas
7. Following directions
8. Summarizing
9. Outlining
10. Reading for accurate detail

(continued)

Table 2–2. *Typical Scope-and-Sequence of Reading Skills Usually Taught at the Elementary Level (continued)*

Sixth Grade

refer to place and time and develop skill in interpreting such expressions

I. Use dictionary and glossary
 1. Further ability to use alphabetical-order guide words, and pronunciation key
 2. Review diacritical marks—introduce circumflex—breve as in sŏft
 3. Review spelling

Word analysis:

A. Phonetic analysis
 1. Review consonant sounds
 2. Diacritical marks—interpreting pronunciation symbols
 3. Review vowel sounds principles

B. Structural analysis
 1. Review compound words
 2. Review hyphenated words
 3. Review prefixes
  a. Review *un-, im-, dis-, re-, in-, anti-, inter-, mis-*
  b. Introduce *trans-, pre-, fore-, ir-, non-*
 4. Review suffixes
  a. Review *-en, -ment, -less, -ish, -ly, -ful, -y, -ed, -shy, -or-, -er, -ous, -ness, -ward, -hood, -ation, -al*
  b. Introduce *-able, -ance, -ence, -ate, -est, -ent, -ity, -ic, -ist, -like*
 5. Review principles of syllabication
 6. Review accented syllables
 7. Apply word analysis in attacking words outside the basic vocabulary

G. Interpreting pictures
H. Evaluating information
I. Interpreting ideas
J. Using facts to form opinions, generalizing

Introduce the skills of

A. Enriching imagery
B. Discriminating between fact and fiction
C. Strengthening power of recall

11. Using index and pronounciation keys
12. Using charts and graphs
13. Reading to answer questions and for enjoyment of literary style

Introduce the following skills:

1. Use of facts and figures
2. Use of headings and type style—especially use of italics
 a. To give importance to a word or expression in a sentence
 b. To show that a sentence has a special importance to the plot of the story
 c. To set off a special title used in a sentence or a reference
3. Use of an index
4. Use of library
5. Use of table of contents
6. Taking notes
7. Reading of information material
8. Reading poetry

Source: Adapted from G. Kaluger and C. J. Kolson, *Reading and Learning Disabilities* (Columbus, Ohio: Charles E. Merrill, 1969).

1. Selection of a standard basal series
   a. Any series that goes from preprimer to the sixth level may be used.
   b. Materials that the child has not previously used should be included.
2. Selection of passages from the basal reader
   a. Choose a selection that makes a complete story.
   b. Choose selections of about 50 words at the preprimer level; 100 words at the primer, first, and second levels; and 100–150 words at the upper levels.
   c. Choose two selections at each level: plan to use one for oral reading and one for silent reading, and take the selection from the middle of the book.
3. Construction of questions
   a. Build five questions for each selection at the preprimer level; six questions for each selection at primer, first, and second levels; and ten questions for each selection at level three and above.
   b. Avoid "yes" and "no" questions.
   c. Include a vocabulary in the questions at the same level as the vocabulary in the selection.
   d. Construct three kinds of questions at each level in about the following percentages: factual, 40 percent; inferential, 40 percent; vocabulary, 20 percent.
4. Construction and preparation of test
   a. Cut and mount the selections on oaktag *or*
   b. Note the pages in the book, put the questions on separate cards, and have the child read the selection from the text itself.

Since the child's word-recognition level would have been determined by one of the previously mentioned word-recognition tests, the teacher can begin this test of comprehension one or two levels below the child instructional level in word recognition. The child is asked to read the first selection aloud, the teacher noting errors in his oral reading (see Figure 2–1). If the test can be reproduced on a spirit-duplicating machine, the following shorthand may be helpful in recording errors:

as|the|boy|went|down|the|street (word by word)
See (repetition)
Jane and Bob were riding ~~their~~ bicycles (omission)
Kim barked loudly at the strange/man (insertion)
"Help," cried the girl on the runaway horse (word asked for)

The child is then asked questions about the selection. This should be followed by a silent selection and questions. The highest level at which a child correctly answers 75 percent of the questions without undue observable symptoms of frustration is an indication of his instructional level.

Cloze Technique

This technique, as described by Clary (1976), can be useful in determining whether a book is suitable for a student.

1. Select a sensible passage of at least 250 words from the middle of the book.
2. Type the first sentence completely.
3. Substitute a blank for every fifth word but leave the last sentence intact.
4. Make an answer key using the omitted words and place it at the bottom of the page.
5. Have the student read and fill in the blanks.

If a student gets less than 40 percent of the exact answers, the book is too difficult.

Example (N. B. Smith, 1968):

The ostrich sat very quietly in the sand, his huge legs folded under him. _____ long and slender neck _____ upward to a great _____. His feather-covered body _____ black except for the _____ plumes of his wings _____ tail. The featherless neck was bluish in color, and it was topped by a head too small for the rest of the body.

Answers:

His   and   height   beautiful   was   curved

In constructing this kind of informal test, the teacher should:

1. Check carefully to see if two or more words could be interchanged without changing the meaning of the passage. If this does occur, more than one answer will have to be counted as correct.
2. The length of the spaces should be uniform and long enough for the student to write the longest word easily.
3. If the first word of a sentence is omitted, the word in the answer key should be capitalized. Make sure that there are at least three or four words with capital letters; otherwise, the student is given the answer just by writing the word with the capital letter in the

blank that begins a sentence. (*Note:* The example is a short passage with only one capital letter, but this is just for illustrative purposes.)

Some commercial publishers have begun to publish materials that use the cloze technique as an instructional device. One in particular is the Scholastic Book Services' *Chillers and Thrillers*, Scope Reading Skills/4 (New York: Scholastic Book Services, 1974).

Informal Reading Inventory

A complete, informal reading inventory (I.R.I.) is usually regarded as a clinical instrument used by reading specialists, although on occasion, a teacher may want to use it. Readers who desire a detailed description of these procedures are referred to the discussion of informal inventories by Johnson and Kress (1969). Although informal reading inventories are too time-consuming for classroom administration, they can provide precise and valuable information about a child's reading difficulty. In the event that a teacher desires a detailed evaluation, he should probably request that an informal reading inventory be administered by the reading specialist.

Initially a child is given a word-recognition test beginning at the pre-primer level. He is given tests until he misses 50 percent of the words on the flash presentation on two successive levels. Starting with the last level at which the child received 100 percent on the flash presentation in the word-recognition test, the child reads two selections (one oral and one silent) at each level and answers questions concerning each selection. When he falls below 90 percent in word recognition, below 50 percent in comprehension (average of oral and silent selection), or is qualitatively frustrated, the child stops reading. Then the examiner reads aloud one selection at each level until the child is unable to answer 50 percent of the questions asked about the material. Levels for word recognition in context and comprehension are computed for each level using the generally accepted criteria as shown by Table 2–3.

Table 2–3. *Criteria for Various Levels*

Level	Word Recognition in Context (percent)	Comprehension (percent)	Observable Behavior
Independent	99	90	No signs of frustration or tension
Instructional	95	75	No signs of frustration or tension
Frustration	Below 90	Below 50	Signs of frustration and/or tension
Hearing capacity		75	

The *independent level* in the table is the reading level at which a child can function on his own. Library books, independent reading, and research work can be carried out at this level. The *instructional level* is the highest level at which the child can profit from instruction. At this level, he can pronounce 95 percent of the running words and can recall about 75 percent of the information. Building on his previous knowledge, the child can profit from instruction in specific word analysis and comprehension skills at this level. The *frustration level* is the level at which the child has great difficulty in pronouncing words or does not understand the concepts or both. *Hearing capacity* is the reading level at which the child can understand materials that are read to him.

It is unnecessary that the teacher attempt to conduct a detailed evaluation of every child in her class. She should do enough assessment work to obtain the needed information but should not become so involved in testing that there is little time left for teaching. In assessment, as in teaching, it is better to move from the simple to the complex. The quick screening instruments will probably serve to adequately place most children at appropriate reading levels; a few children will need a more thorough analysis of reading difficulties; but only an occasional child will need an intensive, detailed evaluation. In these latter cases, other professionals should be enlisted to contribute additional information.

Analysis of Oral Reading Miscues[5]

The assessment procedures described to this point will provide teachers with a number of ideas for instruction. However, each classroom has within it a small number of boys or girls whose reading problems are so persistent that additional, more intensive analysis is required. This statement is based on the belief that children's errors or miscues are not random or capricious, except in the most unusual circumstances. On the contrary, such miscues occur in systematic patterns that can be identified by careful analysis of the child's oral reading. A major goal of such qualitative miscue analysis is to derive ideas on what strategies the child is using that result in the obtained performance patterns. Miscue analysis is helpful in stimulating teachers to develop hypotheses concerning the particular ineffective or inefficient strategies being utilized by the child in the oral reading act. Once the teacher has detected the pattern of the miscues presented by the child, appropriate instructional efforts can follow.

5. We use the term "miscue" rather than "error" for much the same reasons as those articulated by K. S. Goodman (1969); that is, the term "miscue" is less judgmental and avoids the implication that good reading cannot involve departures from the printed text (expected responses).

It is recognized that the complete and comprehensive analysis of each oral reading miscue of a particular child would be too time-consuming for everyday classroom use. For example, the complete coding of the miscues of an average reader would call for approximately 2000 separate decisions. While such detailed analyses may be necessary for research purposes, we believe that a less detailed analysis can provide the classroom teacher with necessary and valuable insight. Teachers interested in the more comprehensive procedures for oral miscue analysis are referred to K. S. Goodman (1969), Y. M. Goodman (1972), and Weber (1968, 1970).

A word of caution on the use of miscue analytic procedures is appropriate. Good readers do not maximally utilize every cue presented in the printed page; that is, they do not make letter-by-letter discriminations, attending to each feature of each letter or even each word. In fact, some authorities (e.g., K. S. Goodman, 1969; F. Smith, 1971) have made strong cases that the really effective and efficient reader is one who is able to derive meaning from the printed page with a minimum use of cues. Thus a good reader forms hypotheses about how the sentence, the paragraph, the story will end. Subsequent reading behavior serves to confirm or disconfirm those hypotheses, which then become part of the "meaning" derived from the page, or become modified, respectively. Accordingly, teachers should not be overly concerned if, on occasion, a child emits a response that is at variance with the printed page. The teacher is properly concerned, however, when the miscues are of a nature and a frequency that the child's comprehension is impaired. Miscue analysis can help the teacher discover what faulty strategies and consistently misleading patterns or rules the child uses that interfere with his reading performance.

Table 2–4 presents the common miscue types. They are of interest to the teacher, but they provide insufficient detail as to the strategies that underlie their use. We suggest that teachers use Table 2–5 to further refine their examination of how the child responds to graphic symbols. Table 2–5 has been organized to indicate that most children's reading substitutions fall readily into graphic, syntactic, and semantic categories. These categories are, of course, not mutually exclusive; for any printed word has graphic, syntactic, and semantic characteristics; and a child may use faulty strategies that apply to these characteristics singly or in combination.

An additional point about Table 2–5 is worth making. It is not accidental that the miscue characteristics are analogous to the aspects of language —phonology, syntactics, and semantics. We point this out again to underline the intimate relationship of the reading act to the child's language proficiency (see the previous section in this chapter, also Chapter 7).

In performing a miscue analysis, teachers structure the situation much as they would in administering an informal reading inventory. In fact, if adequate protocols have been kept from a previous administration of an IRI,

Table 2–4. *Analysis of Oral Reading Miscues: Response Types*

Response Type	Description	Example
Omission	The child omits a word or words.	the big red ball/the big ball[a]
Insertion	The child adds a word or words.	the big ball/the big red ball
Sequence or order	The child makes a response that is expected elsewhere in the text—either immediately preceding or following (horizontal miscue), or immediately above or below the stimulus word (vertical miscue).	John and Harry/John and Harry found the dog./found the Harry
Substitution[b]	The child substitutes a word other than the text indicates. (If the child makes a substitution on the first occurrence of the stimulus word, then on later occurrences makes the expected response, no further analysis is required—see self-correction below.)	The dog ran/The dog red
Sounding out	The child makes several tentative partial responses, voiced or unvoiced.	Patty will play/Patty will p—
Self-correction	The child makes any of the above response types, then spontaneously corrects himself.	That is good/What is—that is good
Dialect	The child makes any of the above, but in accordance with the rules of his dialect.	The boys were scared/The boy be scared

[a] In each example, the printed text or expected response precedes the diagonal line; the child's miscue or the observed response follows.
[b] For more detailed analysis of substitutions, see Table 2–5.

Table 2–5. *Analysis of Substitution Miscues*

Type of Substitution Analysis[a]	Example[b]	Hypothesis or "What the Teacher Does Next"
I. Graphic analysis		
a. No discernible similarity (no shared letters)	king/lady	Probe whether the child is just guessing. Child may have virtually no word-attack skills (test further with commercial or teacher-made word-analysis test).
b. Words similar in overall configuration	leg/boy	Child may be utilizing configural clues—this is a strength that needs to be built on and supplemented with other word-analysis skills.
c. Reversal of single letter	bad/dad	Recheck child's ability to discriminate between b and d, also between other pairs, such as p and q. Provide left–right activities, also specific exercises for discrimination training. See also section on grammatical inappropriateness.
d. Reversal of two or more letters	was/saw	Provide activities as indicated in "c."
e. Beginning letters similar	play/plant	Child is correctly utilizing inital consonant blend cue. He needs to be encouraged to utilize middle and ending graphic cues, also to attend to context. Check other initial letters.
f. Middle letters similar	good/fool	Same as "e" except with middle letters.

Type of Substitution Analysis[a]	Example[b]	Hypothesis or "What the Teacher Does Next"
g. Ending letters similar	that/what	Same as "e" except with ending letters; also extra exercises with "wh" and "th" letters.
h. Single letter omission, deletion, or substitution	very/every	Child needs to be encouraged to look at entire word, also help on using syntactic and semantic.
i. Similar root word: suffix/ prefix miscue	toys/toy	Check for presence of dialect; then activities dealing with singular and plural; also encourage attention to word endings.
II. Syntactic analysis		
a. Beginning position in sentence	The boy . . ./ Who . . .	Check whether child can discriminate between these words when they occur later in the sentence; if so, he is relying heavily on syntactic cues (which is good), but needs more help on word analysis skills.
b. Middle or ending position in sentence	Mary ran far/ Mary ran fast	Child is using syntactic and semantic features of the sentence (good); needs help as in "I.e."
c. Grammatical appropriateness (substituted word has same privilege of occurrence as stimulus word? Sentence grammatical up to and including miscue?)	John found his pet/John found his play	Child relying on initial letter cue (good), but is not showing grammatical awareness. Does child have mastery of oral language? If so, further testing and activities with cloze technique and "guess the end of the sentence game" might be used.
III. Semantic analysis		
a. Stimulus word and child's response unrelated or only partially related	Peter could/ Peter cold	Child is using fairly sophisticated word-analysis skills (teacher can build on this), but needs sequential sentence speaking and reading opportunities. Other activities as in "II.c."
b. Meaning of child's response acceptable in sentence, but not related to stimulus sentence or paragraph	Jerry went home/Jerry went away	Child is thinking about the internal meaning of the sentence (good), but is not relating it to the meaning of the story. Child lacking word-analysis skills.

[a] Category types are not mutually exclusive.
[b] In each example, the printed text or expected response precedes the diagonal line; the child's miscue or the observed response follows.

the teacher may be able to perform usable analyses without asking the child to orally read again. If no IRI protocols are available, the teacher asks the child to read several paragraphs at the instructional level, marking a double-spaced copy with an appropriate code. The miscues emitted by the child are then subjected to an analysis as follows. Using Table 2–5, the teacher categorizes the types of responses made by the child. Special note is made of the child's efforts at "sounding out" (these efforts are invaluable in helping the teacher derive hypotheses concerning the child's word-attack strategies; in fact, the child should be encouraged to "sound out" for this reason), self-correction (which similarly provides valuable insight into how the child monitors his own performance, and whether he utilizes feedback effectively), and dialect considerations. This latter issue is dealt with in Chapter 7 and will not be further explicated, except to say that the child's dialect will affect the interpretation given to graphic, syntactic, and semantic miscues; in fact, the presence or absence of a dialect will determine whether certain departures from the expected responses should be considered miscues at all.

Next, each miscue is analyzed according to its graphic, syntactic, and semantic characteristics. By noting the relative proportion of miscues in each category, the teacher can form a rough idea of whether the child's difficulty is more of the word-analysis type (mostly graphic miscues) or whether the child has linguistic or cognitive difficulty in forming hypotheses about the meaning of the material being read (such difficulty showing up more in syntactic and semantic miscues). We strongly urge teachers to attend closely to this latter miscue type, for it is our belief that linguistic and cognitive aspects of reading have been generally ignored by teachers.

Once the miscue analysis has been completed, the teacher will find it useful to summarize the results on a checksheet such as the one presented in Table 2–6. The use of this checksheet should make it apparent at a glance

Table 2–6. *Sample Record Sheet for Oral Reading Miscues*

Name _____ Age _____ Grade _____ Date _____
Sample of Reading Material on Which Analysis Is Based _____
Number of Words in Sample _____

Response Type	Number of Occurrences	Response Type	Number of Occurrences
Omission _____		Sounding Out _____	
Insertion _____		Self-Correction _____	
Sequence _____		Dialect _____	
Substitution _____			

Substitution Analysis

Graphic analysis		*Syntactic analysis*	
a. No similarity	_____	a. Beginning position	_____
b. Configuration	_____	b. Middle or ending position	_____
c. Single-letter reversal	_____	c. Grammatical appropriateness	_____
d. Several letters reversed	_____	Total syntactic miscues	_____
e. Beginning letters similar	_____		
f. Middle letters similar	_____	*Semantic analysis*	
g. Ending letters similar	_____	a. Meaning unrelated	_____
h. Single-letter miscue	_____	b. Story meaning distorted	_____
i. Root word	_____	Total semantic miscues	_____
Total graphic miscues	_____		

where the child's faulty strategies seem to cluster. The teacher will then have a sound basis for beginning instruction designed to build on strengths and to redress weaknesses. The reading protocol should be attached to the record sheet so that the substance of each miscue type will be readily available as instruction is planned.

Standardized Tests of Reading

Little mention, as yet, has been made of standardized tests of reading because classroom teachers generally are not called upon to administer standardized reading tests to individuals. Most teacher-administered standardized tests are designed for group testing. If a teacher is called upon to select, administer, or interpret a standardized test or to interpret a report in which several standardized tests are used, it is important to have some information about the skills tapped by the test.

In both individual and group standardized tests of reading, certain tests are primarily diagnostic (ascertain specific needs) and some are primarily achievement oriented (evaluate what has been learned). Any standardized achievement test can be used diagnostically. By careful study of the results, individual needs can be estimated. In the manual of administration for almost any test, there is a section dealing with "Suggestions to Improve Skills." The teacher is encouraged to read this section of the manual carefully. There is a great deal more in the test manual than just test directions. Determining an isolated grade-equivalent score or percentile is far less useful to the classroom teacher than finding suggestions to upgrade a child's skills.

Standardized *group* tests are often used by schools in the beginning of the school year to ascertain some general measure of a group's reading ability. Sometimes they are used at the end of the school year to measure achievement. Standardized *individual* tests are often used by reading specialists and school psychologists to determine specific needs. Most standardized group tests yield information in the general categories of vocabulary (word meaning) and comprehension. However, there are many group and individual standardized reading tests that tap many other skills. If called upon to select a standardized test, the following criteria should be considered in selecting the appropriate instrument to meet the particular situation:

1. Does the test claim to measure the skill(s) in which you are interested?
2. Validity. Does the test actually measure what it purports to measure
3. Reliability. Does the test measure accurately and consistently?
4. Ease of administration and scoring. Are the directions for administration clear and easy to follow? Is the test fairly easy to score?

5. Does the test give scores that are adequately defined and standardized?

Farr and Anastasiow (1969) have critically reviewed the more popular standardized reading tests. Their results are summarized in Tables 2–7 and 2–8. When selecting an appropriate test, the teacher will find these tables useful.

VARIOUS APPROACHES TO THE TEACHING OF READING

Some of the common approaches to reading instruction are presented in this section, including techniques that are often used in special classes and reading clinics for teaching specialized word-learning techniques, available supplementary materials, and supplementary exercises which the teacher can use to teach, review, or reinforce specific reading skills. In examining any approach or materials, at least five questions should be asked.

1. Does the material proceed from the simple to the complex?
2. Does the material meet the needs of the children?
3. Is the material based on some knowledge of the language?
4. Does the material lead the child to make his own generalizations?
5. Does the material provide ample opportunities for practice?

Classroom Approaches

At one time reading was taught almost entirely with a basal reading series. Although the basal series is still the most prominent approach to teaching reading, it is not the only classroom method. Other frequently employed systems include the language-experience approach, the individualized reading approach, programmed reading, and augmented alphabets (i/t/a).

The basal approach. These programs consist of reading texts, a teacher's manual, and other supplementary materials, often including workbooks, placement tests, achievement tests, spirit-duplicating practice pads, and audiovisual devices. They usually begin at the readiness level and continue through sixth to eighth grades. The vocabulary is carefully controlled from level to level and skills in both word recognition and comprehension are carefully sequenced. Basal readers are presently undergoing many changes. The "white, middle class, suburban, one father, one mother, one dog, one cat, one pony," motif for stories at the primary level is being expanded to include more varied stories and materials. Many companies are also publishing

Table 2–7. *Evaluation of Technical Information Supplied by Publishers on Elementary-Level Reading Achievement Tests.* [From Roger Farr and Nicholas Anastasiow, *Tests of Reading Readiness and Achievement: A Review and Evaluation* (Newark, Del.: International Reading Association, 1969), pp. 48–51. Reprinted with permission of Roger Farr and the International Reading Association.]

Column key:
1. California Reading Test–Lower Primary
2. California Reading Test–Upper Primary
3. California Reading Test–Elementary
4. Gates MacGinitie, Primary A
5. Gates MacGinitie, Primary B
6. Gates MacGinitie, Primary C
7. Gates MacGinitie, Primary CS
8. Iowa Silent Reading Test, Survey D
9. Metropolitan Achievement Tests: Elementary Test
10. Metropolitan Achievement–Primary I
11. Metropolitan Achievement–Primary II
12. Metropolitan Achievement–Elementary
13. Stanford Achievement–Intermediate
14. Stanford Reading Tests–Primary I
15. Stanford Reading Tests–Primary II
16. Stanford Reading Tests–Intermediate I
17. Stanford Reading Tests–Intermediate II

1	2	3	4	5	6	7	8	9	10	11	12	13	14	15	16	17	Criterion
																	Validity: Does the test measure what it purports to measure?
																	1. Evidence is complete and satisfactory.
a✓	a✓	a✓										✓	✓	✓	✓		2. Evidence as given is satisfactory but not complete enough to support test purposes.
																	3. Data given but indicate test is not valid enough for stated purposes.
			✓	✓	✓	✓	✓	✓	✓	✓	✓						4. Not enough information given.
																	5. No information given.
																	Reliability: Are the test results consistent?
		✓	✓	✓	✓	✓		✓	✓	✓	✓						1. Evidence is complete and satisfactory.
a✓	a✓	a✓										✓	✓	✓	✓		2. Evidence as given is satisfactory but not complete enough to support test purposes.
																	3. Data given but indicate test is not reliable enough for stated purposes.
																	4. Not enough information given.
																	5. No information given.
																	Norms: Are grade or age equivalent scores usable?
												✓	✓	✓	✓		1. Description of norming population is complete and usable.
a✓	a✓	a✓	✓	✓	✓	✓	✓	a✓	a✓	a✓	a✓						2. Description is not complete but norms seem usable.
							✓										3. Description is complete but norms are limited for most purposes.
																	4. Not enough information given.
																	5. No information is given.
																	Subtests and Items
✓	✓	✓					✓	✓	✓	✓	✓						1. Subtests are not long enough for reliable use (only total test scores should be used).
✓	✓	✓	✓	✓	✓	✓	✓	✓	✓	✓	✓	✓	✓	✓	✓		2. Subtests do not seem to be valid measures of subskills (only total test scores should be used).
							✓										3. Several test items are either outdated or misleading or should be used only with special populations

a Additional information is available from the publisher but is not part of the examiner's manual.

Table 2–8. Description of Achievement Tests Reviewed

Name of Test	Subtests	Grade	Publication Date	Authors	Publisher	Time (minutes)
California Reading Test						
Lower Primary	Vocabulary; comprehension	1–2	1970	Tiegs and Clark	California Test Bureau	45
Upper Primary	Vocabulary; comprehension	2.5–4.5				40
Elementary	Vocabulary; comprehension	4–6				40
Gates MacGinitie Reading Test						
Primary A	Vocabulary; comprehension	1	1965	Gates and MacGinitie	Teachers College Press, Columbia University	55
Primary B	Vocabulary; comprehension	2				55
Primary C	Speed and accuracy	3				65
Primary CS	Vocabulary; comprehension	2, 3				17
Survey D	Speed and accuracy	4, 5, 6				65
Iowa Silent Reading Test						
Elementary Test	Rate: comprehension; directed reading; word meaning; paragraph comprehension; sentence meaning; alphabetizing and use of index	4–8	1943	Greene and Kelley	Harcourt, Brace & World	60
Metropolitan Achievement Test						
Primary I	Word knowledge; word discrimination; reading	H–1	1971	Durost et al.	Harcourt, Brace & World	63
Primary II	Word knowledge; word discrimination; reading	2				65
Elementary	Word knowledge; reading	3–4				35
Intermediate	Word knowledge; reading	4–5				45
Stanford Reading Test						
Primary I	Word reading; paragraph meaning		1964	Kelley et al.	Harcourt, Brace & World	55
Primary II	Word reading; paragraph meaning					60
Intermediate I	Word reading; paragraph meaning					50
Intermediate II	Word reading; paragraph meaning					55

materials on *levels* in an attempt to get away from the stigma of "gradedness."

In order for the inexperienced classroom teacher to become familiar with the reading skills and methods of a basal program, she should follow the sequence of stories and carefully use the aids and directions found in the teacher's manual. Flexibility and innovation come with experience. Of course, the teacher should extend the basal approach beyond the basal reader; the reader frequently can be combined with the language-experience approach to broaden the program. As with any program, basal readers are at times subject to improper use. N. B. Smith (1963) has listed some of the misuses of basal readers.

1. Considering the basal program, itself, as the whole program for reading instructions.
2. Using one grade level and basal readers with the entire class, regardless of the different instructional levels of the children.
3. Setting up the goal of having children cover all pages in a certain reader as the end point of a semester's work.
4. Insisting that children should not work in a reader higher than the grade represented in their classroom.
5. Permitting children to keep their basal readers in their desks or take them home, thus providing them an opportunity to become familiar with stories before the teacher is ready to present them.
6. Using the teacher's guide as a detailed prescription to be followed exactly or disregarding it entirely.
7. Confining reading instruction to just reading stories with no period of skill development.
8. Failing to keep records of specific skills on which children need help and not providing extra practice on these skills.
9. Using the basal reader as busy work when the children have nothing else to do.
10. Using workbooks indiscriminately with all children, failing to check workbooks, failing to develop supplementary work with children who are not able to work on them independently.
11. Requiring purposeless re-reading.
12. Using the content of the basal readers as the sole basis for the development of study skills needed in the content areas.[6]

With experience, the teacher can use the manual as a reference of helpful suggestions. At times certain stories may be read out of regular sequence,

6. From Nila Banton Smith, *Reading Instruction for Today's Children,* © 1963, pp. 99–100. By permission of Prentice-Hall, Inc.

if the stories have possibilities for the development of specific skills needed by the students. It is important that the teacher know what is included in the entire manual before she begins to make major changes in the program.

The heart of the basal reading program is the directed reading activity (DRA); this portion is not only applicable to the regular reading program but can be used in any subject area at any level. The following is a skeleton plan for a DRA adapted from Betts.[7]

1. Develop readiness
   a. Arouse interest
   b. Point up background of experience
   c. Develop working concepts; do not conduct isolated drill on new words
   d. Set a purpose or purposes for the specific reading content
2. Guide the first silent reading (this is *not* an independent activity)
   a. Conduct silent reading before oral reading
   b. Encourage pupils to unlock new words in context and to seek the teacher's help, if necessary, in attacking new words
3. Develop comprehension and word-recognition skills
   a. Check understanding in terms of the initially set purposes
   b. Satisfy word-recognition needs; use the contextual setting first
4. Re-reading (not essential for every lesson)
   a. Be certain there are purposes for re-reading
   b. Re-reading may be oral or silent
   c. The entire story does not have to be read
5. Follow-up
   a. Ensure systematic guidance from the teacher to meet individual needs
   b. Aim for the broadening, deepening, or applying of information or of skills
   c. Plan for individual, group, and class instruction

Teachers complain that frequently pupils will not do homework assignments involving use of science or social studies books. Probably, in this day of competition with entertainment and other distractions, the children either rush through the material hurriedly and develop poor study habits, or do not bother to read it at all. However, by using a DRA in a science or social studies lesson, the teacher can be confident that the children are reading the material in an orderly, purposeful manner, learning good study habits, and also developing essential reading skills.

7. Adapted from E. A. Betts, *Foundations of Reading Institution* (New York: American Book Co., 1956). Used by permission of American Book Co.

Individualized reading. In recent years, numerous educators have advocated the use of individualized instruction in reading. It is felt by some that individuals should be given the opportunity to follow their own tastes. Being sociable, children will want to discuss what they read, and will profit by their discussion. If reading instruction is to develop desirable attitudes, habits, and skills, then each teacher must study the needs and interests of his pupils to provide appropriate individualized instruction. The most widely quoted definition of individualized reading has been taken from the work of Lazar (1957), who states:

> Individualized reading is a way of thinking about reading—an attitude towards the place of reading in the total curriculum, towards the materials and methods used, and towards the child's developmental needs. It is not a single method or technique but a broader way of thinking about reading which involves newer concepts about class organization, materials, and the approach to the individual child. The term individualized reading is by no means fully descriptive, but for want of a better term, most proponents of this approach continue to use it (p. 76).

In an individualized reading program, each child reads materials of his own choice and proceeds at his own rate. The pressures of meeting grade-level standards are eliminated and no one is in the low reading group. Each child is taught word recognition and comprehension skills as he needs them so that he can realize their usefulness. Generally, the program permits the child to read a larger amount of material of a wider variety than he would in a more traditional setting. Through individual conferences with the teacher, the student can be guided into new areas of exploration. A child may be very excited about one kind of fiction, for example, mystery stories. The teacher can direct him to research on the work of real detectives, to find out if the author presented the geographical setting correctly, or to investigate other points of the story.

The individualized approach integrates well into the language arts program in the areas of writing, spelling, and speaking. A few of the many activities that can be included are the following:

1. Write a book review giving the positive and negative points of the book.
2. Develop a play from the story and have a group of children perform it for the class.
3. Present a book talk.
4. Draw a map, poster, or illustration for a book or a particular part of it.

Listed here are some of the common criticisms of the individualized reading approach and some answers to these criticisms:

Criticism	Answer
1. A child may select material that is too difficult for him or beyond his background or experience.	1. If the child selects inappropriate material, he should have the right to select another book.
2. A child may never finish the book.	2. It is quite possible that other factors are impeding his progress. Other areas (e.g., vision) should be explored.
3. The skills program will not be balanced or sequenced.	3. Supplementary materials can be developed or secured to balance the skills program.
4. The child may read only one kind of material (e.g., fiction).	4. The teacher should guide the child into other kinds of material.
5. There is no opportunity for group interaction.	5. Children who have read the same book can be grouped for discussions.
6. There is not enough time for teacher–pupil conferences to be worthwhile.	6. Teachers should be familiar with the material and have specific questions to check various skills.
7. The child's needs are never carefully diagnosed.	7. A skilled teacher will have both formal and informal evaluations of a child's reading needs.
8. It is impossible to evaluate such a program.	8. The teacher will evaluate the reading skills of each child, rather than the program.

Language-experience approach. When the language-experience approach is used as a beginning reading program, children describe their experiences and the teacher records what the child says on the chalkboard. These stories are used as the basis for reading lessons. The advantages of using language-experience approach in reading programs include the following: The lesson is based on the experience of the child. The language of the experience story is the child's. The interest level is generally high, since the child is relating and then reading about something that has happened to him. As writing, speaking, and spelling are incorporated into the program, the language-experience approach can be regarded as a total language arts program.

A number of kinds of experience charts can be used. Narrative charts can include an account of an experience of the group. Records of experiments can be developed on charts. Often charts are used to report news events (e.g., many classes place the morning news on experience charts). Fiction stories developed on a cooperative basis can also be placed on charts. The systematic development of an experience chart (or story) involves a number of steps, including (1) preparation of the children, (2) identification of reason for making a chart, (3) preliminary draft, (4) editing and revising, (5) illustrating, and (6) writing the chart in permanent or semipermanent form.

Subjects for charts should come from the real or vicarious experiences of the children. Concepts are developed and clarified through group discussions that give children an opportunity to share information and learn from one another.

A preliminary draft is made on the chalkboard. At this stage the teacher plays an important part in guiding the suggestions, considerations, and revisions. Participation of each pupil should be encouraged. The discussion should be directed at giving the composition unity. The composition should be readable for the group in question with special attention devoted to vocabulary. Its length should depend on the previous experiences of the pupils with this type of activity and their general level of maturity. It is valuable only as long as the children are interested.

The uses of experience charts are many and varied. They can be used in kindergarten and early first grade to develop readiness for formal reading instruction. They can be used at any level to supplement other approaches. Charts can be developed to prepare students for the introduction of a unit in a subject area and also to summarize and unify the unit. The correct use of letter forms and handwriting skills can be developed. Units in areas such as science, social studies, and history can be developed through experience charts. The oral language facility of the children can be improved, as can spelling skills and creative writing skills.

Although this approach is often regarded as only practical for beginning readers, it also can be used effectively in the upper grades with older students, especially if appropriate commercial materials are not available.

Language experience in reading. This approach (Allen and Allen, 1970) uses a basic framework of language experiences to develop reading, listening, speaking, spelling, and writing skills. The program has three major emphases:

1. Extending the experiences of each child to include words that express these experiences orally and in writing, discussing selected topics, listening to and telling stories, writing independently, and making and reading books.
2. Developing skills and procedures for studying the English language and understanding its basic structure by developing an understanding of speaking, reading, and writing relationships, expanding vocabulary, reading a variety of symbols in the environment,

improving skills and forms of personal expression, studying words, and gaining an awareness of characteristics of English.

3. Learning to use a variety of resources to study a given topic, summarizing, outlining, reading for specific purposes, and reading to determine the validity and reliability of statements.

The basis of children's oral and written expression is their sensitivity to the environment, especially their language environment within the classroom and in the world at large; this is the conceptual framework upon which the program rests. Freedom in self-expression, oral and written, is seen as leading to self-confidence in all language usage, including grammar, punctuation, capitalization, spelling, and word recognition. Emphasis is placed on the natural flow of language of the children. The program of instruction values self-expression (oral expression, written expression, reading of the children's written expression by others, and individual authorship). Communication between children is promoted through the use of a variety of materials and activities. This increases the chances of success for more children and hopefully creates positive attitudes toward reading.

Learning centers, where children can work in small groups or individually, are an essential part of this language-experience program. Learning centers might be centers for writing, reading, publishing, language study, mathematics, cooking, games and activities, art, dramatization and puppetry, and viewing and listening. Multisensory materials should be available to the children in the learning centers.

Programmed reading. Programmed reading is a form of individualized approach in which the material is presented to the child in small learning units that have been developed into a carefully organized, logical sequence. The child reads, responds, and then checks his own responses; the responses usually are in the form of yes–no answers, the addition of a single word to complete a sentence, writing a word to answer a question, or filling in letters to complete a word.

There are two types of programming. A *linear* program is comprised of a very structured series of questions arranged so that each item leads the student to make the correct response. If the child errs, he makes the correction immediately before continuing. (Figure 2–3 is an example of linear programming.) The second kind of programming is known as a *branching* program. If the student makes an incorrect response, he is referred to another page or unit where the mistake is explained to him before he continues. An important difference between programmed material and ordinary textbook teaching is that with both types of programmed materials, the reader immediately receives feedback to his response. He does not have to wait until his paper or workbook is graded by the teacher. The programmed

Figure 2–3. *Example of Linear Programming.* [Reprinted from *Programmed Reading Book 4* by C. D. Buchanan, © 1968 Sullivan Associates, with permission of McGraw-Hill, Inc.]

concept has a number of advantages. The child moves in small steps, receives immediate feedback as to the correctness of his responses, and the teacher is freed from correcting drill pages. As a result, the teacher has more time to devote to solving individual problems, explaining new concepts, and leading discussions. Programmed instruction in reading seems most applicable when teaching those concepts that must be fixed by practice or memorization and that should become automatic.

A few of the more serious disadvantages of most programmed reading series should be noted. For example, it is difficult to program material that does not have an exact answer. Also, it is easy for children to cheat (i.e., to look at an answer before trying a frame). Finally, there is insufficient stress placed on the development of comprehension skills. Other objections raised by Spache (1976) are listed below.

1. Despite the claims of the publishers, programmed instruction is not an individualized approach, for in actual practice all children get the same program.
2. The approach tends to reduce reading to a collection of disjointed and possibly unrelated skills.
3. Such instruction is apt to be divorced from the supportive areas of speaking, listening, and writing.

In short, the programmed approach is not a total reading program. In addition, if a child works exclusively with a programmed reader day after day, it is possible for reading to become a laborious and monotonous chore. Therefore, the teacher must be flexible and make every attempt to make the reading period interesting and rewarding. Recognizing this, many publishers of programmed materials make provisions for teachers to expand the program and to include group work.

All programmed materials are not of the "software" variety (e.g., workbooks). Some teaching machines of the "hardware" type are now available. These necessitate the pulling of a knob, the turning of a crank, or the pushing of a lever or button to use them. To date, research has not provided definitive answers regarding the advantages and limitations of such instruments (Cushenberry, 1971).

Peabody Rebus program. Many of the new approaches to teaching reading attempt to circumvent some of the problems facing the beginning reader by providing an intermediate step. Until the Peabody Rebus program was developed (Woodcock, 1967), these intermediate steps have usually been in the form of some phonemic alphabet, such as the initial teaching alphabet (i/t/a). The authors of the Peabody Rebus program, however, believe that rebuses (picture words), rather than spelled words, would be much easier in the initial stages of reading instruction. From this idea evolved the concept that pupils should first learn about the nature of reading and develop basic reading skills in the context of an easily learned rebus vocabulary. The pupils then make the transition to a traditional reading situation through a controlled substitution of spelled words for the rebus.

The Peabody Rebus is a programmed approach to readiness and beginning reading instruction. It is designed to provide a natural bridge between the child's background of spoken language and his new task of learning to read printed words. The author of the Peabody program claims to provide this bridge by immediately introducing the child to the reading process by which he learns to read by using a vocabulary of picture words (rebuses). He feels that pictorial representations of words are remarkably easy for a child to learn and to remember.

The two characteristics of the program that seem to set it apart from other readiness and beginning reading programs are the incorporation of a programmed text format and the use of a rebus as a link between the spoken and written word. As a result of linear programming, much of the teaching load is carried by instructional material, rather than by the teacher. The following instructional procedures are featured in the program:

1. The programmed material provides a progressive and logical series of learning experiences.
2. Each frame requires an active response from the learner.
3. The pupil receives immediate feedback as to the correctness of his response. In the workbook the student applies a streak of water to the ribbed area beneath his choice of answer. The area immediately changes color, green if the response is correct, red if incorrect.
4. The pupil does not proceed until the correct response has been made.

5. The programmed material allows the pupil to proceed at his own rate.
6. A high level of success is provided for the learner.

The readiness level of the Peabody Rebus includes two programmed workbooks (*Introducing Reading—Book One,* and *Introducing Reading—Book Two*). Within each frame there is a simple question or reading task that is carefully built upon the preceding learnings. The program can either supplement or supplant the traditional reading readiness program. The transitional level of this program includes a third programmed workbook (*Introducing Reading—Book Three*) and two rebus readers (*Red and Blue Are on Me* and *Can You See a Flea?*). Children will have a reading vocabulary of approximately 120 spelled words upon completion of the transitional level.

The only items, other than a teacher's guide, that are necessary for the program are copies of the workbooks and some device for applying a streak of water on the ribbed response area. Supplementary materials are available from the publisher and include a set of rebus word cards, small individual sponges, and the Developmental Lessons Kit.

The Peabody creators maintain that first-grade children of average or above-average intelligence can complete a workbook in about 1 week by working 20 to 30 minutes each day. Less mature children will require more time. Fifty to 75 frames a day is appropriate for most pupils.

The Peabody–Chicago–Detroit Reading Project for beginning readers extensively utilized rebuses. This project compared six different approaches for teaching reading to young, mentally retarded children and involved 127 classes of such children in the cities of Detroit and Chicago. One result of this study was the development of an experimental edition derived from the experiences of this program. This edition was field-tested by 53 teachers with a variety of children, including kindergarten, Head Start, first grade, mentally retarded, emotionally disturbed, and remedial readers.

Kindergarten, Head Start, and other preschool programs have found the Readiness Level of Rebus a valuable end-of-program experience, as it provides a stimulating 2- to 4-week introduction to academic learning activities. In the first grade, *Book One* and *Book Two* can be used as a readiness program with any beginning reading approach. Upon completion of the Transition Level, children are ready for the primer level in traditional programs. The Peabody Rebus program also lends itself to teaching non-English-speaking children. The rebuses are first presented in the child's own language, followed by teaching the child the equivalent English word. Remedial readers are attracted by the illustrations and benefit from the emphasis on comprehension skills and context clues in word perception. The carefully sequenced program has also been used extensively with learning disabled and mentally retarded children.

Initial teaching alphabet (i/t/a). The initial teaching alphabet was devised by Pitman (1963), who felt that many beginning readers were confused by using only 26 symbols (the traditional orthography) to represent the 44 common sounds (phonemes) of the English language. His augmented alphabet contains 44 characters (the pictorial representations are called characters, not symbols or letters). There is a one-to-one correspondence between the sound and the character. No distinction is made between the forms of the small and capital letters and no characters are provided for the q and x. Twenty symbols have been added for speech sounds not represented by a single letter of the English alphabet.

Using Pitman's i/t/a, Mazurkiewicz and Tanyzer (1966) have developed the *Early to Read: i/t/a* Program in which children initially learn, through the use of the language-experience approach, that written language represents speech sounds. From this beginning, the children acquire a basic sight vocabulary. Then they begin to read stories with gradually increasing vocabularies.

The program is divided into three phases. In Phase I, the children are introduced to the 44 characters of the i/t/a program and are provided with reading activities in the first five readers. In Phase II, the children are led to higher levels of achievement; and in Phase III, they are taken to a point where they can successfully transfer their reading skills and abilities to the traditional orthography.

The program has a set of teacher's manuals with explicit directions. Once information in the manuals has been mastered, the teacher may add supplementary exercises and activities. The program also is readily adaptable to small-group instruction; provisions for individual needs can be devised by the teacher. The program spans seven books and one workbook for transfer into traditional orthography. No set time for the completion of the program is suggested.

To establish an appropriate instructional level upon completion of the program, placement tests from various publishers or informal testing instruments can be used. Although various grade levels have been suggested, an assessment of reading skills is necessary; otherwise, the child may be placed in a frustrating situation when confronted with traditional orthography. The program has been reported to be successful when used in regular primary, special education, and remedial classes, although research on the use of i/t/a is not conclusive.

Distar. Distar (Englemann and Bruner, 1969) is the product of more than six years of intensive work with preschool children, primarily in the Bereiter–Engelmann experimental program at the University of Illinois. It is a programmed instructional system designed to teach children with below-average communication abilities the prerequisite skills they need to catch up. It is in direct opposition to the programs that advocate readiness classes; there, the emphasis is placed on "performing meaningful activities," while waiting for the child to "mature."

Distar is designed to quickly remediate below-average reading skills by providing exercises in sequencing events, rhyming, and blending—in other words, breaking the reading code.

There are two levels in the program: Reading I and Reading II. Both levels provide a teacher manual and four presentation books. For Reading I, the student materials consist of take-home blending, story, sound—symbol, writing sheets, and workbooks. For Reading II, the students are provided with take-home stories, questions, worksheets, and writing sheets.

Distar can be used with any child who has below-average reading skills, whether he is a preschooler, kindergartener, in the primary grades, an older child needing remedial work, or a child who speaks English as a second language. The children are divided into homogeneous groups, not by how quickly they can learn, but by what they can do at that particular time. All children begin with the first of the 159 lessons in Reading I. Each child changes groups as his performance on tests indicates that he has learned the skills he will need on future tasks. A child may also be moved to a lower group, where he may require individual tutoring.

At the beginning of Reading I, the lowest group should have no more than five children. After the children have mastered the basic reading skills, it may be possible to increase the size of the group. One full, 30-minute lesson should be presented each day. Everything that the teacher is to say and do is spelled out in the manuals. The children sit on chairs in a quarter-circle, each within reach of the teacher. Correct responses are reinforced; wrong answers are corrected.

If the directions are followed, the daily lessons for Reading I will be in this order:

Symbol—Action Games	Begins on first day; presentations 1–17.
Blending—Spelling by Sounds	Begins after Symbol—Action Game 17; presentations 17–60.
Blending, Say It Fast	Begins first day; presentations 1–40.
Take-Home Blending Sheets	Begins first day; presentations 1–5.
Sounds	Begins first day; presentations 1–159.
Reading Sounds	Begins after Sounds 26; presentations 26–159.
Rhyming	Begins after Sounds 6; presentations 6–27.

Symbols—Say It Fast	Begins after Reading Sounds 30; presentations 30–39.
Take-Home Sound Symbol Sheets	Begins on first day; presentations 1–39.
Take-Home Stories and Writing Sheets	Begins after Reading Sounds 40; presentations 40–159.
Workbook	Begins after Sounds 32; presentations 32–159.

Each Reading II presentation is numbered, and each lesson segment should be presented in order. The order presentation is relatively uniform:

Sounds

Reading Sounds

Take-Home Stories and Questions or Read the Items

Take-Home Worksheets and Writing Sheets (as seatwork)

The children are to be periodically tested (the tests are provided). In Reading I, those who fail a test must repeat that series of presentations. Because of this, they may progress faster in some presentations than others; for example, on one day they may be doing Sounds 8 and Blending 15. In Reading II, the tests are consolidated measures of all the skill areas, and a failure results in repetition of all the exercises in the series of lessons. Very little research has been done on either this particular program or the theories of Bereiter and Engelmann, on which it is based. Although the system appears to be well organized and well written, more verification and research is needed.

Words in Color (Gattegno, 1962). This is a synthetic phonics program that uses color as an additional dimension to indicate sounds contained in words. Phonemes (speech sounds) are identified by like colors regardless of the symbols used. The materials used in this program include 29 wall charts. On the first 21 of these, more than 600 words provide the phonic clues to reading. The remaining eight are called the "Phonic Code." On these, various spellings for each sound are arranged in columns. There are 51 columns to include the 51 sounds in this classification of the English language. Other materials, which are printed in black and white, include three phonics readers: the *Word Building Book,* containing tables of signs; worksheets for reinforcement; a *Book of Stories,* used to aid children in writing stories; and *Words in Color Chalk,* used to introduce new signs.

Speech and writing are integral parts of the program. Phonics instruction is stressed and the children learn the sounds of letters rather than the letter names. Vowels are introduced first in this program, one at a time. The sign *a* (white) is first presented on the chalkboard and Visual Dictation is used for learning its sound. As soon as two signs are introduced, combinations and reversals can be ultilized in the Visual Dictation. Book 1 is used in coordination with each vowel as it is learned.

After the vowels are mastered, consonants are introduced. The sign *p* (dark brown) is presented first on the chalkboard. Combinations and reversals are continued with Visual Dictation. Closed simple syllables can be formed by having the teacher's pointer, in a single sweeping movement, connect the three signs. Consonant *t* (magenta) is introduced next and small sentences then can be introduced. The teacher should ask for the response to the whole sentence after pointing out the whole sentence. At this time the *Word Building Book* is introduced; the student uses its materials in the same way the teacher uses the pointer at the chalkboard, only with the eraser end of a pencil. Oral Dictation is used in this book.

Two sounds for the sign *s* are introduced next, *s* (lilac color) as in *is*, and *s* (lime green) as in *us*, thus developing the idea that in English two different sounds may have the same sign. The double sign *tt* is introduced next; it has the same sound and color as the single *t*, teaching the child that two different signs can have the same sound. These exercises are continued and consonant blends can be formed by superimposing the sounds of two words.

The game of transformations is introduced (i.e., transforming one word into another) through the use of the following:

substitutions	test	pest
reversals	pets	step
additions	step	steps
insertions	pet	pest

As the children proceed in the program, new letters and sounds are introduced by introducing new word charts. The *Phonics Code Charts* are not introduced until most or all of the Word Charts have been learned. The *Book of Stories* and the *Worksheet Book* are not introduced until after all of the Word Charts have been learned.

Words in Color is a multisensory developmental program. It can be used for group as well as individual instruction, and students of any age may profit from this approach. The utilization of many sensory pathways would seem to make it adaptable for remedial work and special education classes. However, the large number of colors to be learned may be a problem for some children. Also, Spache (1976) considers Gattegno's reports of his own research with illiterate adults in several foreign countries and his references to trials with migrant children, illiterate adults, first graders, and so on, in this country to be rather vague. Several researchers [e.g., Hill (1967), Lockmiller and Di Nello (1970), and Heilman (1965)] have studied the approach under experimental conditions and report that it is apparently no more efficient than other systems of instruction.

Stern Structural Reading Series (Stern, 1963). This series consists of six combination workbook–readers for grades K–2. Supplementary materials include instructional dominoes and a picture dictionary. The program builds on the oral language of the child and proceeds to the written word, the sentence, the paragraph, and finally the story. The worktexts constitute a complete, primary language arts program and include reading, writing, and spelling skills.

Special Techniques

The following teaching techniques are often used in schools or classes that specialize in children with reading disabilities. A regular class teacher would not usually be expected to use any of these clinical approaches in their entirety. However, they can be modified and adapted to meet the needs of specific children.

The Fernald (VAKT) approach. If a child has a severe word-learning difficulty, and visual–auditory approaches have been unsuccessful, a modification of the Fernald (1943) Word Learning Technique is recommended. Although several authors refer to Fernald's remedial technique for teaching disabled readers as a kinesthetic method, the system is actually multisensory, involving four modalities simultaneously [i.e., visual, auditory, kinesthetic, and tactile (or VAKT)]. The approach is cognitive, for the words learned always originate with the reader, and have contextual or meaningful association.

Fernald, who opened a clinic school at UCLA in 1920, was concerned with the emotional components of failure to learn. "The child who fails in his school work is always an emotional problem" (1943, p. 7). The circular aspect of this dilemma was approached in two ways: by analyzing the problem and by reconditioning the student. Both are positive approaches to remediation that call the child's attention to what he has already learned and assure him that he can learn any words that he wants to learn. To maintain a positive learning climate the following are avoided: (1) emotionally laden situations, (2) the use of methods associated with previous failure, (3) embarrassing situations, and (4) references to the child's problems. Poor readers are divided into two groups: total or extreme disability and partial disability. The VAKT method is used with children from both groups when the disability is failure to recognize words.

Perception of the word as a whole is basic to the Fernald method. The child begins remediation by story writing, initially about anything that interests him, and later concerning his various school subjects. The child "asks" for any word he does not know. It is written for him, learned by him, and used immediately in his story. What he has written is typed for him so that he may read it while its content is still fresh in his mind. For children with extreme disability, almost every word is necessarily taught.

Stage I uses a multisensory approach. As the child requests a word, it is written or printed for him with black crayon in blackboard-size script on a piece of heavy paper. He traces the word with firm, two-finger contact (tactile-kinesthetic), and says the word aloud in syllables (auditory) as he traces. He sees the word while he is tracing (visual), and hears it as he says it (auditory). He repeats the process until he can write the word correctly twice, without looking at the sample. When tracing or writing, the word is always written as a unit, without stopping. If he errs, the child begins again with the first step. Copying a word by alternately looking at the sample and writing a few letters is forbidden. After the lesson, the words are filed alphabetically, to provide a record or source of the words learned.

After a period of tracing, the tactile phase is discontinued and Stage II is begun. Here the child learns a new word by following the looking, saying, and writing steps of Stage I. Vocabulary is still learned in context and involves VAK. There is no arbitrary time limit for the tracing period and usaully the child tends to drop tracing of his own accord.

Stage III dispenses with the kinesthetic mode, and the child learns a new word merely by looking at the sample and saying it to himself.

Stage IV is achieved when the child has the ability to recognize new words by their similarity to words or to parts of words that he has already learned (i.e., when he can generalize his reading skills). Teaching phonics is not considered necessary, for this generalizing process presumably occurs without phonetic analysis. At this stage the child reads to satisfy his curiosity.

The amount of reading necessary before discontinuing remediation and returning the child to the regular classroom reading situation depends on the educational level he must reach. Older children spend more time in Stage IV, as they do not return to the regular instructional setting until they are able to read well enough to make progress at their own instructional level.

In addition to those already stated, Fernald holds several principles:

1. Children are never read to; they must do their own reading.
2. The child never sounds out words, unless he does it while scanning a paragraph for unknown words before beginning to read that paragraph.

3.   At any stage, material must be suited to the child's age and intelligence.

Careful scheduling is important, as the teacher cannot plan to work with one child unless all of the other children are involved in some purposeful activity. The child's resentment at being taken from gym or art also might outweigh any positive accomplishment.   It should be emphasized that the Fernald approach (VAKT) is basically a word-learning technique and the child should have directed reading instruction in a group, or individually, to develop comprehension skills.

The Gillingham (Orton) phonics approach (Gillingham and Stillman, 1970).   This is a remedial, phonics-oriented reading program based on the theoretical work of Orton.   The systematic approaches to reading, spelling, and writing are adapted to all levels from age 6 through high school.   This "alphabetic system" is based on the premise that children who fail to read by group methods do so because group programs rely upon visual-receptive strength.   In contrast, Gillingham's training system stresses auditory discrimination abilities with supplementary emphasis on kinesthetic and tactile modalities.   While phonetic methods help the child to synthesize what he sees with what he hears, visual perception is used minimally.

Gillingham's synthetic approach is essentially a formal skill-building program.   Teachers are encouraged to follow the manual if success is to be expected.   The entire program is built upon eight basic linkages that form the association of auditory, visual, and kinesthetic stimuli.   Once the child has mastered basic sound production, he is introduced to phonograms (one letter or a group of letters that represent a phonetic sound).   Once the phonograms have been mastered, they are used in drill procedures.

The teaching procedure begins with the introduction of the short "a" sound plus several specified consonant sounds.   When these have been learned by the method above, blending is begun.   Several phonogram cards are placed side by side.   Individual sounds are produced in succession and with increasing speed until a fluid rate is achieved.   The day following the initiation of the blending procedure, word analysis begins.   This is achieved on an auditory level with the teacher sounding the word, and the child identifying the letters he hears.   This process leads directly to the Simultaneous Oral Spelling process, in which the teacher says the word, the child says the word, names the letters, then writes the letters as he names them.   This procedure is always used in the production of phonetically pure words.

One of the stipulations of the early program is that the child is given no other printed materials.   If the child remains in a regular class while receiving remedial help, all other subject material must be presented auditorially.

After blending has been established with all of the phonetic sounds, a reader or primer may be introduced. Books are carefully screened to assure that all words included are phonetic and thus suitable for blending. He is then introduced to basic phonetic rules, including syllabication and accent (all of which are included in the manual). When the child is able to synthesize and analyze any combination of phonetic syllables, nonphonetic syllables are introduced and memorized as whole syllables.

Gillingham's program for developing skills combines the use of phonetic study as well as experiences and language stories. Tracing, copying, and dictation are used simultaneously to achieve different purposes. Tracing is useful in learning the formation of letters and establishing a letter sequence for spelling. Copying develops visual memory; after practicing this, a child must produce a model that has been removed from sight. The purpose of dictation is to lengthen the auditory attention span and promote the association between auditory stimuli and visual imagery.

Initially, Gillingham felt that children who were capable of learning by visual methods should do so. However, in "Correspondence" (1958, pp. 119–122), she noted the difficulties children have with spelling and concluded that the kinesthetic and auditory stimuli provided in her program would prevent such difficulties. Therefore, she advised that all children be exposed to the "Alphabetic System,"

The success of this system seems dependent upon its use with children whose auditory discrimination is unimpaired. It is essential that the child's strengths as well as weaknesses be diagnosed. To extend its effectiveness, meaningful interpretations and activities must be introduced despite the admonitions of Gillingham.

Both Dechant (1964) and Gates (1947) have been critical of this system. Their concerns center on the lack of meaningful activities, the rigidity of the teaching procedures, and the tendency to develop labored reading. If valid, these points would certainly limit the usefulness of the system as a total reading program. Interestingly, Harris (1968) noted that even though this approach has been used for many years, he had been unable to locate any comparative research on it.

The Spalding phonics approach. Spalding and Spalding (1962) describes her work as the "new unified phonics method." The sight system of reading is criticized on the basis that it fosters guessing and bad study habits. Her method is believed to be effective with all learners when used exclusively and rigidly. Spalding even recommends it for college students who wish to read more proficiently, though they must start at the very beginning and proceed through each step.

The Spalding method presents 70 phonograms representing the 45 basic sounds in the English language. The teacher introduces each of these sounds (letters are never called by name, only by sound) orally. As students parrot the sound, they are introduced to the graphic symbol that represents the auditory phonogram. The students must write the phonogram in lowercase manuscript form, on ⅜-inch ruled paper, skipping every other line. A precise, rigid notebook is mandated from which there should be no deviation. Instructions are even given on the correct way to erase.

The author has a unique way of teaching the formation of letters. A clockface is used as the background form. For all letters (manuscript, cursive, capital, and lowercase) pencil movement is directed by following a numerical sequence, the numerals corresponding in position to those on a clock dial. For example, the correct pattern for "s" is 2, 12, 10, 4, 6, 8. The program starts with the two-o'clock letters (a, c, d, f, g, o, s, q) and then proceeds to the more complex. After a student has learned to print the graphic symbol, visual cues are no longer given. Much drill is provided wherein the teacher pronounces the phonogram, the students say it, and then the students print it in the best of penmanship.

After the student has mastered the phonograms in the auditory and graphic forms, the instructor begins teaching words. She clearly articulates each phonogram, indicating each by moving her hand in a carefully prescribed manner. The first phonogram is shown by moving the right hand from up to down; the next phonogram by moving the left hand in the same way as the right; continuing to alternate right and left hands for each of the succeeding phonograms until the last, when the right hand crosses the left in horizontal movement. In each move, fingers are extended to indicate the number of letters in each phonogram. These hand motions are thought to create a natural rhythm; the pointing fingers, "a kinesthetic feel for the word." The child sounds each word and then writes it; this is to give the student a chance to think before he has to write.

At this stage in the methodology, the student's notebook becomes increasingly important. Words are presented in groups that follow phonetic rules. The student learns the rules as a logical system, and not by rote memorization; the words printed in the notebook serve to remind him of the rules. Spalding claims that almost all words in the English language are basically phonetic.

In her general comments, Spalding suggests that the entire class be taught at one time; she sees no value in splitting a class into small instructional groups. She further suggests that many teachers fail because they proceed too slowly; when half of the group has mastered one phase of this method, the teacher is to introduce the next phase. As the students master the rules, they are introduced to a primer.

While some aspects of this program seem useful in general, it tends toward rigidity and oversimplication. Spalding assumes that:

1. Any child can benefit from group instruction.
2. The auditory modality is intact.
3. Children have large spoken vocabularies.
4. Students have no need of training for cognitive skills that are a significant part of traditional reading programs.
5. Reading may be defined as the process by which students translate mentally from a graphic symbol to the sound of a familiar sound which represents a word he knows.
6. Students know the correct spacing of numerals on a clock dial.

In addition, Spalding does not explain how a child who mispronounces words will learn to spell and read correctly. Neither does she provide for the student who cannot keep up with his group. Rather, this program is a highly structured phonics system designed for group use. It should be adequate, however, when used with children who can benefit from such an approach.

The nine fundamental points of Spalding's teaching procedure are as follows:

1. Teach the phonograms.
   a. Pupils are shown phonograms and say the associated sound in unison.
   b. Just after the phonogram is pronounced, the students write the letter symbol.
2. Avoid naming the letters; only the phonetic sounds are used. Spalding believes that this procedure facilitates the unification of speech, writing, and reading by eliminating the confusion occurring from using letter names.
3. Always refer to multiple-letter phonograms, such as *ea* or *eigh*, by the sounds associated with them; never spell them letter by letter. The children should learn to think of these phonograms as distinct sounds, not agglomerations of letters.
4. From the beginning of instruction, teach and demand correct writing and pronunciation.
5. After the phonograms have been learned, dictate to the children words from the Ayres list for them to write.
   a. The students should say each phonogram of short words or each syllable of longer words.
   b. Immediately after pronouncing the sound or syllables, the children write the associated letter forms; their writing of the word marks the first time they have seen the word in its written form.

6. The basic rules in spelling are taught as the need arises; such rules are ultimately committed to memory.

7. Irregular forms of words, that is, words which cannot be analyzed phonetically and to which no spelling rules apply, must be taught as sight or "learned" words.

8. Spelling must be emphasized as the basic key to the understanding of both written and spoken language.

9. Reading from books is delayed until the children can read common words easily enough to grasp the meaning of the material.

Color Phonics system (Bannatyne, 1966). This system consists of a set of individual letters and letter combinations printed on small cards; the letters are color coded in such a way that once the principle of the coding has been learned, the child can immediately identify each sound. The system is intended for use with almost every inadequately reading child, although in a few cases specific training in visual–spatial concepts is necessary. Color Phonics is, of course, not recommended for children with color blindness or color agnosia.

The Color Phonics system systematizes the irregular orthography of the English language. The color codings are not as numerous as those in Words in Color. All the consonants and the two consonant combinations *ph* and *qu* are printed in white on charcoal gray, while the vowels, including dipthongs, are printed in color sounds on a white ground. Each letter is mounted on a plaque on the back of which is a picture of some object or situation that represents the key word printed underneath. Each key word contains the appropriate, underlined phoneme. The color-coded approach is unique because the letters can be sequenced and each phoneme can be identified from the name of the color itself. For example, the phoneme *ee*, as sounded in green, is printed in a green color, and the phoneme *ow*, as sounded in brown, is printed in brown, and so on.

The Color Phonics system is quite compatible with the gradual introduction of particular phonemes and phonograms, as suggested in the Gillingham method. The system is not broken up into an extended series of separate exercises. The system operates independently of books. Suitable books can be introduced, once the teacher feels that the child has regained sufficient self-confidence to tackle suitable reading material. Although the system is not rigid, there are certain broad stages which are adhered to in the teaching process.

The system is best used in a one-to-one situation with nonreading children who have auditory sequencing and/or auditory–memory problems. It is a teaching *aid* and should be used with other programs. The technique does not depend on a great deal of organization of verbal content; instead, it requires the student to provide his own content. This is of value when using the system with older children who might react negatively to a system with organized verbal content, such as Words in Color.

Tutoring Individual Children in Reading

Today, adults, high school students, and even elementary pupils are often employed effectively as tutors in the schools. Even though these paraprofessionals may instruct children in basic school subjects, the primary qualifications for a tutor are not necessarily academic, a fact that is reflected in the following guidelines for selecting individuals to serve as tutors; for example, the tutor must:

1. Be dependable, for missing only one or two sessions will destroy the tutoring relationship and allow the child to regress.
2. Be patient and ready to go over material a number of times before the child has finally learned it.
3. Have an understanding of the student's problems and feelings.
4. Have integrity; for example, the tutor must be truthful and never leave the student with the impression that he is doing much better than is actually the case.
5. Be capable of handling well her own interpersonal relations.

Beyond these qualifications, the tutor must be interested in helping children, accept responsibility readily, and follow directions.

Before a tutorial program can be initiated efficiently, certain things must be done and agreed to. First, the child's problems in reading must be assessed carefully. Second, those areas in which the tutor will work must be decided upon. Third, the approach and materials that are to be used should be selected. Fourth, the period of time to be spent on any activity should be estimated. It is very important that the tutor know exactly what is expected, what is to be done, and how to do it. Therefore, some training should be conducted before the tutor begins the program. Left to their own devices without proper training and supervision, the tutor may unwittingly create problems and end up being "more trouble than she is worth."

Record keeping. Each tutor should be given a notebook (preferably looseleaf) in which there are three distinct kinds of pages. The first should be the Tutor's Lesson Plan. On this page, the activities, the procedures, and the amount of time to be devoted to each student can be listed. If special materials are required, they should be mentioned and an indication of where they may be obtained should be made. A sample lesson plan is shown in Figure 2–4.

Figure 2–4. *Tutor's Lesson Plan*

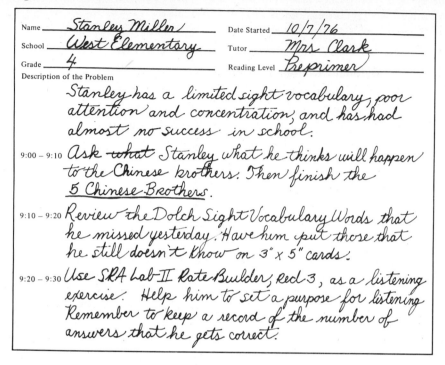

Name _Stanley Miller_   Date Started _10/7/76_

School _West Elementary_   Tutor _Mrs. Clark_

Grade _4_   Reading Level _Preprimer_

Description of the Problem

Stanley has a limited sight vocabulary, poor attention and concentration, and has had almost no success in school.

9:00 – 9:10 Ask Stanley what he thinks will happen to the Chinese brothers. Then finish the 5 Chinese Brothers.

9:10 – 9:20 Review the Dolch Sight Vocabulary Words that he missed yesterday. Have him put those that he still doesn't know on 3" x 5" cards.

9:20 – 9:30 Use SRA Lab II Rate Builder, Red 3, as a listening exercise. Help him to set a purpose for listening. Remember to keep a record of the number of answers that he gets correct.

The second kind of page that should be included in the Tutor's notebook is a Tutor's Log Sheet. On this, the tutor may record any observations about the progress of the child on a particular day that seems pertinent. The availability of this sheet will foster ongoing communications between the tutor and the busy classroom teacher. An example is given in Figure 2–5.

Another kind of sheet is the Teacher's Note. On this page, the teacher can make comments, suggestions, and/or recommendations for changes in the Tutor's Lesson Plan. For an example, see Figure 2–6.

Tutor training. Not only must the teacher assess, prescribe, and gather materials, but she must also make sure that the tutor can and does carry out the program as specified. To accomplish this, the teacher will usually have to provide the tutor with at least some minimal training (e.g., the tutor will have to be taught to complete the forms described in the previous section, to become familiar with the basic methods and strategies used by the teacher, etc.). Of course, it is not possible for the experienced teacher to transfer to the tutor all of the skills and expertise that she has acquired as a result of

Figure 2–5. *Tutor's Log Sheet*

Tutor: Mrs Clark — Student: Stanley Miller
Date: 10/7/76 — Grade: 4 — School: West Elementary

Stanley ~~do~~ could think what might happen but he listened and said, "Now I know!" when we came to it. We reviewed the Dolch Words and he missed 6 of them. He asked me if he could take them home. I told him I'd check with you. He answered all the questions on the rate builder correctly. This is 4 in row— he may be ready for the next color.

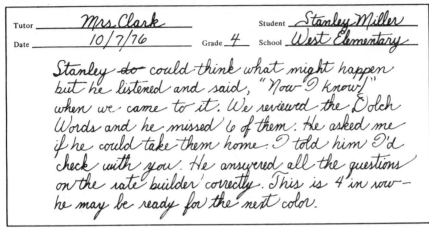

completing a 4-year college program and several years of teaching; but she can make sure that the tutor knows what to do and has the materials to do it.

Whenever possible, the tutor's training should be by example. The teacher should work with a child and demonstrate items of importance in a tutorial lesson, such as:

1. Qualities of good oral reading (e.g., creating interest in a story, setting purposes, anticipating outcomes, etc.).
2. Various ways to use flashcards for drill.
3. Teaching the child to trace words correctly, if this technique is used.
4. Selecting, or helping the child to select, an appropriate book.
5. Using a positive (i.e., reinforcing) attitude in all activities.
6. Keeping comprehensive records.

Figure 2–6. *Teacher's Note*

Tutor: Mrs Clark — Student: Stanley Miller
Teacher: Mr Lobb — Date: 10/7/76

Tell Stanley that we'll need the cards for something else later. He can take them home when we are finished. Try the next color for a listening activity. Have him select another book for the oral reading.

7. Various materials; their location and use.
8. Physical surroundings (e.g., adequate lighting).
9. Use of a dictionary when necessary.

During the training period, rapport between the tutor and the teacher must be established. If this is accomplished properly, the tutor will feel free to ask the teacher any question about the program. Rapport can be enhanced and maintained if, when asked a question, the teacher will carefully consider his response before answering. For example, it is far better for the teacher to say, "I'm sorry; I should have told you that," than to say, "I thought that you'd use your common sense." Negative criticism can shut off communication quickly.

Even when the tutors have received a great deal of training, problems will still arise, because a tutor cannot be expected to learn everything that she needs to know all at once. As a result, she will make gross mistakes occasionally. For example, the tutor may try to get the child to "sound out" words that are not phonetic; or to make sure that a pupil is reading, the tutor may encourage him to whisper or to move his lips when reading silently. From time to time, a tutor may inadvertently threaten a child with such statements as "If you don't do this, I won't like you," or "I can't understand why you don't know this; I've told you a hundred times!" The tutor may not recognize when a child is frustrated. There are many things, some great, some small, that can go wrong in a tutoring program, so the importance of adequate preparation, planning, tutor training, and supervision cannot be stressed too often.

If possible, tutors should be paid. Adult volunteers can fill the necessary gap; but they sometimes leave for a paying job, especially after they get some experience and can qualify for employment in a day-care center, a nursery school, or a private preschool; and they are often undependable. On the other hand, there is a wealth of untapped student talent in the school district that can serve as volunteer tutors. For example, older students can work with younger pupils ("cross-age tutoring"); and children of the same age can, and often do, tutor each other ("peer tutoring").

There exists a fairly impressive body of research that testifies to the merits of student tutoring in reading. For example, Cloward (1967) used sophomore and junior students as tutors for fourth- and fifth-grade boys. The students who tutored four times per week showed a significant gain in reading ability. Lane, Pollack, and Sher (1972) used a group of disruptive adolescents to tutor third- and fourth-grade students of below-level reading ability. Both tutors and students being tutored showed gains in reading and the tutors' antisocial behavior lessened considerably. Erickson (1971) conducted a study in which low-achieving seventh-grade students tutored third graders who were having difficulty in reading. He found that the program had a positive effect on both groups. Early reports on the Youth Tutoring Youth (Kopp, 1972), in which underachieving high school students tutored younger children, indicate that both groups gain valuable reading skills. Some tutors gained as much as 3 years in one semester. J. L. Thomas (1972) reported success with a program in which fifth- and sixth-grade students successfully tutored second graders.

SUPPLEMENTARY MATERIALS

Some pupils may need additional practice materials to ensure mastery of particular skills. The following materials are not designed to take the place of a comprehensive reading program; rather, they are best used in addition to one of the basic reading approaches. In prescribing any of these materials the teacher does not necessarily have to follow the sequence provided by the authors, nor does every child have to complete every page. If a total supplementary program is deemed necessary, the basic program should be evaluated to determine whether it is really meeting the needs of the students.

The teacher should have a variety of supplementary materials for different reading levels in her classroom. A child in a fifth-grade class may need practice in certain phonics skills that are best presented in a third-grade supplementary workbook. The teacher is cautioned against falling into a rigid approach in the use of supplementary materials, where each child is working on the same page in the same book.

The following is a brief sampling of materials that are commercially available. It would be impossible to list all of them, as new supplementary materials are being published every year. When planning a visit to an educational convention or conference, time should be set aside to visit the exhibits of new educational materials.

Skillbooks

Many companies publish supplemental workbook-type materials. Some of these, such as *Phonics We Use* (Meighen and Pratt, 1964), deal only with word-attack skills in grades one to six. Others, such as *Reading for Meaning* (Coleman and Jungeblut, 1965), stress vocabulary development and comprehension. *Be a Better Reader* (N. B. Smith, 1968) can be used in grades four to six to develop work-attack vocabulary, comprehsion, and study skills, as can the *Developmental Reading Text Workbook Series* (Burton, Kemp, Baker, Craig, and Moore, 1975). If this type of material is used in a systematic, planned manner, it can be useful in providing additional practice leading to mastery of particular skills. Care must be exercised so that these are not used inflexibly or as busywork. An additional consideration is the cost; the materials are consumable and must be replaced each year.

Reading Kits

The *Classroom Reading Clinic* (Kottmeyer, 1962) is a kit spanning the elementary grades and containing material to develop work-attack, vocabulary, and comprehension skills. It can be used with individual students or in small groups. In addition to skill-building materials, there are also high interest–low vocabulary library books.

The *SRA Reading Laboratories* (Parker and Scannell, 1961) are designed to offer individualized reading instruction to students in their regular classroom under the direction of the teacher. The kits that are available include:

SRA Reading Lab	*Reading Levels*	*To Be Used in*
Lab 1a	1.2–3.0	First grade
Lab 1b	1.4–4.0	Second grade
Lab 1c	1.4–5.0	Third grade
Lab 11a	2.0–7.0	Fourth grade
Lab 11b	3.0–8.0	Fifth grade
Lab 11c	4.0–9.0	Sixth grade
Lab 111a	3.0–12.0	Junior high

The program enables the teacher to meet individual needs within the classroom. Recently the concept of the "micro-level" was established so that children could progress in smaller steps than was required in older editions of the program. The program is based on a multilevel philosophy that emphasizes the differences in both learning rate and capacity. The SRA Reading Labs are one of the most widely used, individualized supplementary programs for reading instruction. Each kit contains all the materials needed for the program except the *Student's Record Book*, which is purchased separately.

A note of caution should be added. The teacher's manual gives explicit directions necessary to receive the maximum benefit from the program. Major deviations from the prescribed program generally appear to impede its effectiveness. This should not be regarded as a completely independent program; the teacher is needed. Also, the kit should not be used in a haphazard, infrequent fashion. Although this program has many attributes, overuse can lead to boredom on the part of the students.

Supplementary Phonics Programs

The *Phonovisual Method* (Schoolfield and Timberlake, 1960) consists of a large Consonant Chart, a large Vowel Chart, two charts for each pupil, a workbook for each child, and a teacher's manual. The child is taught to recognize and associate sounds with symbols in the following sequence: initial consonant sounds, medial consonant sounds, final consonant sounds, vowel sounds, and blends.

Highest Interest–Low Reading Level Programs

Field Educational Publications has published a number of high interest–low reading level series of reading books. Any of these can be used in directed reading activities or for supplementary reading. The teacher's manuals are sparse in directions, so the teacher must rely on her own background of experience and information to develop the lessons.

Title	Interest Level	Reading Level	Authors
Time Machine Series	K–3	PP–2.5	Darby (1966)
Jim Forest Series	1–6	1.7–3.2	Rambeau, Rambeau, and Gullett (1959)
Morgan Bay Mysteries	4–10	2.3–4.1	Rambeau and Rambeau (1962)
Wildlife Series	3–8	2.6–4.4	Leonard and Briscoe (1966)
Deep Sea Adventure Series	3–10	1.8–5.0	Coleman, Berres, Hewett, and Briscoe (1962)

Reading materials adapted from the adult version of the *Reader's Digest* are available for reading levels one through six. The soft-covered *Reader's Digest Reading Skill Builders* (Raths, Wasserman, Jonas, and Tothstein, 1968) provides interesting stories for directed or supplementary reading. Even the lowest-level books appeal to older students. *Reader's Digest Science Readers* (Raths, Wasserman, Jonas, and Tothstein, 1963), which contain adaptations of science articles, are also available. Owing to the popularity of the *Reader's Digest* as a magazine, the books can be used to develop reading skills with older students without the stigma of childish stories. The publisher presents these books in a variety of packages so that it is possible to obtain a few selections from a wide range of grade levels. This set can be used for adults with reading problems, also.

Reading Efficiency

Although many programs contain exercises to improve reading speed and accuracy, the *Standard Test Lessons in Reading* (McCall and Crabbs, 1961) strives primarily to improve reading efficiency. The series can be used in grades three through high school. There are seventy-eight selections at each level. The lessons can be used as timed, graded exercises to develop speed or for other supplementary activities. The purposes can vary with the needs of the students. The lessons, under timed conditions, yield a grade score for the number correct. It is felt that the grade score should be regarded with some caution.

Study Skills

The *Be a Better Reader* (N. B. Smith, 1968) series is a set of workbooks that emphasizes study skills and reading in academic subject areas. Four areas are covered at each level—literature, science, math, and social studies. There are many exercises in word recognition, vocabulary, and comprehension. Students whose instructional reading level is at least fourth grade can use the materials profitably under the direction of the teacher. In 1971, a set of answer cards was added so that each student can correct his own work.

General Reading Skill Development

Certain supplementary materials dealing with many skills are not easily classified. The *Reading Spectrum* (Weinberg, Deighton, and Sanford, 1964) is an individualized supplementary reading program encompassing skills and recreational reading. The *Spectrum of Skills* can be used in the intermediate grades or junior high school to develop or improve skills in word attack, vocabulary, and comprehension. A student is placed in the appropriate area and color-coded text through a placement test. He can then proceed at his own rate in his area of greatest deficiency. The *Reading Spectrum* contains literature at various reading levels. The accompanying teacher's manual contains summaries of the stories and questions for comprehension checks. The teacher must be available to clarify any questions and give individual assistance.

Reading Exercises (Gates and Peardon, 1963) contains thirteen soft-covered books that can be used with children whose reading levels are between second and sixth grades. The lower-level texts are written in such a way that the material would be appropriate to older children with reading difficulties. The set is broken down into five levels, as follows:

1. Introductory (Levels A and B). These exercises lead the child to the concept of purposeful reading. Each story is followed by questions that call for the ability to recall facts and details, understand the main idea, and follow directions. The exercises are appropriate for superior first graders, average second graders, and below-average readers in the third and fourth grades.
2. Preparatory (Levels A and B). Each exercise is followed by the same types of questions as were posed at the Introductory Level. The exercises are appropriate for above-average second graders, average third graders, and less able readers in grades four and five.
3. Elementary. Each of the three booklets at this level emphasizes a particular aspect of reading—recall of facts and details, understanding of the main idea, and following directions. The materials are written at about a fourth-grade reading level and are appropriate for more able third graders and less capable readers in the fifth and sixth grades.
4. Intermediate. Booklets are organized in the same manner as the texts at the Elementary Level; they are appropriate for above-average fourth graders, average fifth graders, and less able readers in junior high school.
5. Advanced. Booklets are organized in the same manner as the Elementary and Intermediate sets; they are appropriate for above-average fifth graders, average sixth graders, and below-average junior high school students.

The *Specific Skill Series* (Boning, 1970) contains booklets for students who are reading between the second and sixth reading levels. At each level there is a booklet for a specific skill. The skills emphasized are shown by the titles of the booklets: *Using the Context, Getting the Facts, Following Directions, Locating the Answers,* and *Working with Sounds.* The booklets are valuable for follow-up work, supplementary activities, and self-directed work. The teacher must correct the answers and be available to answer any questions. Essentially, the entire class could be working with this material, with each child pursuing a particular skill at a certain level completely independent of everyone else. Careful diagnosis on the part of the teacher is needed to obtain full value from these materials. It is a waste of time for a child to work in skill areas at levels at which he is already competent. No diagnostic placement tests for these materials have been developed to appropriately place children.

The *Reading Skills Lab* program (Durr and Hillerich, 1968) is designed to meet individual needs of students exhibiting skill deficiencies in grades four to six. The areas of weakness are detected by the use of *Diagnostic Tests,* which survey the pupils' strengths and weaknesses and are correlated with the *Reading Skills Lab Books*. The *Lab Books* can then be used to develop specific skills. *Achievement Tests* are provided to check the pupil's grasp of the skill developed. The general skills covered in the program are as follows:

> Level 1 (grade four)
>   A. Unlocking strange words
>   B. Overcoming meaning difficulties
>   C. Reading for different purposes
> Level 2 (grade five)
>   A. Overcoming meaning difficulties
>   B. Reading for different purposes
>   C. Using reference aids
> Level 3 (grade six)
>   A. Studying informative materials
>   B. Using reference aids
>   C. Reading critically

To keep informed about new products and materials that are available on the commercial market, the teacher or school may want to subscribe to *Curriculum Products Review* (1155 Waukegan Road, Glenview, Illinois 60025). This magazine is published nine times a year and can be a valuable reference when considering new materials.

EXAMPLES OF SPECIFIC REMEDIAL TECHNIQUES IN READING

The following list of remedial techniques can aid the teacher in helping certain children overcome specific difficulties in reading. The teacher should carefully file remedial activities so that they can be used again and again. In a few years it is possible to collect a significant number of specific exercises that can be used for individual follow-up to a group reading lesson.

Problem Area	*Suggested Remedial Activity*
I. General word recognition (basic sight vocabulary)	1. The picture dictionary. The child makes a scrapbook that is indexed with the letters of the alphabet. Pictures can be drawn or cut out of magazines. As the child learns a word, he pastes a picture on the page that has that letter. For example, the word "car" would go on the C page. This has advantages over commercial picture dictionaries be-

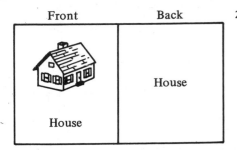

II. Reversals
A. Word

cause it contains the words that the child is learning and he is making it himself. Most useful with nouns.

2. Picture cards and tracing. On one side of the card a picture is placed with a word underneath it; on the other side the word is printed. The teacher presents the card with the word and picture side up and pronounces the word. Then the child pronounces and traces the word until he can recognize the word without seeing the picture. The words can be reviewed from time to time and used as an independent drill. Most useful with nouns.

3. Matching words with pictures. This can be used with words other than nouns. For example, a clear picture of a child running can be used to help teach the word "run." On the back of the card, the picture is reproduced and the child is given three words and must match the word and the picture.

4. Labeling. Attach labels to the door, closet, window, pictures, bulletin board, and other things in the room so that the child will begin to associate the written symbol with the object.

5. Tachistoscope. Cut a piece of oaktag or cardboard to a 5- by 8-inch size. Fold down the top and bottom about ½ inch to hold the word cards. Cut a window in the center to expose the word. Attach a shutter to the outside. Make up word cards with basic sight vocabulary words on them. These can be flashed by quickly opening the shutter. If the child misses a word, it can be reexposed so that he will be able to apply his word-attack skills.

6. Phrase cards. Short phrases, then longer phrases should be introduced. These can be used in the tachistoscope exercise.

1. Place the word on a 5- by 8-inch card in crayon. Have the pupil say the word, trace it, and say it again. He should do this a number of times and then be given an opportunity to read it in a sentence.

2. Hold up a card that is covered with a sheet of paper. Move the sheet of paper to the right so that the letters are exposed in the proper sequence.
3. Use a card with the word printed on it and color lightly the first letter.
4. Place some design (e.g., a diamond) to call the child's attention to the first letter.

B. Letter

1. Place the letter on a 3- by 5-inch card and have the child trace it until he thinks he can write it correctly, then have him practice writing it. This can also be done at the chalkboard.
2. Use pictures illustrating words that begin with the letters the child reverses. For example, for the letters "b" and "d," use a picture of a boat and a duck. Place the picture of the duck to the left of the "d." Paste the picture of the boat next to the lower part of the "b" and to the right of it.
3. Stories may be used to differentiate letters frequently reversed:
This is b
b is on the line
b is tall like a building
b looks to the right

III. Initial sounds
Note: Check teacher's manuals of readiness and primary-level reading books for further suggestions

	ard
h	and
	ouse

1. Dictate a series of three or four words that begin with the same sound. Have the child write the letter that represents the initial sound.
2. On 3- by 5-inch index cards, place an "x" on the left side and three or four phonograms on the right. The child is asked to give the initial sound and then the whole word.
3. Picture dictionary. See item 1.
4. Rotating wheel. Two cardboard circles, one smaller than the other, can be fastened together so that they rotate freely. On the larger one place common phonograms, on the smaller one place initial consonants. By rotating the larger circle, initial consonants can be combined with other phonograms.

IV. Final sounds
Note: teacher's manuals from linguistically based reading series

1. Make a rhyming book to illustrate word families.
2. Ask the child to give a rhyming word for one the teacher has just pronounced.

have many suggestions for developing this skill

```
┌─────────────────────────┐
│    b                    │
│    l                    │
│    m         end        │
│    s                    │
└─────────────────────────┘
```

These can be placed on the chalkboard and the parts that sound alike can be underlined.

3. Make up cards with an initial consonant on the left and an ending on the right. Have the child blend the initial sound with the ending to make new words.

V. Medial vowel sounds

1. Develop practice exercises that make the child focus his attention on the medial vowel sound in the word, as:
   a. The cat sat on a (rig, rog, rug).
   b. The cat sat on a r__g.

2. Make key cards with the vowel colored to call attention to the sound.
   b*a*t b*e*t b*i*t b*o*t b*u*t
   (Bot is a nonsense word, but being so, the child may remember it because it is unique.)

VI. Endings

1. Place three columns of words on cards (or the chalkboard), ask the child to pick out the one that has a different ending from the other two.

VII. Context clues

1. This teaches the child to anticipate meanings. If a new word, such as "toys" is to be introduced, write a sentence like, "Jim saw many _____ in the window of the store." Ask what he might have seen that starts with a "t." (The teacher should read the sentence and have the child simply respond with the word "toys.")

We ride to school on a _____ (bus).
At night I go to_____ (bed).

2. Write a sentence on the chalkboard with only one word that the child does not know the meaning of but can infer through the context. Ask the child to read the sentence silently. When he has read it, ask him if he knows what the last word is. If he is having difficulty, structure further questions until he can infer the right word.

Mary is wearing a new | dress. bless. class.

3. Sentences can be constructed with a number of choices. Have the child underline the correct one to complete the sentence.

I carry my home. I like to live in water. I am in this room. What am I?

4. The teacher or the children can make up riddles. These can be put on spirit-duplicating masters or on the chalkboard. The children must infer the meaning from the context.

VIII. Letter discrimination

put   *hat*

porch   hold
ball   hot
pot   pot
doll   hat
pass   have

1. Place a list of words on the chalkboard and have the child (or children) underline the words that begin with the same letter as the first one.

IX. Phonemic and word discrimination

1. Tell the child (or children) that you are going to read a list of words. Most of them will begin alike (e.g., boat). Every time they hear a word that does not begin like boat, they should clap their hands.
2. Tell the child (or children) to shut his eyes. Pairs of words are read and he must tell if they sound exactly alike or are different.
3. Follow step 2 with exercises on beginning sounds.
4. Follow step 2 with exercises on final sounds.
5. Pronounce a word and its beginning sound. Ask the child to give some more words that begin with the same beginning sound.
6. Follow step 5 with exercises with ending sounds.

X. Compound words

1. Give the child a list of compound words and have him separate them.
2. Give the child two lists of words and have him draw lines from the right column to the left to make compound words.

XI. Root words

1. Present a list of words with variant endings and have the child circle the root word.
2. Present the child with a list of words and a list of endings. Tell him to make up as many *real* words as he can using the endings.

XII. Suffixes

1. Write a sentence on the chalkboard with a derived form of a word in it. Have the child find the root word and then explain how it alters the meaning of the whole word or what the meaning of the suffix is.
   a. Start with words that do not change their spelling when a suffix is added.

b. Introduce spelling variations one at a time and provide practice before moving to another one.

XIII. Prefixes

1. Write sentences on the chalkboard containing words with prefixes. Ask the child to locate the root word. Ask him to explain what the new word means.

Jim locked the door.
Jim____locked the door.

2. Write sentences on the chalkboard. Below each one write the same sentence but leave space for a prefix on one word. Ask the child what prefix can be added to make the sentence mean the opposite.

XIV. Vocabulary development

1. Use any opportunities to introduce new words in discussion and call attention to them, e.g., "The sign over the main door of the school is 'exit.' What do you think it means?"

2. Develop a modified crossword puzzle. In early grades the first letter should be given.

3. Have the child (or children) develop their own crossword puzzles.

XV. Classification

vegetables–house–transportation

carrot–floor–car–airplane
tomato–helicopter–door
potato–train–roof

1. Prepare a list of words that can be separated into general classifications and have the child (children) group them.

XVI. Sequence

1. Cut up or draw a series of pictures that make a complete story when arranged in the proper sequence. Have the child complete the exercise.

2. Prepare strips of paper with single sentences on each one. Ask the child to arrange them to tell a complete story.

3. Write out directions for making something in a scrambled order. Have the child number the steps in the order in which they should happen.

XVII. Following directions

1. Give the child a picture with specific directions as to how it should be colored and have him finish it.

2. Give a child a series of oral directions and have him carry them out in the order in which you gave them; start from the simple and gradually become more complex.

XVIII. Main ideas

1. Read the child (or children) a short story. Write a list of phrases on the chalkboard and have them pick out the one that best tells the main idea. (In some cases, the phrases must be read to the children.)
2. Read a story to the child (or children) and have them make up a title and tell why it is a good one.
3. Exercises similar to 1 and 2 above can be done with the child reading the story and completing the exercise independently.

XIX. Phrase reading

1. Use a piece of cardboard about 10 by 6 inches, cut two slits in it about 2½ inches wide and 1 inch apart. Write a story on a roll of cash register paper (2½ inches wide) and write short phrases or sentences that tell a continuous story. Pull the roll through so that only one phrase is exposed at a time. Have the child read each phrase.

XX. Reading for details

1. Have the child look at pictures and tell what he sees.
2. Have the child read a paragraph with an irrelevant sentence inserted in it. Have him cross out the irrelevant sentence.

XXI. Alphabetizing

1. Make sure that the child knows the sequence of the alphabet.
2. Give the child practice in determining which letter comes before and after a specified letter.
3. Practice alphabetizing by first letter, then second letter, and so on.

XXII. Verbal relationships
Find two fruits:
apple dog pig plum

1. Make a list of exercises that give practice in word meaning.

Problems in Mathematics Achievement 3

Nettie R. Bartel

Because of the far-reaching effects of disability in mathematical skills, it is somewhat surprising to note that, until recently, relatively little attention had been paid to this significant problem area. Perhaps this has been the case because so much time and effort was being expended in the attempt to make children literate; perhaps it reflected the fact that many children with virtually no understanding of mathematical principles were able to hide behind a facade of rote ability in computation. Even with the introduction of the newer materials described in a subsequent section of this chapter, the concerned teacher will still find comparatively fewer programs, tests, methods, and materials for instructing children with matematical difficulties than in the other areas. Considerable resourcefulness and ingenuity on the part of the teacher are essential for the effective teaching of those children who seem to have particular difficulty in mathematics.

This chapter reflects the relative paucity of research and development activities concerning children with problems in mathematics. First, an overview is provided for establishing the goals of a mathematics program. Attention is then directed toward the question of pupil readiness for mathematics instruction. This is followed by a description of types of difficulty in mathematics. The fourth section is designed to assess mathematical difficulties; it includes a section on standardized mathematics testing and a fairly detailed set of procedures to be utilized by the teacher in the diagnostic instructional cycle. A final section deals with the instruction of children who have problems in mathematics.

ESTABLISHING GOALS IN MATHEMATICS

Any mathematical activity should be undertaken only if it is responsive to some goal or objective that has been established for a particular child or for a group of children. Teachers will find many sources that will help to articulate the goals of the mathematics program: curriculum guides, professional publications, scope-and-sequence charts accompanying commercial materials, Bloom's Taxononomy of Educational Objectives (1956), and the landmark 1963 report of the Cambridge Conference on School Mathematics.

An example of a set of broadly stated mathematical goals is that developed by Buffie, Welch, and Paige (1968, p. 6):

1. Development of computational facility.
2. Development of mathematical understanding.
3. Development of rational power (including divergent, logical, and creative thinking).
4. Development of a positive attitude toward mathematics.

To this list of four goals, we add another:

5. Development of an understanding of how mathematics computation and concepts are utilized in real-life situations.

This goal is added in recognition of the fact that, for most persons, mathematics will serve as a tool in daily living. For example, in one study, the researchers analyzed daily newspapers and periodicals and found the following to be necessary prerequisites to a reader's comprehension (Adams, 1924; cited in Burns, 1962):

1. Time—hour, day, week, month, year.
2. Recognizing numbers—street, house, telephone.
3. Money—coins and bills under $100.
4. Simple ratios.
5. Units of measure—length, volume, weight.
6. Mathematical expressions and terms (less than, larger than, etc.).
7. Practical problems.

Moreover, Norton and Norton (1936) cited the following mathematical requirements as most representative of daily living:

1. Basic addition, subtraction, multiplication, division.
2. Common fractions.
3. Measurements—length, volume, weight.
4. Use of money—buying and selling
   borrowing and repaying
   rent and mortgages

insurance
budget

Recent technological developments with calculators make this a highly likely item to be used in daily living; hence, children need to be familiarized with their existence and use.

MATHEMATICAL READINESS

Insufficient readiness may seriously affect the performance of a child at any level of arithmetic functioning. This being the case, some children are unable to learn to count because they do not have a clear notion of one-to-one correspondence. Some children fail to master long division because they have not yet learned to multiply. So—this section discusses readiness as it relates both to beginning instruction in mathematics and to the more advanced mathematical functions.

Basic Readiness

Basic to the development of arithmetic-related abilities is the child's ability to classify. *Classification* refers to the grouping of objects according to some common distinguishing characteristic. In order to do this, the child must be able to discriminate between objects on the basis of some relevant aspect of color, size, shape, or pattern. The ability to make these discriminations is usually attained by a child sometime between two and seven years, during the period which Piaget has called the pre-operations period (Piaget, 1965). Initially, motor actions, then internalized behaviors, are utilized in the child's coming to an awareness of various classifications (Piaget and Inhelder, 1963). In accordance with the general Piagetain principle of actions preceding perceptions, children should be encouraged to enact as many concepts as possible and to manipulate two- and three-dimensional objects in the initial stages of classificatory behavior. During the latter part of this period, acquisition of language is believed to facilitate the ability to classify.

The ability to classify may be assessed a number of different ways. Children may be shown an array of objects and asked "Which does not belong"? when all items except the one share a common characteristic: for example, "Which does not belong . . . dog, cat, tree, bird?" Since three of the items share the category "animal," the correct answer is "tree." The Sesame Street jingle, "One of these things is not like the others; one of these things doesn't belong" is exemplary of the kind of exercise that helps to establish whether a child has learned to classify. It should be recognized that classification tasks vary greatly in difficulty, depending on the characteristic that must be discriminated and on the salience of that characteristic.

Learning the concept of *one-to-one correspondence* is essential for subsequently learning to count and for mastering addition and subtraction. The concept underlies such seemingly intuitive abilities as placing the correct number of table settings for a given number of people or for distributing candies or other treats on the basis of one or two per child. Whether the pupil understands one-to-one correspondence or not can be quickly established by asking him to give each child in his row a piece of paper or to get enough pencils for each child in a reading group. Teaching children the idea of one-to-one correspondence should begin with situations in which there are only two objects in each set. Gradually, the numbers to be corresponded is increased. Only when one-to-one correspondence in a wide variety of settings has been firmly established should the children be instructed in many-to-one correspondence. Initially, items in each set should be identical. Later, children can be asked to match dissimilar objects, such as matching pieces of bubble gum with pennies. Pictures of objects are introduced only when the youngster has developed a firm grasp of the concept and has demonstrated success with concrete objects.

Seriation or *ordering* in its simplest form can be accomplished by a two- or three-year-old child who successfully places a series of rings of graduated sizes on a cone. More complex seriation tasks involve lining up disks of graduated diameter or height in ascending or descending order. More difficult are tasks that require the child to seriate on the basis of numbers in a series of sets—sets of one, two, or three objects in order. It is apparent that ability to seriate underlies the entire number system. Work in seriation can most meaningfully be done with three-dimensional objects. The Montessori materials, the Stern materials, and the Cuisenaire rods (discussed later in this chapter) offer excellent training in seriation and ordering. Lacking any of these materials, the teacher can teach seriation with bottles, crayons, pencils, or cards of varying sizes.

The child's *understanding of space and spatial representation* has both perceptual and cognitive aspects. Perceptual aspects are dealt with in Chapter 8; hence, it is sufficient to state here that a firm grasp of spatial relations is important not only for traditional geometry (geometric forms), but for understanding sets and fractions, and the basic arithmetic processes of addition, subtraction, multiplication, and division. Here again, according to Piaget, motor actions should precede strictly perceptual tasks (Piaget and Inhelder, 1963; Stephens, 1971). Visual–perceptual activities should be supplemented with opportunities for tactual explorations of objects.

Before meaningful formal instruction (counting, adding) in arithmetic can occur, the child must have achieved *flexibility* and *reversibility* of thought, as well as the concept of *conservation*. Flexibility of thought is demonstrated by the child's ability to see that colored geometric shapes can be sorted first on the basis of one criterion, namely color, then shifted to another criterion, shape, and finally to possibly a third criterion, size. Flexibility also characterizes the conceptual process of observing that an individual or object belongs to several categories and subcategories at once; e.g., a person may be both a mother and a daughter, or two cups of water equal both one pint and half a quart (Stephens, 1971). Flexibility is also necessary for a child to recognize that 10 equals 5 + 5, but it may also equal 4 + 6 or 9 + 1.

Reversibility is essential for the child to grasp the relationship between addition and subtraction; e.g., 5 + 4 = 9 and 9 − 4 = 5. In younger children, reversibility can be readily demonstrated with the Cuisenaire and Stern materials. Only with considerable experience in the manipulation of objects can the child achieve a firm grasp of the concept that no matter how objects are arranged they can always be returned to their original pattern. Thus, if
$\begin{smallmatrix} \cdot & & \cdot \\ \cdot & & \cdot \end{smallmatrix}$ is rearranged to $\begin{smallmatrix} \cdot & & \cdot & & \cdot \\ & \cdot & & \end{smallmatrix}$, its basic value is still the same, and it can be reversed back.

The concept of conservation, closely related to that of reversibility, refers to the fact that the number of units within an object or set remains the same regardless of changes made in the shape of the unit or the arrangement of the set (Figure 3–1). The familiar Piagetian experiments of the ball of clay rolled into a long roll, or of water poured into a tall, thin glass versus a low, wide glass are examples of conservation. While the question of whether conservation can be directly taught is debatable, allowing the child plenty of opportunity to manipulate clay and to rearrange units of sets will permit reinforcement of the notion of conservation.

Figure 3–1. *Amount of Water in the Two Containers Is the Same; Amount of Clay in the Two Shapes Is the Same*

Readiness for More Advanced Mathematics

Readiness for higher-level mathematical operations was the topic of a study reported by Brownell (1951). The particular type of mathematics task that he investigated was division by two-place divisors. Prior to the study, he identified the mathematics skills that children must have in order to perform the division task. The specific subskills that he considered prerequisite for "readiness" for two-place divisor division are the following:

1. Multiply a two-place number by a digit:

    23
    × 6

2. Add, to the extent of carrying in multiplication:

    48
    +48

3. Subtract, without and with borrowing:

    323   323
    − 21   − 27

4. Divide, in the sense of knowing the algorithm: 3) 7 .

Next, Brownell developed a Test of Readiness for Division by Two-Place Divisors—a test of skills 1 to 4 above. Using 80 percent correct as a criterion, he concluded that almost half of the children were "not ready" to begin instruction in two-place division. Yet their teachers already had begun such instruction.

This study is illustrative of the need for establishing the criteria for "readiness" clearly. Whether one is dealing with initial mathematics instruction or with the introduction of a more advanced topic, the teacher's effectiveness and efficiency is enhanced by appropriate timing in the presentation of teaching tasks. The real test of "readiness" for a given mathematical topic is not whether that topic comes next in the workbook but whether the pupils have mastered the prerequisite skills (as demonstrated in Brownell's study) or have achieved the cognitive operations underlying the topic to be introduced. Establishing the state of a child's readiness is an important component of mathematical diagnosis, and is dealt with next.

CAUSES FOR DIFFICULTY IN MATHEMATICS

When a child demonstrates difficulty in mathematics performance, the teacher will want to undertake a preliminary appraisal of possible reasons for the problem. This initial appraisal is usually informal in nature and highly subjective. At this point, the teacher is attempting to generate hypotheses as to the possible reasons for the difficulty; she will then try to confirm these initial hypotheses using more objective means. Depending on what is discovered, the teacher may refine, reformulate, or implement an intervention on the basis of that first hypothesis. Descriptions of some of the more general reasons underlying mathematics difficulty are presented below.

1. *Ineffective instruction* probably accounts for more cases of problems in arithmetic than any other factor. Children who are the victims of poor teaching can frequently be identified by their relatively good performance in arithmetic concepts that are frequently acquired incidentally (e.g., size relationships or value of coins), as compared to skills that are usually acquired as the result of specific instruction ("carrying" in addition or long division). Remediation is usually effective if planned on the basis of a diagnosis of specific deficits.

2. *Difficulties in abstract or symbolic thinking* will interfere with the child's ability to conceptualize the relationship between numerals and objects that they represent, the structure of the number system (base of 10), and relationships between units of measurement. Teachers of children with these difficulties frequently turn in frustration from attempting to get the child to master concepts to emphasizing the rote manipulation of numerals. This may create a facade of arithmetic competence, when in fact the child does not understand what he is doing.

3. *Reading problems* frequently characterize those children who perform well on tests of computation or on oral story problems, but who do poorly in typical workbook or standardized test situations in which they must be able to read the problem to understand which mathematical process to perform.

4. *Poor attitudes or anxiety* about mathematics may inhibit the performance of some children. Careful observation on the part of the teacher may provide the first indication that this is at the root of the child's problem. Does the child avoid mathematics? Does he "play sick" when it is time for mathematical activities? The teacher may also wish to use one of the instruments developed for assessing attitudes toward arithmetic. An example of one such instrument is presented later in the chapter.

ASSESSMENT OF MATHEMATICS PERFORMANCE

To engage in appropriate and efficient instruction, the teacher must employ a set of assessment procedures that permit her to have a detailed picture of each child's strengths and weaknesses in mathematics. Most teachers discover quickly that the standardized survey type of mathematics achievement tests yields relatively little information. Therefore, it becomes necessary for the teacher to study in depth the areas of difficulty pointed out by the survey test. For example, the child who is shown to be having computational difficulties is given a much more detailed inventory of computation problems. The teacher appraises the child's performance on the various computation tasks to determine the types of errors that trouble the child. Further probing of the child's errors is done through intensive analysis of his written work and/or through an oral interview in which the child "thinks out loud" while solving problems. The entire process can be conceived of as a search on the part of the teacher for the faulty concepts and strategies being used by the child. Initial testing is gross and provides only the most general clues to the teacher. Successive assessment efforts, based on clues obtained from previous testing, help the teacher to "zero in" on the child's difficulty. Having discovered the problem, the teacher then plans an intervention to correct the difficulty. If the child shows improvement, the teacher may conclude that the problem was correctly identified, and followed by appropriate instruction. Continued failure by the child must lead to reexamination of the diagnostic process and/or of the subsequent instruction.

The Use of Standardized Tests

A teacher could establish a child's overall performance level by having him "try out" in various mathematics texts, programs, or instructional sysems. We believe, however, that it is much more efficient and reliable to administer a norm-referenced test that will give the teacher a general idea of the child's functional level in mathematics. Such survey tests may be either of the group-administered or individually administered type. Some of the most widely used survey tests of mathematical functioning are presented in Table 3–1.

The authors of a few mathematics programs provide their own placement tests to help teachers establish the child's entry level into the program. Of course, such tests are usually applicable to only that program.

Even for children whose survey test performance indicates grade-level or near-grade-level functioning, we recommend that the teacher peruse the errors made by the pupil. The purpose of this activity is to check if the child's performance is reasonably even across the various types of mathematics problems; it is possible to obtain a fairly average score by excelling in one area, say addition, even if performance in another area, say multiplication, is very poor. The analysis of errors and error patterns has been found to be particularly helpful for pupils who are new to the teacher.

To help the teacher establish whether a child's difficulty is related to fear or dislike of mathematics, we have included an example of a test of attitudes toward mathematics (Table 3–2).

Table 3–1. *Commonly Used Standardized Survey Tests of Arithmetic Achievement*

Test (Author)	Grade Level	Reliability Coefficient	Skills Measured	Special Features
California Achievement Test (Tiegs and Clark, 1970)	1–9	.70–.97	1. Computation 2. Concepts and problems 3. Total	May be used diagnostically Weak students may obtain fair scores by guessing
Iowa Test of Basic Skills—Arithmetic (Lindquist and Hieronymous, 1956)	1–9	.89–.91	1. Arithmetic concepts 2. Problem solving 3. Total	Convenient Much verbal content
Metropolitan Achievement Tests—Arithmetic (Durost et al., 1971)	3–9	.82–.95	1. Computation 2. Problem solving 3. Concepts 4. Total	Traditional
Stanford Achievement Series in Arithmetic (Kelley et al., 1964)	1–10	.77–.89	1. Concepts 2. Computation 3. Application	Traditional
SRA Achievement Series in Arithmetic (Thorpe, Lefever, and Naslund, 1969)	1–9	.80–.96	1. Concepts 2. Reasoning 3. Computation 4. Total	Provides hand-book for diagnostic analysis
Wide Range Achievement (Jastak and Jastak, 1965)	1–10	.94–.97		Individually administered Takes only 5–10 minutes

Table 3–2. *Evaluation of Attitudes Toward Arithmetic*

Check (X) only the statements that
express your feeling toward arithmetic.

_____ 1. I feel arithmetic is an important part of the school curriculum.
_____ 2. Arithmetic is something you have to do even though it is not enjoyable.
_____ 3. Working with numbers is fun.
_____ 4. I have never liked arithmetic.
_____ 5. Arithmetic thrills me and I like it better than any other subject.
_____ 6. I get no satisfaction from studying arithmetic.
_____ 7. I like arithmetic because the procedures are logical.
_____ 8. I am afraid of doing word problems.
_____ 9. I like working all types of arithmetic problems.
_____ 10. I detest arithmetic and avoid using it at all times.
_____ 11. I have a growing appreciation of arithmetic through understanding its values, applications, and processes.

(continued)

Table 3–2. *Evaluation of Attitudes Toward Arithmetic (continued)*

_____12. I am completely indifferent to arithmetic.
_____13. I have always liked arithmetic because it has presented me with a challenge.
_____14. I like arithmetic but I like other subjects just as well.
_____15. The completion and proof of accuracy in arithmetic gave me satisfaction and feelings of accomplishment.

Before scoring your attitude scale, place an (X) on the line below to indicate where you think your general feeling toward arithmetic might be:

11	10	9	8	7	6	5	4	3	2	1
Strongly favor				*Neutral*				*Strongly against*		

Scoring the scale. The scale is designed to show attitudes for or against arithmetic. Each item has a scale value (see below). Individuals will usually have both favorable and unfavorable feelings toward arithmetic. By adding all responses and dividing by the total number of responses, one can secure a general average for each individual. Each test item will provide data for pupil guidance. For example, a pupil may like the logical aspects of arithmetic (No. 7) but will be afraid of word problems (No. 8). Scaled values will also show the intensity of feelings toward arithmetic.

Method of Scoring Arithmetic Attitude Test

Place the scale value for the items you checked on the test in the left margin of the page. Total all items checked and divide by the total number of items you checked. This will give you an average score on the test. Compare this average with the estimated placement shown on the line indicating your general feeling toward arithmetic. Individual items will reveal highly favorable or unfavorable attitudes.

Scale Value	Test Item	Scale Value	Test Item
7.2	1	2.0	8
3.3	2	9.6	9
8.7	3	1.0	10
1.5	4	8.2	11
10.5	5	5.2	12
2.6	6	9.5	13
7.9	7	5.6	14
		9.0	15

Source: Wilbur H. Dutton and L. J. Adams, *Arithmetic for Teachers,* © 1961. Reprinted by permission of Prentice-Hall, Inc., Englewood Cliffs, N.J.

While standardized survey tests are used to answer the questions "What is the child's relative status in mathematics?" the standardized "diagnostic" tests deal with "What is the child's status in the various areas of mathematics, e.g., addition, subtraction, fractions, etc.?" A number of tests

Table 3–3. *"Diagnostic" Tests of Mathematics Performance*

Test	Skills Measured	Grade Level	Special Features
Fountain Valley Teacher Support System in Mathematics (1976)	1. Numbers and operations 2. Geometry 3. Measurement 4. Application 5. Statistics/probability 6. Sets 7. Functions 8. Logical thinking 9. Problem solving	K–8	Criterion-referenced Self-scoring Areas of weakness keyed to math text or program
Basic Educational Skills Inventory in Math (1972)	All mathematical areas	Elementary	Criterion-referenced Keyed to a retrieval system that refers teacher to materials designed to develop skills that the child missed
Patterns Recognition Skills Inventory (Sternberg, 1976)	Levels of readiness for all areas of math Reasoning skills	Ages 5–10	Concept-referenced diagnostic inventory Requires no reading by student Developmentally sequenced
Diagnostic Tests and Self-Helps in Arithmetic (Brueckner, 1955)	1. Computation with whole numbers 2. Operations with fractions, decimals, percentage 3. Measurement	3–8	Each diagnostic test is correlated with corrective self-help exercises
Los Angeles Diagnostic Tests: Fundamentals and Reasoning (Armstrong and Clark, 1947)	1. Computation with whole numbers 2. Reasoning		
KeyMath Diagnostic Arithmetic Test (Connelly, Nachtman, and Pritchett, 1976)	1. Content 2. Operations 3. Applications	K–6	Convenient and attractive to administer Requires almost no reading or writing Not really diagnostic (not enough items), but useful for identifying problem areas

that have been commercially developed for appraising a pupil's performance in greater detail are listed in Table 3–3. Although these tests purported to be "diagnostic," none of them provides sufficient opportunity to probe strengths and weaknesses adequately. They are helpful, however, for identifying broad areas that need further analysis. The type of analysis that is most effective for the detailed probing of children's mathematical difficulties can only be done by the teacher himself.

Teacher-Made Diagnostic Inventories

The teacher's first step in developing an inventory is to choose the content to be assessed. One way to do this is to study the scope-and-sequence-chart of the mathematics program that is being used in the school (most mathematics series present these near the beginning of the teacher's manual) or from Table 3–4. The contents of the table have been organized in such a

Table 3–4. *Typical Scope and Sequence of Elementary Mathematics*

		Grade						
		K	1	2	3	4	5	6
I.	*Readiness for Mathematics*							
	Classification	•	•	•	•	•	•	•
	One-to-one correspondence	•	•	•	•	•	•	•
	One-to-many correspondence					•	•	•
	Seriation or ordering	•	•	•	•	•	•	
	Space and spatial representation	•	•	•	•	•	•	•
	Flexibility and reversibility	•	•	•	•	•	•	•
	Conservation	•	•	•	•	•	•	
II.	*Mathematical Concepts*							
	Same, equal, as much as	•	•	•	•	•	•	•
	More than, greater, greatest, larger, largest	•	•	•	•	•	•	•
	Bigger, biggest, longer, longest	•	•	•	•	•	•	•
	Less than, fewer, fewest, smaller, smallest	•	•	•	•	•	•	•
	Shorter, shorter, most, least	•	•	•	•	•	•	•
	Enough, not enough, more than enough	•	•	•	•	•	•	•
	Left, right		•	•	•	•	•	•
	Above, below, up, down, next to, between		•	•	•	•	•	•
	Putting together, add, plus		•	•	•	•	•	•
	Take apart, take away, subtract, minus		•	•	•	•	•	•
	How many in all? How many are left?		•	•	•	•	•	•
	Odd, even			•	•	•	•	•
	Open, closed		•	•	•	•	•	•
	$=, >, <$		•	•	•	•	•	•
	Factors, primes, multiples							•
III.	*Sets*							
	Definition	•	•	•	•	•	•	•
	Elements of sets	•	•	•	•	•	•	•
	Kinds of sets							
	Identical	•	•	•	•	•	•	•
	Equal and equivalent	•	•	•	•	•	•	•
	Unequal and nonequivalent						•	•
	Empty set	•	•	•	•	•	•	•
	Union of sets (addition)	•	•	•	•	•	•	•
	Subset (subtraction)	•	•	•	•	•	•	•
	Intersection of sets						•	•

	Grade						
	K	1	2	3	4	5	6
IV. *Whole Numbers*							
Abstracting idea of cardinal number from equivalent set	•	•	•	•	•	•	•
Counting: one through ten	•	•	•	•	•	•	•
Concepts and counting: numbers above ten		•	•	•	•	•	•
Concept of zero	•	•	•	•	•	•	•
Skip counting by twos, threes, fives, tens		•	•	•	•	•	•
V. *Operations on Whole Numbers: Addition and Subtraction*							
Properties							
Closure and nonclosure			•	•	•	•	•
Commutativity and noncommutativity			•	•	•	•	•
Associativity and nonassociativity			•	•	•	•	•
Inverse relation of addition and subtraction			•	•	•	•	•
Ways of conceptualizing							
Union of sets or forming of subsets			•	•	•	•	•
Number line			•	•	•	•	•
Addition and subtraction with zero			•	•	•	•	•
Addition and subtraction with horizontal notation			•	•	•	•	•
Addition and subtraction with vertical notation			•	•	•	•	•
Addition and subtraction without regrouping							
One-place numbers	•	•	•	•	•	•	•
Two-place numbers		•	•	•	•	•	•
Three-place numbers			•	•	•	•	•
Numbers with more than three digits				•	•	•	•
Addition and subtraction with regrouping							
Two-place numbers			•	•	•	•	•
More than two-place numbers				•	•	•	•
Column addition		•	•	•	•	•	•
VI. *Operations on Whole Numbers: Multiplication and Division*							
Properties							
Commutativity of multiplication			•	•	•	•	•
Associativity of multiplication				•	•	•	•
Distributive property of multiplication and division over addition				•	•	•	•
Inverse relation of multiplication and division			•	•	•	•	•
Ways of conceptualizing							
Union of sets or partitioning into equivalent sets			•	•	•	•	•
Repeated addition or successive subtraction			•	•	•	•	•
Arrays				•	•	•	•
Number line				•	•	•	•
Multiplication and division with horizontal notation			•	•	•	•	•
Multiplication and division with vertical notation			•	•	•	•	•
Use of zero in multiplication and division			•	•	•	•	•
"One" as the identity element			•	•	•	•	•
Multiplication and division with 10's, 100,'s, etc.				•	•	•	•

(continued)

Table 3–4. *Typical Scope and Sequence of Elementary Mathematics (continued)*

	K	1	2	3	4	5	6
Computation without regrouping							
One-place factor or divisor, one-place sums, dividend				•	•	•	•
One-place factor or divisor, two-place sums or dividends				•	•	•	•
Computation with regrouping							
One-place factor or divisor, two- or three-place sums or dividends				•	•		•
Two-place factors or divisiors, any number sums or dividends					•	•	•
Three- or four-place factors or divisors							•
Multiple multiplication					•	•	•
VII. Fractions							
Definition			•	•	•	•	•
Ways of conceptualizing							
Number line				•	•	•	•
Arrays or subsets				•	•	•	•
Geometric figures			•	•	•	•	•
Computation							
Addition and subtraction of simple fractions with common denominators				•	•	•	•
Addition and subtraction of simple fractions with mixed denominators					•	•	•
Addition and subtraction of mixed fractions with common denominators				•	•	•	•
Addition and subtraction of mixed fractions with mixed denominators					•	•	•
Multiplication and division							•
Decimal fractions							•
VIII. Measurement							
Measurement of length (inch, foot, yard, mile, metric)			•	•	•	•	•
Measurement of area (English and metric units)						•	•
Measurement of weight (ounce, pound, ton, metric units)					•	•	•
Measurement of liquids (cup, pint, quart, metric units)	•	•			•	•	•
Dry measures (quart, peck, bushel, metric units)				•	•	•	•
Measurement of quantity (dozen, gross)				•	•	•	•
Measurement of temperature (Fahrenheit, Celsius)				•	•	•	•
Measurement of time (clock, calendar)	•	•	•	•	•	•	•
Measure of money (coins, paper bills)	•	•	•		•	•	•
IX. Geometry							
Geometric shapes (circle, square, rectangle, triangle)	•	•	•	•	•	•	•

	K	1	2	3	4	5	6
						Grade	
Geometric shapes (pentagon, hexagon, octagon, parallelogram)				•	•	•	•
Spatial relationships	•	•	•	•	•	•	•
Point, line, line segment, ray, intersection					•	•	•
Parallel line, curved line, straight line						•	•
Radius, diameter						•	•
Angles, arc degrees							•
Closed-line plane, open-line plane						•	•
Area and perimeter						•	•
Three-dimensional shapes (sphere, cube, cone)						•	•

way as to enable the teacher to quickly identify, on the basis of a child's grade level, what mathematics skills and capabilities he should have. For example, if the child is in second grade and is having difficulty with subtraction, the teacher looks in column 2 of part V of the table. The table (based on commonly used commercial texts and curriculum guides) indicates that the child should understand the properties of subtraction, be able to conceptualize subtraction as the inverse of addition, be able to use the number line to subtract, be able to use both vertical and horizontal notation, be able to subtract up to two-place numbers without regrouping and two-place numbers with regrouping. Of course, the teacher may wish to include more difficult items on the inventory, if she wishes to establish whether the child has skills beyond that usually developed in second grade.

The next step is to establish whether the child has the necessary underlying concepts and capacities required for the subtraction tasks. Here the teacher is referred to Figure 3–2, which outlines the general hierarchical interrelationships between and among various areas of mathematical functioning. In each case, the source of an arrow may be considered to be a necessary prerequisite for full mastery of the capability to which the arrow is pointing. Thus, in the subtraction example, the child would need to have evidenced the readiness capabilities of Box A and mastery of basic mathematical concepts and vocabulary of Box B. (For fuller development of these, the reader is referred to the preceding section on Readiness and to Part II, Mathematical Concepts of Table 3–4.)

An alternative approach is to conduct a task analysis and/or concept analysis of each of the terminal skills desired in the subtraction area. The reader is referred to Chapter 1 for an explication of these procedures. (For an excellent description of how to proceed with a mathematical task analysis, see also Reisman, 1972.)

The final step in determining what should go into the diagnostic inventory is to decide in what form and under what conditions the child is supposed

Figure 3–2. *Summary of Scope and Sequence in Typical Elementary Mathematics*

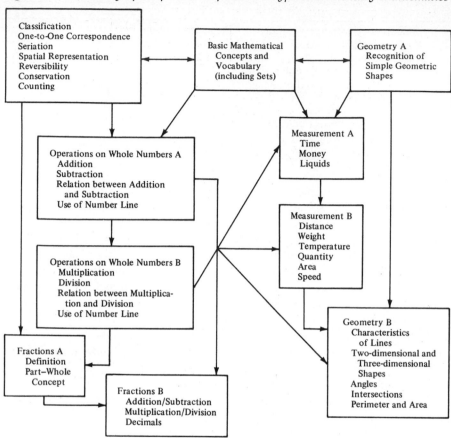

to be able to perform the task. This decision should be stated in *precise, observable* terms. (See Chapter 1 for a fuller discussion on the stating of objectives.)

Now the teacher is ready to begin to write the actual items. They may be adapted from commercial texts, tests, or workbooks; or the teacher may write her own. An example of a subtraction inventory, adapted from Burns (1965), and limited to the vertical format, is presented in Table 3–5.

To further probe the child's understanding of concepts underlying subtraction proficiency and to assess his ability to perform subtraction problems in a variety of formats and contexts, Burns (1965) has suggested a series of follow-up exercises. These are presented in Table 3–6.

Table 3–5. *Sample Analytical Inventory: Subtraction*

Problem Type	Exercises for Child to Complete			
Basic subtraction facts without zero	1. $\begin{array}{r} 4 \\ -\ 2 \\ \hline \end{array}$	2. $\begin{array}{r} 8 \\ -\ 1 \\ \hline \end{array}$	3. $\begin{array}{r} 17 \\ -\ 3 \\ \hline \end{array}$	4. $\begin{array}{r} 15 \\ -\ 6 \\ \hline \end{array}$
Basic subtraction facts involving zero		5. $\begin{array}{r} 7 \\ -\ 7 \\ \hline \end{array}$	6. $\begin{array}{r} 9 \\ -\ .0 \\ \hline \end{array}$	
Higher-decade subtraction fact requiring no regrouping		7. $\begin{array}{r} 79 \\ -\ 6 \\ \hline \end{array}$		
Higher-decade subtraction fact requiring regrouping		8. $\begin{array}{r} 75 \\ -\ 9 \\ \hline \end{array}$		
Higher-decade subtraction fact, with difference in ones' place		9. $\begin{array}{r} 25 \\ -\ 23 \\ \hline \end{array}$		
Higher-decade subtraction fact; zero in ones' place in minuend		10. $\begin{array}{r} 20 \\ -\ 3 \\ \hline \end{array}$		
Subtraction of ones and tens with no regrouping required		11. $\begin{array}{r} 47 \\ -\ 24 \\ \hline \end{array}$		
Three-digit minuend minus two-digit subtrahend; no regrouping		12. $\begin{array}{r} 169 \\ -\ 45 \\ \hline \end{array}$		
Subtraction of ones, tens, hundreds; no regrouping		13. $\begin{array}{r} 436 \\ -\ 215 \\ \hline \end{array}$		
Two-digit minuend minus two-digit subtrahend; regrouping tens and ones in minuend required		14. $\begin{array}{r} 46 \\ -\ 38 \\ \hline \end{array}$	15. $\begin{array}{r} 72 \\ -\ 34 \\ \hline \end{array}$	
Three-digit minuend minus two-digit subtrahend; regrouping tens and ones in minuend required (zero in difference)		16. $\begin{array}{r} 272 \\ -\ 64 \\ \hline \end{array}$		

(continued)

Table 3–5. *Sample Analytical Inventory: Subtraction (continued)*

Problem Type	Exercises for Child to Complete					
Three-digit minuend minus two-digit subtrahend; regrouping hundreds and tens of minuend required	17.	528 − 54				
Subtraction of ones, tens, hundreds; regrouping tens and ones in minuend required	18.	742 − 208	19.	750 − 374		
Subtraction of ones, tens, hundreds; regrouping hundreds and tens in minuend required	20.	724 − 183	21.	307 − 121		
Subtraction of ones, tens, hundreds; regrouping entire minuend required	22.	531 − 173				
Four-digit minuend minus three-digit subtrahend; regrouping entire minuend required	23.	1076 − 247	24.	5254 − 968	25.	5805 − 978
Subtraction of ones, tens, hundreds, thousands; regrouping hundreds, tens, and ones of minuend required	26.	4553 − 1258				
Subtraction of ones, tens, hundreds, thousands; regrouping entire minuend required	27.	9563 − 2687				
Five-digit minuend minus four-digit subtrahend; regrouping entire minuend required	28.	23238 − 3879				
Five-digit minuend minus four-digit subtrahend; regrouping entire minuend (involving zeros) required	29.	10000 − 7192				
Five-digit minuend minus five-digit subtrahend; regrouping entire minuend required	30.	30503 − 19765				

Table 3–6. *Follow-Up Exercises for the Analytical Test of Subtraction*

1. Make a dot drawing to represent the fact that 17 take away 8 leaves 9.
2. What subtraction fact does this drawing illustrate?

12 cookies in all

00000000000

left   eaten

3. Show on the number line how the answer to 31 minus 12 might be found.
4. Start at 57 and count down by 5's to the first number in the thirties. To do this, say, "57, 52, 47," and so on.
5. Write three different ways to read the number statement, $24 - 8 = 16$ (as "8 from 24 leaves 16").
6. What is the result when zero is subtracted from a number?
7. What is the result when a number is subtracted from itself?
8. What pairs of one-digit numbers would make each a true sentence?

   $\square + \square = 9 \qquad \square + \square = 11 \qquad \square + \square = 13$

9. What basic subtraction fact helps you to subtract 6 from 53?
10. Start with 13, subtract 6, add 3, subtract 4, subtract 3. Where are you?
11. There is a two-digit minuend and a one-digit subtrahend whose difference is 9. What might they be?
12. Think the answers to the following questions. Then write the answers.
    a. 7 from 18 leaves how many?
    b. 68 and how many more equals 72?
    c. The difference between 77 and 24 equals what number?
    d. Is 19 minus 12 equal to 7?
    e. When 203 is taken from 526, what is left?
    f. Is 60 from 388 equal to 328?
    g. Does 65 minus 9 equal 56?
    h. If you think 36 from 64, what do you get?
    i. How many are left if 19 is subtracted from 52?
    j. 525 is how much less than 3478?
13. In subtracting 1 ft 3 in. from 3 ft 1 in., to what name would you change one of the measures?
14. When 16 is subtracted from 51, to what number name is the 51 changed?
15. Do the following subtractions, using numerals and words.

    a. $\begin{array}{r} 20 = 2 \text{ tens } 0 \text{ ones} = \\ -\ 3 = \qquad\quad 3 \text{ ones} = \end{array}$ b. $\begin{array}{r} 31 = 3 \text{ tens } 1 \text{ one} = \\ -\ 17 = 1 \text{ ten } 7 \text{ ones} = \end{array}$

    c. $\begin{array}{r} 500 = 5 \text{ hundreds } 0 \text{ tens } 0 \text{ ones} = \\ -\ 125 = 1 \text{ hundred } 2 \text{ tens } 5 \text{ ones} = \end{array}$

16. Use the words hundreds, tens, and ones to show the renaming of 413 in subtracting 187 from 413.

17. What do the digits at the top of the work mean?

    a. $\begin{array}{r} {\scriptstyle 3\ 13} \\ 4\!\!\!/3 \\ -\ 18 \\ \hline 25 \end{array}$ b. $\begin{array}{r} {\scriptstyle 6\ 12} \\ 7\!\!\!/2 4 \\ -\ 183 \\ \hline \end{array}$ c. $\begin{array}{r} {\scriptstyle 9\ 10} \\ {\scriptstyle 4\ 1\!\!\!/0} \\ 5\!\!\!/0\!\!\!/0 \\ -\ 125 \\ \hline \end{array}$

(continued)

Table 3–6. *Follow-Up Exercises for the Analytical Test of Subtraction (continued)*

18. Write the number sentence for this word problem. There are 527 pupils in the Madison School, of whom 283 are boys. How many girls are there?
19. How can an equivalent addition question be written for the subtraction question $42 - 26 = n$?
20. Does $n + 17 = 42$ represent an addition or a subtraction situation?
    Does $n - 17 = 25$ represent a subtraction situation?
21. For each addition statement, write the subtraction statement that "undoes" it. The first one is done for you.

    $6 + 4 =$ $36 + 7 =$ $58 + 17 =$
    $10 - 6 = 4$
       or
    $10 - 4 = 6$

22. Write the missing numeral for each of the following statements:

    $19 - \boxed{} = 7$ $\boxed{} - 47 = 24$ $36 - 28 = \boxed{}$

23. Subtract $6.98 from $10.00.
24. Subtract. Check your answers by subtracting the difference from the minuend. Check again by adding the difference and the subtrahend.

162	806	1422	8461
75	436	766	7298

Source: P. C. Burns, Analytical testing and follow-up exercises in elementary school mathematics. *School Science and Mathematics*, 1965, *65*, 34–38. With permission.

The Oral Interview

All existing evidence shows that most computational errors are caused by children's problems with number facts or by their using faulty algorithms. Diagnosis of difficulty with number facts can usually be discovered and confirmed by an examination of the child's written work. However, to establish the faulty rules or strategies that the child is using in his computational procedures, it is frequently necessary to engage the child in an oral interview. The oral interview may be used to search for the child's error strategies, or it may be used to confirm (or disconfirm) the "hunches" that the teacher has derived from an examination of the child's written work. Because of the time-consuming nature of the oral interview, the teacher will want to confine its use to "hard-core" problems. The procedures described below have been adapted from Cawley (1976) and Lankford (1974), as well as from the authors' experience.

1. *Select one problem area at a time.* The problem selected should be sequentially prior to the others in a task analysis or on Figure 3–2. For example, if a student is having difficulty in both addition and multiplication, clear up the addition problems first. Once this

has been accomplished, the child will need to be retested on written multiplication before oral probing in that area. It may be that correction of the faulty addition strategy modifies the difficulty in multiplication.

2. *Begin with the easiest problems first.* To help give the child a sense of confidence, present him first with a problem that he probably can perform correctly. Then provide him with examples that are of increasing difficulty (for him).

3. *Tape or keep a written record of the interview.* If tape is used, the child should be told that his explanations are being recorded. A similar explanation should be given if a written record is made.

4. *The child simultaneously solves the problem in written form and "explains" what he is doing orally.* The teacher must remember that the oral interview is a diagnostic exercise, not an instructional lesson.

5. *The child must be left free to solve the problem in his own way without a hint that he is doing something wrong.* Avoid giving clues or asking leading questions. If the child directly asks whether the answers are correct, the teacher should tell the child that he should concentrate on "telling in his own words" how he is solving the problem.

6. *Avoid hurrying the pupil.* Depending on the complexity of the operations being diagnosed, the oral interview can take from 15 to 45 minutes.

Analysis of Errors

The identification and interpretation of a child's errors, whether evidenced in his written work or in the oral interview, is the basis on which the teacher develops an appropriate instructional program. It is important, therefore, for the teacher to be proficient in the analysis of pupil errors. This section identifies some of the common types of errors made by pupils (see Table 3–7) and provides some examples of error analyses. Errors made in verbal problem solving are dealt with in the next section.

In a recent study, Lepore (1974) investigated the types of computation errors made by 79 mildly handicapped children aged 12 to 14 on 38 problems in addition, subtraction, multiplication, and division. As can be seen in Table 3–8, the type of error most frequently made is that of "renaming" (sometimes called "regrouping" or "borrowing" or "carrying"). Procedural errors were also well represented, as were errors due to lack of knowing the number facts required for the computations. While we hesitate to draw firm conclusions from this study (because we do not know how representative it

Table 3–7. *Types of Arithmetic Habits Observed in Elementary School Pupils*

Addition

Errors in combinations
Counting
Added carried number last
Forgot to add carried number
Repeated work after partly done
Wrote number to be carried
Irregular procedure in column
Carried wrong number
Grouped two or more numbers
Splits numbers into parts
Used wrong fundamental operation
Lost place in column
Depended on visualization
Disregarding column position
Omitted one or more digits

Errors in reading numbers
Dropped back one or more tens
Derived unknown combination from familiar one
Disregarded one column
Error in writing answer
Skipped one or more decades
Carrying when there was nothing to carry
Used scratch paper
Added in pairs, giving last sum as answer
Added same digit in two columns
Wrote carried number in answer
Added same number twice

Subtraction

Errors in combinations
Did not allow for having borrowed
Counting
Errors due to zero in minuend
Said example backwards
Subtracted minuend from subtrahend
Failed to borrow; gave zero as answer
Added instead of subtracted
Error in reading
Used same digit in two columns
Derived unknown from known combination
Omitted a column
Used trial-and-error addition
Split numbers

Deducted from minuend when borrowing was not necessary
Ignored a digit
Deducted 2 from minuend after borrowing
Error due to minuend and subtrahend digits being same
Used minuend or subtrahend as remainder
Reversed digits in remainder
Confused process with division or multiplication
Skipped one or more decades
Increased minuend digit after borrowing
Based subtraction on multiplication combination

Multiplication

Errors in combinations
Error in adding the carried number
Wrote rows of zeros
Carried a wrong number
Errors in addition
Forgot to carry
Used multiplicand as multiplier
Error in single zero combinations, zero as multiplier
Errors due to zero in multiplier
Used wrong process—added
Error in single zero combinations, zero as multiplicand

Confused products when multiplier had two or more digits
Repeated part of table
Multiplied by adding
Did not multiply a digit in multiplicand
Based unknown combination on another
Errors in reading
Omitted digit in product
Errors in writing product
Errors in carrying into zero
Counted to carry
Omitted digit in multiplier

Errors due to zero in multiplicand
Error in position of partial products
Counted to get multiplication combinations
Illegible figures
Forgot to add partial products

Split multiplier
Wrote wrong digit of product
Multiplied by same digit twice
Reversed digits in product
Wrote tables

Division

Errors in division combinations
Errors in subtraction
Errors in multiplication
Used remainder larger than divisor
Found quotient by trial multiplication
Neglected to use remainder within problem
Omitted zero resulting from another digit
Counted to get quotient
Repeated part of multiplication table
Used short division form for long division
Wrote remainders within problem
Omitted zero resulting from zero in dividend
Omitted final remainder
Used long division form for short division
Said example backwards

Used remainder without new dividend figure
Derived unknown combinations from known one
Had right answer, used wrong one
Grouped too many digits in dividend
Error in reading
Used dividend or divisor as quotient
Found quotient by adding
Reversed dividend and divisor
Used digits of divisor separately
Wrote all remainders at end of problem
Misinterpreted table
Used digit in dividend twice
Used second digit or divisor to find quotient
Began dividing at units digit of dividend
Split dividend
Counted in subtracting
Used too large a product
Used endings to find quotient

Source: G. T. Buswell and Leonore John, *Diagnostic Studies in Arithmetic* (Chicago: University of Chicago Press, 1926). Used with the permission of the publisher.

Table 3–8. *Analysis of Computation Errors*

Type of Error	Addition	Subtraction	Multiplication	Division
Procedural	5	16	144	58
Number facts	12	60	55	16
Regrouping	33	232	42	
Omissions and reversals	16	35	4	
Gaps (problems combining one-place with two- or three-place numbers)	7	19		
Use of zero	0	84	25	11
Add/subtract errors in multiplication/division problems			17	2

Source: Adapted from Lepore (1974).

is), we believe it can increase the efficiency of a classroom teacher by providing clues to the types of errors to look for first. An additional caution is that it is highly likely that types of errors made by students reflect the type of mathematics instruction that those students have been exposed to. (This information is not provided in the Lepore study cited above.) Therefore, we urge teachers to keep records of the types of difficulty encountered by pupils of a given type at a given level in a given mathematics program.

A more systematic analysis of error types, easily adapted for classroom use, was reported by Roberts (1962). The "failure strategies" employed by children usually fall into one of the categories outlined in Table 3–9.

Roberts found in his group of third graders that the most common type of error was in use of a defective algorithm. Only the lowest-functioning children made more errors of another type—and these were random responses.

The utilization of the child's written work and his statements during an oral interview in the diagnostic–instructional sequence is illustrated in Table 3–10. In each case, what the child does and what he says lead the teacher to a tentative hypothesis concerning the source of difficulty. Once having identified the problem, the teacher is able to make a good guess as to what instructional procedures will be effective with the child. Possible teaching strategies for each instance are examplified in the column "What the teacher does next."

Table 3–9. *Failure Strategies Employed by Elementary Pupils*

	Example	
Strategy	*Problem*	*Pupil Response*
Wrong operation (the pupil performs an operation that leads to an incorrect result	38 $-\ 11$	$\begin{array}{r} 38 \\ -11 \\ \hline 49 \end{array}$
Obvious computational error (the pupil makes an obvious error in basic number facts)	42 $\times\ \ 3$	$\begin{array}{r} 42 \\ \times\ 3 \\ \hline 146 \end{array}$
Defective algorithm (the pupil makes procedural errors as he tries to apply the correct process)	562 $-\ 387$	$\begin{array}{r} 562 \\ -387 \\ \hline 225 \end{array}$
Random response (the pupil's response does not relate in any discernible way to the problem)	742 $\times\ \ 59$	$\begin{array}{r} 742 \\ \times 59 \\ \hline 123 \end{array}$

Source: Adapted from Roberts (1962).

INSTRUCTION IN MATHEMATICS

Once the child's performance has been analyzed in detail, instruction can begin. The nature of decisions to be made by the teacher shifts now to considerations of materials, methodologies, and approaches. This section begins with a discussion of a few principles that will assist the teacher in making sound instructional decisions. This is followed by descriptions of several instructional approaches which lend themselves to use with children having particular difficulty in mathematics. Because of the particular difficulty experienced by many children with verbal problem solving, this aspect of instruction has been singled out for special attention. A final section on one aspect of instruction—record keeping—concludes this chapter.

The Place of the Discovery Method

More than any other issue, the field of mathematics education has been dominated by a discussion of the extent to which teachers should use a "discovery approach" in teaching. The widespread adoption of this style of teaching is based on the belief that children learn more thoroughly and better retain principles and concepts that were acquired through a "discovery" process rather than through didactic instruction on the part of the teacher. Although Jerome Bruner of Harvard University has been a leading advocate of the discovery approach, other individuals have articulated it as well (e.g., Shulman, 1967; Kersh, 1965; Worthen, 1967). In using the discovery method, the teacher limits the number of cues that are given to the child to assist him in solving a particular problem. The cues that are withheld might be process cues, e.g., telling him to do such-and-such, or product cues, e.g., giving "hints" as to where to look for the answer.

The debate over the discovery method takes on particular significance when one is talking about the instruction of children who have problems in mathematics performance. One could define such children as those for whom cues that were sufficient for their peer group are not sufficient. That is, whatever the quantity and type of cues that made it possible for their classmates to learn did not work for this group. To talk further cue reduction for these children, then, seems almost irresponsible. Should children with mathematics problems be presented only with expository-type teaching? Although there is no research evidence one way or the other, we believe such a course to be unwise. *All* children, including those with learning difficulties, should be exposed to a variety of teaching styles and instructional approaches. Naturally, we do not advocate persisting with an approach that has been manifestly ineffective. What we are asserting is that there is more than one way to teach mathematics to children and discovery learning should

Table 3–10. *Sample Inventory of Subtraction of Whole Numbers: Error Analysis*[a]

Problem Presented	What the Child Writes	What the Child Says (Oral Interview)	Error Analysis Teacher's Hypotheses	What the Teacher Does Next
$\begin{array}{r} 7 \\ -\ 3 \\ \hline \end{array}$	$\begin{array}{r} 7 \\ -\ 3 \\ \hline 2 \end{array}$	7 take way 3 = 2.	Doesn't know number fact?	Present same problem in another form (rule out random error). Check other subtraction facts. Provide practice with physical objects, worksheets, number line, flashcards, games, etc. Retest before going to more difficult subtraction.
$\begin{array}{r} 15 \\ -\ 6 \\ \hline \end{array}$	$\begin{array}{r} 15 \\ -\ 6 \\ \hline 11 \end{array}$	6 take away 5 is 1; 1 stays the same.	Faulty algorithm; doesn't understand integrity of minuend and subtrahend; doesn't know number fact?	Check further to see if child always subtracts smaller number from larger. Review addition and subtraction at enactive and iconic level (Bruner) with one-digit numbers, then two-digit. Have child respond orally before returning to written form.
$\begin{array}{r} 85 \\ -\ 3 \\ \hline \end{array}$	$\begin{array}{r} 85 \\ -\ 3 \\ \hline 52 \end{array}$	3 from 8 is 5; 3 from 5 is 2.	Problem worked left to right; problem with place value (subtracting ones from tens).	Review place value at the enactive, iconic, and symbolic levels; provide practice with subtraction algorithm in simpler two-digit problems.
$\begin{array}{r} 85 \\ -\ 9 \\ \hline \end{array}$	$\begin{array}{r} 8\,{}^{1}5 \\ -\ 9 \\ \hline 86 \end{array}$	The 8 goes down here; then you have to change the 5 to 15, then subtract 9 from 15.	Problem worked left to right; doesn't understand effect of regrouping ones on tens.	Provide experience with place value—manipulating bundles of straws (1's, 10's, 100's), pocket chart, or Stern materials; then provide workbook pictorial practice. Finally, rework symbolic problems.

Problem	Child's explanation	Diagnosis	Remediation
91 − 83 ‾‾‾ 1	Since you can't take 3 from 1, the answer is 1; also because 8 from 9 is 1.	Problem in regrouping; possible problem in number fact.	Review place value (tens and ones); perform several problems of this type on the pocket chart, or with Cuisenaire rods. Provide successful experience on problems of this type before returning to numeral form.
523 − 284 ‾‾‾ 249	This 2 (in tens place) should be 12, that makes this 5 a 4. Now 12 − 8 = 4 and 4 − 2 = 2. To take 4 away over here (ones column) you make the 3 to a 13; 13 − 4 = 9; change 12 to 11.	Sequence is the problem here. The child performed all the steps correctly but in the wrong order.	Practice right-to-left sequence in problems not involving regrouping. Use place-value box or chart to show why sequence affects results.
300 − 157 ‾‾‾ 053	You have to get ones from the three because there aren't any here (pointing to 0's); 3 take away 2 makes the 3 a 1. Now we have 10 ones, and 10 tens, and we can subtract.	Relationship of empty sets of ones to tens to hundreds a problem. Child doesn't understand conversion from one unity to another.	Provide child with experience in converting tens to ones and hundreds to ones. (It might be very effective to use dollars, dimes, and pennies first; then use the paper-and-pencil mode.) First provide practice using only tens and ones together, then hundreds and tens together, then hundreds and ones together, finally conversions involving all three units in one problem.

a For an excellent discussion and numerous examples of error analysis, the reader is referred to R. B. Ashlock, *Error Patterns in Computation: A Semiprogrammed Approach* (Columbus, Ohio: Charles E. Merrill, 1972).

not be ruled out for any child. Similarly, to rely exclusively on the discovery method seems to us to be just as foolhardy.

Flexibility in Using Instructional Approaches

As stated in the preceding section, the effective teacher utilizes more than one approach, depending on the child, the task, and the situation. Olson (1972), noting that children can acquire the same knowledge when instructed in different modes, has presented a model that relates mode of experience to the acquisition of an underlying system of knowledge and skills (Figure 3–3). Note that a child may acquire the concept of the diagonal, for example, by direct or directed reinforced experience; he may achieve the same capability by observing that someone demonstrate the concept; or he may be verbally instructed through a symbol system (in this case, the English language). Olson's proposal has enormous implications for the teacher of mathematics (and to all teachers). If he is correct, teachers have considerably more choice than they may have thought they had in selecting an instructional mode.

Figure 3–3. *Proposal for Relating Three Modes of Experience to the Acquisition of an Underlying System of Knowledge and Skills*

Cognitive Development		Categories of Behavior (Modes) from Which Information May Be Extracted		Informational Coding (Alternatives Specified by:)
Knowledge	Skills			
Diagonal	Checkerboard Drawing Speaking	Contingent experience	Direct	Reinforcement consequent upon one's acts (learning theory)
			Directed (instructional)	
Chair	Sitting Drawing Describing	Observational learning	Observation	Modeled alternatives (social learning theory)
Objects	Locomotive		Modeling (instruction)	
Events	Prehensive			
Space	Linguistic	Symbolic systems	Communication	Coded alternatives (cognitive theory)
Time	Mathematical			
	Iconological		Instruction	

(Information extraction processes)

Thus, at times they may select procedures derived from learning theory (reinforcement consequent upon one's acts), at other times from social learning theory (modeled alternatives), or from cognitive theory (coded alternatives).

The same general thinking underlies a series of research studies and a mathematical developemnt project at the University of Connecticut (Cawley, 1971, 1976). Cawley and his coworkers have postulated an *interactive unit model* (see Table 3–11) that refers to the interaction of teacher and pupil in

Table 3–11. *Project MATH Interactive Unit (Example Selected: Teaching the Concept of "Open" and "Closed")*

		INPUT, usually by teacher (T)			
		constructs	*presents*	*states*	*writes*
OUTPUT, usually by pupil (P)	*writes*	T demonstrates "open" and "closed" with containers; P models with containers.	T presents containers to P; P opens or closes items as requested.	T states "open" or "closed"; P must form open or closed figure with yarn.	T writes "open" or "closed" on chalkboard; P closes or opens containers.
	states	T constructs examples of open and closed containers; P points to his own sample that matches T's.	T presents containers or pictures to P; P selects open or closed as requested.	T states "open" or "closed"; P points to appropriate picture.	P circles workbook picture that has "open" printed at top of page.
	presents	T constructs examples of open and closed containers; P correctly says "open" or "closed," as required.	T presents open and closed items to P; P states whether they are open or closed.	T asks P to name open and closed objects in the room.	P reads word from board, then states which items correspond.
	constructs	T constructs examples of open and closed containers; P correctly writes "open" or "closed," as required.	T presents pictures of open and closed items to P; P writes "open or closed."	T describes items; P writes "open" or "closed."	T writes "open" or "closed' 'at top of page; P writes word under pictures.

Definitions

Construct (do)	To pile, build, arrange, manipulate two- or three-dimensional objects or materials.
Present (see)	To display in fixed representations either two- or three-dimensional stimuli.
Identify (see)	To point to or otherwise mark nonsymbolic options in a multiple-choice task.
State **(say)**	To orally state.
Graphically symbolize (say)	To write with symbols (letters/numerals) or to draw.

Source: Adapted from J. F. Cawley, Learning Disabilities in Mathematics: A Curriculum Design for Upper Grades (unpublished manuscript, University of Connecticut, Storrs, Conn., 1976).

the mathematics teaching–learning situation. The instructional require-ments for the teacher vary from constructing something, presenting some-thing, saying something, or writing something. The child, when interacting with the teacher, can construct something, identify something, say some-thing, or write something. The various combinations of teacher input and student output are sixteen in number. This flexibility permits maximum discretion on the part of the teacher in planning for individuals or groups of children. Thus, if a child is a nonreader, for example, there are still twelve other ways that he and the teacher can interact in the instructional setting. (Other aspects of the materials developed by Cawley et al. are presented lated in this chapter.)

The teacher can evidence flexibility in mathematics instruction in other ways, e.g., in permitting pupils to have a choice in selecting the materials with which they wish to work, or in encouraging pupils to use unusual or alternative algorithms in working mathematical problems. Most textbook-prescribed algorithms are based on convention and on "efficiency," but there are equally acceptable ways of performing the same operation. For example, students having an inordinate amount of difficulty with subtraction involv-ing borrowing (see Table 3–10) may wish to use the alternative algorithm known as the "equal addition method" (Ashlock, 1972). Thus, the problem is

$$\begin{array}{r} 773 \\ -\ 254 \\ \hline \end{array}$$

The solution by this method is

$$\begin{array}{r} 77\,{}^{1}3 \\ -\ 2\,{}_{6}54 \\ \hline 519 \end{array}$$

The rationale for this approach is the principle of compensation: whatever is added to the minuend must be added to the subtrahend. Thus, 10 ones are added to the minuend; 1 ten is added to the subtrahend to compensate. Then, subtraction proceeds normally.

Project MATH (Cawley, 1976, 1978)

Rationale. Project MATH is designed for children in preschool through sixth grade. This comprehensive program is developmental in nature and is designed to (1) provide a multiple-option format for teachers and pupils so that pupils who have difficulty learning one way may be reached through another, (2) increase successful learning for children having difficulty, (3) maximize opportunities to apply mathematics to everyday living, (4) provide a balanced approach that facilitates pupil growth in social and emotional aspects, as well as intellectual, and (5) increase the teacher's individualization of instruction.

Materials and techniques. There are four kits in Project MATH, each covering approximately 1½ grade levels. Each level has two parts: the *Multiple Option Curriculum* (consisting of Instructional Guides, Learner Activity Books, manipulative materials, supplementary materials, evaluation and record-keeping materials), and the *Verbal Problem Solving Component* (consisting of a Guide of Verbal Problem Solving, large picture cards, and small picture cards). The Instructional Guides at each level cover a number of major mathematical strands, each containing a developmental sequence of mathematics concept designed especially for children with handicaps to learning. The strands are Geometry, Sets, Patterns, Numbers, Measurement, and Fractions. Each Instructional Guide is keyed to a particular Input–Output combination (interactive unit). (See Table 3–10 for an example of several Input–Output combinations.) Students' placement in the Multiple Option Curriculum, and their mastery of major concepts in the curriculum, is measured with the Math Concept Inventory.

Evaluation. Each element of Project MATH has been validated through extensive field testing.

Montessori Materials (Montessori, 1964, 1965a, 1965b)

Theory and rationale. The Montessori approach encompasses the entire physiological and psychological development of the child. Montessori (1965a) has organized her didactic materials into three major areas: motor education, sensory education, and language. The learning of arithmetic is seen as integrally related to the education of the senses, and most of the sensory training materials are readily adaptable for arithmetic activities. Montessori advocates a careful sequential development of basic numerical concepts rather than presenting "certain preliminary ideas" in haste (Montessori, 1965a, p. 165).

Training techniques. The Montessori materials are designed to be self-teaching. The basic materials include sets of solid cubes, cylinders, rods, prisms, and other geometric shapes and plane geometric forms; they also include counting boxes, sandpaper numerals, arithmetic frames and heads, counting frames, and bead chains. The materials may be used for learning seriation and ordering, one-to-one correspondence, shape and size, volume and length, counting, place value, addition, subtraction, multiplication, division, and factors.

To illustrate how the Montessori materials are employed for teaching basic arithmetic concepts, the use of cylinders is described. The materials themselves consist of four sets of cylinder boxes, each containing ten cylinders. The cylinders illustrate: (1) same height, change in diameter; (2) corresponding changes in height and diameter; (3) same diameter, change in height; and (4) opposite changes in diameter and height. One set at a time, the cylinders are removed from the box and randomly arranged. Through a series of trials and errors, the child replaces each cylinder until he finds the proper fit between the space in the box and the cylinder. He may also line up the cylinders in order of ascending or descending height or diameter without the use of the boxes.

The purposes of the activities are to observe and make comparisons between objects in terms of one or two dimensions—height and diameter. The child also learns seriation and ordering.

Program evaluation. The work of Montessori may be considered the forerunner of developmental theory concerning motor, sensory, and intellectual development, later refined and reformulated by Piaget, Bruner, and others. The use of concrete materials in the classroom as representations of abstract principles appears to be a major strength of the Montessori methods. After reviewing nineteen experimental studies of the effectiveness of this approach, L. Goodman (1974) concluded that Montessori's techniques had not yet been proved to be particularly useful.

Cuisenaire–Gattegno Rods

Rationale and theory. The Cuisenaire rods (Davidson, 1969) are intructional aids that seem particularly relevant to a modern mathematics curriculum. They are capable of generating pupil interest and enthusiasm while promoting a dialogue between learner and teacher. The rods are based on a definition of mathematics as a process of observation and a discovery of relationships. They were designed for the purpose of teaching conceptual knowledge of the basic structure of mathematics, rather than simply the manipulative skills. The teacher's role in the setting provided by the rods is to observe and ask questions about what the children are discovering for themselves, rather than to instruct or explain. It would appear that if a child works out facts and ideas for himself, he will learn and retain them better. Using rods, a kindergartener is introduced to algebraic equations and a basic appreciation of place value and the number system. The rods were invented by George Cuisenaire in 1953, and have been further developed by Caleb Gattegno.

Training techniques. There are 291 Cuisenaire rods, made of wood, and varying in length and color. The rods combine color and length to embody algebraic principles and number relationships. They are 1 centimeter square in cross section and from 1 to 10 centimeters long. There are five color families. The red rods represent the quantities of 2, 4, and 8; the blue–green rods, 3, 6, and 9; the yellow rods, 5 and 10; the black rod, 7; and the white cube, 1.

Since the rods have no numerals on them, children who have not yet developed an adequate number background can use the materials to explore logic as well as relationships between quantities. Children who possess basic number awareness can work with the rods in terms of the principles identified with particular number operations.

Introduction of the rods at any given grade level is done in the following four stages: (1) Independent exploration; that is, the child is permitted to "play" with the rods. (2) Independent exploration and directed activities with the rods, in which relationships are observed and discussed without the use of mathematical notation. The following aspects of mathematics are explored at this point:

Equivalence
Trains (sequences)
Patterns
Greater than and less than
Staircase (seriation)
Complements
Trains of one color
Transformations
Odds and evens

(3) Directed activities in which mathematical notation is introduced and used without assigning number value to the rods. Opportunities for independent exploration are still needed. (4) Directed activities in which the use of mathematical notation is extended and number values are assigned to the rods. Independent exploration will go beyond the directed activities.

Care should be taken to use rods for proper purposes, that is, discovery and verification. The method would be valueless if children were unable to do sums without the help of the rods. As soon as the situation is well understood, the child must be encouraged to work it out in his head.

Four booklets that accompany the rods treat such topics as cardinality, ordinality, factors, equivalence, permutations, transformations, complements, various forms of measurement, inequalities, proportions, basic whole numbers and rational number operations, number properties, and so forth.

While the booklets are concerned with various aspects of basic mathematics, they cannot be considered a complete program.

Although these materials can be used in grades kindergarten through six, they are usually emphasized through grade three. They may be used with an entire class, a small group, or an individual child. They have been successfully utilized with children possessing a varied range of abilities: the deaf, mentally retarded, gifted, and emotionally disturbed, as well as with other children who need visual and tactile reinforcement for effective learning.

Program evaluation. Research on the Cuisenaire–Gattegno materials has not been conclusive, but it has indicated that the rods are at least as effective as more traditional mathematics approaches. In addition, these materials minimize drill and rote learning and promote discovery and understanding by the individual child according to his own developmental level. Student interest and enthusiasm is usually high. The concreteness of the materials and their manipulation by a tactile modality make them particularly useful for children with whom a traditional mathematics program has been unsuccessful.

The Cuisenaire rods have been criticized on the grounds that children become too dependent on them and are unable to function at a symbolic, abstract level without them. However, used judiciously in conjunction with other models and approaches, the Cuisenaire rods have a place as supplemental materials in a modern mathematics curriculum for children with learning problems.

Individually Prescribed Instruction (IPI)—Mathematics

(Learning Research and Development Center, University of Pittsburgh, 1969, 1972)

Rationale. The program is based on the view that providing adequately for individual differences requires the individualizing of both goals and instructional resources. IPI permits students to pace themselves, to develop self-direction and self-initiation, to encourage self-evaluation, and to demonstrate mastery in mathematics skills. Although extensively validated, the program is still being revised.

Training techniques. IPI—Mathematics is organized into about 40 units, each of which deals with a number of related objectives—for example, numeration, place value, addition, fractions, and money. Each unit is divided into several levels; the levels correspond roughly to grade levels. Thus, the unit on addition encompasses levels A through H; the unit or division begins at level D and continues to level H. When the child begins the program, the teacher selects one of the units into which the child will be placed. A highly specific test covering the objectives in that unit is then given the child to determine precisely which objectives he has not yet mastered. Instructional resources keyed to those objectives are then prescribed for the child. Upon completion of the instructional material, the child is retested for mastery of the objectives at that level. The cycle is repeated until the child "passes" all the objectives in that unit.

Evaluation. The IPI test model is one of the most thoroughly developed and comprehensive approaches available. The program continues to the refined, based on field validation. A number of other individualized programs are based on basic research conducted in the development of the IPI. (IPI programs in science, spelling, reading, and handwriting are also avialable.)

Structural Arithmetic (Stern, 1965)

Rationale. This system is based on the assumption that arithmetic is the basis for the further study of mathematics and science; it presumes that mathematical concepts can and must be developed at the beginning of school life. Furthermore, the program assures mastery in computation by developing an insight into number relationships. This is achieved by having the child experiment with concrete materials that reveal the structure of our number system.

The goals of this approach are to develop mathematical thinking and nurture an appreciation for its exactness and clarity. Mathematical thinking can only develop if the child has obtained insight into the characteristic structure of the entire set of concepts to which specific addition or subtraction facts belong, or if he has developed insight into structural relationships that make transfer of learning possible. All experiments in *Structural Arithmetic* are designed to develop concepts that lead the child to arrive at generalizations essential to the understanding and mastery of arithmetic.

Structural Arithmetic hopes to achieve its goals through the following approaches:

1. By the use of concrete materials which allow the child to discover a number fact for himself.
2. By following a carefully arranged sequence of experiments through which the child advances step by step from simple number concepts to the mastery of arithmetical computation and problem solving.
3. By presenting functional illustrations in the workbooks which help the child reconstruct any forgotten number fact.

It is hoped that the child will experience the following achievements resulting from his use of structural materials:

1. Immediate success in arithmetic. (There will be a carryover from work with concrete materials to ability to do abstract figuring.)
2. Development of self-reliance. (The child can check answers and correct himself; he will become accustomed to always checking for correctness.)
3. Preparation for the mathematical thinking necessary in the later development of mathematics.

Training techniques. The materials for *Structural Arithmetic* (SA) are packaged in four kits, appropriate for kindergarten level and grades one through three. Materials for each grade include a teacher's manual, pupils' workbooks, and manipulatable materials (number markers, number guide, number track, number stand and accompanying slides, pattern board, unit box with unit blocks, subtraction shield, number cases, and a box of 100 cubes).

The approach in SA is based on measuring. The numbers are represented by blocks that measure 1 unit, 2 units, 3 units, and so on. With these devices the child can discover all existing number relations by himself. He finds out by measuring not only what block combinations yield 10, but also discovers processes of carrying and borrowing, multiplying and dividing. They are as well adapted for use with groups as for individual instruction.

Problem solving is an important part of SA. Pupils are prepared step by step for solving problems. They begin by listening carefully to oral problems and then demonstrate the problems with the manipulative materials. In SA 1, problems are presented by pictures without any printed words. In this way, a child's lack of reading ability will not hold him back. Word problems are introduced in SA 2 and used through SA 3. The vocabulary is kept simple throughout. In addition to work with structural materials, most of the lessons contain suggestions which teachers may use to provide an opportunity for pupils to do oral computation. Mastery tests appear at the end of each workbook and are also used throughout the SA program.

Each lesson is planned in the teacher's guide to help the teacher set up experiments that guide pupils to make appropriate discoveries and generalizations. From each experiment the pupils are to gain insight into an arithmetical procedure. To check whether the demonstration was successful, the teacher should present examples which the children can solve without the structural materials or pencil and paper. Following this the children continue using the topic of the day's experiment in their workbooks. There are provisions for additional experiments for the child who is having difficulty, and enrichment activities for the child who wishes to work independently.

Program evaluation. *Structural Arithmetic* is a complete mathematics program that is flexible, well organized, and concrete. The teacher's guide is very thorough and includes detailed teaching suggestions. The program has been successful with mildly retarded and learning disabled children, as well as in regular classes. The materials are nonconsumable.

SRA's Criterion-Referenced Measurement Program/Mathematics (SRA, 1975)

Rationale. This program is based on the assumption that the teaching process is cyclical and that instruction should be preceded by assessment (mastery tests) to determine prerequisite skills. Accompanying instruction is continuous diagnosis, which permits the instruction to be precisely focused so that appropriate remediation can occur. Then to determine mastery of material taught, the child is once more assessed (repeat mastery test). The mastery (evaluation) and diagnosis (instruction) may be used together or separately. They may be used as a self-contained unit.

Training techniques. The diagnosis series consist of two labs, level A for grades one to four and level B for grades three to six. All diagnosis labs are organized to provide immediate feedback. Each of these labs contains criterion-referenced tests called "probes." Items on the "probes" are keyed to other SRA material to existing textbooks published by others and are constantly updated, through prescription guides which are published on an ongoing basis. Probes are correlated to the mastery items. The mastery tests, in turn, provide the teacher with overall information about a child's mastery of specific skills. Three test items have been developed for each skill objective. For example, in the whole-number-computation portion of the test, objective CT-11 is given as: "Given an addition problem in the horizontal format with two one-digit addends whose sum is 12, 13, or 14, the learner will identify the sum." Items on the Mastery Test which assessed the child's level on this objective are: $7 + 6 = \square$, $9 + 3 = \square$, and $6 + 8 = \square$. Correct performance in all three items is taken to indicate mastery. For schools that do not wish to utilize all of the objectives listed in the "Mathematics Catalog of Objectives," custom-made tests can be assembled by SRA which include only those objectives desired by the school system. Mastery results are available as individual student profiles or group reports.

Evaluation. Although this program is too new to have accumulated any educational research, it clearly embodies many educational ideas currently in vogue. Objectives are clearly stated. Criteria for mastery of the objectives are explicit. A student's profile is systematically taken into account for establishing entry-level and subsequent instruction into the program. Maximum flexibility is achieved in the program's being keyed to existing materials in mathematics instruction.

The Learning Skills Series: Arithmetic
(Hunter and LaFollette, 1976)

Rationale. This series of pupil workbooks and teacher manual was originally developed for adolescent, slow-learning youngsters who were labeled "educable, mentally handicapped." However, the materials found such wide use with "normal" young men and women that the 1976 edition claims to be appropriate for slow-learning teenagers however they are designated. Accompanying the workbooks are four placement tests, performance on which determines entry level into the workbook series. These placement tests are computational in nature, indicating the authors' belief that computation is the basis for sound performance in arithmetic. The objectives of the series are stated, however, in broader terms, e.g., "to help students develop mature mental and emotional attitudes, a sense of responsibility and self-direction, a practical reading and spelling vocabulary, longer attention spans, honest work habits, self-confidence, and some basic pre-vocational knowledge and skills" (Teacher's Manual, p. 1).

Training techniques. As indicated above, the series consists of pupil workbooks, teacher's manual, and placement tests. The teacher's manual is organized to enable the teacher to work with up to four ability levels within a regular classroom setting. That is, each chapter has differentiated objectives, depending on the capacity of the child or the group of children who will be working with it. For example, the very first chapter has as its objectives for level A pupils to give meaning to counting, to show that adding is an easier way to count and to emphasize the idea of subtraction as "how many are left." For level B pupils, a more complex objective is introduced: to expose the idea of subtraction with borrowing. For level C and D pupils, the main purposes of the chapters are to reinforce existing addition, multiplication, and division skills. The chapters in the series are untimed, permitting teachers maximum flexibility for planning review or moving quickly to topics with which the pupils are already familiar. The first three chapters of the series are primarily computational. An attempt is made to relate computational skills to such everyday activities as reading road maps, recipes, timetables, thermometers, clocks, and newspaper advertisements. In subsequent chapters, pupils learn to maintain personal expense account sheets and write checks, to keep daily temperature graphs, to set up a household budget and maintain household expense sheets, to learn to plan and prepare meals (computational aspects), and to do basic geometry.

Features of the series includes inclusion of metric measurements as an option, and a conscious effort to represent different minority groups and individuals of both sexes in illustrations and examples.

Evaluation. No formal evaluation using controlled research was available. However, a perusal of the material and comments of teachers who have used the materials indicate considerable success when used with adolescents who had previously had very little success in mathematics. Of particular benefit is the emphasis on acquisition of practical skills for a population of individuals who will in all likelihood enter the job market shortly after completing the series.

Distar Arithmetic I, II, III
(Englemann and Carnine, 1976)

Rationale. The Distar Arithmetic Kits are consistent with the Distar philosophy that intensive and systematic preplanning and structuring of the skills required for mastery in the basic subject areas is the most effective way of teaching. The authors state that the underlying concept is "that virtually all children can learn if we teach them carefully" (Distar Arithmetic II, Teacher's Guide, p. 1). Each kit is designed to provide a teacher with all the techniques, information, and materials needed to teach students effectively.

Training techniques. Each Distar Arithmetic Kit consists of a Teacher's Guide, several Teacher's Presentation Books, workbooks for each child, and, depending on the level, geometric figures cards, form boards, fact cards, and card stand. The teaching technique itself is a highly structured one in which the teacher presents to the child in a highly prescriptive fashion what he is required to say and do. What the teacher says and does is specified. Lessons are rapidly paced to maintain the student's interest. By requiring pupils to respond orally (and in revised kits in written form to a greater extent) on a continuing intensive basis, children remain actively involved and hopefully at a high level of interest. Subskills are introduced in sequence, with simple concepts first and more complicated ones later. The program shows what mistakes children are likely to make and what the teacher should say and do in response to such mistakes. Program objectives are clearly stated and criteria for mastery are explicit.

Evaluation. More than most programs, the Distar series has undergone extensive field testing. Data regarding this field testing from SRA indicate that children demonstrate success mastering the specified objectives.

Individualized Computation Skills Series
(Simon, 1975)

Rationale. This program is designed to help the learner develop mastery of basic computation through self-diagnosis, self-study, and self-practice. All materials are cross-referenced so that the learner will spend time on those computation skills that he has not yet mastered.

Training techniques. The materials consist of three sets of self-diagnostic tests, individualized study units, learn-and-practice sheets, and answer cards organized into eight units that deal with the computation of whole numbers, fractions, decimals, and percents. Although no grade level is specified, the materials would seem to be appropriate for the elementary grades.

Ideally, the learner should be able to use these materials entirely on his own in much the same way as the SRA individualized reading kits would be used. That is, each child completes a diagnostic test, grades it himself, and, depending on his score, either goes back to redo a practice sheet or goes on to the next one in sequence. A class record sheet is provided so that the teacher can easily keep track of the children's performances on each of the tests and on the practice sheets.

Evaluation. No research has been reported on the use of this program. However, it would seem to be a useful supplementary set of materials for a classroom in which there are one or more pupils needing additional work in developing computational skills. While the materials are said to be self-study materials, it is likely that the teachers will want to monitor a child's progress by periodic checks.

Other Suitable Materials

While it is possible to adopt most regular mathematics materials for children with special learning problems, we have found a few textbook series that are particularly useful. These series are summarized in Table 3–12.

Verbal Problem Solving

Probably no area of mathematics performance causes more difficulty for students than verbal problem solving (Ashlock, 1970, p. 193). It is not known what all the causes for poor problem-solving ability are, but they almost certainly include the following:

1. *Lack of practice.* Some teachers do not fully recognize the com-

plexity of problem solving, and fail to teach it in a systematic way. Considerable time must be alloted for the successful development of problem-solving skills.

2. *Inadequate development of underlying capabilities.* Task analysis and research have indicated that the following are related to ability to solve mathematical problems:

    a. *Ability to perform required computations is a necessary sub-skill.* Pace (1961) found that an understanding of the four fundamental operations (addition, subtraction, multiplication, division) is vital for problem solving.

    b. *Ability to read with understanding.* That reading problems are frequently implicated in problem-solving difficulties is exemplified by Heddens and Smith (1964). This study found that the typical commercial mathematics text has a readability level above that of the assigned grade level. The reading aspect of mathematical problems is further affected by the fact that many words have a different meaning in a mathematical context than in everyday life. For example, "set" in mathematics refers to a grouping of items; in ordinary usage it is a verb, as in "set the table." The point is that even if the child can read the word "set," it does not follow that he knows its mathematical usage. Other such special terms include "order," "base," "prime," "power," and "roots." Treacy (1944) found that poor problem solvers had trouble with a number of reading skills, particularly those that had to do with interpreting vocabulary.

    c. *Ability to estimate answers.* Checking the "reasonableness" of an obtained answer requires the ability to estimate. Poor problem solvers tend not to be proficient in this skill (Kliebhan, 1955).

    d. *Acquisition of prerequisite concepts and cognitive structures.* There is reason to believe that the capacities described in the section on "Readiness" are necessary for children to solve mathematical problems. For example, Steffe (1968) reported that ability to conserve was related to problem-solving performance.

    e. *Ability to organize required problem-solving steps in sequence.* Although the evidence is mixed as far as the necessity for teaching specific problem-solving steps to most children (Wilson, 1967; Lerch and Hamilton, 1966), we advocate the use of such procedures for children who are having inordinate difficulty. The procedure to be followed is outlined in Table 3–13.

Table 3–12. *Summary of Mathematic Series Adaptable for Children with Learning Problems*

Name (Author)	Components	Content	Method or Approach	Provisions for Students with Difficulties	Special Features
Holt School Mathematics	Student text Teacher text Cassettes Sound filmstrip Transparencies Jumbo screen Blocks and boxes Workbooks Drill masters Diagnostic tests Test masters Guide for individualizing	Sets, number operations and properties, problem solving numeration sentences, reasoning, probability and statistics, geometry, measurement, graphs, tables, scale drawings	"Guided discovery." Emphasis on getting students to discover patterns.	Suggestions for individualizing. Each lesson presented at three levels: *A*—minimal course with time for reinforcement and recycling; *B*—regular course; *C*—enriched course.	Strong problem-solving emphasis. Extra practice exercises provided.
Math Around Us	Teacher text Student text Punch-out materials Duplicating masters Test booklets Practice and activities book Optional: Geoboards, lab activities, metric booklets		Teaching strategy is to: 1. Motivate 2. Teach 3. Practice 4. Apply	Lesson notes in teacher's text have suggestions for "helping the low achiever" and "additional material for individualizing."	Built-in testing program. Emphasis on skills and applications. Extensive use of photographs "that bring the real world into the book."

Ginn Elementary Mathematics (Scott, Immerzeel, and Wiederanders, 1972)	Pupil's book Annotated teacher edition	Computation, functions, number systems, numeration, number theory, geometry, measurement, problem solving, probability and statistics, application	Steps to learning: 1. Image 2. Symbol 3. Organization 4. Generalization 5. Practice 6. Application	Plenty of opportunity for working with concrete materials. Each lesson has behavioral objectives and evaluation criterion.	Emphasis on math structure. Systematic variation of teaching strategy.
Modern School Mathematics (Duncan et al., 1970)	Teacher's book, Pupils' books	Numerals and numbers, sets, number sentences, mathematical operations, application, problem solving, geometry, measurement, functions	Spiraled discovery approach	Three levels in "Assignment Guide"—for minimum, average, or maximum course of study. General suggestions for less-able students. Controlled reading level. Regular diagnostic chapter tests.	Emphasis on patterns and structures. Use of set language.

Table 3–13. *Suggested Steps in Verbal Problems Solving*

	Problem A	Problem B
	Mary has 3 apples. Betty has 2 oranges. Peter has 4 apples. How many pieces of fruit do the girls have?	Bill has 7 quarters, 3 dimes, and 4 pennies. How much money will he have left if he spends 45 cents for candy?
A. Preview: read the problem		
1. Identify unknown words	None	None
2. Identify words with unusual usages	None	None
3. Identify any "cue" words, e.g., "total," "in all," "how many were left"	None	"How much . . . have left"
B. Re-reading: information processing		
1. Identify what is given		
a. Is renaming required?		
i. unit conversion	No	Quarters and dimes to cents
ii. categorization (superordinate, subordinate categories	Apples and oranges to fruit	No
b. Is sufficient information given?		
c. Is irrelevant or distracting information given?	"Peter has 4 apples."	
2. Identify what is asked for; formulate hypothesis		
a. What process is required? (comparing, combining, etc.)	Combining	Conversion, combining, separating
b. What unit or category is required (minutes, inches, apples, dollars, etc.)	Fruit	Dollars and cents
C. Refine hypothesis: operations analysis Decide what operations need to be performed Possible strategies:	Combining: addition	Combining: addition; then separation: subtraction
1. Substitute easier numbers in the problem	Not applicable	Bill has (10 cents). How much money will he have left if he spends 5 cents for candy? Solution pattern: subtract money spent from origi-

	Problem A	Problem B
	Mary has 3 apples. Betty has 2 oranges. Peter has 4 apples. How many pieces of fruit do the girls have?	Bill has 7 quarters, 3 dimes, and 4 pennies. How much money will he have left if he spends 45 cents for candy?

	Problem A	Problem B
		nal amount of money, or; original money − money spent = *required answer*. Now substitute numbers from Problem B.
2. Use manipulative objects, number line, or doodles drawn on paper to help "visualize" the problem.		
D. Write the mathematical sentences	$3 + 2 =$ *required answer*	$7 \times .25 = a$ $3 \times .10 = b$ $4 \times .01 = c$ $a + b + c = d$ $d - .45 =$ *required answer*
E. Perform the operation	$3 + 2 = 5$	$7 \times .25 = 1.25$ $3 \times .10 = .30$ $4 \times .01 = .04$ $1.75 + .30 + .04 = 2.09$ $2.09 - .45 = 1.64$
F. Check the answer		
1. Recheck reason and computation.	Repeat steps A–E	Repeat steps A–E
2. Estimate the answer and compare to obtained answer.	Will vary	Will vary
G. State the result		
In terms of E (above) In terms of B.2.b (above)	The girls now have 5 pieces of fruit.	Bill will have $1.64 left.

Source: Adapted from K. Kramer, *The Teaching of Elementary School Mathematics* (Boston: Allyn and Bacon, 1970); J. F. Cawley, Learning Disabilities in Mathematics: A Curriculum Design for Upper Grades (unpublished manuscript, University of Connecticut, Storrs, Conn., 1976); and from author's experience.

Figure 3–4. *Summary Checksheet*

Name of Pupil	One-place whole numbers without carrying	Two-place whole numbers without carrying	Three-place whole numbers without carrying	Two-place whole numbers with carrying 10's	Three-place numbers with carrying 10's	Three-place numbers with carrying 10's, 100's	Mixed digit addition with carrying	Simple fractions common denominators	Mixed fractions common denominators	Simple fractions mixed denominators	Mixed fractions mixed denominators	Decimals—one decimal point	Decimals—two or more decimal points
Mary B.	9/26	10/4	10/14	1/21	1/30	2/14	5/10						
Tommy S.	9/2	9/30											

Record Keeping for Diagnostic Teaching

Employment of the diagnostic, analytic procedures outlined in the previous sections obviously call for precise record keeping. The teacher will want to keep at least two kinds of records for each child's performance in mathematics. The first type is in the form of a summary checksheet for a group of children or for an entire class and is used to plan individual and group activities. A portion of such a table is shown as Figure 3–4.

Checksheets such as this can be used to keep a record of when each child has finally achieved mastery of given areas or mathematics achievement. During the period from when the child is first instructed in a given performance area until the time that he achieves mastery, more detailed record keeping is required. Take the example of a child who has just been introduced to a new unit on long division. The objective is to teach the child to perform division problems of the type

$$3 \overline{)\, 7965} \quad \text{(one-digit divisor, no remainder)}$$

Figure 3–5. *Example of Untimed Number-Correct Record Keeping*

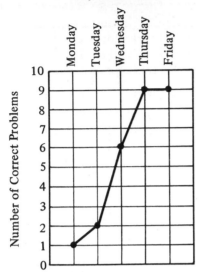

Figure 3–6. *Example of Rate-per-Minute Record Keeping*

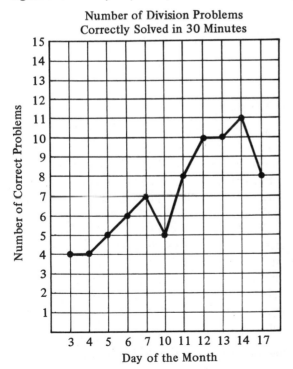

Each day the child is presented with ten problems of this type. A record of his performance might look as shown in Figure 3–5. After the child has demonstrated adequacy in performing division problems of this type, the teacher might wish to encourage a child to work more quickly by recording his performance on a rate-per-minute index, or as the number performed in a given number of minutes. An example of this type of recording is given in Figure 3–6.

Improving Spelling Skills

Donald D. Hammill

4

Proficiency in spelling is a highly prized but frequently unattained outcome of language arts instruction. Most children are taught by means of a school-wide spelling program and readily become fluent spellers. However, many others, with comparable mental ability and interest, do not learn to spell adequately. When deficiencies are first observed, the teacher should immediately take steps to help the child overcome his problem. This chapter is designed to aid teachers to better understand spelling skills, and to acquire information about appropriate assessment techniques and various developmental and remedial teaching programs directed toward improvement in spelling.

A GENERAL OVERVIEW OF SPELLING

Spelling is the forming of words from letters in both written and oral forms, according to accepted usage. The written form is the more important to the child, as he is constantly expected to write about his ideas and feelings. The "spelling bee," an oral form, is primarily a technique employed to develop the skill of spelling, and is actually used in the hope that the skill developed will transfer to the written form. While spelling may receive less attention in the modern school, most children who are poor spellers are placed at a considerable disadvantage in our society. Otto and McMenemy (1966, p. 203) paraphrasing Hildreth, have presented three cogent arguments for teaching children to spell:

1. Ability to spell enables the writer to concentrate on the ideas he wishes to convey rather than on the mechanics of writing.

2. Ability to spell is often regarded as evidence of scholarly achievement. Justifiably or not, incorrect spelling often creates an unfavorable impression beyond its true significance.
3. Correct spelling facilitates the reading of what is written. It is a common courtesy the reader has a right to expect.

In the past, spelling was viewed as a school subject to which the child was introduced during the second grade or at the end of the first grade. Teachers assumed that their pupils were ready to learn the skill at this appointed time, as in fact most pupils were. Often the initial exposure to spelling was handled in an unimaginative manner; it was expected to be mastered by the rote memorization of selected words. When failures were noticed, more memorization was the prescribed cure. If after great effort and frustration on both the part of the teacher and the pupil, the child could not produce the expected competency, the deficiency was overlooked or forgotten. The additive nature of education, however, compounded the problem; spelling, like handwriting and reading, is a tool subject; and deficits in this skill can influence the child's entire school experience.

Several educators, notably Personke and Yee, have attempted to generate models that can be employed to explain spelling behavior. When well conceived and presented, the models can help teachers to understand the total spelling process. This is essential if the teacher is to know how and where breakdowns in spelling occur and what might be done to correct or bypass problem areas.

Personke and Yee (1966, 1968) have postulated a model for spelling that includes a series of five sequenced channels or options which the spelling process may take. Although these channels are distinct, they are also complementary and imply that a spelling program that utilizes only one or a few of the channels will not prepare the speller to cope with all the spelling situations he might encounter. A schematic presentation of the model is provided in Figure 4–1. The reader will note that internal and external feedback and inputs are accounted for in the model. The important elements of the model are the channels (i.e., processes) associated with spelling behavior. These include the:

Memory channel. The speller writes a word from memory, then looks at it to see if it is correct.
Memory–kinesthetic bypass. The speller has so overlearned a word that it can be written without any conscious thought. For example, words such as "and" or "the" are produced without hesitation.
Checking channel. The speller refers to an external input (e.g., dictionary, spelling book, another person) prior to writing the word.
Proofread channel. The speller checks a word that he has written through the use of an external input.

Proofread rewrite detour. The speller checks written words through external agents; if a word is incorrect, he rewrites the word correctly.

The creators of the model point out that the most efficient process is the memory–kinesthetic bypass, since it enables the pupil to spell correctly and quickly without an undue amount of thinking. However, this process is useful only for words already mastered. Subsequently, in teaching spelling, attention should be directed toward adequacy in all channels. Two articles

Figure 4–1. *Theoretical Model of Spelling Behavior.* [From C. Personke and A. H. Yee. The situational choice and the spelling program. *Elementary English*, 1968, 45, p. 33. *Reprinted with the permission of the National Council of Teachers of English and the authors.* Also in *Comprehensive Spelling Instruction: Theory, Research, and Application* (New York: Intext Educational Publishers, 1971).]

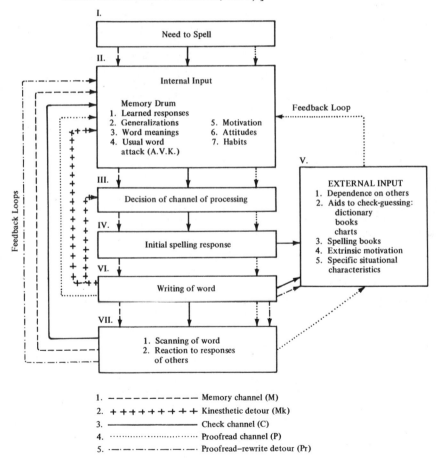

are devoted to the model. In the first, Personke and Yee (1966) present and explain their model; in the second (1968), they attempt to demonstrate its practical significance. Although this model may contribute somewhat to a teacher's theoretical understanding of spelling, it is of limited practical value.

These short, summary statements regarding this model, or any of the other models described in this book, are in no way intended as comprehensive presentations; they are intended merely to inform teachers that models do exist. The teacher is directed to the original sources for detailed discussions of the models. The information gained from these sources may then be considered in planning an effective spelling program.

ASSESSING SPELLING SKILLS

When a child fails in spelling, the teacher immediately needs the answers to several pertinent questions:

1. Does the child have sufficient mental ability to learn to spell?
2. Are his hearing, speech, and vision adequate?
3. What is his general level of spelling ability?
4. Has he areas of specific weakness in spelling?
5. What systems, techniques, or activities might be used to remediate his difficulties?

The answers to questions one to four are crucial and prerequisite to answering question five. In most cases, there will be no question as to the pupil's mental or sensory adequacy, and the teacher can proceed directly to assessing the child's spelling deficits. This section is devoted to a discussion of procedures that might be used to assess spelling readiness and specific spelling skills.

Assessing Spelling Readiness

There is a temptation to refer to spelling readiness in the broadest of terms; e.g., the child should be motivated to learn to spell or he should have adequate auditory and visual memory. Unfortunately, such phrases are so indefinite that they are of little value to teachers. Although R. M. Smith (1968), Frostig and Maslow (1973), Westerman (1971), and many others believe on a theoretical level that "auditory and visual reception," "auditory and visual memory," "auditory and visual discrimination," "association of auditory and visual stimuli," "motor expression," and "vocal expression" are skills basic to successful spelling, the assessment of spelling readiness confined to these broad, possibly hypothetical categories is not profitable. For instance, there is no doubt that in some "abstract" sense, the ability to associate auditory and visual stimuli is involved in some ill-defined way in the act or spelling; however, the practical question remains: Which particular associative tasks are prerequisites to spelling? Clearly, not all associations are important. The association of letters with their sounds is likely to be essential (or is it, since some deaf individuals are fluent spellers?), while association of spoken words with pictures is probably less critical to spelling. It is important for teachers to note that when attempts have been made to empirically study the relationship of tests of psycholinguistic processes, sensory modalities, and perceptual abilities to tests of spelling, the resultant correlation coefficients have been consistently too small to have any educational usefulness. Readers who have a particular interest in this topic are referred to the review of thirteen relevant studies on pages 48–50 in Newcomer and Hammill (1976).

For most school children, teachers should consider average mental ability and sensory integrity (i.e., adequate hearing and sight) as the primary prerequisites for spelling. Pupils exhibiting normal intelligence, language, sight, and hearing who fail in spelling should be subjected to a thorough teacher evaluation using procedures discussed in this chapter. But this assessment should focus on a study of the child's performance in tasks directly related to spelling, rather than on "underlying" psycholinguistic processes. To our knowledge, the precise constellation of skills that are predictive of spelling success are as yet mostly unknown or unresearched.

Norm-Referenced Spelling Tests

The norm-referenced standardized tests that are available to teachers range widely regarding the types and breadth of information provided. Some yield information only on a child's general spelling ability (e.g., most achievement tests) and some yield information on several different spelling skills. The latter devices are frequently called diagnostic tests. For the most part, these tests usually involve selecting correctly spelled words or writing dictated words.

The main shortcoming of most achievement tests with which many teachers are familiar is that they yield a single score which is compared to a set of standardized norms and which results in a grade equivalent. Although this information is useful for some purposes (e.g., in determining the spelling level of a particular school or school district or in identifying poor spellers), it often is not helpful to teachers. With reference to most of the commercially available tests, Westerman (1971) has commented:

> Unfortunately, most of these instruments serve but one major function: to discover how many words a child can spell as compared to others in his class thus providing a so-called "grade level" score (p. 35).

In light of Westerman's remarks, it should be noted that achievement tests are designed to measure skills broadly; they do not readily lend themselves to error analysis. Examples of these tests include the spelling subtests from the popular achievement batteries, e.g., the Wide Range Achievement Test (Jastak and Jastak, 1965), the Metropolitan Achievement Tests (Durost et al., 1971), and the Iowa Tests of Basic Skills (Lindquist and Hieronymous, 1956).

Diagnostic tests, on the other hand, are designed to provide information about an individual's functioning ability in several different areas. Unfortunately, there are few diagnostic spelling tests available, and none of them permit the measurement of all the abilities that comprise spelling. To the extent that the diagnostic tests fail to do this, the teacher must supply his own information, gathered from employing the informal evaluation techniques presented in the next section. One of those multiability tests of spelling are discussed below.

A new norm-reference diagnostic test, called the Test of Written Spelling, has been developed by Larsen and Hammill (1976). The 60 words that comprise the test were chosen because they appear in each of the ten spelling series that are used most often in the schools. Thirty-five of these words are "predictable," in that their spelling is consistent with certain phonological (i.e., phoneme–grapheme correspondence) rules or generalization (e.g., had, spring, pile, salute, legal); and 25 words are "unpredictable" in that their spelling conforms to no useful phonological or morphological rules (e.g., people, knew, eight, fountain, community). Test results can be interpreted in terms of the student's mastery of the predictable words, the unpredictable words, or the total number of words.

The test is standardized on a nationwide sample of 4544 children who share the national characteristics relative to geographic location, sex, and urban–rural residence. Studies indicate that the TWS is reliable (i.e., internally consistent) at all grade levels between two and nine (coefficients in the 80s and 90s), and that its results correlate strongly with the spelling subtests of the Durrell Analysis of Reading Difficulty (.90), Wide Range Achievement Test (.80), California Achievement Test (.80), and the SRA Achievement Series (.69).

In general, norm-referenced tests with the most complete standardizations offer the teacher little more than a grade-equivalent or grade-level score. On the other hand, the tests that attempt to provide a more complete analysis of an individual's spelling ability tend to have inadequate standardizations. The teacher, therefore, has the option of using a test with a comparatively sound research base but offering little information, or of using a test that attempts to tap more components of spelling but has no reported reliability.

The teacher should be selective in the type of tests used and should consider the following three suggestions:

1. Know what the test measures and what its limitations are before giving it to the child: for example, what type of children were used for the standardization and what is the reported reliability and validity of the test.
2. Be prepared to supplement the test where possible with other formal measures.
3. Use informal evaluation techniques whenever specific information about the child's spelling abilities is required, and as a guide to planning a remediation program.

Criterion-Referenced Testing in Spelling

Norm-referenced tests such as those just mentioned are usually comprised of statistically selected items because they are built to be relatively short, highly reliable measurement devices. Criterion-referenced tests, on the other hand, are constructed to include a broad spectrum of items, reflecting most, if not all, of the elements that make up the skill being measured. Builders of criterion-referenced measures are not unduly concerned with the statistical characteristics of the items being chosen. The purpose of criterion-referenced testing in educational practice is not to determine where the child stands relative to other children but to identify those components of the ability being assessed that are in need of training. While these tests may or may not be accompanied by rough norms, they will invariably be quite suitable for item analysis.

This type of assessment helps the teacher to determine a child's instructional level while also measuring progress toward the task goal. The following advantages to this approach are suggested by Westerman (1971). Criterion-referenced tests:

1. Indicate the skills a child has and those he needs.
2. Provide an objective measure of progress as the child moves from task to task.
3. Are designed by the teacher and are based upon what content is to be taught and who is to learn it.

While there are many more or less criterion-referenced measures of spelling from which the teacher may choose, only one will be presented in this book, Kottmeyer's (1970) Diagnostic Spelling Test (see Table 4–1). The test is administered using a dictation format; e.g., the examiner says to the child or children, "Not. He is *not* here," after which he or they write the word "not."

Table 4–1. *Diagnostic Spelling Test*

Give list 1 to any pupil whose placement is second or third grade.
Give list 2 to any pupil whose placement is above grade three.
Grade scoring, list 1:

Below 15 correct:	Below second grade
15–22 correct:	Second grade
23–29 correct:	Third grade

Any pupil who scores above 29 should be given the list 2 test.
Grade scoring, list 2:

Below 9 correct:	Below third grade
9–19 correct:	Third grade
20–25 correct:	Fourth grade
26–29 correct:	Fifth grade
Over 29 correct:	Sixth grade or better

Any pupil who scores below 9 should be given the list 1 test.

List 1

Word   Illustrative Sentence

1. not—He is *not* here.
2. but—Mary is here, *but* Joe is not.
3. get—*Get* the wagon, John.
4. sit—*Sit* down, please.
5. man—Father is a tall *man*.
6. boat—We sailed our *boat* on the lake.
7. train—Tom has a new toy *train*.
8. time—It is *time* to come home.
9. like—We *like* ice cream.
10. found—We *found* our lost ball.
11. down—Do not fall *down*.
12. soon—Our teacher will *soon* be here.
13. good—He is a *good* boy.
14. very—We are *very* glad to be here.
15. happy—Jane is a *happy* girl.
16. kept—We *kept* our shoes dry.
17. come—*Come* to our party.
18. what—*What* is your name?
19. those—*Those* are our toys.
20. show—*Show* us the way.
21. much—I feel *much* better.
22. sing—We will *sing* a new song.
23. will—Who *will* help us?
24. doll—Make a dress for the *doll*.
25. after—We play *after* school.
26. sister—My *sister* is older than I.
27. toy—I have a new *toy* train.
28. say—*Say* your name clearly.
29. little—Tom is a *little* boy.
30. one—I have only *one* book.
31. would—*Would* you come with us?
32. pretty—She is a *pretty* girl.

List 2

	Word	Illustrative Sentence
1.	flower	A rose is a *flower*.
2.	mouth	Open your *mouth*.
3.	shoot	Joe wants to *shoot* his new gun.
4.	stood	We *stood* under the roof.
5.	while	We sang *while* we marched.
6.	third	We are in the *third* grade.
7.	each	*Each* child has a pencil.
8.	class	Our *class* is reading.
9.	jump	We like to *jump* rope.
10.	jumps	Mary *jumps* rope.
11.	jumped	We *jumped* rope yesterday.
12.	jumping	The girls are *jumping* rope now.
13.	hit	*Hit* the ball hard.
14.	hitting	John is *hitting* the ball.
15.	bite	Our dog does not *bite*.
16.	biting	The dog is *biting* on the bone.
17.	study	*Study* your lesson.
18.	studies	He *studies* each day.
19.	dark	The sky is *dark* and cloudy.
20.	darker	This color is *darker* than that one.
21.	darkest	This color is the *darkest* of the three.
22.	afternoon	We may play this *afternoon*.
23.	grandmother	Our *grandmother* will visit us.
24.	can't	We *can't* go with you.
25.	doesn't	Mary *doesn't* like to play.
26.	night	We read to Mother last *night*.
27.	brought	Joe *brought* his lunch to school.
28.	apple	An *apple* fell from the tree.
29.	again	We must come back *again*.
30.	laugh	Do not *laugh* at other children.
31.	because	We cannot play *because* of the rain.
32.	through	We ran *through* the yard.

List 1

	Word	Element Tested
1.	not	⎫
2.	but	⎪
3.	get	⎬ Short vowels
4.	sit	⎪
5:	man	⎭
6.	boat	⎫ Two vowels together
7.	train	⎭
8.	time	⎫ Vowel–consonant-*e*
9.	like	⎭
10.	found	⎫ *ow–ou* spelling of *ou* sound
11.	down	⎭

(continued)

Table 4–1. *Diagnostic Spelling Test (continued)*

	Word	Element Tested
12.	soon	Long and short *oo*
13.	good	
14.	very	Final *y* as short *i*
15.	happy	
16.	kept	*c* and *k* spellings of the *k* sound
17.	come	
18.	what	
19.	those	*wh, th, sh, ch,* and *ng* spellings and *ow spelling* of long *o*
20.	show	
21.	much	
22.	sing	
23.	will	Doubled final consonants
24.	doll	
25.	after	*er* spelling
26.	sister	
27.	toy	*oy* spelling of *oi* sound
28.	say	*ay* spelling of long *a* sound
29.	little	*le* ending
30.	one	
31.	would	Nonphonetic spellings
32.	pretty	

List 2

	Word	Element Tested
1.	flower	*ow–ou* spellings of *ou* sound
2.	mouth	*er* ending, *th* spelling
3.	shoot	Long and short *oo, sh*
4.	stood	Spelling
5.	while	*wh* spelling, vowel–consonant-*e*
6.	third	*th* spelling, vowel before *r*
7.	each	*ch* spelling, two vowels together

	Word	*Element Tested*
8.	class	Double final consonant, *c;* spelling of *k* sound
9.	jump	
10.	jumps	Addition of *s, ed, ing;*
11.	jumped	*j* spelling of soft *g* sound
12.	jumping	
13.	hit	Doubling final consonant
14.	hitting	before adding *ing*
15.	bite	Dropping final *e* before *ing*
16.	biting	
17.	study	Changing final *y* to *i* before
18.	studies	ending
19.	dark	
20.	darker	*er, est* endings
21.	darkest	
22.	afternoon	Compound words
23.	grandmother	
24.	can't	Contractions
25.	doesn't	
26.	night	Silent *gh*
27.	brought	
28.	apple	*le* ending
29.	again	
30.	laugh	Nonphonetic spellings
31.	because	
32.	through	

Source: Teacher's Guide for Remedial Reading by William Kott-meyer, © 1970, with permission of McGraw-Hill, Inc.

After the child has completed the test, the number of correct spellings are totaled and first interpreted in a norm-referenced fashion using the data offered just below the heading "Directions for Diagnostic Spelling Test." They are next interpreted in a criterion-referenced manner. For example, if the child misspelled "not," it is likely that he has not yet mastered the phonological rule governing the short vowel /o/. Analysis of the child's errors on the test should result in the development of a relatively data-based remedial program.

Informal Assessment Procedures

Information gleaned from the informal assessment of children's spelling behavior will be of considerable value to teachers in planning individualized programs of study. This evaluation is based primarily on the teacher's direct observation of a child's behavior in a variety of spelling situations and on her analysis of many samples of a pupil's spelling work. In short, informal assessment is actually directed, structured, and/or analytic observation.

Preliminary assessments may be made by the teacher's careful scrutiny of the child's spelling lessons and his work habits. In particular, Linn (1967, pp. 62–63) suggests that teachers evaluate pupil performance in terms of the following questions. Can the child recall the letter and sound symbols quickly and accurately? Can he produce them on paper correctly? Can he fuse the sound parts of words together into whole words? Does he reverse letters in sound parts? Can he remember what the teacher has written on the board a few minutes after it is erased? Does he learn words when he hears the letter sequence rather than when he sees it? Does he appear to block out or not hear sounds? Can he write the correct symbol for single sounds when they are dictated to him orally? Can he identify sounds? Errors in these areas are clues to specific spelling problems.

Brueckner and Bond[1] have systematized informal observations by suggesting the following guidelines for teachers to use:

1. Analysis of Written Work, including Test Papers
   a. Legibility of handwriting
   b. Defects in letter forms, spacing, alignment, size
   c. Classification of errors in written work, letters, or tests
   d. Range of vocabulary used
   e. Evidence of lack of knowledge of conventions and rules
2. Analysis of Oral Responses
   a. Comparison of errors in oral and written spelling
   b. Pronunciation of words spelled incorrectly
   c. Articulation and enunciation
   d. Slovenliness of speech
   e. Dialect and colloquial forms of speech
   f. Way of spelling words orally:
      (1) Spells words as units
      (2) Spells letter by letter
      (3) Spells by digraphs
      (4) Spells by syllables
   g. Rhythmic pattern in oral spelling

1. L. J. Brueckner and G. L. Bond, The Diagnosis and Treatment of Learning Difficulties. In E. C. Frierson and W. B. Barbe (Eds.), *Educating Children with Learning Disabilities* (New York: Appleton-Century-Crofts, 1955). Reprinted by permission.

      h.   Blending ability

      i.   Giving letters for sounds or sounds for letters

      j.   Technique of word analysis used

      k.   Quality and error made in oral reading

      l.   Oral responses on tests or word analysis

      m. Analysis of pupil's comments as he states orally his thought process while studying new words

3. Interview with Pupil and Others
   a. Questioning pupil about methods of study
   b. Questioning pupil about spelling rules
   c. Questioning pupil about errors in convention
   d. Securing evidence as to attitude towards spelling

4. Questionnaire
   a. Applying checklist of methods of study
   b. Having pupil rank spelling according to interest
   c. Surveying use of written language

5. Free Observation in Course of Daily Work
   a. Securing evidence as to attitudes towards spelling
   b. Evidence of improvement in the study of new words
   c. Observing extent of use of dictionary
   d. Extent or error in regular written work
   e. Study habits and methods of work
   f. Social acceptability of the learner
   g. Evidences of emotional and social maladjustment
   h. Evidences of possible physical handicaps

6. Controlled Observation of Work on Set Tasks
   a. Looking up the meanings of given words in dictionary
   b. Giving pronunciation of words in dictionary
   c. Writing plural forms and derivatives of given words
   d. Observing responses on informal tests
   e. Observing methods of studying selected words
   f. Estimating pupil success when using a variety of methods of studying selected words

Of course, it is useful for teachers to know which words the child cannot spell. Therefore, each child who has difficulty in spelling should have his own list of frequently misspelled words. Since some words are more likely to be misspelled than others, the teacher should at some time assess the child's performance on the list of 100 demons,[2] or commonly misspelled words.

2. From A. Kuska, E. J. D. Webster, and G. Elford, *Spelling in Language Arts 6* [Ontario, Canada: Thomas Nelson & Sons (Canada) Ltd., 1964]. Reprinted by permission of the publisher, Thomas Nelson & Sons (Canada) Limited.

Teachers should select words from the list that correspond to the child's grade level. The demons are:

ache	families	neither	sandwich
afraid	fasten	nickel	scratch
against	fault	niece	sense
all right	February	ninety	separate
although	forgotten	ninth	shining
angry	friendly	onion	silence
answered	good-bye	passed	since
asks	guessed	peaceful	soldier
beautiful	happened	perfectly	speech
because	happily	piano	squirrel
beginning	here's	picnic	stepped
boy's	holiday	picture	straight
buried	hungry	piece	studying
busily	husband	pitcher	success
carrying	its	pleasant	taught
certain	it's	potato	their
choose	kitchen	practice	there's
Christmas	knives	prettiest	through
clothes	language	pumpkin	valentine
climbed	lettuce	purpose	whose
course	listening	quietly	worst
double	lose	rapidly	writing
easier	marriage	receive	yours
eighth	meant	rotten	
either	minute	safety	
enemy	neighbor	said	

Once the misspelled words are determined, they may be taught by rote or the misspellings can be subjected to error analysis.

For each child with a spelling problem, a careful analysis of errors should be made to discern if a pattern of errors exists. For analysis and error tabulation, use both material dictated from spelling lists and material provided by uncorrected continuous prose, such as a story a child has made up. Edgington[3] has provided a sample of types of errors that exist in children's spelling work:

> Addition of unneeded letters (for example, *dressses*)
> Omissions of needed letters (*hom* for *home*)
> Reflections of child's mispronunciations (*pin* for *pen*)
> Reflections of dialectical speech patterns (*Cuber* for *Cuba*)
> Reversals of whole words (*eno* for *one*)

3. From R. Edgington, But He Spelled Them Right This Morning, *Academic Therapy Quarterly*, 1967, 3, 58–59. Used with permission of the author and publisher (Academic Therapy Publications, San Rafael, California).

Reversals of consonant order (*lback* for *black*)
Reversals of consonant or vowel directionality (*brithday* for *birthday*)
Reversals of syllables (*telho* for *hotel*)
Phonetic spelling of nonphonetic words or parts thereof (*cawt* for *caught*)
Wrong associations of a sound with a given set of letters, such as *u* has been learned as *ou* in *you*
"Neographisms," or letters put in a word which bear no discernible relationship with the word dictated
Varying degrees and combinations of these or other possible patterns

TEACHING CHILDREN TO SPELL

Since pupils vary considerably in intellectual capacity and specific areas of weakness, spelling programs and remedial techniques should also vary with regards to level, theoretical orientation, vocabulary, manner of presentation, and format. The teacher cannot expect that a single spelling series will be suitable for all pupils. Therefore, she should have knowledge of an assortment of instructional alternatives. This section will review briefly several developmental and remedial systems and a few game activities which might facilitate spelling competence if employed effectively.

Developmental Methods

A long-standing and sometimes confusing controversy exists among authorities regarding the teaching of spelling. [See Yee (1966) for a detailed discussion of the topic.] Teachers should be aware of this debate because many of the spelling materials and methods used today reflect the controversy. Very simply, the conflict centers on the relative merits of using rules to enhance spelling competence. Some educators recommend the teaching of spelling rules that utilize a phonetic or sound–letter approach (Hanna and Moore, 1953; Hodges and Rudorf, 1965). They have found support in the work of Hanna, Hanna, Hodges, and Rudorf (1966), who programmed a computer with rules and made it "spell" 17,000 words, which it did with remarkable (50 percent) accuracy. Thirty-seven percent of the words were spelled with only a single error. A review of this project is in Hanna, Hodges, and Hanna (1971).

Others point out that English spelling forms are linguistically so irregular that spelling should be taught using almost no rules whatsoever. Still others suggest the limited teaching of rules (Archer, 1930; Horn, 1957). Spelling instruction, following this latter view, involves a gradual accumulation of necessary and practiced words and includes the introduction of rules whenever warranted.

Whatever the merits of the arguments may be, most of the developmental spelling series in common use today seem to adhere to the idea that American English spelling is sufficiently rule-governed that a basic linguistic approach can be utilized. By linguistic approach, we mean one that emphasizes the teaching of phonological, morphological, and syntactic rules or word patterns. Justification for this statement is based on the recent survey of spelling instructional methodologies reported by Hammill, Larsen, and McNutt (1977). They contacted a nonselected group of 100 third- through eighth-grade teachers and asked them to specify the particular methods that they used to teach spelling. In all, these teachers were instructing 2956 students residing in twenty-two states.

The three basal spelling series utilized most often by teachers in this sample were *Spell Correctly* (Benthul, Anderson, Utech, Biggy, and Bailey, 1974), used with 26.0 percent of the children; *Word Book* (Rogers, Ort, and Serra, 1970), used with 16.7 percent of the sample; and *Basic Goals in Spelling* (Kottmeyer and Claus, 1968, 1972), used with 14.2 percent of the students. Various other spelling programs were employed with 29.6 percent of the student sample, while the teachers reported that 13.4 percent of the children were receiving no specific spelling instruction.

The authors of the three most-used basal spelling series in this sample all maintain that their method of teaching spelling is based on "linguistic theory." This being the case, a brief description of linguistics would probably be useful. Linguistics, the study of language, may be subdivided into four discrete but related topics: (1) phonology, the study of speech sounds; (2) morphology, the meaningful units of speech; (3) syntax, the rules that govern sentence formation or word order; and (4) semantics, the process by which a global understanding is gained from the presented language. While linguistic theories usually encompass all four areas of study, when they are applied to teaching spelling, two elements appear to receive a majority of the emphasis: phonology and morphology. A more specific explanation of these two areas follows.

Phonology refers to speech sounds with the term "phoneme" being of prime interest. A phoneme is a group of sounds that are so similar that they are considered equivalent. Although there may be slight variations in the production of a phoneme, for all intents and purposes it is a single speech sound with various letters or groups of letters being capable of representing the same phoneme. There are approximately 36 phonemes in our language. Graphemes are the letter(s) or combination of letters that represent a phoneme. For example, the phoneme /k/ may be represented by the grapheme "k," "c," or "ck."

Morphology refers to the smallest units of meaningful speech, morphemes. A morpheme may be a word (e.g., *boy*, because it cannot be broken into smaller units that yield meaning) or even a single letter (e.g., the plural marker /z/ in boys). Morphology includes the inflections and changes in words which alter their meanings (e.g., prefixes and suffixes).

While each of the three most-used basal spelling series utilizes aspects of linguistic theory, this should not imply that the series are identical. To aid in identifying some of the differences, a brief description of the three spelling series follows.

The words for each unit in the *Spell Correctly* series are divided into basic lists and enrichment lists which are topical or thematic in organization. The basic words constitute approximately 90 percent of the words most students use in their daily writing, with each group or list focusing on one particular spelling pattern. The patterns generally are phonological (e.g., short *a* words) or morphological (e.g., prefixes that mean "not") in nature. In addition to the general spelling lessons, *Spell Correctly* integrates many skills from a language arts curriculum (e.g., dictionary skills) as well as containing various enrichment or extension activities for the more able student.

The authors of the *Word Book* program state that the presented words are grouped according to their particular spelling patterns: rhyming patterns (e.g., bit, fit, hit), nonrhyming patterns (e.g., did, dig, dip), and vowel-changing patterns (e.g., pat, pet, put). Additionally, the words of the core vocabulary comprise 80 percent of the spelling needed by an elementary child, while the upper levels emphasize words that are important to adult living. It should perhaps be noted that the authors do not state how the core words or the words needed for adult living were chosen. Emphasis is also placed on integrating various communication skills (e.g., speaking and listening skills). Unlike the other two series, many of the units in the *Word Book* program emphasize various topics not related to spelling (e.g., Going to Bed on Time, Nature in the Spring, A Wise Constitution).

As with *Spell Correctly, Basic Goals in Spelling* presents basic word lists and word lists for enrichment. The basic words were chosen because research revealed that they are commonly used in the writing vocabulary of pupils at each level. While morphological relationships are included, the stress according to the series authors is on sound–symbol relationships, indicating the importance of phonology. Rather than having the teacher state spelling rules for the students to memorize, the authors of the programs stress the importance of allowing the students to observe similarities of sound and spelling in words and to formulate generalizations (i.e., rules) on their own.

That the authors of this system and the others previously described have depended heavily on linguistic theory to develop their programs is even more evident when one examines the scope-and-sequence charts in which the skills supposedly being taught are depicted. The charts associated with the Basic Goals in Spelling series will serve as an example and are reproduced in Tables 4–2 and 4–3.

Table 4–2. *Linguistic Skills Taught in the Primary Grades*

	Examples of Vocabulary	
Skills Taught	*Grade 2*	*Grade 3*

Auditory Recognition of Phonemes

Consonant sounds:

1. The eighteen key consonant sounds: *b, d, f, g, h, j, k, l, m, n, p, r, s, t, v, w, y, z.*

   Key pictures: ball, dog, fish, girl, hat, jug, kite, lamp, moon, nail, pig, rabbit, sun, top, vase, wagon, yarn, zebra

2. The *sh, ch, wh, th,* and *ng* sounds.

   Key pictures: shoe, chair, wheel, three, ring

   Short vowel sounds

   Key pictures: apple, elephant, Indian, ostrich, umbrella

Graphemic Representation of Phonemes

Consonant sounds:

1. The regular consonant sounds	bed, hat, sun, yes	must, trip, ask, zoo
2. The *sh, ch, ng, wh,* and *th* sounds	fish, much, sing, which, this, with	shoe, child, sang, while, those, thank
3. The *nk* spelling of the *ngk* sounds		drunk, drank
4. The *x* spelling of the *ks* sounds	box, fox	next
5. The *c* spelling of the *k* sound	cold	cup
6. The *c* and *k* spellings of the *k* sound	cat, kept	ask, cake
7. The *ck* spelling of the *k* sound	duck, black	chicken, clock
8. The *s* spelling of the *s* and *z* sounds	sun, as	gas, has
9. The *gh* spelling of *f*		laugh
10. Silent consonants	doll, hill, who, know, would	bell, grass, walk, catch, wrote, night

Vowel sounds:

1. The short vowel sound regularly spelled in initial or medial position	am, did	bad, send, stop
2. The long vowel sound spelled by		
a. a single vowel at the end of a short word in open syllables	go, be	paper, table
b. two vowels together	meat, rain	soap, cream, train
c. vowel–consonant–silent *e*	home, ride	game, side, snake
3. Other long vowel spellings		
a. the *ow* spelling of long *o*	snow, grow	window
b. the *ay* spelling of long *a*	day, play	always, yesterday
c. the final *y* spelling of long *e*	baby, very	city, study, sorry
d. the final *y* spelling of long *i*	my, why	cry, try
4. Additional vowel sounds and spellings		
a. the *oo* spelling of *u̇* and *ü*	good, soon	cook, shoot
b. the *ow* and *ou* spellings of the *ou* sound in *owl* and *mouse*	down, house	flower, ground

		Examples of Vocabulary	
	Skills Taught	Grade 2	Grade 3
	c. the *oy* spelling of the *oi* sound	boy, toy	
	d. vowel sounds before *r*		
	the *er* spelling of ə*r* at the end	over, teacher	ever, another
	the *or* spelling of ə*r* at the end		color
	er, ir, or, and *ur* spellings of *er*	her, bird, work, hurt	person, third, word, turning
	the *or* and *ar* spellings of ô*r*	for	horse, warm
	the *ar* spelling of ä*r*	car	star, party
5.	Unexpected spellings		
	a. unexpected single vowel spellings	from, off, cold	kind, full, cost
	b. unexpected vowel-consonant-silent *e*	give, done	whose, sure
	c. unexpected spellings with two vowels together	been, said	bread, great, friend
	d. other unexpected vowel spellings	they, eye	aunt, says, could
6.	The *le* spelling of the ə*l* sound		people, table

Using Morphemes to Make Structural Changes

1.	The *s* or *es* plural	cats, cows	cups, buses, dishes
2.	Changing *y* to *i* before *es*		cry, cries
3.	The *s* or *es* for third person singular	live, lives	jumps, races, misses
4.	The *s* to show possession	yours, ours	
5.	The *d* or *ed* ending for past tense	played	asked, laughed
6.	The *ing* ending	blowing	reading, thinking
	with doubled consonant		clapping, beginning
	with dropped silent *e*		skating, moving
7.	The *er* noun agent ending	singer, player	painter, builder
8.	The *er* and *est* endings	old, older	high, higher, highest

Devices to Aid Spelling Recall

1.	Syllabication	yel low, go ing	bas ket, ta ble
2.	Recognizing compounds	today	airplane, something
3.	Recognizing rhyming words	pet, get	hand, land

Miscellaneous

1.	Homonyms	to-too-two	its-it's, eight-ate
2.	Antonyms	last-first	cry-laugh
3.	Alphabetizing	periodic activities requiring the use of the first, second, third, fourth, and fifth letters	

Source: "Linguistic Skills Taught in the Primary Grades," reprinted by permission of the publisher from *Basic Goals In Spelling*, 3rd ed., Teacher's Edition, Grade 2, by William Kottmeyer and Audrey Claus. Copyright © 1968 by McGraw-Hill, Inc.

Table 4–3. *Linguistic Skills Taught in the Intermediate Grades*

	Examples of Vocabulary		
	Grade 4	Grade 5	Grade 6

Graphemic Representation of Phonemes

Of consonant phonemes:

		Grade 4	Grade 5	Grade 6
1.	The regular consonant sounds	sad	belt	fact
2.	The *sh, ch,* and *ng* consonant sounds	ship	shade	shelf
		rich	chest	chain
		hang	among	gang
3.	The voiced and unvoiced *th* sounds	bath	sixth	thread
		those	either	leather
4.	The *ch* spelling of the *k* sound	schoolhouse	echo	orchestra
5.	The *wh* spelling of the *hw* sounds	wheel	whistle	whale
6.	The *g* spelling of the *g* or *j* sound	frog	gate	cigar
		bridge	damage	pledge
7.	The *c* spelling of the *k* or *s* sound	cage	cool	cabbage
		circus	princess	juice
8.	The *ck* spelling of the *k* sound	luck	attack	ticket
9.	The *x* spelling of the *ks* sounds	fix	expect	expedition
10.	The *qu* spelling of the *kw* sounds	queen	quarter	acquaint
11.	The *nk* spelling of the *ngk* sounds	monkey	trunk	plank
12.	The *ph* spelling of the *f* sound	elephant		alphabet
13.	Silent consonants	answer	ghost	delightful

Of vowel phonemes:

		Grade 4	Grade 5	Grade 6
1.	The short medial vowel regularly spelled	cap	bunch	slept
2.	The long sound spelled with vowel-consonant-silent *e*	bone	prize	blaze
3.	The long sound spelled with two vowels together	tie	beads	coach
4.	The long sound regularly spelled in open syllables	hotel	locate	soda
5.	The various spellings of vowels before *r*	fur	term	stairs
		born	artist	skirt
6.	The *ou* and *ow* spellings of the *ou* sound	count	outfit	growl
		cowboy	shower	surround
7.	The *ow* spelling of the *ō* sound	unknown	crow	narrow
8.	The *oo* spelling of the *u̇* and *ü* sounds	hook	loose	bloom
		stood	choosing	shook
9.	Unexpected spellings	bush	lose	wolf
		true	grew	route
10.	The *oi* and *oy* spellings of the *oi* sound	noise	join	spoil
		enjoy	voice	voyage
11.	The *o, al, au,* and *aw* spellings of the *ô* sound	north	crawl	author
		tall	chalk	naughty
12.	The spellings of the *əl* and *l* sounds	castle	model	carnival
		jungle	central	barrel
13.	The *y* spelling of the *ē* sound	busy	worry	crazy

	Examples of Vocabulary		
	Grade 4	Grade 5	Grade 6

Using Morphemes to Make Structural Changes

1.	The *d* or *ed* ending	recalled untied	excited earned	continued contracted
2.	The *s* or *es* ending	socks chimneys churches	beads beaches	insects sandwiches
3.	The irregular plurals	feet		calves geese
4.	The changing of *y* to *i* before *es*	bodies	colonies	pantries
5.	Forming plurals of nouns which end in *o*			pianos potatoes
6.	The *ing* ending	interesting	bending	stretching
7.	Doubling a final consonant before *ing*	stepping	chopping	snapping
8.	Dropping the final silent *e* before *ing*	trading	ruling	shaking
9.	The *er* and *est* endings	paler palest	cleaner cleanest	tinier tiniest
10.	The *ly* ending	finally	especially	dreadfully
11.	The number suffixes	fifteen fifty	thirteen sixty	
12.	Suffixes to change the part of speech	kindness friendly	playful improvement	harmless attractive
13.	Prefixes to change root or root-word meanings	unlock replace	exchange promote	dishonest incorrect

Devices to Aid Spelling Recall

1.	Syllable division of vowel-consonant/consonant-vowel words	bottom	contest	costume
2.	Syllable division of vowel/consonant-vowel words	hotel	select	museum
3.	Syllable division of vowel-consonant/vowel words	cabin	salad	proper
4.	Remembering unexpected spellings	minute	gloves	thread
5.	Choosing the correct homonym	whole	hymn	principal
6.	Spelling compounds by parts	upstairs	watermelon	schoolmate

Source: "Linguistic Skills Taught in the Intermediate Grades," reprinted by permission of the publisher from *Basic Goals In Spelling,* 3rd ed., Teacher's Edition, Grade 6, by William Kottmeyer and Audrey Claus. Copyright © 1968 by McGraw-Hill, Inc.

Remedial Techniques for Spelling

Many children exposed to the traditional, classroom-presented spelling programs reviewed in the previous section do not reach expected levels of achievement. As an alternative, the teacher may decide to employ one of the remedial spelling systems which differ considerably from the classroom series. The pupil is taught in a one-to-one relationship or in small groups and the activities usually incorporate kinesthetic elements in varying degrees. Some children are supposedly helped by relying on the "feel" of the word. The following are examples of specific teaching techniques in spelling which can also be used for remediation.

1. Fernald's (1943) multisensory approach is reported to be highly successful with some children. The child traces the letters (tactile–kinesthetic), sees the tracing (visual), says the letters aloud (vocal), and hears what he says (auditory). For this reason, the approach is often referred to as the VAKT (visual–auditory–kinesthetic–tactile) technique.

   Fernald's techniques are usually reserved for clinical use with children who have serious problems in spelling. This is somewhat unfortunate; for though the activities are highly individualized, they can easily be adapted to work in a regular classroom as well as in a remedial group. When teaching remedial spelling, Fernald recommends that teachers adhere strictly to the following procedures:

   a. The word to be learned should be written on the blackboard or on paper by the teacher.
   b. The teacher pronounces the word very clearly and distinctly. The children pronounce the words.
   c. Time is allowed for each child to study the word.
   d. When every child is sure of the word, it is erased or covered; and the child writes it from memory.
   e. The paper should be turned over and the word written a second time.
   f. Some arrangement should be made so that it is natural for the child to make frequent use, in his written expression, of the word he has learned.
   g. Finally, it is necessary that the child be allowed to get the correct form of the word at any time when he is doubtful of its spelling.
   h. If spelling matches (i.e., spelling "bees") are desired, they should be written instead of oral.

   In her book, Fernald described in detail just how each of these steps is to be carried out, what verbal instructions are given to the child, and how spelling vocabulary lists are used to select the "foundation" words that should be taught first. Of all the approaches to the remedial teaching of spelling, this one is perhaps the most popular.

2. The Gillingham alphabetic system (Gillingham and Stillman, 1970) stresses the child's ability to build sounds into words through the

application of visual, auditory, and kinesthetic associations, sometimes called the "language triangle." The child links a sound with a letter form, establishes a visual memory pattern for a particular word, and then reinforces that pattern by writing the word.

3. The sensory approach has been advocated by Montessori (1965a) and many other educators. The basic procedure involves some system of color-cueing for vowels, consonants, and sight words which must be memorized. Words may be traced over, used orally in a sentence, visually studied, traced, and sounded out, until the word can be spelled and written independently.

4. The phonovisual method (Schoolfield and Timberlake, 1960) is a phonetic system that provides direct training in visual and auditory discrimination. Wall charts are used to orally introduce consonants and vowels. The introduction of consonant and vowel sounds is well organized and pictures on the charts provide the pupil with familiar visual images to associate with the letter sound.

5. A visual method (Getman et al., 1968), based on Getman's theory of spelling as visualization, trains for visual memory. The pupil repeatedly traces over a word on the chalkboard, saying the name of each letter as he traces. Tracing in the air with eyes closed continues until the child thinks that he can "see" the word in his mind.

Game Supplements for Spelling Instruction

The teacher will find the literature replete with games and other activities reported to be beneficial as supplements to a spelling program. While games provide diversification in the method of presentation and help to foster interest in the teaching effort, the experienced teacher knows that they are intended as supplements and not as substitutions for a spelling program. Several examples of spelling games follow.

Tongue Twisters.   Objective: Awareness of initial consonants.

Direction: Think of a sentence in which most of the words start like "Funny father."

Example: 1. Funny father fed five foxes.
2. *Polly Page put a potato in her pocket.*

Variation: The teacher writes the child's twister on the board.

Direction: How are many of these words similar? Draw a line under the similar parts.
Help the children to see that most of the words start with the same sound and letter.

Bingo.   For grades three to six.

Fold paper into 16 squares. Children are asked to give

a word. A scribe writes the word on the board or challenges the donor to spell the word. The children all write the correctly spelled word on any one of the 16 squares. When all the squares are filled, a child is selected to come forward. With his back to the board, he spells any one of the words a selected caller gives him. Each correctly spelled word enables the class to place a marker on the corresponding Bingo square. The first child to complete a row or a diagonal calls "Bingo" and wins the game. The teacher keeps a list of the words called and checks off the winner. These Bingo squares may be kept for repeated playing.

Treasure Hunt. A team game for grades two to six. Select teams, set a time limit of two minutes, and write a base word on the board at the head of each team's column.

Direction: Each child can write only one word, a new one or a corrected one. At a given sign, the first child from each team races to the board and writes any word that can be made with letters in the base word. Each child races back, hands the chalk to the next child, and goes to the end of the line. Continue until the teacher calls time. The group with the longest correct list in a specified limit is the winner.

Example: The given base word is *tame.*
Children may write: tam
                                    am
                                    me

Anagrams. Children can make anagram or scribble games for independent activities.

Variations: 1. Make words by adding a letter in vertical or horizontal order.

Example: C a t
                over
                    e
                    r
                    y

2. Start with a common word. Change one letter each time the word is spelled. Example: dime—dome—home—hope. Each player must have a scribe to record his colleague's completed word, or he must record his own words. Winners are those who can complete the greatest numbers of correctly spelled words. Teachers act as final judges of correct spelling.

Telegraph.   Objective: Quick thinking and correct spelling. A team game for grade five.

Establish a goal of 6 or 10 points for game, and a time limit of four slow counts or four seconds for the hesitant speller.

Direction: Each child is given one or two letters of the alphabet. The teacher pronounces a word to team one. The letters of the telegraph begin to respond in proper order. If the response is correct, they get one point and another word to transmit.

The opposing side gets a word when

1. a member of the team has failed to give his letter in the four-second time limit or by four counts;
2. if the completed word was misspelled;
3. someone on the team "helped" to spell the word.

Example: The word is battle. The letters respond in proper order, b a t t l e.

Scoring: One point is scored for each correctly spelled word; a game is 8 or 10 points.

Variation: A group game for primary grades

1. Letters used or needed for the spelling of the teacher's list are printed on 2- by 6-inch cards. Each child receives a card. The teacher pronounces a word. The telegraph letters take their places in the proper order at the front of the room.

2. Letters may be placed in a chart holder or on the blackboard ledge.

The teaching of spelling, a tool subject, should be integrated as much as possible into the total language arts program. Too often, however, the activities, methods, and materials used to teach spelling have little or no relationship to the rest of the language arts program. Westerman (1971) notes that frequently one set of words is used in teaching reading, another set in spelling (usually designed to meet the needs for different sound patterns), and still other sets for speaking and listening. A coordinated program, on the other hand, is more efficient for the teacher and motivating for the child.

Donald D. Hammill • Mary Poplin

5

Writing, a highly complex process involving the integration of visual, motoric, and conceptual abilities, is one of the highest forms of communication, and hence usually the last to be mastered. It is actually an expressive form of a graphic symbol system used for conveying thoughts, feelings, and ideas. "Writing," a generic term that encompasses the entire expressive graphic process, includes (1) the generation of ideas for writing, (2) syntax, and (3) penmanship or handwriting, terms which are used synonymously in this book. Writing is closely related to language, reading, and spelling.

Normally, the child first learns to comprehend and use speech, to read, and later to express ideas through writing. Therefore, adequate oral language experience is vital to the normal development of written language. The deaf, who learn to read and write in the presence of a handicapping hearing deficit, achieve these abilities as a result of highly specialized teaching techniques which are by no means universally successful.

Since writing is both a skill and a means of self-expression, more than drill aspects should be emphasized in teaching. Consequently, as with reading, training in writing should be correlated with work in other academic areas. The general aims of writing instruction are to help children to write legibly and neatly, without undue strain, and to teach them to express their ideas adequately through this medium. However, a review of the pertinent educational literature suggests that teachers seem to be more interested in viewing writing as a skill rather than as a form of expression, for discussions of legibility, speed, and penmanship predominate.

SPECIFIC PROBLEMS IN WRITING

Every child will experience some difficulty in learning to write. Reversals, omissions, and poor spacing are characteristic of a young child's writing. It is the persistence of such errors over a long period of time that is indicative of a writing problem. Perhaps the most comprehensive recent study of disorders of written language has been made by Myklebust (1965; Johnson and Myklebust, 1967). He suggests that such difficulties are associated with deficiencies in visual–motor integration (dysgraphia), revisualization (memory), and formulation (syntax). Myklebust's researches relative to disorders of written language are most thorough; they are based on the study of children who exhibit severe problems in this area. Most teachers, however, will encounter problems of lesser severity and will find it more useful to conceive of difficulties in writing as being associated with readiness, penmanship, and/or conceptual writing. In this trichotomy, readiness refers to the basic perceptual–motor, linguistic experiences presumed to be prerequisite to writing; penmanship refers to legibility and speed in writing; and conceptual writing refers to the grammatical accuracy and meaningfulness of the product.

ASSESSING DIFFICULTIES IN WRITING

One goal of assessment in writing is to identify children who are unable to write with sufficient efficiency to meet minimum standards of speed and quality for their personal daily needs. Once the pupils are identified, an equally important goal is to determine the specific problems in writing in need of remediation. Unlike the reading, arithmetic, and perception areas, writing has generated few standardized tests. For the most part, when assessing the child's skills, the teacher will have to rely upon informal procedures or loosely standardized devices. In this book, these techniques have been divided into those pertaining to measuring writing–readiness skills, penmanship (legibility, productivity), and conceptual writing (correctness, meaning).

Measuring Writing-Readiness Skills

The primary writing-readiness abilities are adequate language and experience, for these allow the child to have something meaningful to say through written composition. The secondary readiness abilities have to do with those perceptual–motor skills that are necessary to execute graphic symbols in a legible or neat manner. This section is devoted primarily to the latter; language readiness is discussed in detail in Chapter 7. It should be stressed that several prerequisite skills for writing—the copying of geometric forms and the development of laterality (handedness), ocular control, and visual perception—have not been clearly established as having anything major to do with proficiency in either penmanship or written composition

(Wiederholt, 1971; Harris and Herrick, 1963). However, since many educators do consider these to be readiness skills for writing, they deserve some mention. A list of possible readiness skills and techniques for their evaluation follows:

1. Visual–motor integration
   a. Eye–hand coordination
      (1) "Imitation of Movement" (Kephart, 1971). These tasks require the child to transfer a visual pattern into a motor pattern.
      (2) Eye–Hand Coordination subtest of the Frostig Developmental Test of Visual Perception (Frostig et al., 1964)
   b. Copying
      (1) Slingerland's (1970) test: Far point, subtest 1; Near point, subtest 2
      (2) Copying subtest from the Metropolitan Readiness Test
      (3) Spatial Relations subtest from the Frostig DTVP
   c. Ocular control. Roach and Kephart's (1966) Purdue Perceptual–Motor Survey
   d. Left–right progressions
      (1) Does the child begin to read at the left side of the page?
      (2) Does he read words or phrases, in reverse order?
      (3) Put two dots on the blackboard. Does he connect them from left to right?
      (4) When given paper and pencil tasks does he begin at the left side of the page?
   e. Small-muscle coordination
      (1) Observe the child stringing beads, using a pegboard, holding his pencil
      (2) Review child's school records. Did the kindergarten, first-grade, or second-grade teachers comment that he had poor small-muscle coordination?
      (3) Compare samples of his writing with samples from other children his age

2. Laterality
   a. Handedness
      (1) Case history of handedness
      (2) Keep a record of the activities for which he uses his right or left hand
      (3) Ask the child to pretend he is
         (a) Eating
         (b) Brushing his teeth

(c)   Throwing a ball

(d)   Writing

Then have him actually do these things with the appropriate utensils.   A child will often use his dominant hand for the pretended activities and his nondominant hand that he was forced to use for the real activity in instances where the child was switched.

(4)   Observe the child in the classroom and have the mother keep a record at home of which hand he prefers for

(a)   Throwing a ball

(b)   Picking up objects

(c)   Coloring

(d)   Cutting

(e)   Writing

b.   Eyedness

(1)   Fold a 9- by 12-inch paper in half two times.   Tear off a corner for a peephole.   Have the child hold it in both hands at waist level, arms outstretched.   Tell him to fixate on a small object on eye level at midline.   Then have the child lift the paper and look through the peephole. The eye used to sight the object may be said to be dominant.

(2)   Have the child sit at his desk and mark an "X" about ¼ inch high on a sheet of paper.   Give him a small tube, 3 or 5 inches long, made of a rolled sheet of paper.   Have him hold the tube in both hands and look at the "X" through the tube.   Then ask him to bring the tube slowly back closed to his eye without losing sight of the "X." Notice to which eye he brings the tube.   Do this several times.

3.   Tactile

a.   Use figures (letters and numbers) cut from sandpaper.   Place several into a bag.   Ask the child to reach into the bag and identify, by touch alone, the figure he has drawn.

To us, the skills mentioned above are decidedly offtask as far as writing readiness is concerned.   Because of this opinion, we prefer a more direct approach to writing-readiness assessment, one that can be used to identify young children who are likely to become poor writers later in their school life and to pinpoint the specific areas of writing readiness that are in need of training.   To achieve these purposes, the teacher can use the Handwriting subscale of the Basic School Skill Inventory (Goodman and Hammill, 1975).

This scale, the BSSI, was constructed primarily on the results of extensive interviews with kindergarten and first-grade teachers. In these interviews, the teachers were asked to describe the actual behaviors that seemed to distinguish between children who were "ready" for school and those who were not. The behaviors that related to writing were singled out and used to form the Handwriting subscale of the BSSI.

The BSSI can be used either in a norm-referenced fashion (i.e., to identify children who are "low in writing readiness" and thereby need special help) or in a criterion-referenced fashion (i.e., to decide what skills are to be taught and in what order). To use the scale, teachers select a particular child to be assessed, find the time at school or home to read each item carefully, and using their own knowledge about the child's classroom performance relative to the item, decide whether or not the pupil can do the task. The child is not taken aside and "tested" unless the teacher lacks sufficient familiarity with the pupil's writing behavior to answer the questions (i.e., the scale items). The ten items that comprise the subscale are reproduced in Table 5–1.

Table 5–1. *Handwriting*

Materials:	primary pencil
	lined primary writing paper
	crayons
	drawing paper
	card containing a common word

All the items on this subscale relate to the child's proficiency in using a pencil. For the most part, these abilities have to be taught by teachers or parents; it is unlikely that a child will master the pencil entirely through incidental experience. Children who do well on the subscale are likely to be ready for instruction in either manuscript or cursive writing.

22. *Does the child print from left to right?*
    To earn a pass on this item, a pupil should evidence some consistent knowledge of left–right progression in writing. His letters or words may be illegible, poorly formed, misspelled, or otherwise inadequate and still be recorded as a pass if, in the execution of his written efforts, he proceeds in a left-to-right sequence. This sequence does not even have to be on a straight line; diagonal writing is permissible, as long as it is basically left to right.

23. *When printing, does the child exhibit an easy three-finger grasp near the tip of his pencil?*
    For most pupils, writing is accomplished most easily when the pencil is grasped with the thumb and the next two fingers. Using either hand, the child should hold the pencil loosely near the pencil tip. Holding the pencil in the palm of the hand is a nonscorable grip.

24. *Can the child print his first name?*
    The intention of this item is to determine whether the child can write (manu-

script or cursive) his first name on command. The product does not have to be properly formed. The result must, however, be recognizable as being the child's actual name. Writing one's name from a model is not acceptable here.

25. *Does the child maintain a proper sitting and writing position?*
Observe whether the child keeps his head reasonably erect, uses the nonwriting hand to hold the paper in a steady position, etc.

26. *Can the child draw a triangle with three sharp angles and no openings?*
This is a copying task; therefore, avoid asking the child to "draw a triangle." Some children may execute the task on command, thus demonstrating both understanding of the term *triangle* and motor competence in drawing the figure. However, this task is designed to determine adequacy in pencil use, not language proficiency. Many children, who may not know the meaning of the word *triangle,* have the motor ability to draw the form correctly.
    Show the child a model and ask him to draw the same shape. To earn a pass, the child's drawing must have three sharp angles and no openings. It may be constructed with one continuous line or with several lines.

27. *When given a common word on a card, can the child copy the word correctly on his own paper?*
Place a card containing a common word on the child's desk. The pupil must copy the example correctly to receive a plus for the item.

28. *Can the child draw a picture of a person with a recognizable head, body, arms, and legs?*
To pass this item, the child's drawing must include the four body parts indicated. Stick figures are permissible, provided the parts are definitely connected and recognizable. Eyes, nose, mouth, ears, neck, fingers, and other details are desirable but not necessary.

29. *When a common word is written on the chalkboard, can the child copy it correctly on his own paper?*
A child's ability to copy from the chalkboard requires his focusing on the work at the board, retaining the images of the letters, and transferring the images to his own paper. To earn a pass, the pupil must copy the word correctly.

30. *When printing, can the child stay on the line?*
This is a relatively difficult task for many children. In scoring the item, you are concerned with the child's skill at organizing and spacing his letters squarely on the line, not with the legibility or quality of the letters themselves.

31. *Can the child print his last name?*
To receive credit for this item, a child should make a solid attempt at writing his last name. The name may be misspelled and some of the letters may be reversed or poorly formed. The point here is that the child has enough of an idea about the written form of his name that he will attempt to write it.

Source: L. Goodman and D. D. Hammill, *The Basic School Skills Inventory* (Chicago: Follett, 1975). Reprinted by permission of authors and publisher.

Children can easily be identified as candidates for special attention in handwriting readiness by consulting the following normative information:

Pupil's Age	Scores Indicating That a Child Is Poor in Handwriting Readiness
4-0 to 4-5	0
4-6 to 4-11	0 and 1
5-0 to 5-5	0–3
5-6 to 5-11	0–5
6-0 to 6-11	0–7

Pupils ranging in age from 5-6 to 5-11 who "pass" five or fewer of the BSSI tasks would be identified as being poor in handwriting readiness when compared to their age-mates. Those who scored six points or more are apparently doing as well in handwriting-readiness activities as other children their age. Teachers should consider preparing individual remedial programs for each student who is found to be poor in readiness for writing and should use the BSSI tasks that were not passed as a guide for selecting goals and activities.

Assessing Penmanship Errors

As children learn to write, some pupils will begin to make numerous errors in penmanship. As a result, their writing may be illegible, too slow, or otherwise unsatisfactory. These same children may be "ready" in the sense that they have mastered left–right progression, a "proper" pencil grip, staying on the line, etc. The experienced teacher has no difficulty in identifying these children. But new teachers or teachers who wish to quantify their observations will find several measures useful.

A popular device for assessing the cursive and manuscript handwriting of pupils in grades 1 through high school is Zaner-Bloser's Evaluation Scale (1968), previously known as the Freeman Scale (Freeman, 1959). To administer this test, the teacher writes a particular sample sentence on the chalkboard. After several practice efforts, the pupils copy the example on a piece of paper. They are allowed 2 minutes to complete the task. Papers are collected and assigned to one of three groups (i.e., "good," "medium," or "poor") on the basis of the teacher's judgment. Each paper is then matched against a series of five specimen sentences that are appropriate to the child's grade placement. Each of the sentences represents a different quality of penmanship, ranging from "high for grade" to "poor for grade." The use of the specimen sentences permits teachers to make rough estimates about the adequacy of a child's penmanship as compared to youngsters in the same grade. To examples of Zaner-Bloser's evaluation sentence charts, one for manuscript and one for cursive writing, are provided in Figures 5–1 and 5–2.

Other scales, using similar formats, are available and teachers might on occasion want to review some of them. For example, the Ayers Scale (1920)

Figure 5–1. *Evaluation Scale for Manuscript Writing.* [Used with permission from *Creative Growth with Handwriting.* Evaluation scale, second grade. Copyright © 1974. Zaner-Bloser, Inc., Columbus, Ohio.]

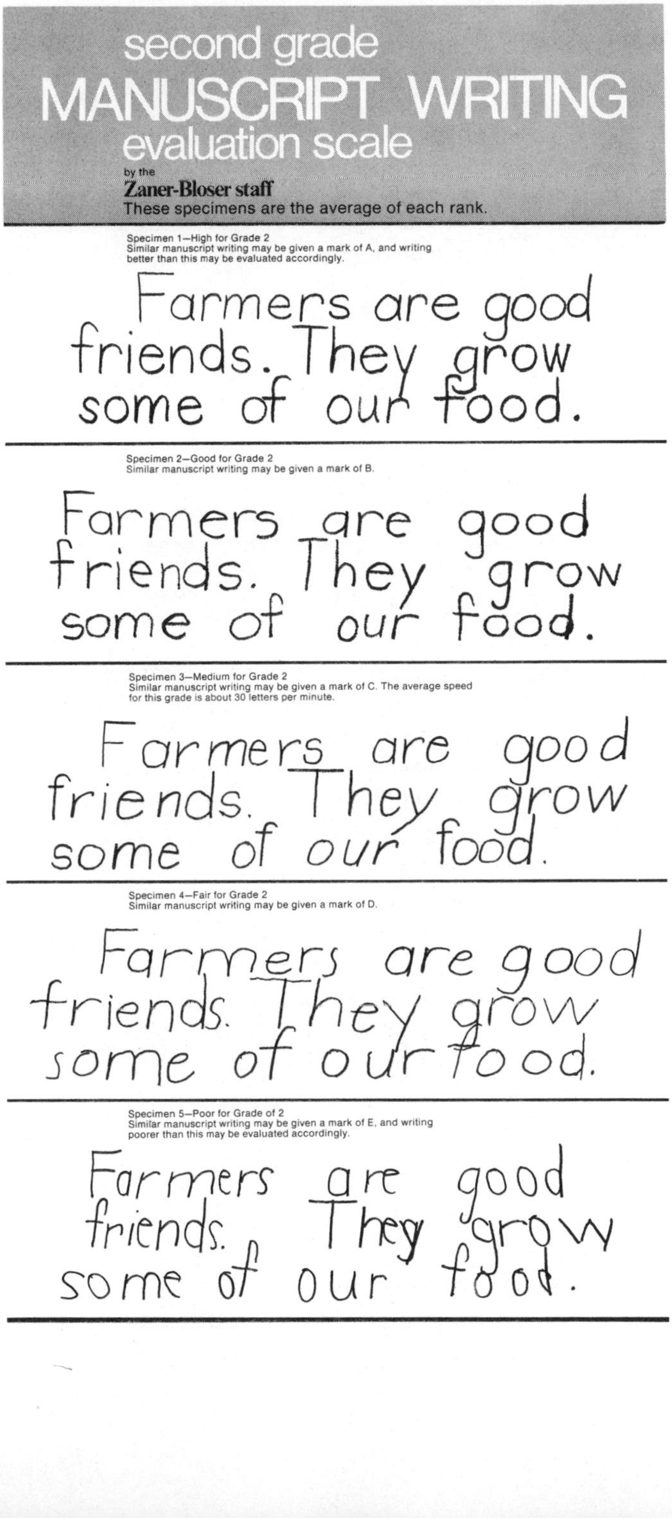

second grade
MANUSCRIPT WRITING
evaluation scale
by the
Zaner-Bloser staff
These specimens are the average of each rank.

Specimen 1—High for Grade 2
Similar manuscript writing may be given a mark of A, and writing better than this may be evaluated accordingly.

Farmers are good friends. They grow some of our food.

Specimen 2—Good for Grade 2
Similar manuscript writing may be given a mark of B.

Farmers are good friends. They grow some of our food.

Specimen 3—Medium for Grade 2
Similar manuscript writing may be given a mark of C. The average speed for this grade is about 30 letters per minute.

Farmers are good friends. They grow some of our food.

Specimen 4—Fair for Grade 2
Similar manuscript writing may be given a mark of D.

Farmers are good friends. They grow some of our food.

Specimen 5—Poor for Grade of 2
Similar manuscript writing may be given a mark of E, and writing poorer than this may be evaluated accordingly.

Farmers are good friends. They grow some of our food.

Figure 5–2. *Evaluation Scale for Cursive Handwriting.* [Used with permission from *Creative Growth with Handwriting.* Evaluation scale, fifth grade. Copyright © 1974. Zaner-Bloser, Inc., Columbus, Ohio.]

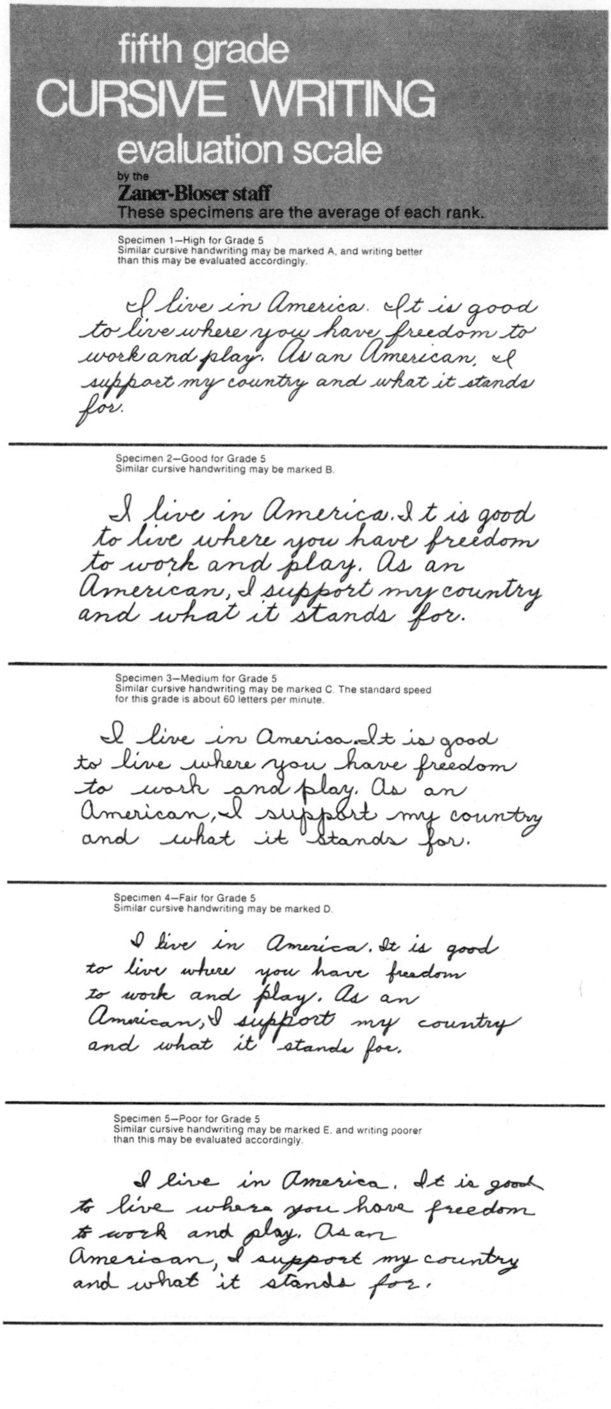

fifth grade
CURSIVE WRITING
evaluation scale

by the
Zaner-Bloser staff
These specimens are the average of each rank.

Specimen 1—High for Grade 5
Similar cursive handwriting may be marked A, and writing better
than this may be evaluated accordingly.

I live in America. It is good to live where you have freedom to work and play. As an American, I support my country and what it stands for.

Specimen 2—Good for Grade 5
Similar cursive handwriting may be marked B.

I live in America. It is good to live where you have freedom to work and play. As an American, I support my country and what it stands for.

Specimen 3—Medium for Grade 5
Similar cursive handwriting may be marked C. The standard speed
for this grade is about 60 letters per minute.

I live in America. It is good to live where you have freedom to work and play. As an American, I support my country and what it stands for.

Specimen 4—Fair for Grade 5
Similar cursive handwriting may be marked D.

I live in America. It is good to live where you have freedom to work and play. As an American, I support my country and what it stands for.

Specimen 5—Poor for Grade 5
Similar cursive handwriting may be marked E, and writing poorer
than this may be evaluated accordingly.

I live in America. It is good to live where you have freedom to work and play. As an American, I support my country and what it stands for.

is also sometimes used in the schools, but it is not recommended, because it deals only with cursive writing and is not graded. Less well known, but similar scales by Thorndike (1910) and West (1957) are also available. A fine description and critical review of these and other legibility scales is provided by Herrick and Erlebacher (1963), Anderson (1968), and Starkel (1975).

Use of the Zanner-Bloser Evaluation Scale and these other devices will permit only the grossest evaluation of a child's handwriting. For example, they allow the examiner to determine if the pupil's penmanship skills are seriously behind, level with, or appreciably above his age-mates, but they do not yield the kinds of specific information about the child's handwriting that can be used to formulate a remedial program. To derive maximum value from this procedure, teachers must subject the child's written products to a thorough analysis of errors.

Having determined, through direct observation or through the use of one of the scales just mentioned, that a problem does exist, the teacher can use Freeman's (1965) checklists as a guide to error analysis. (He offers one checklist for manuscript and another for cursive.) These checklists, reproduced in Table 5–2, direct the teacher's attention to such aspects of penmanship as letter size, proportion, formation, spacing, and slant.

While the use of these checklists will provide the teacher with some valuable information, they yield no data about the particular letters that are illegible. Therefore, when engaged in a complete analysis of the errors in a child's handwriting, the teacher should keep in mind the work of Newland (1932), who studied the handwriting of 2381 people and analyzed the errors they made. He identified the most common illegibilities made in cursive handwriting by elementary school pupils and classified the errors into 26 major groups. Surprisingly, almost half of the illegibilities were associated with the letters *a, e, r,* and *t.* If teachers are familiar with these common errors, they will find it easier to recognize them in their pupils' written work. The 10 most common errors were:

1. Failure to close letters (e.g., *a, b, f,* etc.) accounted for 24 percent of all errors.
2. Top loops closed (*l* like *t, e* like *i*) accounted for 13 percent.
3. Looping nonlooped strokes (*i* like *e*) accounted for 12 percent.
4. Using straight up-strokes rather than rounded strokes (*n* like *u, c* like *i*) accounted for 11 percent.
5. End-stroke difficulty (not brought up, not brought down, not left horizontal) accounted for 11 percent.
6. Top short (*b, d, h, k*): 6 percent.
7. Difficulty crossing *t*: 5 percent.
8. Letters too small: 4 percent.

Table 5–2. Helping in Analyzing and Grading Handwriting

Name

Your Manuscript Handwriting has been thoughtfully analyzed and rated according to the chart below. Any item checked in Section I is outstandingly good and worthy of mention. If an item in Section II is checked, it is faulty and needs improvement. To improve your manuscript handwriting, you will want to study both lists and then review the lesson giving special attention to all items checked—the good ones, to be continued; the faulty ones, to be corrected.

Section I Good
- [ ] Appearance of work
- [ ] Size
- [ ] Quality of line
- [ ] Vertical writing
- [ ] Form of letters
- [ ] Spacing
- [ ] Alignment
- [ ] Proportion
- [ ] Figures
- [ ] Margins

Section II Room for Improvement

Position of Hand, Arm, Body, or Paper
- [ ] Incorrect

Size of Writing
- [ ] Too large
- [ ] Too small
- [ ] Varying in size
- [ ] See your text

Proportion
- [ ] Not primary (half to whole relationship)
- [ ] Changing
- [ ] See your handwriting aid

Quality of Pencil Line
- [ ] Too heavy
- [ ] Too light
- [ ] Varying
- [ ] Kinky (looks slow)
- [ ] Wild and uncontrolled

Slant of Writing
- [ ] Too slanting
- [ ] Not vertical (back slant)
- [ ] Irregular (too many different slants)

Figures
- [ ] Poor figures

Manuscript Handwriting Grading Slip

Form of Letters
- [ ] Poor circles
- [ ] Places illegible
- [ ] Poor straight strokes
- [ ] Parts of letters disconnected
- [ ] Capital letters weak

Spacing
- [ ] Within letters
- [ ] Between letters
- [ ] Between words
- [ ] Between lines
- [ ] Too wide
- [ ] Crowded
- [ ] Irregular
- [ ] Poorly arranged on page
- [ ] Margins uneven

Alignment of Letters
- [ ] Off the line in places
- [ ] Low letters uneven in height

Fluency
- [ ] Too fast
- [ ] Too slow

Name

Your Manuscript Handwriting has been thoughtfully analyzed and rated according to the chart below. Any item checked in Section I is outstandingly good and worthy of mention. Any item checked under Section II is faulty and needs improvement. To improve your handwriting, you will want to note the items checked and then review the lesson giving special attention to them—the good ones, to be continued; the faulty ones, to be corrected.

Section II Room for Improvement

Position of Hand, Arm, Body, or Paper
- [ ] Incorrect

Size of Writing
- [ ] Too large
- [ ] Too small
- [ ] Varying in size
- [ ] See your text

Proportion
- [ ] Not primary (half to whole relationship)
- [ ] Not upper grade
- [ ] Changing

Cursive Handwriting Grading Slip

- [ ] Uneven in height
- [ ] Capital and loop letters uneven
- [ ] Minimum letters vary
- [ ] Intermediate letters vary

Form of Letters
- [ ] Angular letters
- [ ] Letters too round
- [ ] Letters too thin
- [ ] Places illegible
- [ ] Beginning strokes poorly made
- [ ] Ending strokes poorly made
- [ ] Poor loop letters

Section I   Good

- ☐ Appearance of writing
- ☐ Margins
- ☐ Slant of writing
- ☐ Quality of pen or pencil line
- ☐ Spacing in and between words
- ☐ Letter forms
- ☐ Size of writing
- ☐ Alignment of letters
- ☐ Figures
- ☐ Proportion

Fluency
- ☐ Too fast
- ☐ Too slow

Spacing
- ☐ Within letters
- ☐ Between letters
- ☐ Between words
- ☐ Between lines
- ☐ Too scattered (wide)
- ☐ Crowded
- ☐ Irregular
- ☐ Poorly arranged on page
- ☐ Margins uneven

An Explanation of the Cursive Handwriting Grade Slip

On nearly every writing paper there are some good features. It is the intent of this "Good" section on this grading slip to pick out the good features and commend the pupil. This tends to instill confidence in his own ability to write. Any of these ten items that are checked good are representative of the best things on the paper.

- ☐ See your handwriting aid

Quality of Pen or Pencil Line
- ☐ Too heavy
- ☐ Too light
- ☐ Varying
- ☐ Kinky (looks slow)

Slant of Writing
- ☐ Too slanting
- ☐ Too nearly vertical
- ☐ Irregular

Alignment of Letters
- ☐ Off the line in places

Section I   Good
- ☐ Appearance of writing
- ☐ Margins
- ☐ Slant of writing
- ☐ Quality of pen or pencil line
- ☐ Spacing in and between words
- ☐ Letter forms
- ☐ Size of writing
- ☐ Alignment of letters
- ☐ Figures
- ☐ Proportion

Section II   Room for Improvement

Position: This refers to the position of the hand, arm, body, or paper.

Incorrect

When position is checked on the grading slip, it means one of four things:

1. Position of your body is incorrect.
2. Position of the paper is incorrect.
3. Position of your hand and arm is incorrect
4. You are holding the penholder or pencil wrong.

- ☐ Upper   ☐ Lower

Capital letters weak
- ☐ Too small   ☐ Too large
- ☐ Small letters need strengthening
- ☐ Disconnected letters in words
- ☐ Down-strokes not uniform

Figures
- ☐ Poor figures

How can we tell this by looking at your writing?

If your writing is too nearly vertical or too slanting, there is something wrong with position. Either the body position is not right, the paper is being held at the wrong slant, or you are not writing in front of your eyes and pulling the down-strokes toward the center of your body (for the left-hander, pull down-strokes toward the left elbow).

If the bottoms of the letters are shaded, there is too much pressure being put on the pen or pencil at the bottom of each letter. The pen or pencil is being held incorrectly.

Position and slant go hand in hand. If your paper and body are in the correct position, and if you write directly in front of your eyes and pull all of the down-strokes or slant-strokes toward the center of your body, the slant of your writing will be accurate, uniform, and regular.

Source: F. W. Freeman, *Reference Manual for Teachers. Grades One Through Four* (Columbus, Ohio: Zaner-Bloser, 1965), pp. 21–23. Used with permission of the author and publisher.

9. Closing *c, h, u, w*: 4 percent.
10. Part of letter omitted: 4 percent.

Newland's research concerning common errors can easily be incorporated into a simple criterion-referenced assessment procedure that can be used to identify the letters that are illegible in a child's writing and to estimate the particular kinds of errors being made in the formation of those letters. For example:

1. The first step is to obtain a sample of the child's ability to write the letters that are most likely to be illegible. To do this, the teacher might have the child write five to ten *a*'s in a row in cursive, then an equal number of *b*'s, of *e*'s, *h*'s, *m*'s, *n*'s, *o*'s, *r*'s, and *t*'s. These particular letters are selected because the research suggests that they are the ones that are most often produced in a defective, unreadable fashion. The child's paper might look like the following:

2. An alternative to step 1 might be to take an example of the child's spontaneous or elicited written work and circle all the *a*'s, *b*'s, *e*'s, *h*'s, etc.
3. The next step is to evaluate the way a pupil forms his letters according to the criteria listed below:

	Wrong	Right
1. *a* like *o*		
2. *a* like *u*		
3. *a* like *ci*		
4. *b* like *li*		
5. *d* like *cl*		
6. *e* closed		
7. *h* like *li*		

8. *i* like *e* with no dot	*e*	*i*
9. *m* like *w*	*m*	*m*
10. *n* like *u*	*u*	*n*
11. *o* like *a*	*a*	*o*
12. *r* like *i*	*i*	*r*
13. *r* like *n*	*n*	*r*
14. *t* like *l*	*l*	*t*
15. *t* with cross above	*t*	*t*

If the manner in which the child forms the letters differs from that suggested in the column marked "right," one can assume that illegibility (i.e., nonreadability) will be increased. The handwriting examples under the "Wrong" column indicate the most common errors made in the formation of the eight letters. These particular errors are often referred to in the language arts literature as the fifteen handwriting demons and are purported to cause or contribute to most of the illegibilities in children's cursive writing.

The procedures outlined in this section will enable teachers to identify (1) the students who need help in penmanship, (2) the general areas requiring attention (e.g., slanting, spacing, etc.), (3) the individual letters being mis-formed, and (4) the specific kinds of errors causing the illegibilities. It is this kind of information that teachers can use to individualize remedial programs for children.

Assessing Conceptual Writing

Conceptual writing refers to the quality (i.e., the abstractness, appropriateness, and creativeness of the ideas expressed) and to the properness of the grammatic conventions employed. The effort to assess conceptual writing begins with deciding which skills are to be evaluated. To do this, the teacher must have a clear idea as to what abilities constitute expressive writing, the skills that comprise these abilities, and the order of their development. This information can be obtained readily by consulting a scope-and-sequence chart for written expression (e.g., the one provided in Table 5–3).

Table 5–3. *Scope and Sequence of Conceptual Writing Skills*

	Grade 1	Grade 2	Grade 3
Capitalization	The first word of a sentence The child's first and last names The name of the teacher, school, town, street The word "I"	The date First and important words of titles of books the children read Proper names used in children's writings Titles of compositions Names of titles: Mr., Mrs., Miss	Proper names: month, day, common holidays First word in a line of verse First and important words in titles of books, stories, poems First word of salutation of informal note, as "Dear" First word of closing of informal note, as "Yours"
Punctuation	Period at the end of a sentence which tells something Period after numbers in any kind of list	Question mark at the close of a question Comma after salutation of a friendly note or letter Comma after closing of a friendly note or letter Comma between the day of the month and the year Comma between name of city and state	Period after abbreviations Period after an initial Use of an apostrophe in a common contraction such as isn't, aren't Commas in a list
Vocabulary	New words learned during experience Choosing words that describe accurately Choosing words that make you see, hear, feel	Words with similar meanings; with opposite meanings Alphabetical order	Extending discussion of words for precise meanings Using synonyms Distinguishing meanings and spellings of homonyms Using the prefix *un* and the suffix *less*
Word Usage	*Generally in oral expression* Naming yourself last Eliminating unnecessary words (my father he); use of *well* and *good* Verb forms in sentences: is, are did, done was, were see, saw, seen	*Generally in oral expression* Double negative Use of *a* and *an*; *may* and *can*; *teach* and *learn* Eliminating unnecessary words (this here) Verb forms in sentences: rode, ridden took, taken grow, grew, grown	Use of *there is* and *there are*; *any* and *no* Use of *let* and *leave*; *don't* and *doesn't*; *would have*, not *would of* Verb forms in sentences: throw, threw, thrown drive, drove, driven wrote, written tore, torn

Grade 4	Grade 5	Grades 6, 7, and 8
Names of cities and states in general Names of organizations to which children belong, such as Boy Scouts, grade four, etc. Mother, Father, when used in place of the name Local geographical names	Names of streets Names of all places and persons, countries, oceans, etc. Capitalization used in outlining Titles when used with names, such as President Lincoln Commercial trade names	Names of the Deity and the Bible First word of a quoted sentence Proper adjectives, showing race, nationality, etc. Abbreviations of proper nouns and titles
Apostrophe to show possession Hyphen separating parts of a word divided at end of a line Period following a command Exclamation point at the end of a word or group of words that make an exclamation Comma setting off an appositive Colon after the salutation of a business letter Quotation marks before and after a direct quotation Comma between explanatory words and a quotation Period after outline Roman numeral	Colon in writing time Quotation marks around the title of a booklet, pamphlet, the chapter of a book, and the title of a poem or story Underlining the title of a book	Comma to set off nouns in direct address Hyphen in compound numbers Colon to set off a list Comma in sentences to aid in making meaning clear
Dividing words into syllables Using the accent mark Using exact words which appeal to the senses Using exact words in explanation Keeping individual lists of new words and meanings	Using antonyms Prefixes and suffixes; compound words Exactness in choice of words Dictionary work; definitions; syllables; pronunciation; macron; breve Contractions Rhyme and rhythm; words with sensory images Classification of words by parts of speech Roots and words related to them Adjectives, nouns, verbs—contrasting general and specific vocabulary	Extending meanings; writing with care in choice of words and phrases In writing and speaking, selecting words for accuracy Selecting words for effectiveness and appropriateness Selecting words for courtesy Editing a paragraph to improve a choice or words
Agreement of subject and verb Use of *she, he, I, we,* and *they* as subjects Use of *bring* and *take* Verb forms in sentences: blow, blew, blown drink, drank, drunk lie, lay, lain take, took, taken rise, rose, risen	Avoiding unnecessary pronouns (the boy he . . .) Linking verbs and predicate nominatives Conjugation of verbs, to note changes in tense, person, number Transitive and intransitive verbs Verb forms in sentences: am, was, been say, said, said	Homonyms: *its,* and *it's; their, there, they're; there's, theirs; whose, who's* Use of parallel structure for parallel ideas, as in outlines Verb forms in sentences: beat, beat, beaten learn, learned, learned leave, left, left lit, lit, lit

(continued)

Table 5–3. *Scope and Sequence of Conceptual Writing Skills (continued)*

	Grade 1	Grade 2	Grade 3
Word Usages	ate, eaten went, gone came, come gave, given	know, knew, known bring, brought drew, drawn began, begun ran, run	chose, chosen cilmbed broke, broken wore, worn spoke, spoken sang, sung rang, rung catch, caught
Grammar	Not applicable	Not applicable	Nouns: recognition of singular, plural, and possessive Verbs: recognition

Grade 4	Grade 5	Grades 6, 7, and 8
teach, taught, taught raise, raise, raise lay, laid, laid fly, flew, flown set, set, set swim, swam, swum freeze, froze, frozen steal, stole, stolen	fall, fell, fallen dive, dived, dived burst, burst, burst buy, bought, bought Additional verb forms: *climb, like, play, read, sail, vote, work*	forgot, forgotten swing, swung, swung spring, sprang, sprung shrink, shrank, shrunk slid, slid, slid
Nouns, common and proper; noun in complete subjects Verb in complete predicate Adjectives: recognition Adverbs: recognition (telling how, when, where) Adverbs modifying verbs, adjectives, other adverbs Pronouns: recognition of singular and plural	Noun: possessive; objective of preposition; predicate noun Verb: tense; agreement with subject; verbs of action and state of being Adjective: comparison; predicate adjective; proper adjective Adverb: comparison; words telling how, when, where, how much; modifying verbs, adjectives, adverbs Pronouns: possessive; objective after prepositions Prepositions: recognition; prepositional phrases Conjunction: recognition Interjection: recognition	Noun: clauses; common and proper nouns; indirect object Verb: conjugating to note changes in person, number, tense; linking verbs with predicate nominatives Adjective: chart of uses; clauses; demonstrative; descriptive, numerals; phrases Adverb: chart of uses; clauses; comparison; descriptive; *ly* ending; modification of adverbs; phrases Pronoun: antecedents; declension chart—person, gender, case; demonstrative; indefinite; interrogative; personal; relative Preposition: phrases Conjunction: in compound subjects and predicates; in subordinate and coordinate clauses Interjection: placement of, in quotations Noun: antecedent of pronouns; collective nouns; compound subject; direct object; indirect object; object of preposition Verb: active and passive voice; emphatic forms; transitive and intransitive; tenses; linking verbs Adverb: as modifiers; clauses; comparing adverbs; adverbial phrase, use of *well* and *good* Adjectives: as modifiers; clauses; compound adjectives Pronouns: agreement with antecedents; personal pronoun chart; indirect object; object of preposition; objective case, person and number; possessive form Preposition: in phrase Conjunction: coordinate; subordinate; use in compound subjects; compound predicates; complex and compound sentences

(continued)

Table 5–3. *Scope and Sequence of Conceptual Writing Skills (continued)*

	Grade 1	Grade 2	Grade 3
Sentences	Write simple sentences	Recognition of sentences; kinds: statement and question Composing correct and interesting original sentences Avoiding running sentences together with *and*	Exclamatory sentences Use of a variety of sentences Combining short, choppy sentences into longer ones Using interesting beginning and ending sentences Avoiding run-on sentences (no punctuation) Learning to proofread one's own and others' sentences
Paragaraphs	Not applicable	Not applicable	Keeping to one idea Keeping sentences in order; sequence of ideas Finding and deleting sentences that do not belong Indenting

Source: Adapted from W. Otto and R. McMenemy, *Corrective and Remedial Teaching* (Boston: Houghton Mifflin, 1966); H. Greene and W. Petty, *Developing Language Skills in the Elementary School* (Boston: Allyn and Bacon, 1967).

In this chart, the scope is constituted of capitalization, punctuation, vocabulary, word usage, grammar, sentence construction, and paragraph construction. These are the major aspects in the writing curriculum. The specific skills and the order in which they are to be assessed (or taught) is represented in the sequence. In this particular case, the skills in the sequence are grouped according to grade levels.

The contents of the chart suggest the breadth of skills that can be assessed by the teacher but do not indicate the precise evaluation procedures to be used. As in the case of penmanship assessment, there are no really satisfactory standardized tests that can be used to evaluate children's performance in this area. Because this is the case, teachers must rely on subjective interpretation of children's written-work samples, on criterion-referenced tests that they have constructed for their own use, and on teacher-made checklists.

Grade 4	*Grade 5*	*Grades 6, 7, and 8*
Command sentences Complete and simple subject; complete and simple predicate Adjectives and adverbs recognized; pronouns introduced Avoiding fragments of sentences (incomplete) and the comma fault (a comma where a period belongs) Improving sentences in a paragraph	Using a variety of interesting sentences: declarative; interrogative; exclamatory; and imperative (*you* the subject) Agreement of subject and verb; changes in pronoun forms Compound subjects and compound predicates Composing paragraphs with clearly stated ideas	Development of concise statements (avoiding wordiness or unnecessary repetition) Indirect object and predicate nominative Complex sentences Clear thinking and expression (avoiding vagueness and omissions)
Selecting main topic Choosing title to express main idea Making simple outline with main idea Developing an interesting paragraph	Improvement in writing a paragraph of several sentences Selecting subheads as well as main topic for outline Courtesy and appropriateness in all communications Recognizing topic sentences Keeping to the topic as expressed in title and topic sentence Use of more than one paragraph Developing a four-point outline Writing paragraphs from outline New paragraphs for new speakers in written conversation Keeping list of books (authors and titles) used for reference	Analyzing a paragraph to note method of development Developing a paragraph in different ways: e.g., with details, reasons, examples, or comparisons Checking for accurate statements Use of a fresh or original approach in expressing ideas Use of transition words to connect ideas Use of topic sentences in developing paragraphs Improvement in complete composition—introduction, development, conclusion Checking for good reasoning Use of bibliography in report based on several sources

Consider the case where a second-grade child is suspected of having a conceptual writing problem. If the individual conducting the evaluation were interested in the pupil's mastery of capitalization, she would have to consult the chart to identify the capitalization forms that are characteristically taught in school between kindergarten and the end of second grade.

Examples of the child's written work could then be evaluated in terms of these expected forms to learn which have been acquired by the child, which are insecurely mastered, and which are missing altogether. The main defect with the analysis of work samples is that the samples selected for evaluation may not adequately represent the child's writing weaknesses and strengths. For example, often in executing spontaneous written products, such as essays or stories, some children write only sentences that contain the grammatic forms that they know how to use. Therefore, error analysis of their work may result in a distorted view of the skills that they have and have not acquired. Put another way, if error analysis is to work well, the products that are to be evaluated must include adequate opportunities for the errors of interest to occur and to be observed. Because this may or may not be the case where spontaneously written products are concerned, the teacher may want to use additional procedures.

The teacher could generate a sentence (i.e., a test item) that contains the particular element being evaluated (e.g., the capitalization of proper names, the use of a colon to separate the hour from minutes, the use of a comma to set off introductory clauses, etc.). Presumably, one or two sentences would be developed to correspond with each item on the chart. Next, the sentences would be typed in such a manner that the specific element being tested would be left unpunctuated (or punctuated erroneously). The list of sentences could then be presented to the child, who is asked to correct any errors that he recognizes in the sentences. Example sentences might include:

1. The boy's name was bill.
2. School is out at 3 30.
3. After the movie was over Mary went to the store.

In the first sentence, children who strike out the "b" and replace it with a "B" are telling the teacher that they understand the capitalization rule that pertains to first names. Those who insert a semicolon after "Mary" in the third sentence, who see nothing wrong with the sentence, or who place a comma after "movie" are showing that they do not apply the rule concerning the punctuation of introductory clauses. The educational implications of the children's performance on such a criterion-reference device are obvious—teach them the forms that they do not know and give them ample, meaningful opportunities to practice their newly acquired knowledge.

If this criterion-referenced approach is attempted, special care should be taken to make sure that the vocabulary used in the sentences is well known to the children being evaluated. A child who cannot comprehend the meaning of a written sentence certainly cannot be expected to punctuate it properly. Most pupils who have difficulty with writing are enrolled in the upper elementary grades; therefore, a suitable vocabulary level for the test sentences can be obtained by consulting Thorndike and Lorge (1944) for a listing of the words that appear most often in the reading material of children aged six through eight, i.e., third grade and below. If these words are used to construct the test sentences, teachers can have every reason to believe that the children being evaluated will understand the vocabulary of the sentences used to assess writing mechanics ability. If the teacher has any reason to suspect that the child cannot read the sentences, the child should be asked to tell in his own words what the sentence means. If the pupil is unable to do this, the sentence should be reworded utilizing an appropriate vocabulary.

Also, the teacher will want to adhere very closely to the developmental sequence found in Table 5–3, for it indicates the order in which grammatic forms are usually taught in the schools. Using the three sentences above as examples, teachers would find that children are generally taught (1) during kindergarten and first grade that the first and last names of a person are capitalized, (2) between second and fifth grades that colons separate hours from minutes, and (3) between fourth and sixth grades that commas are used to set off an introductory clause. This information is of considerable value for teachers who must prepare special programs for individual children, because it enables them to sequence both the goals that underlie training and the activities that are to be used to ameliorate deficits according to most desirable levels.

The assessment of the content of a composition is considerably more difficult than the evaluation of writing readiness, penmanship, or most of the skills included in Table 5–3, although the problems are hardly insurmountable. The experienced teacher can probably read a child's essay and score it properly according to the criteria specified in the Carlson Analytical Originality Scale (Carlson, 1965) (see Table 5–4). This scale requires that the teacher rate the child's written content on five dimensions (i.e., its story structure, novelty, emotion, individuality, and style).

Of course, since the ratings tend to be subjective, they are only as good as the talent and experience of the individual doing the evaluation. Therefore, it is important to take a few precautions to minimize the evaluator's subjectivity and to increase her reliability. Whoever are designated to evaluate the quality of the ideas expressed in children's written work should take steps to calibrate their judgments by acquiring a set of "internalized norms." This can be done by standardizing the topics of the written pieces that are to be assessed. For example, if examiners are called upon most often to assess the work of children in grades three through six, they should select three topics, e.g., "My Favorite Television Show," "The Place I'd Most Like to Visit," "The Person I Admire Most," and have a sample of ten to twenty representative students at each grade level write a short composition on each topic. Reading approximately sixty essays all on the same topic will usually equip examiners with a better-than-intuitive knowledge of what constitutes average, below-average, and above-average quality with regard to a given topic and will probably enable them to complete Carlson's scale items with some assurance.

This section is concluded with a description of one attempt at developing a standardized test of conceptual writing [i.e., the Picture Story Language Test (Myklebust, 1965)]. The test is purported to measure such important areas as productivity, syntax (i.e., grammar), and quality of content. In administering the test, the composition is then evaluated according to the child's productivity and correctness and the composition's meaning. Pro-

Table 5–4. *Carlson Analytical Originality Scale Scoring Key for Scoring Original Stories*

Name of child _____   Name of teacher _____

Story type _____   Total score on scale _____

Scale Division A—Story Structure

1.	Unusual title	0 1 2 3 4 5
2.	Unusual beginning	0 1 2 3 4 5
3.	Unusual dialogue	0 1 2 3 4 5
4.	Unusual ending	0 1 2 3 4 5
5.	Unusual plot	0 1 2 3 4 5

Scale Division B—Novelty

6.	Novelty of names	0 1 2 3 4 5
7.	Novelty of locale	0 1 2 3 4 5
8.	Unique punctuation and expressional devices	0 1 2 3 4 5
9.	New words	0 1 2 3 4 5
10.	Novelty of ideas	0 1 2 3 4 5
11.	Novel devices	0 1 2 3 4 5
12.	Novel theme	0 1 2 3 4 5
13.	Quantitative thinking	0 1 2 3 4 5
14.	New objects created	0 1 2 3 4 5
15.	Ingenuity in solving situations	0 1 2 3 4 5
16.	Recombination of ideas in unusual relationships	0 1 2 3 4 5
17.	Picturesque speech	0 1 2 3 4 5
18.	Humor	0 1 2 3 4 5
19.	Novelty of form	0 1 2 3 4 5
20.	Inclusion of readers	0 1 2 3 4 5
21.	Unsual related thinking	0 1 2 3 4 5

Scale Division C—Emotion

22.	Unusual ability to express emotional depth	0 1 2 3 4 5
23.	Unusual sincerity in expressing personal problems	0 1 2 3 4 5
24.	Unusual ability to identify self with feelings of others	0 1 2 3 4 5
25.	Unsual horror theme	0 1 2 3 4 5

Scale Division D—Individuality

26.	Unusual perceptive sensitivity (social and physical environment)	0 1 2 3 4 5
27.	Unique philosophical thinking	0 1 2 3 4 5
28.	Facility in beautiful writing	0 1 2 3 4 5
29.	Unusual personal experience	0 1 2 3 4 5

Scale Division E—Style of Stories

30.	Exaggerated tall tale	0 1 2 3 4 5
31.	Fairy tale type	0 1 2 3 4 5
32.	Fantasy-turnabout of characters	0 1 2 3 4 5
33.	Highly fantastic central idea of theme	0 1 2 3 4 5
34.	Fantastic creatures, objects, or persons	0 1 2 3 4 5
35.	Personal experience	0 1 2 3 4 5
36.	Individual story style	0 1 2 3 4 5

Source: R. K. Carlson, *Sparkling Words: Two Hundred Practical and Creative Writing Ideas* (Berkeley, Calif.: Wagner Printing Co., 1965; distributed through the National Council of Teachers of English, Urbana, Ill.).

ductivity is defined as the number of words, sentences, and words per sentence and is, of course, more related to penmanship (specifically, speed) than to conceptual writing. Correctness (syntax) refers to accuracy in the use of words, word endings, and punctuation. Meaning is defined as ideation. Reliability data in the manual are insufficient and the information provided is at best equivocal. While interscorer reliability is adequate, the results of other reliability procedures provide only mixed support. For example, the reliability of Words per Sentence and for Syntax was determined at five age levels. For the Words per Sentence scale, only one of the five coefficients exceeded .80; for Syntax, only two. Although the test lacks sufficient reliability to be used as a diagnostic device with confidence, teachers can adapt it into a useful, informal, observational technique.

TEACHING WRITTEN LANGUAGE

Before describing selected procedures for teaching written language, several points should be mentioned. Teaching handwriting to left-handed children presents a few special problems, though in general the techniques used with right-handed pupils will suffice with slight variation. Readers are referred to the work of Fletcher (1967), Anderson (1968), or Lerner (1976) for discussions of the modifications for left-handed pupils. Current thinking dictates that a child who is definitely left-handed should be allowed to write with his preferred hand. Forcing him to use the right hand is not recommended.

Often teachers are undecided whether to teach manuscript or cursive initially. Learner (1976) has briefly summarized the arguments for each.

> The arguments for beginning with cursive writing are that it minimizes spatial judgment problems for the child and that there is a rhythmic continuity and wholeness that is missing from manuscript writing. Further, errors of reversals are virtually eliminated with cursive writing; and by beginning with the cursive form in initial instruction, the need to transfer from one form to another is eliminated. Many children with learning disabilities find it difficult to make the transfer to cursive writing if they have first learned manuscript writing.
>
> The advantages of manuscript writing are: it is easier to learn since it consists of only circles and straight lines; the manuscript letter form is closer to the printed form used in reading; and some educators feel it is not important for a child to transfer to cursive writing at all since the manuscript form is legal, legible, and thought by some to be just as rapid (p. 255).

The research suggests that in most cases it does not matter which style is taught, though the common practice is to begin with manuscript and to introduce cursive at about the third-grade level. The following instruction procedures relate to teaching writing readiness, penmanship, and conceptual writing.

Stimulating Writing Readiness

Most six-year-old children are ready to begin to write. At this age both the visual–motor integrations necessary for forming letters and the visual–auditory discriminations required for making sound–letter associations are usually developed. However, written language does not develop on the basis of maturation alone, for the child needs proper instruction in order to acquire skill in writing. Some of the competencies purported to underlie success in writing are as follows.

1. Eye–hand coordination, especially necessary for using a pencil, is required in the production of legible handwriting.
2. The child needs to be able to "see" what he has written in order to guide his hand movements and to monitor his work for errors.
3. The ability to discriminate the features of letters and words is an important component of readiness.
4. Adequate speech and life experiences provide the ultimate basis for writing.
5. The ability to combine letters and sequence them in proper order is a major aspect of writing.
6. Spelling is usually helpful to a child who is beginning to write.
7. Mastery of left and right progression is essential.
8. Interest in learning to write is extremely important.

When children lack these fundamental abilities, it is necessary to begin instruction at the readiness level. But before the teacher can prepare a specific writing-readiness program for a child, he will have to determine the areas of readiness deficiency. Does the child lack the basic language prerequisites while evidencing adequate visual–motor skills? Or, does he speak and use verbal concepts which are at expected levels for his age but fail miserably in copying, drawing, and coloring exercises? Proper intervention depends on accurately estimating the nature of the readiness problem. In the former case, a heavy language program is indicated, while selected perceptual–motor activities, closely related to penmanship, will probably suffice in the latter case.

Most writing-readiness teaching programs emphasize penmanship readiness and consequently are concerned with activities which, in this book, are discussed in Chapter 8. Most commercial companies offer readiness-training workbooks and programs.   A few examples of these readiness activities are:

1.   Practicing how to hold chalk, crayons, pencils.
2.   Tracing circles, slants, and other shapes by means of chalkboard templates.
3.   Arranging pictures in a left-to-right and a top-to-bottom sequence.
4.   Dot-to-dot games, scribbling, drawing, cutting, and pasting.
5.   Tracing of letters cut out of sandpaper.

Teaching Penmanship

The procedure for teaching handwriting skills necessary for legible writing are subdivided by Reger et al. (1968, pp. 220–224) into four developmental levels.[1]   The teacher should begin with Level I and move to Level IV as the pupil masters the skills.   It should be noted that while this sequence could be used as a program for all pupils, it is intended for use with children who experience difficulty in handwriting.   Most children will respond adequately to one of the developmental systems described later in this chapter.

   Level I—introductory movements. Using the chalkboard as a prop, the teacher discusses how the movements of writing are made; for example, "First we go up and then we go down."   The teacher demonstrates on the board. Or she says, "We go away from our body and then towards our body."   The children make the movement at the board while they look at the model but not at the board.   They say "up" when they are going up and "down" when they are going down.   The movements should be rhythmic and free flowing.   The children should stand at least 6 inches from the board. Supplementary chalkboard activities are provided by Ramming (1968).

   After the child has had several days of practicing the movement on the board following the procedure above, the auditory clue is eliminated and the child makes the movement on the board while he looks at the model but not at his hands.   Then the outlined procedures are repeated, this time on paper or large newsprint, using crayon. Reger et al. (1968, p. 221) suggest the movements shown in Figure 5–3.

   The teacher will also want to keep in mind Spalding and Spalding's observation (1962, p. 74) that only the six different pencil strokes shown in Figure 5–4 are necessary for making lowercase manuscript letters. One or

1. Material in this section was drawn from *Special Education: Children with Learning Problems* by Roger Reger, Wendy Schroeder, and Kathie Uschold.   Copyright © 1968 Oxford University Press, Inc. Used with permission.

Figure 5–3. *Introductory Movements*

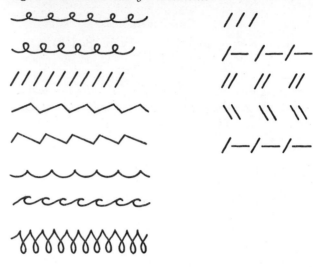

Figure 5–4. *Pencil Strokes Needed for Lowercase Letters.* [From R. B. Spalding and W. T. Spalding, *The Writing Road to Reading* (New York: William Morrow, 1962), p. 74. Used by permission of the authors and publisher.]

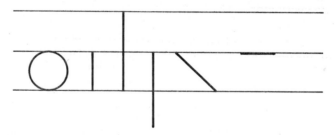

two of these movements can be introduced each week in conjunction with Reger's exercises. If a child has difficulty with any of the movements, additional practice should be given as often as possible. Before introducing a new movement, the previous ones should be reviewed.

Level II—introducing movements on the chalkboard. The same procedures are repeated, but the child is allowed to look at the paper. It should be kept in mind that: (1) the child should have correct posture when he performs the movements; (2) the slant of the paper should be correct, and dependent on the hand used; (3) the hand position should be proper. Teachers can usually find detailed descriptions of the proper positions for writing in

Figure 5–5. *Movements for Cursive Writing.* [Adapted from W. M. Cruickshank, F. A. Bentzen, F. H. Ratzeburg, and M. Tannhauser, *A Teaching Method for Brain-Injured and Hyperactive Children* (Syracuse, N.Y.: Syracuse University Press, 1961).]

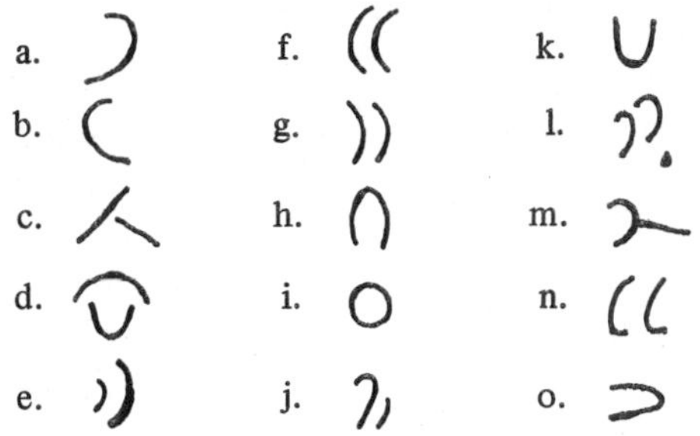

the teacher manuals that accompany the various commercially available writing programs.

The movements on paper should be done first on paper with 1-inch spaces. The letters should be three spaces high initially, then two spaces, and finally one space high. The teacher can line the paper with magic markers, using blue for the top line, green for the middle line, and red for the bottom line. This helps the children stay on and within the lines. Serio (1968) is a source of information regarding writing materials, especially pencils and paper with colored lines.

Level III—movements for cursive writing. Follow the procedures set forth under Level I using the movements shown in Figure 5–5. Begin on the chalkboard and eventually progress to newsprint using crayon or magic marker.

Spalding and Spalding (1962) offer an alternative by suggesting that cursive writing is an adaptation of manuscript writing and that it is only necessary to teach five connecting strokes (Figure 5–6).

Level IV—movements for writing. Using letters, progress from the chalkboard (repeating the procedures stipulated under Level I), to 1-inch-lined paper where three lines have been drawn with red, green, and blue magic markers, and finally progress to regular lined paper. Materials for this level include: (1) Overlays with each letter made on the transparency with magic marker, blank overlays, and overhead projector. (2) The different

Figure 5–6. *Cursive Writing.* [From R. B. Spalding and W. T. Spalding, *The Writing Road to Reading* (New York: William Morrow, 1962), pp. 88–89. Used by permission of the authors and publisher.]

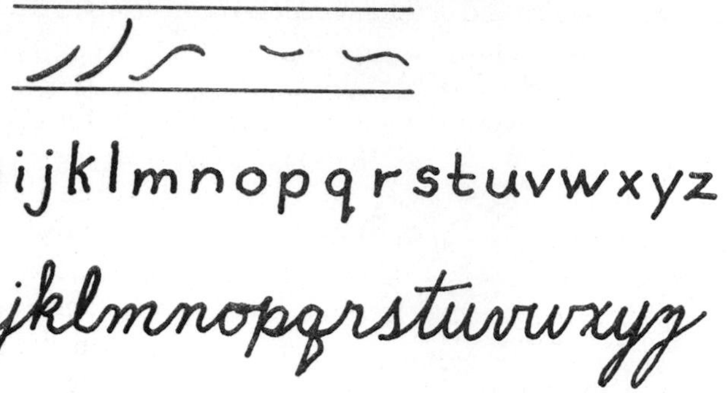

abcdefghijklmnopqrstuvwxyz

abcdefghijklmnopqrstuvwxyz

parts of the letter are made in different colors with magic markers to show the various movements. (3) To show the direction of the letters, such as *s, z,* and others, cinematic materials are used. A Polaroid filter mounted on a clear plastic wheel that is motorized is placed over the transparency. The letters then move from left to right, or right to left, to show the child the direction of the letter.

In general, the following sequence is appropriate for teaching at this level:

1. Name the letter.
2. Discuss the form of the letter while the child looks at it.
3. On a blank overlay, make the letter for the children.
4. Using the Polaroid filter wheel, show the children the direction of the letter.
5. Develop the kinesthetic feel for the form of letters with use of sunken and raised script letterboards (may be purchased from the American Printing House for the Blind).
6. The child makes the letter while he looks at the model.
7. His eyes are on the model, not on his hand.
8. Help him compare his work with the model.
9. Auditory clues may be given to help the child who has difficulty with the letter, or the child's hand may be held as he makes the letter. Some children may need to write the letter in salt or sand (on a salt tray).
10. Have the child write the letter on the chalkboard without the model.
11. Have the child write the letter on newsprint without a model, eyes averted.
12. Have the child write on paper with eyes on the paper.

In following this sequence, 1-inch-lined paper should be used with the writing space divided into three parts (by colored magic markers). If the top line is always blue, the middle line green, and the bottom line red, the teacher can then say to the child "Start on the red line, go up to the blue line, come down to the red line," depending on the letter. The lines should be dark and heavy so the child will be able to stay within them.

The teacher puts a model of the letter on the child's paper, and the letter form and direction are discussed. The position of the paper for left- and right-handed children is demonstrated, and each child's paper is checked for proper positioning. Masking tape or marks on the desk are used to show the child how he should position the paper.

The writing posture is discussed and demonstrated: elbow on the desk, nonwriting hand holding the paper, fingers on the pencil correctly, feet on floor, proper head tilt. Before each writing assignment, the correct habits for writing should be reviewed.

The child traces the model of the letter and makes a row of letters. The teacher should watch him carefully to determine his success with the letter and to decide where he needs help. The child is then taught to write within the 2-inch-lined area, next uses 1-inch lines, and finally writes on regular primary paper. The same procedure as mentioned above should be followed.

The order in which the letters are presented to the child is not clearly established and varies from program to program. Dubrow (1968) offers a sequence based on the movements involved in cursive production.[2]

1. The swing-up letters: *i, u, w, t, r, s*
2. The swing-up-and-over letters: *n, m, v, x*
3. The swing-up-and-turn-back letters: *e, l, b, h, k, f*
4. The swing over-and-turn-back letters: *c, a, g, d, q*
5. Some more swing-up letters: *o, p, j*
6. Some more swing-up-and-over letters: *y, z*

When the child has succeeded in writing the letters accurately, he should be taught to connect letters and then to write simple words. As the child progresses, simple sentences should be copied and gradually the child should be encouraged to attempt to write without copying. It is at this point that handwriting becomes an expressive language ability. The time of the writing period will vary from class to class and from child to child. If one child can tolerate writing only one line, he should write only that much. If another child can write a whole page, he should be allowed to do so. The sequence just outlined is basically a remedial one and can be supplemented

2. H. C. Dubrow, *Learning to Write* (Educators Publishing Service, Inc., Cambridge, Mass., 1968). Used by permission.

by activities drawn from Gillingham and Stillman (1970), Spalding and Spalding (1962), and Johnson and Myklebust (1967).

The "applied behavioral analysis" technique is particularly productive when specific errors in penmanship have been noted and selected for improvement. For example, the teacher may have decided as a result of observation or testing that the child's difficulty is centered in letter illegibility, improper spacing, sloppiness, slowness, and/or unacceptable slanting. One of these problems, probably the one that is the most annoying to the teacher, is chosen as the target for retraining; and the principles of ABA are implemented. The dynamics of managing an ABA program are based on the ideas expressed in the behavior-modification section in L. Brown's chapter (see pp. 213–261). Individuals interested in this approach should read the section referred to as well as Lovitt's (1975b) description of how the technique has been used to help improve children's penmanship skills.

The experienced teacher will recognize readily that the procedures just outlined probably cannot be used with all the children in a regular class. They are best reserved for use in special remedial classes with an enrollment of 6–10 pupils or with those few pupils in the regular class who are developing problems in writing. Although this book is primarily concerned with the management of children with problems, the teacher must have considerable knowledge of the "developmental" teaching systems. For example, in teaching handwriting to a whole class of children, one system may work quite efficiently with 80 percent of the pupils, another system with the remaining 20 percent. By using several developmental systems, remedial procedures may not be necessary at all. In 1960, four companies, Zaner-Bloser, Palmer, Scale, and Noble and Noble, accounted for 50 percent of all instructional materials used in the United States for teaching handwriting. As they are all similar, only one set of materials, Noble and Noble, will be described.

The Noble and Noble program, *Better Handwriting for You*, contains a series of eight workbooks and teacher editions prepared by Noble (1966). Books 1 and 2 present manuscript writing and Books 3 through 8 deal with cursive writing. There is a transitional book between Books 2 and 3 which begins with manuscript and introduces cursive. Throughout, the teacher is given instructions regarding management of the left-handed pupil, correct position for holding the pencil, proper positions for the paper, and correct positions for writing on the chalkboard or at the desk.

In the first book, upper- and lowercase letters and numbers are introduced. Numbers and arrows are used to teach the sequence and direction of strokes necessary to write the various graphic forms. Models and ample opportunity to copy them are provided in the workbooks. In Books 7 and 8, devices are presented whereby the pupil can evaluate the quality of his writing; he is presented with the 15 handwriting demons, or the errors that cause most illegibilities, and the 100 spelling demons.

A program comprised of six programmed texts with several unique features is provided by Skinner and Krakower (1968). The first three deal with the formation of capital and lowercase letters and numbers; the remainder are concerned "with the evaluation of handwriting, and the practical uses of both manuscript and cursive writing" (p. 1). The paper in the workbooks is specially treated so that a correct mark appears yellow with a gray dot in it, while an incorrect mark is all yellow. This use of color allows the pupil to monitor his own work for correctness. Every attempt is made to present the writing exercise within a relevant and varied framework. Therefore, the writing activities include the filling out of bank deposit forms, library cards, and applications for Social Security numbers, among other exercises. The authors have made a concerted effort to provide interesting and relevant activities and as a result their program offers a marked contrast to others.

Teaching Conceptual Writing

The term "conceptual writing" refers to the syntactic and semantic aspects of a child's written product. It is manifested in the ability to capitalize and punctuate, to use vocabulary and grammatical forms, and to construct sentences and paragraphs. Obviously, a certain level of competence in all these abilities is essential if a child is ever to use writing as a means of self-expression. Before attempting to remediate problems in any of these areas, teachers must first be aware of (1) the goals of individualized instruction in writing, (2) the language-experience approach to teaching conceptual writing, (3) the scope and sequence of the specific skills usually taught, and (4) the instructional activities that can be used to help a child attain a desired level of competence.

Goals of individualized instruction. The goals of instruction in conceptual writing are threefold. The first goal is to teach students at least the minimum competencies that they will need to succeed in the school curriculum. The second goal is to instruct them in those writing abilities that will be required for success outside the school (e.g., letter writing, completion of forms, note taking, etc.). The third goal is to teach them to express their creativity is writing poetry, fantasies, and stories. Each of these goals is important and the teacher should keep them in mind when planning an intervention program for a particular student.

The language-experience approach to teaching conceptual writing. In general, teachers usually use a variation of the "language-experience" approach to teach conceptual writing. In using this technique, the teacher's knowledge of a particular child's background and interests serves as the basis of instruction. The teacher begins by recording a student's verbal description of objects and events on a chart or board. Contents of the chart are discussed with the child, and attention is called to the various mechanical and compositional aspects of written expression, as well as to the relationships existing between the child's experiences and between oral and written language. Gradually, the student assumes more and more responsibility for the writing of his own expressions. At first, he is asked to write only those words that the teacher knows are well within his speaking vocabulary. Eventually, the child is asked to write complete compositions reflecting his thoughts about some interesting topic or experience. The theme of these essays can be provided by the teacher or, as is more often the case, by the student himself.

At all times, the student is encouraged to write creatively; and the emphasis of instruction is always on the quality of ideas expressed and on motivation for writing. In time, the more mechanical and rule-governed aspects of writing are introduced; but care is taken to make sure that the increasing curricular focus on these skills does not interfere with the child's desire to write creatively. This approach to teaching conceptual writing is most effective when it is integrated with the teaching of other areas in the language arts curriculum (e.g., reading, spelling, penmanship, etc.). Readers who want more information on using the language-experience approach to teach writing are referred to Parts II and III of Fernald (1943); Chapters 6, 8, and 9 of J. Smith (1967), and Chapters 7–9 of Burns et al. (1971).

"Proofreading," the reading of a written product for the purpose of identifying errors, is an integral part of all approaches to teaching conceptual writing. Students are usually taught to proofread soon after they begin to read and write original compositions. Children can proofread their own work, the work of other pupils, or special pieces containing selected errors that have been composed by the teacher. Regardless of the material to be proofread, students will find the following questions designed by Burns, Broman, and Wantling (1971, pp. 241–242) to be helpful guides to developing proofreading ability:

1. Listen and look at each group of words to be sure it is a good sentence. Make sure that you kept your sentences apart.
2. Listen and look for mistakes in punctuation. Be sure that you have put in punctuation marks only where they are needed. Did you end sentences with the mark required?
3. Listen and look for mistakes in using words correctly. Be sure that you have said what you mean and that each word is used correctly with other words. Is there any incorrect verb or pronoun usage?
4. Look for mistakes in using capital letters. Did you capitalize the first words and all important words in the title? Did you begin each sentence with a capital letter?

5. Look for misspelled words. Use the dictionary to check the spelling of any word about which you are not sure.
6. Check for legibility of writing and directions about spacing, title, and the like.

Scope and sequence for conceptual writing skills. In teaching written expression, the teacher must have a clear understanding of the theoretical basis and the specific sequence of skills that make up the instructional program that is to be used. The teacher can use this information as a guide for assessing a child's strengths and weaknesses in that program and also as a framework for planning short- and long-term objectives. The easiest way to obtain the needed knowledge about a particular approach is to prepare and study a scope-and-sequence chart in which the skills and conceptual ideas incorporated in the program are depicted. Fortunately, the authors of many programs provide teachers with scope-and-sequence data for their materials.

The theoretical constructs (i.e., the major aspects of the curriculum) are represented in the "scope" of the chart, while the skills of a particular construct and the order in which they are to be taught are displayed in the "sequence." An example of a scope-and-sequence chart that is useful for assessment and remedial purposes in conceptual writing was presented in Table 5–3. The scope of this curriculum is comprised of capitalization, punctuation, vocabulary, word usage, grammar, sentence construction, and paragraph construction. These categories represent the major conceptual ideas involved in the program. The skills that make up these categories are grouped according to grade levels (i.e., the sequence). This chart serves as a guide for identifying the skills that need to be taught, for deciding the order in which the skills are to be introduced, for recording an individual's progress, and for facilitating systematic instruction.

The procedures for using a scope-and-sequence chart to assess skills in conceptual writing were described on pages 185–193. Having used these procedures to determine the skills that a particular child does not have, e.g., the use of a period after initials and abbreviations (punctuation skills found at the third-grade level in Table 5–3), the teacher is ready to plan an appropriate course of instruction.

Instructional activities. Once a suitable scope and sequence has been acquired and a child's skill deficits have been identified, the teacher is ready to choose instructional activities that are appropriate to the student's needs and situation. The activities described in the remainder of this chapter are representative of those which can be used to teach punctuation, capitalization, vocabulary, word usage, grammar, and sentence and paragraph construction. When applied to children having problems in writing, these activities should be used in conjunction with the language-experience approach discussed earlier.

Punctuation and capitalization. The strategies for teaching punctuation and capitalization are basically similar. For example, to teach skills in either area, the teacher (1) utilizes the language-experience approach to collect passages of the student's written work, (2) calls attention to each incidence in the essay where punctuation or capitalization is required, (3) discusses the need to use the skill to enhance meaning, (4) shows how to use the required skill properly, (5) provides activities for practice, and (6) arranges an opportunity for the pupil to demonstrate competence in spontaneous writing. To facilitate instruction in punctuation and capitalization, the teacher may want to use variations of the following activities. For example, students can:

1. Match items on a list of punctuation marks with possible functions (stop, yield, etc.). *Examples:*
    period = stop
    comma = yield
2. Punctuate and/or capitalize written passages. *Example:* billys cat was lost but it was found quickly
3. Proofread the work of their classmates and underline possible errors. The paper can be returned to the classmate for correction, or the student who did the proofreading may correct the error.
4. Write passages dictated by the teacher. The sentences dictated involve various examples of punctuation and capitalization.
5. Be taught to listen for drops in the teacher's voice when she is dictating. These drops indicate the end of a sentence or the need for a comma. Young students can clap their hands when they recognize a point where a punctuation mark should be placed.
6. Be told to write sentences demonstrating a particular kind of form. *Example:* Write a sentence as if you were talking to Mr. Smith (quotation marks).

Vocabulary, word usage, and grammar. These are related abilities; therefore, they can often be taught simultaneously using similar instructional activities. A child's vocabulary is the supply of words that he comprehends and uses in speaking and writing. The goal of vocabulary-development activities is to increase this supply of words in number and complexity. Word usage, on the other hand, refers to the "appropriateness" of the child's selection of vocabulary in terms of accepted standards. This differs from grammar, in that grammar is the way in which words are structured or organized to form a complete thought. An example will illustrate these differentiations more clearly:

I am not going to school.	(The basic sentence)
I am not *attending* school.	(Improvement due to vocabulary)
I *ain't* going to school.	(Unacceptable usage—ain't)
I am going *not* to school.	(Incorrect organization of words—grammatical error)

One of the most important issues in the discussion of vocabulary, word usage, and grammar is the consideration of the student's oral language and past experiences. In no instance should the teacher expect a student's written composition to reflect a vocabulary, a usage pattern, or a grammar that he does not use in speaking. Therefore, it is important for the teacher dealing with these aspects of written expression to allow the student to utilize those forms with which he is familiar. For example, in preparing experience charts, the student's own words and structure should be recorded. An attempt to remediate these kinds of problems in written language must be preceded and accompanied by "remediation" in oral language. Information on teaching oral language is found in Chapter 7.

The following list is an accumulation of suggested activities to increase *vocabulary* skills. They are drawn from Greene and Petty (1967), Burns et al. (1971), Otto, McMenemy, and Smith (1973), and our own experience.

1. List on the board new words encountered in classroom and out-of-school activities.
2. Read stories, descriptions, poems, etc., aloud to the students and follow up with group discussions.
3. Have a student go on "word hunts" outside the classroom. He will enjoy collecting words from billboards, warning signs, traffic signs, etc. These may also be used as the child's weekly spelling list.
4. Discuss and use words appearing in reading material.
5. Let the student keep a list of words that he likes or wants to use. As an alternative, he can write the new words on an index card and file them with others in a "word box."
6. Make lists or charts of special-interest words, such as those related to football, television, and cooking.
7. Build words from root words by adding prefixes, suffixes, etc.
8. List words that rhyme with others and discuss their meanings.
9. Suggest topics for oral written expression whereby students must employ the new vocabulary items.
10. Utilize word games, such as Scrabble.
11. Find synonyms and antonyms for new words.
12. Have students take turns bringing in new words for the day.
13. Use dictionary drills and emphasize proper use of reference books.

It is important for the teacher interested in remediating *word-usage* problems to select only a few items to attack at any one time. A list of common "errors" to be eliminated is that of Pooley (1960), Table 5–5. The teacher can utilize this list in targeting the particular usages to be attacked. The most important factor in correcting word usage and grammatical errors

Table 5–5. *Word-Usage Errors to Be Eliminated in Elementary Grades*

1. The elimination of all baby-talk and "cute" expressions.
2. The correct uses in speech and writing of *I, me, he, him, she, her.*
3. The correct uses of *is, are, was, were* with respect to number and tense.
4. Correct past tenses of common irregular verbs such as *saw, gave, took, brought, bought, stuck.*
5. Correct use of past participles of the same verbs and similar verbs after auxiliaries.
6. Elimination of the double negative; *we don't have no apples,* etc.
7. Elimination of analogical forms: *ain't, hisn, hern, ourn, theirselves,* etc.
8. Correct use of possessive pronouns: *my, mine, his, hers, theirs, ours.*
9. Mastery of the distinction between *its,* possessive pronoun, and *it's,* contraction of *it is.*
10. Placement of *have* or its phonetic reduction to *v* between *I* and a past participle.
11. Elimination of *them* as a demonstrative pronoun.
12. Elimination of *this here* and *that there.*
13. Mastery of use of *a* and *an* articles.
14. Correct use of personal pronouns in compound constructions: as subject (*Mary and I*), as object (*Mary and me*), as object of preposition (to *Mary and me*).
15. The use of *we* before an appositional noun when subject; *us* when object.
16. Correct number agreement with the phrases *there is, there are, there was, there were.*
17. Elimination of *he don't, she don't, it don't.*
18. Elimination of *learn* for *teach, leave* for *let.*
19. Elimination of pleonastic subjects: *my brother he; my mother she; that fellow he.*
20. Proper agreement in number with antecedent pronouns *one* and *anyone, everyone, each, no one.* With *everybody* and *none,* some tolerance of number seems acceptable now.
21. The use of *who* and *whom* as reference to persons (but note, *Who did he give it to?* is tolerated in all but very formal situations; in the latter, *To whom did he give it?* is preferable).
22. Accurate use of *said* in reporting the words of a speaker in the past.
23. Correction of *lay down* to *lie down.*
24. The distinction between *good* as adjective and *well* as adverb, e.g., *He spoke well.*
25. Elimination of *can't hardly, all the farther* (for *as far as*), and *Where is he (she, it) at?*

Source: R. C. Pooley, Dare Schools Set a Standard in English Usage? *English Journal,* 1960, *49,* 179–180. Copyright © 1960 by the National Council of Teachers of English. Reprinted by permission of the publisher and the author.

is to provide ample opportunity for the student to utilize the correct forms in oral expression. The following list provides some suggested activities to increase efficiency in word usage.

1. Provide frequent opportunities for practice. Repetition should be emphasized.
2. Utilize the tape recorder in oral language activities.
3. Provide usage activities throughout the day, not only during a language time.
4. Rephrase students' incorrect usage in situations where it will not prove embarrassing.
5. Have students clap, etc., when they hear a usage error as the teacher reads a selection.
6. Give students opportunities to mark incorrect usage in written expressive tasks.
7. Play games substituting correct and incorrect usage in sentences.
8. Dramatize characters in plays utilizing different usage forms.
9. Attend primarily to those most socially unaccepted usage forms.

Grammatical skills will be susceptible to most of the approaches mentioned for vocabulary and word usage. Initial instruction in the various grammatical structures will be best taught through oral and written examples and repetition. Following instruction in the simple sentences and questions using the noun + verb, noun + verb + noun, etc., the teacher will want to include instruction, group activities, and games which experiment with noun and verb phrases and, later, with clauses. For example,

The dog ran.
The big dog ran.
The big gray dog ran.
The big gray and white dog with a red collar . . .
. . . ran over the hill.
. . . ran over the green hill toward them.

Exercises such as these can often be extended into the absurd and not only incorporate new vocabulary but provide for enjoyable class interactions. Burns et al. (1971, p. 21) provide twelve items in which students should be instructed so that they can manipulate grammatic structures and patterns to create sentence variations. These are quoted below with the permission of the authors. They will provide a useful guide in sequencing of instruction.

1. Elements (as adverbs) can be recorded:
   Marie stood by quietly.   Quietly Marie stood by.
2. Indirect objects may be rearranged:
   He gave a ball to John.   He gave John a ball.

3. The use of "there" provides an alternative:
    A visitor was upstairs.   There was a visitor upstairs.
4. Adjectives can be used:
    The cat is dirty.   The dirty cat . . . (or The cat that is dirty . . .)
5. Possessives may be formed:
    Bill has a dog.
    The dog is gentle. } Bill's dog is gentle.
6. Comparisons may be made:
    John is strong.
    Tom is stronger. } Tom is stronger than John.
7. Relatives (such as *that, which, who, whom*) can be utilized:
    The girl played the piano. } The girl who played the piano
    The girl is my sister.   } is my sister.
8. Appositives can be employed:
    Clara is my youngest sister. } Clara, my youngest sister,
    She went to California.   } went to California.
9. Noun phrase complements may consist of a "that clause"; infinitive clause ("for . . . to"); or gerundive clause (genetive or possessive form), such as:
    That Bill arrived late bothered Sue.
    For Bill to have arrived late bothered Sue.
    Bill's having arrived late bothered Sue.
10. Coordination:
    The phone rang. } The phone rang, but no
    No one answered it. } one answered it.
11. Subordination:
    The man was strong.
    He was tall. } The man was strong, tall,
    He was handsome. } and handsome.

    The wind was strong.
    The leaves fell to the ground. } The leaves fell to the ground because (as, since, when) the wind was strong.
12. Sentence connection:
    I am not going to the movie. } I am not going to the movie;
    I am going to the dance. } however, I am going to the dance.

Activities employed to develop grammatic skills for children with learning problems will primarily be oral. Some examples of suggested activities are listed below:

1. Repeat and expand or elaborate child's utterances to form more complete or complex sentences.
2. Give students ample opportunities to participate orally in class:

—describing objects or events
—retelling a story
—discussing an experience or activity

Sentence and paragraph construction. To be competent in forming written sentences and paragraphs, children have to coordinate all the skills involved in punctuation, capitalization, vocabulary, word usage, and grammar. In addition, they must organize content as well. West (1966) has prepared a list of problems that are commonly associated with children's sentence construction. These include: fragments, run-on and comma splices, sentences that are too simple or too complex, misplaced or dangling modifiers, pronouns without proper referents, lack of variety in sentence structure, pronoun–antecedent and subject–verb disagreements, overuse of expletives and passive voice, and tense-sequence problems. Each of the errors will have to be attended to individually by applying and/or adjusting instructional activities such as those that follow. The teacher should:

1. Have students arrange a string of written words that will form a sentence. *Examples:*

fast	the	dog	black	ran
The	black	dog	ran	fast.

2. Have students mark errors in given sentences or have them mark, correct, and rewrite the incorrect portions.

3. Have students complete partially written sentences. *Examples:*
   Mary went to the store to buy _____.
   Mary went to the store to buy _____, _____, and

   _____.
   Mary went _____.

4. Do much group work in composing (e.g., experience charts, writing letters to classmates, etc.).

5. Begin conceptual writing instruction with one-word composition, progress to simple sentences, and gradually increase the number and complexity of the sentences used in the exercises.

6. Encourage and provide opportunities for students to dictate letters and stories.

7. Utilize dictation and proofreading exercises in the writing program.

8. Give students a group of written statements comprised of both complete sentences and fragments; ask them to select those that are fragments.

9. Have students underline subject and verb as clues to determining which are complete sentences and which are fragments.

10. Have students match predicate and verb phrases.
11. Give students an outline or form for a sentence to be constructed. *Examples:*

Noun	Verb	Noun	Noun
John	gave	Bill	the ball.

12. Have students practice using connectives, such as *and, but, for, which, when, because,* etc. *Examples:*

    Willie was tired, _____ he got up early this morning.
    Susie ran well, _____ Judy won the race.

Once a student can compose complete sentences, the teacher should begin instruction in paragraph formation. Four major points should be stressed in teaching children to write paragraphs: the content to be expressed, the topic sentence, the order and flow of sentences and ideas within the paragraph, and the concluding sentence. Activities for each are provided below. The teacher may:

1. Collect statements made by students during a discussion, write them on the board, and have the students select those that go together.
2. Let students order the statements selected above.
3. Give students selections whereby they must locate inappropriate sentences in paragraphs.
4. Give students paragraphs that contain appropriate but poorly sequenced sentences; have the students rearrange the sentences into a more meaningful order. The teacher may want to see if the young pupil can tell an experience in sequence or arrange comic strips and tell a story from the frames before attempting this task.
5. Utilize opportunities, such as class or school newspapers, to motivate students to compose.
6. Employ dictation and proofreading activities.
7. Introduce students to the concept of outlining.

In conclusion, teachers should be ever mindful that in using any of the activities described in this chapter, care must be taken to ensure that students are required to perform only those tasks in which they can experience some degree of success. As the child succeeds, the complexity of the tasks can be increased gradually until eventually he will have mastered the targeted skills or areas completely.

Teacher Strategies for
Managing Classroom Behaviors

6

Linda L. Brown

Teachers are expected to manage an appreciable number of the behavior problems that arise in their classrooms. Aggressive behavior such as fighting, stealing, or destroying property is obviously harmful to the children involved and also temporarily disrupts the ongoing educational program in the classrooms in which it occurs. Passive behavior such as withdrawal, refusing to begin or complete work, or crying excessively is equally regrettable in that it prevents the affected child from participating fully in the academic and social activities in the classroom. All of these behaviors, whether passive or aggressive, require the teacher's time and attention as do a myriad of less serious—although not necessarily less aggravating—problems, such as throwing spitwads, poking classmates, or running noisily through the corridors.

We are confident that teachers are quite capable of assessing and managing the vast majority of the behavior problems that exist in their classrooms. To help in this endeavor, a variety of strategies that teachers can use to handle problem behaviors will be presented in this chapter. The assessment techniques that are described encourage the teacher to approach the problem behavior directly and to pay special attention to situational and environmental variables which may contribute to or aggravate the problem. An eclectic selection of management techniques is also presented to assist the teacher in managing or changing the child's behavior patterns in the classroom.

ASSESSING PROBLEM BEHAVIORS

Teachers often observe behaviors that interfere with children's school learning or that are symptomatic of emotional stress. For example, Jim cries every

213

morning while on the school bus, unusual behavior for a fourth-grade student; Mary "cuts" high school English repeatedly but attends her other classes regularly; Willie is given to spitting on other people and pulling out patches of his hair; Nellie is friendless, frequently involved in fighting and teasing episodes, and is verbally abusive to her classmates; Sarah constantly talks out in class and is almost never in her seat; and David is abnormally reticent and withdrawn. If the situation is thought to be serious, the teacher will want to prepare a written description of (1) the precise behaviors that have led to the conclusion that the pupil is having problems, (2) the situations under which the behaviors occurred, and (3) any other information about the child and the classroom that might be relevant.

Once a child has been identified as needing help and a thorough behavioral description has been made in writing, the teacher may have reason to document the presence and severity of the difficulty through more objective means. Such documentation may be necessary to qualify a youngster for certain services, to assist the teacher in choosing those behaviors which require immediate attention, to probe more fully and systematically areas of perceived difficulty, and to demonstrate that behavioral change has occurred as a result of treatment. Six assessment strategies for teachers to use in measuring problem behaviors will be presented in this chapter: the use of (1) direct observation, (2) behavioral checklists and inventories, (3) Q-sorting, (4) techniques for analyzing the physical environment, (5) procedures for examining interaction in the classroom, and (6) standardized tests.

Direct Observation

The most convenient method a teacher can use to measure problem behavior is to observe it directly in the classroom. The three direct-observation techniques about to be discussed have been described by Hall (1971c). They are (1) automatic recording, (2) analysis of permanent products, and (3) observational recording.

Automatic recording. Automatic recording involves the measurement of behavior by machines. For instance, in biofeedback such behaviors as pulse, heart rate, blood pressure, and galvanic skin response are measured by sensitive mechanical devices. In laboratories where animal research is conducted, such machines are used frequently to record the movements or responses of the laboratory animals. These machines are costly to purchase and to repair, and they are rigid in their functioning, usually incapable of being adapted to measure more than a single behavior or set of behaviors. For these reasons, automatic recording devices are rarely used in school settings. They are mentioned here only to familiarize teachers with their existence.

Analysis of permanent products. This technique is infinitely more useful to teachers. In using this approach, the teacher evaluates the product of a behavior rather than the behavior itself. For example, a student's spelling paper is the "permanent product" of taking a spelling test. The number of correctly spelled words (or correct algebra problems, complete sentences, etc.) can be counted and verified easily. While it is often used by teachers to measure pupil status or progress in academics, the technique is seldom employed to assess "affective" behaviors because they do not usually have permanent products associated with them.

Observational recording. Observational recording of classroom behavior problems can be accomplished in one of six ways: (1) maintaining anecdotal records, (2) event recording, (3) duration recording, (4) interval recording, (5) time sampling, or (6) planned activity check. Data obtained from these observational techniques should be recorded in a systematic way which can be interpreted quickly and easily. Anecdotal records, of course, must be presented in narrative form. The most common way of recording data gathered through the other five techniques is by graphing them, as in Figure 6–1. The teacher can easily "eyeball" these graphs to note trends or to see when the rate or duration of a behavior begins to increase or decrease.

1. *Anecdotal records* provide an account of everything that is done to, with, for, by, or around the target child. Obviously, no individual teacher can take the time to gather all the anecdotal data

Figure 6–1. *Graph of Frances' Swearing Behavior During Algebra Class*

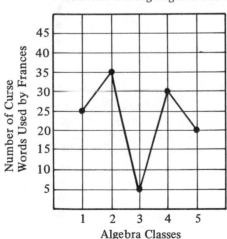

that are required for a comprehensive record. Occasionally, other personnel such as trained volunteers, aides, or student teachers can be assigned some responsibility for gathering these data. Ideally, a videotape recording of the child's entire school day should be available for analysis but, of course, this is not practical in most situations. A coding system or some form of shorthand may be devised to permit the observer to record as much data as possible in a short amount of time and space. The shorthand is transcribed later into narrative form which can be understood by individuals who are unfamiliar with the coding system. A coded entry in an anecdotal record might look like this: "1025 — sci ctr — X pokes SL — SL cries, X pokes more — M, SR, PR also in ctr — M calls △, others tell X to quit — △ comes to ctr." Translated, this means that at 10:25 in the science interest center, the target child (X) poked Susan Lily (SL) until she cried, after which he continued poking her. The other children in the science center (M, SR, and PR) told the target child to quit poking and M called the teacher (△), who then came to the science center. Anecdotal records are especially useful when a teacher is unable to identify the pattern of a student's problem. By analyzing a continuous recording of the student's behavior over a period of time, the teacher may learn that the behavior occurs only in certain situations or at certain time periods in the day or that every occurrence of the problem behavior is followed by a positive reward (e.g., by increased teacher attention and interest). While from time to time these variables can be identified from reading an anecdotal record, in most instances, continuous recording is not a time-efficient measurement device for the classroom teacher to employ.

2. *Event recording* is a frequently used observational recording technique. It is, simply, a recording of the number of times a defined behavior occurs (i.e., it is a behavioral frequency count). Using this technique, a teacher learns that Frances used 27 curse words during the 30-minute algebra class on Monday, 33 on Tuesday, 8 on Wednesday, 28 on Thursday, and 19 on Friday. These data are recorded in the form of a conventional graph in Figure 6–1.

3. *Duration recording* is used when a teacher is more concerned with how long a behavior lasts than with the frequency of occurrence. Knowledge of the duration of a child's temper tantrum, for instance, may occasionally be more important than a recording of the number of outbursts occurring during a given time period. Another example is provided by Linda, who has difficulty attending to the task at hand. It could be that she exhibits only one

instance of off-task behavior during the seatwork period; regrettably, that one instance lasts for 20 minutes.

4. *Interval recording* combines the two previously described techniques, giving the teacher a measure of both the frequency and the duration of a behavior. An observation period is divided into equal, usually short, time periods (e.g., the 5 minutes after recess may be divided into thirty 10-second intervals). The teacher observes continuously during the 5-minute session and notes whether or not the defined behavior occurs during each of the shorter intervals. For instance, if Pat talked without permission during twenty-five of the thirty 10-second intervals, the results would be reported as 83 percent of the time spent talking out. The form on which the teacher recorded Pat's talking (T) would probably look something like the following:

T 1	T 2	T 3	T 4	T 5	T 6
T 7	T 8	T 9	T 10	11	12
T 13	T 14	T 15	T 16	T 17	T 18
T 19	T 20	T 21	T 22	T 23	T 24
T 25	T 26	T 27	T 28	29	30

The duration of the talking could be easily calculated: Pat was talking during twenty-five 10-second intervals, or for 4 minutes and 10 seconds. Event data could also be extracted: Pat talked out twice, from the first through the tenth 10-second interval and from the fourteenth through the twenty-eighth interval. The data could be graphed in any of the three ways shown in Figure 6–2.

5. *Time sampling* is very similar to interval recording, but it does not require the teacher to observe continuously throughout the observation period. The observation period is again divided into equal, usually longer, time periods. For instance, Mr. Nixon, the world history teacher, may divide his 50-minute class period into five 10-minute intervals. He then conducts a time sampling of Henry, who is supposed to be answering the questions at the end of Chapter 14 in the world history textbook. After (not throughout) each 10-minute interval, Mr. Nixon would observe to see if Henry were or were not answering the questions. If Henry was working (W) four of the five times that Mr. Nixon observed him,

Figure 6–2. *Methods of Graphing Data*

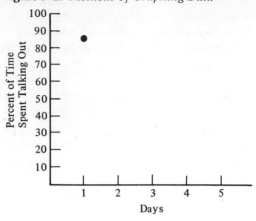

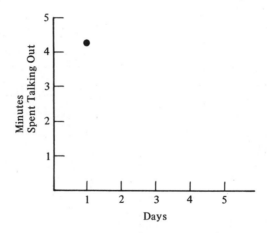

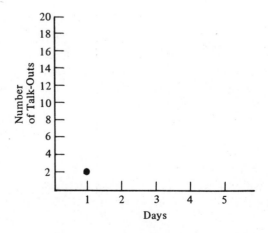

he would be recorded as working 80 percent of the time. An example of Mr. Nixon's time sampling record is as follows:

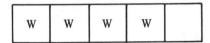

6. *Planned activity check* (sometimes called "placheck") is used to measure the behaviors of groups of children. Teachers using this technique would be interested in the percentage of students engaged in a defined behavior. Perhaps a teacher would want to make a placheck of the children working on an assignment in an interest center. The teacher would first count the number of students working and would then count the number of students actually in the interest center. If ten students were in the center and only four were engaged in the assignment, the placheck record would be 40%. Placheck records are often taken on a time sampling basis. For example, Mr. Nixon, the world history teacher, may do placheck every 10 minutes during his 50-minute class period. If 25 students are in the class and if 24 are working at the first check, 20 at the second check, 25 at the third and fourth checks, and 5 at the final check, the placheck records would be 96, 80, 100, 100, and 20 percent, respectively. Mr. Nixon might conclude that studying behavior dropped off during the final 10 minutes of his class, particularly if this pattern continued over a period of time. He might adjust his planning to make better use of that final 10 minutes.

Behavioral Checklists and Inventories

On some occasions, the teacher may find it helpful to assess problem behaviors by using checklists and/or inventories. The items on these checklists typically relate to a variety of both normal and problem behaviors and do not concentrate solely on behaviors that are disturbing and disruptive. In addition, checklists are constructed for use with several children, not for a single student; they derive some objectivity from this characteristic. Teachers may find checklists particularly useful in identifying those children who are passive or withdrawn, behaviors that otherwise might go unnoticed in a busy classroom. Many teachers use checklists when they must narrow their target behaviors or must find precise descriptions of target behaviors. Some of the published checklists discussed in the next section also give teachers guidelines for determining the seriousness and/or severity of the behavior problems which they have defined.

Checklists are relatively easy to use and require little time to complete. The individual who is responding, usually a teacher, parent, clinical professional, or perhaps the child himself, reads a list of behaviors and checks whether or not each behavior has been observed. Some checklists are scored on a Likert-type scale which asks if the behavior occurs never, sometimes, frequently, or whatever. Most published checklists then provide rough norms against which the results may be evaluated. Published checklists and inventories, as well as criteria that teachers may use to devise their own checklists, are presented below.

Published checklists. Most published behavior checklists and inventories evidence neither a high reliability nor a demonstrated validity. Despite this, however, they have some value when used for general observation and assessment. Seven of the more popular published checklists will be discussed here: the Peterson–Quay Behavior Problem Checklist, the Coopersmith Self-Esteem Inventory and Behavior Rating Form, the American Association on Mental Deficiency's Adaptive Behavior Scale, three of the Devereux behavior rating scales, and the Walker Problem Behavior Identification Checklist. Some of these checklists and many others which are not mentioned here are reviewed in the first volume of Buros' (1972) *Seventh Mental Measurements Yearbook*. Teachers are encouraged to read the Buros reviews before selecting a published checklist.

1. The Peterson–Quay Behavior Problem Checklist (Quay and Peterson, 1967) is one of the more widely used devices. Despite its rather low reliability, the teacher may find that this instrument will yield information concerning the severity of behavior problems. Behaviors are measured and classified according to four dimensions: conduct disorders (aggression), personality disorders (anxious, withdrawn), inadequacy–immaturity, and subcultural (socialized) delinquency. Four "warning" items tap a fifth category, autism or psychotosian behavior. Examples of items used in the Behavior Problem Checklist follow.

1. Oddness, bizarre behavior (autism).
5. Doesn't know how to have fun; behaves like a little adult (personality disorder).
20. Short attention span (inadequacy–immaturity).
26. Loyal to delinquent friends (socialized delinquency).
36. Truancy from school (socialized delinquency).
46. Destructiveness in regard to his own and/or other's property (conduct problems).

2. The Coopersmith Self-Esteem Inventory (Coopersmith, 1968) is a self-report device for elementary-age students. The short (25 items) and

long (58 items) forms have reported reliabilities in the middle .60s. Both forms can be administered to students who are nonreaders. The following items were extracted from the Self-Esteem Inventory.

2. I'm pretty sure of myself.
14. I'm proud of my schoolwork.
23. I can usually take care of myself.
46. Kids pick on me often.
51. I'm a failure.

The Behavior Rating Form which accompanies the instrument is completed by the teacher and is purported to identify those problem behaviors that may contribute to the child's self-concept. The Behavior Rating Form contains such items as:

2. Does this child hesitate to express his opinions, as evidenced by extreme caution, failure to contribute, or subdued manner in speaking situations?
7. When this child is scolded or criticized, does he become either very aggressive or very sullen and withdrawn?
12. Does this child attempt to dominate or bully other children?

3. The American Association on Mental Deficiency's Adaptive Behavior Rating Scale (Nihira, Foster, Shellhaas, and Leland, 1969) is a useful instrument for assessing the social development of mentally retarded and emotionally maladjusted individuals, ages three through adulthood. Divided into two domains, the first section of the scale measures skills and habits considered important for daily functioning (cleanliness, money handling). The second part provides measures of maladaptive behavior. The Adaptive Behavior Scale can be administered by teachers and results can be used to identify behavioral deficiencies that require modification. The mean reliability for the scale is .67. The following items are included in the scale:

1. Threatens or does physical violence.
11. Uses angry language.
19. Lies or cheats.
21. Is withdrawn.
27. Has strange and unacceptable habits.
42. Has hypochondriachal tendencies.

4. There are three Devereux scales, the Devereux Adolescent Behavior Rating Scale (Spivak, Spotts, and Haimes, 1967), the Devereux

Elementary School Behavior Rating Scale (Spivak and Swift, 1967), and the Devereux Child Behavior Rating Scale (Spivak and Spotts, 1966).

The Adolescent Behavior Rating Scale (ABRS) is appropriate for use with normal and emotionally disturbed students from ages thirteen to eighteen years. A variety of problem behaviors are identified, including dependency, the need for approval, and peer dominance. The median inter-observer reliability of this instrument is .82.

The Elementary School Behavior Rating Scale (ESBRS) is appropriate for use with students in kindergarten and in grades one through six. Its median stability reliability is .87. This scale "provides a profile of 11 dimensions of *overt* problem behaviors that experienced teachers have judged as relevant to classroom achievement." Questions included in these scales are similar to those described above in the Coopersmith Behavior Rating Form.

The Child Behavior Rating Scale (CBRS) was devised for emotionally disturbed and mentally retarded children from ages eight to twelve. The respondent on this scale must have an "intimate living arrangement" with the child who is being rated, which precludes its use by most teachers in settings other than residential institutions. A total of seventeen scores can be derived, ranging from immature behavior to social aggression, poor coordination, and the need for independence. The one-week test–retest reliability of the instrument is .83. The following items are from the CBRS:

1. Approach strangers who come to visit the unit or home?
8. Have a fixed facial expression which lacks feeling?
21. Intentionally tells lies?
27. Tease or bully other children?

5. The Walker Problem Behavior Identification Checklist (Walker, 1970) was designed to assess problem behaviors of students in grades four, five, and six. The split-half reliability of the checklist is reported to be .98. The instrument yields a total score and scores on five behavioral aspects: acting out, withdrawal, distractibility, disturbed peer relations, and immaturity. The following items are typical of those found in the Walker checklist:

1. Complains of other's unfairness and/or discrimination towards him.
18. Argues and must have the last word in verbal exchanges.
27. Has temper tantrums.
31. Has rapid mood shifts: depressed one moment, manic the next.
37. Has no friends.
41. Does not complete tasks attempted.

50. Frequently stares blankly into space and is unaware of his sur-
    roundings when doing so.

Teacher-made checklists. Instead of using published checklists, teachers will find that in some instances—perhaps most—it is most beneficial for
them to develop a behavior checklist criterioned to a particular classroom
situation and/or child. Bower and Lambert (1971) discussed teacher-made
behavior checklists and concluded that items should describe behaviors seen
specifically (1) in the target child, (2) in the target child's interaction with
other students in the class, and (3) in the teacher's interaction with the target
child. More recently, Wiederholt, Hammill, and Brown (1978) have suggested that these same three categories of behaviors should be sampled by
checklist items. These authors go on to recommend that a teacher-made
checklist should include no more than 30 items. They provide a sample
teacher-made checklist, which is reproduced in Figure 6–3.

Figure 6–3. *Teacher-Made Checklist for Measuring Problems in Social and Emotional Development*

Teacher Checklist: This measure was designed to be used by teachers in any classroom to make them more aware of their students' behavior. This list might help
identify behavior that otherwise might be overlooked or misunderstood. From
here the teacher might want to take frequency counts of identified behavior, or in
some other way further analyze the situation.

		Frequently	*Not Frequently*
1.	Self-Image		
	A. Makes I can't statements		
	B. Reacts negatively to correction		
	C. Gets frustrated easily		
	D. Makes self-critical statements		
	E. Integrity: cheats		
	tattles		
	steals		
	destroys property		
	F. Makes excessive physical complaints		
	G. Takes responsibility for actions		
	H. Reacts appropriately to praise		

(continued)

	Frequently	Not Frequently

2. Social Interaction
   A. Seeks attention by acting immaturely: thumbsucking, babytalking, etc.

   B. Interacts negatively

   C. Fails to interact

   D. Initiates positive interaction

   E. Initiates negative interaction

   F. Reacts with anger, verbally

   G. Reacts with anger, physically

3. Adult/Teacher Relationships
   A. Seeks attention by acting immaturely

   B. Excessively demands attention

   C. Reacts appropriately to teacher requests

   D. Inappropriately reacts to authority figures

4. School-Related Activities
   A. Attends to task

   B. Exhibits off-task behavior

   C. Interferes with the other students' learning

   D. Show flexibility to routine changes

Date the checklist and complete one for each child. Once the checklist has been completed and reviewed a narrative report can be written with explanations and suggestions for the future. For the list to be effective, the teacher must use the results to actually make changes in her classroom.

Source: Developed by the following teachers and used with their permission: Lee Person, Becky Beck Browning, Margaret Hughes Hiatt, and Margaret Morey-Brown. Reprinted with permission of the authors and publisher of J. L. Wiederholt, D. D. Hammill, and V. Brown, *The Resource Teacher* (Boston: Allyn and Bacon, 1978).

Q-Sorting

The Q-sorting technique can be used by teachers to compare two interpretations of a single set of behaviors. For example, a teacher might describe behaviors associated with reading (e.g., reads well, doesn't like to read, reads at home) or even social attributes (e.g., dates a lot, can't dance, has friends). The teacher would then compare how a child or teenager viewed the various

Figure 6–4. *Parent Q-Sort Items*

1. Does assigned chores.	13. Eats between meals.
2. Does his homework on time.	14. Is overweight.
3. Goes to bed without problems.	15. Is destructive of property.
4. Comes home when he should.	16. Gets ready for school on time.
5. Argues with parents.	17. Makes own decisions.
6. Has friends.	18. Chooses own clothes.
7. Likes school.	19. Is unhealthy.
8. Cries or sulks when he doesn't get his own way.	20. Fights with brothers and sisters.
9. Throws temper tantrums.	21. Has a messy room.
10. Likes to watch TV.	22. Responds to rewards.
11. Likes to read.	23. Does acceptable schoolwork.
12. Plays alone.	24. Is a restless sleeper.
	25. Stretches the truth.

items from both realistic and idealistic points of view. Commercial Q-sorts are available and teachers can easily devise Q-sorts of their own which will match the classroom situations and behaviors of particular interest to them. Directions for constructing one of these, as well as suggestions for its use, will be presented in this section.

The first step in using the Q-sort technique is to devise a list of descriptor statements such as those in Figure 6–4. Although most Q-sorts have 25 or 36 items, any number of descriptor statements may be included as long as the items can be sorted into a perfect pyramid form as in Figure 6–5. The descriptor statements are written on small cards, one item per card, which are read to or by the students who are responding.

After reading through the items, students sort them onto a formboard such as the one in Figure 6–5. All the squares on the pyramidlike form must be used: none may be left blank and none may be used twice, although students may rearrange the items until they are satisfied with their responses. Students sort the items twice. On the first sort they place the items into categories that are supposed to reflect how they believe they really are; this is called the *real sort*. The second time, the students sort the items into the categories as they wish they were; this is called the *ideal sort*.

Students' responses are recorded on the form shown in Figure 6–6 and a simple correlation is calculated between the two sorts. For example, if a student sorted item 1 as "A Little Like Me" on the *real sort*, a 4 would be recorded in the first column (S-1). If the student rated the same item as "Unlike Me" on the *ideal sort*, a 7 would be recorded in the second column (S-2). The difference between the sorts is 3, and this is recorded in the D column. The difference squared (D^2) is 9. The D^2 column is summed and the total (ΣD^2) is substituted into the formula at the bottom of the page. This formula will result in the correlation coefficient; it will not be larger

Figure 6–5. *Q-Sort Formboard*

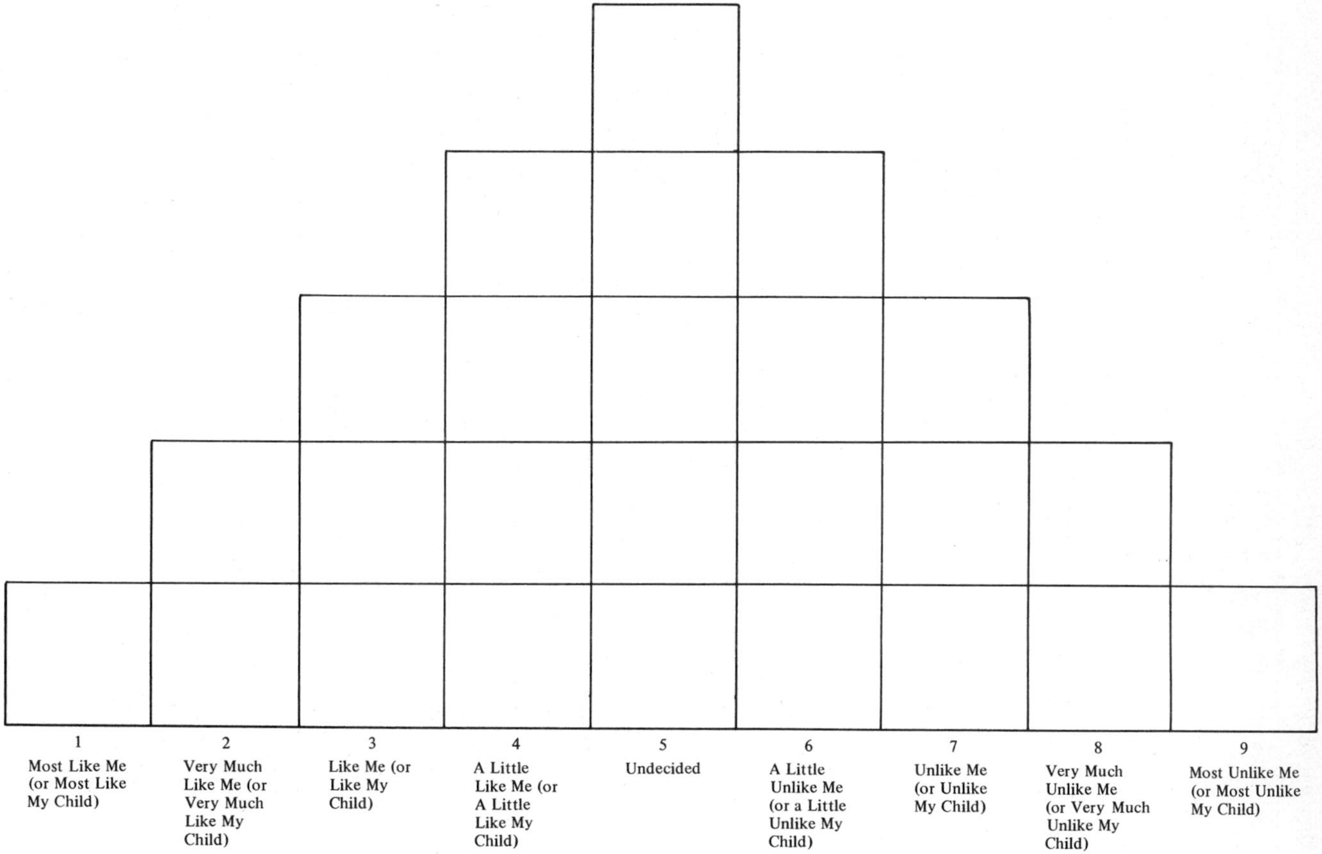

1	2	3	4	5	6	7	8	9
Most Like Me (or Most Like My Child)	Very Much Like Me (or Very Much Like My Child)	Like Me (or Like My Child)	A Little Like Me (or A Little Like My Child)	Undecided	A Little Unlike Me (or a Little Unlike My Child)	Unlike Me (or Unlike My Child)	Very Much Unlike Me (or Very Much Unlike My Child)	Most Unlike Me (or Most Unlike My Child)

Figure 6–6. *Q-Sort Record Form.* [Reprinted with permission of the author and publisher of R. Kroth, The behavioral Q-sort as a diagnostic tool, *Academic Therapy*, 1973, *8*, 327 (Academic Therapy Publications, San Rafael, California).]

Name of Subject _____ Sex _____ Date Tested _____

Address _____ Phone _____ Date of Birth _____

School _____ Teacher _____ Grade _____ Age _____

Name of Examinee _____ Relationship to Child _____

Card No.	Column S-1	Column S-2	D	D^2
1				
2				
3				
4				
5				
6				
7				
8				
9				
10				
11				
12				
13				
14				
15				
16				
17				
18				
19				
20				
21				
22				
23				
24				
25				
			$\Sigma =$	

$$n = 1 - \frac{\Sigma D^2}{200}$$

than $+1.00$ or smaller than -1.00. The farther the correlation is from $r = .00$, the greater the agreement between the *real* and *ideal sorts*.

In most instances, the teacher will be less interested in the correlation between the two sorts than in those individual items which have large discrepancies between them. Items with great discrepancies between the sorts can provide the teacher with some possible target behaviors for intervention. If the child rates an item such as "Likes to read," as "Like Me" on the *ideal sort* but as "Very Unlike Me" on the *real sort*, the teacher may have identified an area in which the child is ready to begin work for improvement.

Kroth (1973a) has an excellent article on the uses of the behavioral Q-sort and interested teachers will want to read it. He suggests that the Q-sort could be administered to children's parents and teachers, with the *real sort* representing the way they believe the children behave and the *ideal sort* representing the way they wished the children would behave. The use of the technique in this way would permit analysis of various combinations of Q-sort responses: e.g., the child's *ideal sort* compared with the parent's *ideal sort*, the regular classroom teacher's *real sort* compared with the resource teacher's *real sort*, the child's *real sort* compared with the teacher's *real sort*, and so on. Again, particular discrepancies may be more important than the correlation between the sorts. If the child's regular class teacher rates "Likes to read," as "A Little Unlike My Child" and the special education teacher rates this same item as "Like My Child," a source of conflict *may* have been identified.

Q-sort items can be read to nonreaders, although this has not been particularly successful. Children who cannot read the items have great difficulty in manipulating the cards, especially when only a few slots are left on the formboard and some switching is necessary. Children who are easily frustrated also have difficulty with the Q-sort because they are forced to limit each category to a specific number of items. Most children, however, enjoy the activity and can complete it independently after brief instructions have been given.

Techniques for Analyzing the Physical Environment

Not all of the behavior problems that occur in school can be understood fully by looking only at the behaviors of individual children. Many of the difficulties experienced by children are caused by problems existing within the physical environment of the classroom and the school. For this reason, teachers will want to examine the classroom environment for physical variables that may be stimulating and/or maintaining problem behaviors. Redl (1959) identified four variables relating to physical aspects of the school which can be manipulated to prevent or ameliorate behavior problems. These variables are space, equipment, time, and props. Careful examination of each of these variables may be indicated when teachers are assessing children's behavior problems.

In assessing these variables, the teacher must first be aware that they can cause or contribute to classroom behavior problems. The teacher will then want to ask such questions as: Does the child need more space for a particular activity? Does he need to move around the class more? Does he need smaller space boundaries in which to work? Could the problem be avoided by using (or discarding) certain pieces of equipment? If the activity were rescheduled for a different time, would the behavior problems associated with it decrease? Is his attention being drawn away from a lesson or activity and focused on a nonrelevant but highly seductive item (e.g., a noisy pencil sharpener)? If the answer to any of these questions is yes, the teacher will want to document the existence and/or severity of the problem by using one of the measurement techniques described earlier (e.g., event recording, time sampling, and so on). For instance, if the teacher believes that a child's problems are caused partially by having too much work space, the following sequence would be appropriate for both assessment and intervention. First, the teacher would define and measure the problem behavior(s). The teacher would then alter the troublesome variable. In this instance, excess space could be handled by providing the child with a study carrel or a small, well-defined study area. The teacher would note any changes in the target behavior after the study carrel was introduced. If no change occurs, the teacher can be relatively certain that space is not a relevant variable in the child's current problems. If changes are noted, the teacher will have a ready-made prescription to relieve the behavior problem. Each of Redl's four variables (i.e., space, time, equipment, and props) will be explained briefly below.

Space. This item refers to the amount of physical area allotted to a particular activity and the ways in which that space affects children's behaviors. Redl notes that it is difficult to hold the attention of a small group of children located in the gymnasium. Equally disruptive behaviors may arise when too many students are crowded into a small area, as when all the fifth-hour social studies classes are sent into one classroom to view a film.

Time. The period of the day when an activity is scheduled is important. Most elementary school teachers intuitively utilize this element in their planning: the bulk of the basic academic work is scheduled for the early morning, and "winding-down" activities are employed after recesses and lunch periods. A hot, sweaty child who has just returned from a stimulating game of kickball can hardly be expected to buckle down immediately to a sheet of long-division problems. Unfortunately, teachers in secondary schools have little control over scheduling. They work in a system that assumes, probably fallaciously, that high school students do not require these same considerations. Woe to the English teacher who must present the delights of Chaucer to a class in which many of the students have just returned from band practice or physical education!

Equipment. Materials and equipment that are required for each activity should be identified and acquired before the activity is initiated. Is the necessary equipment available, is it in working order, can the students operate it? In individualized instruction, a student's ability to use equipment is an important factor in his ability and willingness to continue working without disruption. Such equipment can be highly motivating or highly frustrating and disruptive. In group instruction, the teacher's attention may be divided as a consequence of preoccupation with arranging or setting up materials and equipment. Students who are wondering just how much they can get by with when the teacher isn't looking are likely to begin testing classroom rules. The flow of activity is again disrupted when the teacher is forced to stop arranging equipment to manage the problem behaviors. It may be difficult to resume a steady pace.

Props. Most classrooms are filled with items or "props" which teachers use to set the classroom stage. Those items which hold students' attention during a mathematics lesson do not suddenly lose their seductive charms when instruction is switched to social studies. Many of these items are more attention holding, seductive, and alluring than either the teacher or the lesson at hand. When this occurs, disruptive behaviors are sure to ensue. By the same token, disinterested behaviors will be elicited when the props supporting a lesson are not interesting and seductive. The teacher's job will be to determine those props which contribute to the program, those which detract from the program, and those which should be present occasionally and absent at all other times.

Procedures for Examining Classroom Interaction

By now it should be apparent that many of the behavior problems that one finds in a classroom do not spring from a single cause. Rather, they are products of the interaction of two or more variables. This section will examine techniques used to measure the type and quality of teacher–child, child–peer, and child–environment interactions. Five procedures will be presented: sociometrics, Dyadic Interaction Analysis, Flanders' Interaction Analysis Categories, the Florida Climate and Control System, and ecological assessment. With the exception of sociometrics, each of these procedures is extremely time consuming and should only be employed in those situations where the time investment is warranted (e.g., where particularly troublesome or severe cases are involved). Each technique provides valuable information, but if the teacher does not need detailed information of this nature, simple observation may suffice.

Sociometrics. This way of obtaining peer ratings is a nominating technique originally developed by Moreno (1953). This sociometric procedure may be used to determine each child's position within the class by analyzing choices made by each child with respect to all other children in the group. Thorndike and Hagen (1969) have stressed that in order to understand the individual child and the climate of the class, it is important to appraise the role of the individual child within that group.

In applying this technique to the classroom situation, each child is asked to choose one or two children with whom he would like to play, eat, work, or engage in any class activity. This information can aid in understanding the social structure within the group by plotting the nominations on a sociogram as illustrated in Figure 6–7. In this example, ten children were asked to choose two children with whom they would like to work on an art project.

In examining the diagram, it becomes apparent that John was most highly desired as a partner, while Bill was an "isolate," neither making nor receiving any nominations. Jim was an unchosen member of the group;

Figure 6–7. *Example of a Sociogram*

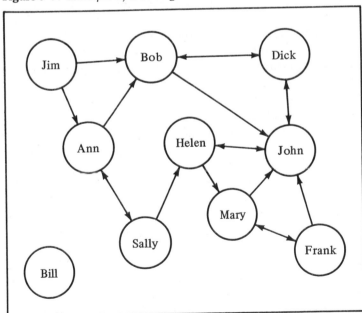

although he did choose two children he was not selected by any member of the group.

After the teacher has determined which child is isolate or without friends, he may begin to seek out the causes. Frequently, the explanations are quite simple, such as being new to the class, living outside the community, or being older than the other children. The teacher can now be sensitive to structuring situations in which the isolate can interact with others and share his skills. Sometimes the causes are more complicated, but when they are understood, the teacher can help the child develop necessary social, athletic, or academic skills that will enable him to enter into the mainstream of the group's social system. Isolation may also be the result of attitudes toward minority-group members. In that case, the teacher should focus on *group* attitudinal and behavioral changes instead of changes within the isolated member.

Fiske and Cox (1960), Hollander (1965), Lindzey and Borgatta (1954), and Reynolds (1966) have offered evidence which suggests that sociometric peer rating is one of the most dependable rating techniques. It not only assesses the present status of the group but also acts as a valuable tool for measuring the effectiveness of teacher intervention.

Another use of sociometrics, infrequently practiced, acts as feedback to the teacher's behavior. Often the teacher consciously or unconsciously praises or rebukes the same children. This habit could be corroborated or disproved by asking the class to "Write the name of a class member whom Ms. Jones likes best" or "Write the name of the class member whom Ms. Jones does not like." If the teacher receives a variety of names in response to these questions, she is not isolating the same children. If only one or two names are reported by the class, the teacher actually may be betraying her own preferences, causing the other class members to feel rejected or anonymous.

Dyadic interaction analysis. Brophy and Good (1969) devised this system to identify and measure interactions occurring between a particular student and the classroom teacher. Observations are gathered in daily sessions over a period of time. A coding system is used to record the five types of dyadic interactions identified by Brophy and Good and to note the duration of each interaction. The system also indicates who initiated the interaction and clarifies the order of events. The five interaction classes are: (1) *response opportunities,* those occasions when the student is responding to a question from the teacher; (2) *recitation,* activities such as oral reading or giving an oral report, when the child will be talking (appropriately) for a relatively long period of time; (3) *procedural contacts,* interactions related to "administrivia" and the general functioning of the classroom; (4) *work-related contacts,* contacts that follow the student's completion of an activity;

and (5) *behavioral contacts*, contacts involving discipline and behavior management. This system is especially useful in situations where knowledge is needed of the interaction between a single student and the teacher.

Flanders' interaction analysis categories. The Flanders system (Flanders, 1970) does not focus on any one child's interactions with the teacher. Instead, it codes and analyzes interactions between the teacher and all the students in the class. It is a system which is more valuable for teachers who wish to modify their own behavior in the classroom than for teachers who are interested in those few children who are exhibiting behavior problems. Flanders identifies ten behaviors which are recorded in 4-second intervals. The ten behaviors include seven teacher responses and initiators, two student behaviors, and a no-behavior or silence category. The teacher responses include: (1) accepting students' feelings, (2) praising or encouraging students, and (3) accepting/using students' ideas. Teacher initiators are: (4) asking questions, (5) lecturing, (6) giving directions, and (7) criticizing. The two student behaviors are: (8) responding to the teacher and (9) initiating talk or conversation. The final category is: (10) silence or confusion. Observation periods should be short, perhaps a maximum of 30 minutes at a time, and data should be taken for several days.

The Florida climate and control system. This approach (Soar, Soar, and Ragosta, 1971) is most elaborate and would take considerable time to learn to use properly because of the excessive numbers and kinds of codes that are employed. It is difficult to imagine a teacher using this system to gather information for personal purposes, although its thoroughness makes it ideal for use in research projects when trained observers can be employed. In addition to coding more than 50 incidences of student and teacher interaction, the Florida system also codes variables related to the physical environment of the classroom, including the size and type of class, the nature of the classroom activity at the time of the observation, the student and teacher tasks, the structure of the classroom, the seating arrangement, and the use and type of various displays in the classroom.

Ecological assessment. Ecological assessment is a procedure that is gaining popularity. It assesses the child's status in the various "ecologies" or environments in which he functions. Within the school setting, the teacher can assume that children change ecologies each time they change classrooms, teachers, or even specific areas within the same classroom (e.g., when children move from a supervised reading group to an art interest center). On a few occasions, the teacher may also examine nonschool ecologies such as home, church, and various clubs.

Laten and Katz (1975) have defined five phases in conducting an ecological assessment. These include (1) assimilating referral data, (2) identifying ecological expectations, (3) organizing behavioral descriptions, (4) summarizing data, and (5) establishing goals. The first phase, referral, involves gathering broad intake data from each of the ecologies in which the child functions. Of particular interest at this time is the degree of success which the child enjoys in each ecology. The expectations or requirements that each ecology demands of the child are identified in the second phase. What level of academic proficiency is expected? What social behaviors are required? Are there any special demands? In general, the teacher attempts to learn what things the child must do in each ecology in order to succeed and meet the requirements. Behavior descriptions are organized during the third stage. What does the child do? How does he behave? What skills does he possess and use? Particular attention is given to determining the child's behaviors with regard to the expectations which were identified in the preceding phase. Descriptions are also gathered of the professional skills and support services that each ecology can provide. The data are then summarized. Finally, goals are established for the child and for the professionals within each ecology. Reasonable goals for improvement are defined for the child as well as guidelines for the material and personnel support that will be provided in each category. In addition to Laten and Katz, the reader is referred to Wiederholt, Hammill, and Brown (1978) for a summary of the ecological assessment process.

Standardized Tests of Personality

Occasionally, a teacher will be provided with the results of standardized tests of personality or character which have been administered to a child. These are usually found in cumulative folders of children who have been referred to another professional in the school or to an agency specializing in disturbed or disruptive children. In assessing a referral, school counselors, psychologists, and other mental health specialists often use standardized personality measures as well as many of the observational techniques and checklists which have already been described in this chapter. Personality tests are rarely, if ever, given by classroom teachers. However, since the results of tests are frequently shared with them, teachers should probably have some basic information about commonly used personality measures.

One broad category of personality testing involves the use of self-report devices, e.g., sentence-completion tests or checklists completed by the child. Sentence-completion tests contain sentence stems that the child is asked to complete. Typical sentence stems might be:

The thing I like most about school is _____.

My mother _____.

I am afraid when _____.

Personality inventories might also be included in an assessment of a problem area. These tests present the child with a series of statements, e.g., "I am happy," "People usually like me," which the child rates as true, false, or some noncommital response ("Not sure," "Cannot say"), or with a series of questions (e.g., "Are you frequently ill?" "Do you like to attend parties?" to which the child responds yes or no). Tests of this type include the Minnesota Multiphasic Personality Inventory (MMPI) (Hathaway and McKinley, 1951), the California Test of Personality (Thorpe, Clark, and Tiegs, 1942), and the Bell Adjustment Inventory (1961). Locus-of-control tests, such as the Bialer Children's Locus of Control Scale (1961) or the Children's Intellectual Achievement Responsibility Questionnaire (Crandall, Kathovsky, and Crandall, 1965), are also classified in this category.

Projective instruments constitute another major type of standardized personality measure. Cronbach (1970) asserts that these instruments are of two types, tests in which the type of problem solving is important (stylistic tests) and tests in which the content of the solution is important (thematic tests). The Rorschach Inkblot Test (Rorschach, 1954) and the Bender Visual Motor Gestalt Tests (Bender, 1938) are stylistic. The Thematic Apperception Test (TAT) (Murray, 1943) and the Children's Apperception Test (Bellak and Bellak, 1961) are thematic in nature. In projective testing the child is presented with a stimulus such as an inkblot, a drawing, or a picture and is then asked to describe what is seen or to tell a story about the picture. Analyses of children's drawings are also frequently included in these assessments. The Draw-A-Person (Urban, 1963) and House–Tree–Person (Buck, 1948) Tests are popular examples. Drawings from the Bender may also be used. Rough standards for interpretation are usually included in the manuals accompanying these measures. Yet, even when these are available, the results of projective testing are quite subjective. They are, therefore, highly dependent on the competence and experience of the examiner. After studying the extent to which the use of these projective tests yielded valuable information, Kessler (1966) concluded that the derived information can usually be obtained from other sources, notably from teacher assessment. For a more detailed discussion of projective testing, the reader is referred to Anastasi (1968), Kessler (1966), Thorndike and Hagen (1969), and Ullmann and Krasner (1969).

MANAGING PROBLEM BEHAVIORS

The intervention strategies about to be presented have become strongly associated with specific schools of thought. For instance, the various behavior modification strategies were developed and are used primarily by individuals holding a behavioral point of view, while a technique such as life-space interviewing evolved from the work of analytically oriented professionals. Analytic professionals often scoff at the uses of behavior modification, and the behaviorists almost invariably advise against the use of analytic techniques.

To us, the division of management techniques according to discrete philosophical categories seems to be a useless activity that will only reduce the number of tools available for use by today's teachers. We believe that each of the techniques described in this section has value in some situations and that all of them are well within the teacher's ability to use.

The first important aspect of an intervention plan (i.e., establishing a goal for behavioral improvement and assessing the current level of the behavior problem) has been discussed earlier. In this section five methods for managing behavior are described: behavior modification; contracting; Long and Newman's techniques for managing surface behaviors; Trieschman's strategies for managing temper tantrums; life-space interviewing; and projective techniques such as role playing, play therapy, puppetry, and art and music therapy. Commercially available programs that purport to assist in the development of children's affective domains will also be reviewed.

Behavior Modification

Rationale. Classroom management, consequence management, or behavior modification has its roots with the behavioral learning theorists, Thorndike, Pavlov, Watson, and Jones. Ayllon (1965) and Ferster and Skinner (1957) expanded and refined the theory and popularized its clinical use, enabling the behavioral specialist to use it in modifying deviant behavior. Clinical experimentation with individual children and adults brought this approach into the foreground in the 1960s, with the renewed interest in the interaction between people and their environment. In short, behavior modification is a systematic, highly structured approach to altering behavior. Its use will have the effect of strengthening, weakening, or maintaining target behaviors. For a more detailed description of the specific techniques involved, the reader is referred to Hall's (1971a, 1971b, 1971c) series of pamphlets entitled *Behavior Modification,* to Miller's (1975) *Principles of Everyday Behavior Analysis,* and to Axelrod's (1977) *Behavior Modification for the Classroom Teacher.*

Procedures. A plan to modify a target behavior is comprised of four phases: (1) the acquisition of baseline data, (2) the selection and implementation of a particular modification technique, (3) the verification of results, and (4) the application of the program in the classroom.

1. *Taking baseline data.* The selection of any intervention technique is predicated upon the assumption that the teacher has already defined the target behavior and has taken "baseline" data regarding its frequency or duration. Hall's direct observation techniques described on pages 214–219 are employed often in gathering baseline information. To ensure a representative sample of a child's behavior, five measurement periods are usually devoted to collecting baseline data. The effects of intervention strategies can then be determined objectively by comparing the baseline with subsequent increases or decreases in the targeted behaviors. The data graphed in Figure 6–1 represent baseline data.

2. *Selecting a treatment.* Reinforcement and punishment are the two basic treatments in behavior modification. These will be discussed in some detail in this section. Extinction, differential reinforcement, shaping, discrimination training, generalization, modeling, and token economies will also be presented.

a. *Reinforcement.* A "reinforcer" is any event that occurs after a behavior and that increases the frequency or duration of the behavior and/or increases the likelihood that the behavior will reoccur (Hall, 1971b). The graph depicting the frequency of a behavior that is being reinforced will show an upward trend. Teachers may assume that being smiled at, receiving an A grade, or being given 5 minutes of free time are reinforcing events, at least to most children; but this conclusion is only justified when there is an increase in the behaviors which these events follow. In fact, the teacher will quickly discover that many children who exhibit problem behaviors are not reinforced by the "usual" things.

Some behaviorists will refine this definition of reinforcement by describing its negative and positive instances. For instance, the reader may have encountered the terms "negative reinforcement" (e.g., a reinforcement procedure in which something aversive or negative is removed from the environment) and "positive reinforcement" (e.g., a reinforcement procedure in which something pleasant or positive is added to the environment). These refined definitions can be quite confusing. Therefore, we have elected to use Hall's definition cited above because it is simple, practical, and straightforward.

Observation of children will probably give the teacher ample ideas of things which are likely to be rewarding for them. Additional information can be obtained by asking individual children to complete an interest inventory or by directly asking children what they like to do. The teacher can then select a potential reinforcer from the lists that have been developed. If the event proves to be reinforcing, that is, the target behavior increases, the teacher will continue to use the reinforcer, alternating it occasionally with other reinforcers to prevent the pupil from becoming tired of "the same old thing." Overuse of a reinforcer will eventually result in satiation and in the loss of reinforcement power. If the event does not prove to be a reinforcer (i.e., if the target behavior does not increase), the teacher must select another potential reinforcer from the student's reinforcement menu.

The reinforcer may be primary or secondary. Examples of primary reinforcers are the following:

Food	Playing ball in the gym
Penny prizes	Drawing paper
A drink of water	Crayons
Lavatory privileges	Chewing gum

Secondary reinforcers are social as opposed to tangible or physical. Following are several examples:

Receiving a star or an A
Moving one's seat close to the teacher
Verbal praise
Sending a praising note home to parents
A pat on the shoulder
A hug

It should be reemphasized that one of the goals of behavior modification is to encourage a child or class of children to work for social reinforcement. Thus, whenever food or toys are given as a consequence, they must be accompanied by social reinforcement—verbal praise, a smile, a star, or a hug. In doing this, the primary reinforcement becomes associated with social approval. Eventually, the social reinforcement will have the same effect as a tangible item.

Reinforcement can be delivered on either a ratio or an interval schedule, and in both cases the arrangement or reinforcement can be fixed or variable. With *ratio* schedules, the number of responses emitted is important. The rate of reinforcement is largely self-controlled, because the more behaviors that the students emit, the more reinforcement they will receive. For this reason, ratio schedules usually yield fairly high rates of responding. *Interval* schedules, however, deliver reinforcement after a specified amount of time has elapsed, rather than after a particular number of behaviors. Reinforcement on interval schedules is controlled by the teacher, not by the student; a set amount of time must pass before reinforcement can be delivered, regardless of the number of behaviors students have emitted. Consequently, interval schedules tend to yield low rates of responding. On a *fixed* schedule, reinforcement occurs at a regular interval or after a set number of responses. Fixed schedules are characterized by pauses in responding after reinforcement, because the children know when reinforcement will occur. Reinforcement in *variable* schedules, however, occurs at irregular intervals or after varying numbers of responses. Variable schedules are therefore characterized by fairly steady rates of responding, because the children are not certain just when reinforcement will be delivered.

Thus, reinforcement can be of four varieties: fixed ratio, variable ratio, fixed interval, and variable interval. Behaviors reinforced on *fixed ratio* schedules would result in high rates of behavior with pauses. Behaviors reinforced on *variable ratio* schedules would have high steady rates of responding. *Fixed interval* schedules would yield low rates of responding with pauses. *Variable interval* schedules would result in low steady rates of responding. Cumulative graphs of typical behavior patterns on each of these schedules are shown in Figure 6–8.

On a continuous fixed ratio schedule (CFR), every behavior or response is reinforced. This is a valuable schedule for stimulating behaviors that may not occur frequently. On the other hand, it is an inefficient means of maintaining behaviors, because the acquired behavior disappears rapidly when reinforcement is withdrawn. The behaviors that we exhibit in using vending machines are frequently cited as examples of those maintained on a CFR schedule. The insertion of a quarter into a pop machine is almost always rewarded with a can of soda. This is CFR: every behavior is reinforced. If the machine is broken, however, the insertion of a quarter will not be reinforced by the appearance of a can of soda. One might insert a second quarter, but it is unlikely that an individual would continue to put money into the machine. Because of this, one of the intermittent schedules described below is preferred for maintaining a behavior after it has been acquired on a CFR schedule.

On a fixed ratio schedule (FR), reinforcement follows a fixed number of responses. For example, a behavior that is reinforced on an FR-3 schedule would be reinforced after every third response (i.e., after the third, sixth, ninth, twelfth, etc., behaviors). In fact, CFR could also be called an FR-1 schedule. Piecework is an example of behaviors maintained on an FR schedule. Fruit pickers who are paid by the basket are reinforced on an FR schedule, as are children who receive free time after completing a set amount of work. An FR schedule results in high rates of behavior with pauses after reinforcement has been delivered. On a variable ratio schedule (VR), reinforcement follows an average number of responses. On a VR-3 schedule, reinforcement might follow any behaviors, as long as the average number of responses per reinforcement is three. Gambling on slot machines is a common example of behavior that is maintained on a VR schedule. The

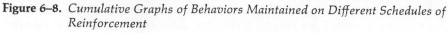

Figure 6–8. *Cumulative Graphs of Behaviors Maintained on Different Schedules of Reinforcement*

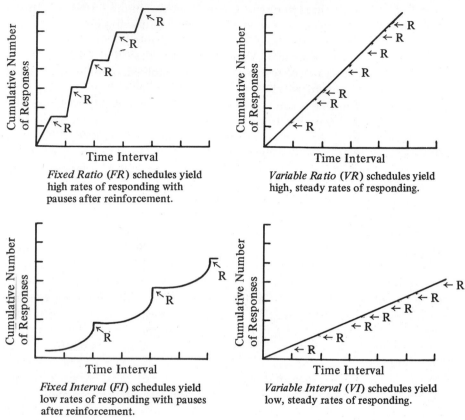

Fixed Ratio (FR) schedules yield high rates of responding with pauses after reinforcement.

Variable Ratio (VR) schedules yield high, steady rates of responding.

Fixed Interval (FI) schedules yield low rates of responding with pauses after reinforcement.

Variable Interval (VI) schedules yield low, steady rates of responding.

Note: R ↑ indicates when reinforcement was delivered.

machines are calibrated to provide reinforcement (a jackpot) after an average number of coins has been inserted. A VR schedule results in a high, steady rate of responding.

On a fixed interval schedule (FI), reinforcement follows the first behavior to occur after a fixed period of time has elapsed. FI-2 minutes means that reinforcement will follow the first behavior to occur after 2 minutes, 4 minutes, 6 minutes, and so on. It does not matter if the student emits one behavior or one hundred behaviors during the 2-minute interval; reinforcement will only occur after the allotted time has passed. The FI schedule yields a low response rate with pauses after reinforcement. On a variable interval schedule (VI), reinforcement follows the first behavior to occur after an average amount of time has passed. This schedule yields low steady rates of behavior. Reinforcing incompatible responses involves rewarding action that is incompatible with the bothersome behavior: for example, talking aloud. The teacher decides to reward a child for completing ten arithmetic problems. In order to accomplish this task and to obtain the reward, the child is too busy to talk. The desired behavior is incompatible with talking aloud. Not only does this approach reduce disturbing behavior, but it also increases desirable academic performance (Table 6–1). Although reinforcing incompatible responses has not received as much emphasis as other behavior-modification techniques, it appears to be a most applicable and effective procedure for classroom use.

Regardless of the reinforcement schedule which a teacher elects to employ, it is imperative that reinforcement be delivered as quickly as possible to avoid reinforcing the wrong behavior. The child should know why reinforcement is delivered. It will help, if the teacher verbalizes this as the points, tokens, etc., are delivered (e.g., "Good, Billie! You worked quietly for 2 minutes"). It is also important to remember that the reinforcement is delivered *only* as a consequence of the desired behavior.

If free time is the reinforcer which is being used, then free time should not be available to the target child in his regular daily schedule.

b. *Punishment.* A "punisher" is any event that follows a behavior and that decreases the frequency or duration of the behavior and/or decreases the likelihood that the behavior will reoccur (Hall, 1971b). The frequency graph of a behavior that is being punished will show a downward trend. Again, the assumption that such things as expulsion from school, low grades, or standing in the hall are punishing must be proved. Let's look at a brief example. Brett swears in class and his teacher decides to punish this behavior by sending him to the principal's office. If Brett's swearing increases, the teacher must assume that going to the principal's office is, in fact, reinforcing for Brett, not punishing.

Earlier we discussed negative and positive reinforcement. The reader may also encounter descriptions of two punishment procedures. That is,

Table 6–1. *Simultaneous Effects of Reinforcing Incompatible Responses*

Target Behavior	Behavioral Results
Disturbing, annoying	Decrease
Desirable academic performance	Increase

punishment can be achieved by adding something aversive to the environment or by removing some pleasurable consequence. The important thing for the teacher to note is if the target behavior decreases.

The teacher will select a punishment procedure if the goal is to decrease a behavior. A reinforcement procedure will be used to increase a behavior. Obviously, the precise definition of the target behavior is crucial to this. For instance, a teacher could elect to reinforce a child for only talking with permission, to punish the same child for talking without permission, or to do both. In the vast majority of instances, it is more desirable to reinforce than to punish a child. Whenever punishment is to be used, it should be accompanied by reinforcement if at all possible. Punishing a behavior tells the student only that the behavior is unacceptable; it does not, in any way, indicate which behavior(s) is/are considered appropriate.

The effectiveness of a punisher is governed by many of the same variables which effect reinforcers. Punishers will be more powerful if they are delivered immediately, if the student knows why they are delivered, and if delivery of punishment is contingent upon a specific behavior. In addition, punishers and reinforcers are most effective when they are not overused (e.g., when the child is not satiated).

Punishment has the effect of arresting or suppressing behavior without eliminating or extinguishing it. It is beneficial only when applied to specific acts (running out into the street) rather than to generalized situations (being a naughty child). Momentarily stopping an undesirable behavior has positive effects when it is accompanied by the demonstration and reinforcement of alternative responses.

The teacher must be aware of the possible negative effects of using punishment. The emotional side effects, such as guilt, fear, withdrawal, and frustration, may lead to other maladaptive behaviors. In addition, the punishing teacher may serve as a negative, aggressive model for other children.

c. *Extinction*. Extinction occurs when a reinforcing event is withdrawn and the behavior which it followed decreases. For example, Carolee frequently talks without permission and is corrected by the teacher. If Carolee's talking without permission increases, we can assume that the teacher's corrections reinforced the unwanted behavior. Extinction would occur if Carolee's talking out behavior decreased after the teacher withdrew the apparent reinforcement (the corrections) and ignored the talking out. As teachers, we often unwittingly reinforce undesirable behaviors, as Carolee's teacher did. Extinction, then, is a tool that can be invaluable.

d. *Differential reinforcement*. Differential reinforcement involves two or more different responses: one response is reinforced and the other(s) is/are extinguished. For example, Marty frequently made self-deprecatory remarks (one response), only rarely noting something that he did well (a second response). His teacher ignored the negative remarks (extinction) and reinforced the positive remarks (by attending to them). Eventually, Marty spoke more highly of himself as a result of differential reinforcement. Differential reinforcement is valuable because its use reduces or eliminates undesirable behaviors while simultaneously encouraging behaviors considered to be appropriate.

e. *Shaping.* Shaping is the differential reinforcement of successive approximations of a behavior. Let's consider the example of Karen, a first grader who is out of her seat 60 percent of the time in the reading period. Using differential reinforcement, the teacher extinguished Karen's out-of-seat behavior (by ignoring it) and reinforced her in-seat behavior (by praising it). The goal for Karen is to be in her seat throughout the reading period. Successive approximations of this goal would be increasing percentages of time spent in her seat to receive reinforcement, perhaps 50 percent, then 55 percent, and so on. The final goal (i.e., for her to be in seat 100 percent during reading) would be achieved through a shaping process. In fact, education itself is primarily a process of shaping.

f. *Discrimination training.* Discrimination training involves a single behavior which is reinforced in the presence of one stimulus and is extinguished in the presence of other stimuli. For instance, Matt is reinforced for responding "two" when he is asked to supply the answer to "1 + 1 = _____." However, that same response ("two") is extinguished when Matt is asked to supply the answer to all other questions, such as "2 + 3 = _____" and "1 + 2 = _____." Discrimination training has occurred here as well as with the freshmen who learn that they may use the pencil sharpener whenever they want to in Ms. Penny's English I class but that they must get permission to use it in Mr. Schroeder's algebra class. Discrimination training might also be used to teach a retarded adolescent that kissing is acceptable with some people (e.g., with relatives) but that it is not acceptable with strangers, on the job, etc.

g. *Generalization.* Generalization is the occurrence of a discriminated response (e.g., one learned through discrimination training) in the presence of a novel or unknown stimulus. Matt has also learned (through discrimination training) to respond "red" when he sees red circles and squares and to refrain from making that response when he sees circles and squares of other colors. Generalization has occurred if Matt responds "red" when presented with novel stimuli such as red triangles and does not respond "red" when presented with blue, green, or yellow triangles. Generalization is the desired outcome of any intervention plan, regardless of the methodology employed. Students must be able to generalize what is learned, or every situation they encounter will be new. The following steps will facilitate the generalization of a student's behavior from one school situation to another or from school to home.

1. Place the behavior on intermittent reinforcement.
2. Fade the reinforcer from primary to social.
3. Have another adult (parent or student volunteer) participate in the treatment.
4. Have an extinction period, returning to no treatment.
5. Contract with the student to monitor his behavior by keeping his own record and turning it in at the end of the week for reinforcement.
6. Use tokens to bridge the gap between primary and social reinforcement and to encourage delay in gratification.

It is understandable that the time requirements for this technique appear to be lengthy; they are essential, however, for successful application. Once this procedure has been practiced, its time efficiency increases markedly.

h. *Modeling.* In modeling, verbal instructions or imitation are used to teach a child a new behavior. According to Miller (1975), instructional training involves three steps: a verbal description of the desired behavior, a demonstration by the learner of the described behavior, and reinforcement following the demonstration of the behavior. Imitation training also consists of three stages: demonstration by the teacher of the target behavior, an imitation by the learner of the demonstrated behavior, and reinforcement of the imitation. Instructional training is said to take place when, for instance, the teacher says, "Please sit at your desk," the child complies, and the teacher smiles and says, "Thank you." Imitation training occurs when the teacher makes the short *a* sound, the child imitates it, and the teacher says, "Good."

Modeling also occurs when one child observes that another child who is engaging in instructional or imitation learning is being reinforced (or punished) for complying (or not complying). The child who observes that Mark is permitted to go to recess as soon as he has complied with the teacher's instruction to clear off his desk is quite likely to follow suit and clear off his desk, too (if recess is reinforcing). Likewise, the same behavior will result if he sees that the recess privilege is withdrawn from a child who failed to comply with this request.

i. *Token economies.* Reinforcers may be delivered in "token economies," settings where the children receive tokens with which they can later buy tangible items or privileges. The child completes a task (his "job"), such as correctly working five arithmetic problems or sitting quietly in the reading circle, and is paid at the completion of his job with a token. Poker chips, pieces of paper, and stars are examples of items that can be used as tokens. Tokens (like money) are then exchanged in the economy for things the child wants: 5 tokens may buy a piece of gum, 10 may buy a luncheon date with the teacher or some free time, 50 may buy a field trip, and 500 may buy a day off.

There are a number of advantages to a token economy system. The problem of satiation is avoided because the "store" where tokens are exchanged provides a wide variety of reinforcers on the "menu." The system also eases the problem of thinning the reinforcement schedule, because a child can eventually do more work for each token. Five minutes of independent work may earn one token today. A month later, it may take 6 or 7 minutes of independent work to earn a token. Token systems demand that the children exercise some delay of gratification while providing immediate, tangible reinforcement.

Verification of results. Most teachers will readily recognize the effects of the intervention and will not see the need to experimentally verify the results. In some instances, however, it is important to demonstrate formally that the changes achieved through a behavior-modification plan are not the result of other happenings. It is possible, for instance, for Sandy's teacher to instigate a behavior-modification program to reduce the girl's aggressive behavior. The behaviors may disappear, but there is no proof that the change in behavior has resulted from the program which the teacher instituted rather than from a visit by Sandy's grandmother or other variables at home. A reversal or return to baseline is one form of verification. This involves a cessation of the intervention program for a brief period to see if the target behavior begins to approximate its previous baseline level. The program is then reinstituted and the results are verified if the behavior again changes. Many teachers object to using the reversal procedure because they believe they are "pulling the rug out from under" a pupil by reinforcing a particular behavior and then momentarily withdrawing the reinforcement. Multiple baseline is another verification procedure that is frequently utilized. This procedure involves the use of the same intervention program for several children exhibiting similar behavior problems or for one child exhibiting a variety of behavior problems. If similar results are achieved on each of the multiple baselines after intervention has been initiated, verification has taken place. Certainly behavior modification results of an experimental or research nature should be verified through these or other means, although the classroom teacher may find these procedures to be too cumbersome and time consuming to implement on a regular basis.

Classroom application. There is an abundance of research reporting the significant effects of behavior modification with different populations of children. Since it is impossible here to describe all the research, several studies are cited that have particular relevance to problem children. Token economies were set up in most of these studies, where children received points, poker chips, etc., to be traded in at a specified time for desirable reinforcers.

Wadsworth (1971) investigated the efficacy of two different types of instructional approaches to increase motivation in reading for learning-disabled boys. He found that the reinforcement technique was significantly more effective than clinical tutoring in facilitating increased reading motivation and achievement. In another study (Glavin, Quay, and Werry, 1971), a token economy was established in a classroom of poorly disciplined children. It was successful in decreasing deviant behaviors (such as jumping out of the seat), while simultaneously increasing attention and academic performance. Perline and Levinsky (1968) and Sulzbacker and Hauser (1968) report similar results with mentally retarded children.

In a class of seventeen emotionally disturbed nine-year-olds, O'Leary and Becker (1967) attempted to use a token reinforcement system to eliminate deviant behaviors. They were successful in decreasing these behaviors from a range of 66 to 91 percent to a range of 3 to 32 percent. Preschool problem children were involved in a study by Allen, Turner, and Everett (1970). Using contingency reinforcement, disruptive behaviors (hitting, kicking, spitting) were significantly reduced while appropriate behaviors, such as play and motor skills, were increased.

Contracting

Contracting for behavioral change is a popular and effective method for giving students some responsibility for changing their own behavior. A contract is a *two*-way agreement. The child agrees to behave in a certain fashion or to do a certain task at or within a given period of time. The teacher (or parent or other school personnel) agrees to deliver specific kinds of support during the contract and a particular payoff when the contract has been fulfilled. Sample behavioral contracts are shown in Figures 6–9 and 6–10. For additional sample contracts, the reader is also referred to Kohfeldt's (1974) excellent little book, *Contracts*.

Long and Newman's Techniques for Managing Surface Behaviors

Rationale. Perhaps the most succinct discussion of the management of surface behaviors is offered by Long and Newman (1971). These techniques are intended for use as "stop-gap" devices to prevent escalation of behavior problems or to avoid negative contagion. If necessary, they may be explored in depth (clinical exploitation) at a later time.

Figure 6–9. *Formal Contract.* [Reprinted with the permission of the author and publisher of P. Hawisher, *The Resource Room: Access to Excellence* (Lancaster, S.C.: S.C. Region V Educational Service Center, 1975).]

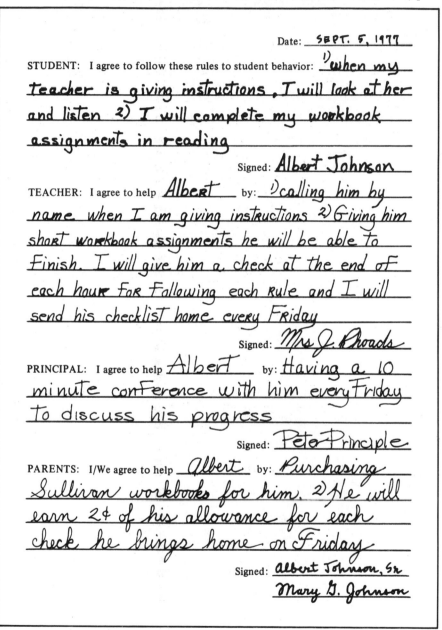

Date: SEPT. 5, 1977

STUDENT: I agree to follow these rules to student behavior: 1) when my teacher is giving instructions, I will look at her and listen 2) I will complete my workbook assignments in reading

Signed: Albert Johnson

TEACHER: I agree to help Albert by: 1) calling him by name when I am giving instructions 2) Giving him short workbook assignments he will be able to finish. I will give him a check at the end of each hour for following each rule and I will send his checklist home every Friday

Signed: Mrs. J. Rhoads

PRINCIPAL: I agree to help Albert by: Having a 10 minute conference with him every Friday to discuss his progress

Signed: Pete Principle

PARENTS: I/We agree to help Albert by: Purchasing Sullivan workbooks for him. 2) He will earn 2¢ of his allowance for each check he brings home on Friday

Signed: Albert Johnson, Sr.
Mary G. Johnson

Figure 6–10. *Informal Contracts.* [Reprinted with the permission of the author and publisher of P. Hawisher, *The Resource Room: Access to Excellence* (Lancaster, S.C.: S.C. Region V Educational Service Center, 1975).]

Date: *October 12, 1974*

STUDENT: *I agree to use only good student language today. When I talk I will speak quietly.*

Signed: *Phillip Carson*

TEACHER: *Phillip* will earn the following reward: *to wear the Good Citizenship Button tomorrow*

Signed: *Mr. Stanley*

Date: *November 13, 1975*

I will *not hit Susie this week*

I will *say "darn it" when I am angry*

I will _____

Signed: *Jim*

I will arrange for: *Jim to see a movie on Friday if he has 19 teacher signatures by that time.*

Signed: *Mrs Reagan, Counselor*

Monday	Tuesday	Wednesday	Thursday	Friday
JRB	JRB	JRB	JRB	JRB
LM	LM	LM	LM	LM
R Trayer	R Trayer	R Trayer	R Trayer	R Trayer
VFT	VFT	VFT	VFT	VFT

Procedures. Twelve interference techniques are described: planned ignoring, signal interference, proximity control, interest boosting, tension decontamination through humor, hurdle lessons, restructuring the classroom program, support from routine, direct appeal to value areas, removing seductive objects, antiseptic bouncing, and physical restraint. *Planned ignoring* closely resembles the extinction procedure, which was described in the previous section. The basic assumption is that many behaviors will disappear more quickly if they are ignored than if the teacher attempts to intervene in some way. *Signal interference* involves the use of some cue, usually a nonverbal one, which will let the student(s) know that particular behaviors should be abandoned. The "school marm" look which most teachers develop is an example of signal interference. *Proximity control* is a device that teachers have often used. The teacher's presence in a potential trouble spot is usually sufficient to stop many surface behaviors which are disrupting the program (such as whispering and note passing) and to prevent the spread of these behaviors. *Interest boosting* and *hurdle lessons* are very similar techniques. In the former, the teacher makes an attempt to demonstrate interest in the child as an individual. The latter involves individual attention, too, though it usually centers around providing academic assistance to alleviate frustration. *Restructuring the classroom program* and *support from routine* are opposite techniques. Both require that the teacher be sensitive to needs within the classroom: Do the students require a fresh outlook or will a familiar, no-surprises approach be more supportive? *Direct appeal to value areas* can be effective only when the teacher and the students share the same values or when the teacher is aware of those values which the students have internalized. *Removing seductive objects* has a direct relationship to the props which Redl discussed and which were presented earlier in this chapter. It is frequently easier to remove seductive objectives than it is to manage the behaviors which they may elicit from children. *Antiseptic bouncing* is used to remove a child from the classroom without any punitive overtones. It is a useful technique to prevent the spread of contagious behaviors such as giggling or false hiccoughing or to give an embarrassed or angry child an opportunity to regain control. Usually the child is asked to run an errand or to perform some other chore outside the class. *Tension decontamination through humor* reflects the power of a sense of humor. Many tense situations can be defused by a single good-natured or humorous remark from the teacher. The final management technique, *physical restraint*, is used on those rare occasions when a child has lost control completely. Physical restraint is intended to prevent the child from injuring himself or others and to communicate the teacher's willingness to provide external control. Most teachers already use many, if not all, of these management techniques. Their power as intervention strategies will be increased if teachers will use them consciously and on a planned basis.

Trieschman's Strategy for
Managing Temper Tantrums

Rationale. Trieschman (1969) hypothesizes that a temper tantrum is not a single behavior but a series of events with definite stages. He identified six stages, which were given descriptive names: the Rumbling and Grumbling stage, the Help–Help stage, the Either–Or stage, the No–No stage, the Leave Me Alone stage, and the Hangover stage. Tantrums are managed by dealing with the behaviors in each stage. If the early stages are managed appropriately, the author asserts that tantrums might occur less frequently or might possibly be prevented from occurring at all.

Procedures. During the Rumbling and Grumbling stage, the child is generally grumpy. He appears to be "dribbling (as opposed to gushing) hostility" (p. 176). The child is seeking an issue over which to throw the tantrum he has already decided to have. In many instances, the issue which the child selects is one that lacks a satisfactory solution. For instance, the child may demand that an irreparably broken toy be mended immediately. Management is aided by identifying the pattern of Rumbling and Grumbling. Frequently, the tantrum issue will have a similar time and place (e.g., right before lunch or only in the P.E. class), which will fall into a recognizable pattern. The teacher who recognizes the pattern can usually help the child to verbalize the problem rather than to act out the "front issue" for the problem. This is usually accomplished through life-space interviewing, a technique which will be discussed later.

The Help–Help stage is the first really loud, noisy stage of the tantrum. The child "has found his issue and is now signaling his need for help. The signal he uses is usually a very visible and deliberate rule-breaking act" (p. 179), which is designed to attract adult attention. The child senses that he is losing internal control and is demanding that an authority figure intervene and impose external control. Management primarily involves teaching the child to signal his need for help in a more appropriate manner, to substitute an appropriate signal for the inappropriate rule-breaking signal. It may be necessary at this point to utilize the physical restraint technique described by Long and Newman while verbalizing to the child the teacher's desire to help him control his behavior. It is best, according to Trieschman, to avoid pointing out that the child broke a rule: he knows he broke the rule, for he broke it deliberately.

The Either–Or stage represents the child's attempt to show that he can still control the situation by setting out either–or alternatives. The child is also trying to insult the adult or authority figure who is attempting to help him by making fun of the adult's personal characteristics. The most important part of the management at this stage is to model appropriate anger for the child. "Helpfully modeling reasonable anger is something a child could imitate more easily than boundless patience and complete passivity in the face of fury" (p. 186). Any either–or proposition that can be accepted should be promoted by the adult and additional alternatives may also be proposed.

The No–No stage is the one in which the child will respond negatively to any suggestion or statement by the adult. It is frequently impossible to manage a tantrum that has reached this stage. Sometimes the tantrum can be pushed back to the previous, Either–Or, stage. If good rapport exists between the child and the teacher, it may even be possible to point out the foolishness of the No–No stage by stating questions in such a way that the child actually complies with your wishes by saying, "No." This technique can certainly backfire, however, and should be used with extreme caution so that the child does not come to believe that the teacher is making fun of him or that he is once again "the goat." The noisy part of the tantrum usually dies down at the end of this stage.

The Leave Me Alone stage is relatively quiet and is often mistaken for a return to normal behavior. It is not. The noise is gone and the child may be more amenable to assistance from the adult. The child is not, however, ready to resume interaction with the world and should not be expected to do so. The child's desire to be left alone should be respected, although the adult should remain within eyeshot or earshot to assure the child that external control is still available if it is necessary. As little conversation as possible is advisable at this stage.

During the Hangover stage, two states of affairs may arise. Some children will experience a "clean drunk" after their tantrums. They have no painful memories of the tantrum and appear to have returned to normal. Other children experience a hangover and feel quite guilty and embarrassed about the incident. The memory is painful. The latter condition is desirable. If a child experiences a clean drunk, it may be possible to induce a hangover that can then be exploited, probably through life-space interviewing. Signal words can be devised, as can other alternative behaviors which are more acceptable than tantruming. "Reviewing the sequence of events . . . and learning alternative coping skills is constructive" (p. 192).

Life-Space Interviewing

Rationale. Life-space interviewing (LSI) is a psychoeducationally oriented technique aimed at dealing with the everyday interactional problems that occur in the classroom. Originally designed for use by teachers assigned to cope with crisis situations, LSI can be effectively used within the classroom. Rational and semidirectional in its approach, LSI attempts to structure a situation so that children can work out their own problems. The teacher's role is one of listener and facilitator in the decision making enacted by the children involved. The technique is nonjudgmental and presents immediate concrete consequences to the children without the typical value appeals that adults frequently make in reaction to behavioral outbursts.

Procedure. A description of an actual incident in which LSI was used is perhaps the most effective way of explaining the approach.

> In the middle of a handwriting lesson, Johnny and David suddenly broke out into a violent fight—cursing, yelling, and hitting each other. The teacher told the rest of the class to continue working and asked the two boys involved in the fight to come up and talk about what just happened.

The LSI approach would proceed in the following manner.

Step 1. The teacher asks Johnny what happened, telling David that he will have equal time to explain as soon as Johnny finishes. The aim of this step is to get at each child's *perception* of what happened. The facts are not important, but rather each child's understanding of the incident. At this point the teacher simply listens.

Step 2. Through objective questioning, the teacher tries to determine if what is offered as the boys' explanations for fighting is really the crux of the problem. Are they fighting over the ownership of a pencil, or is this the manifestation of a deeper worry? Frequently, children bring arguments or hostilities to school that have developed at home or at recess. Questioning by the teacher is an attempt to discover how extensive the problem is, without making any interpretations.

Step 3. After the boys have had a chance to thoroughly express their feelings about the fight and why they think it happened, they are asked what they feel they *can* (not *should*) do about it. By asking this, the values of the child are usually brought to the surface. If their suggestions for remedy are acceptable to all three involved, the interview is terminated here. A note of caution to the teacher should be made at this point: do not oververbalize. By being given a structured and guided opportunity to deal with *their* problems, children can often reach an acceptable solution, without extensive suggestions by the teacher.

Step 4. If the problem is not resolved at this point, the teacher takes a more direct role. She points out the reality factors of the situation and the consequences of the behavior if it occurs again. Once more, value judgments are minimized. The teacher should not moralize about the impropriety of cursing and fighting; she should simply say that the rules of the school prohibit fighting in class and explain the consequences.

Step 5. By talking with the boys, their motivation for change can be explored. If there is no discernible remedy for the situation, the teacher can make suggestions, such as breaking the pencil in half or flipping a coin.

Step 6. The final step is to develop a follow-through plan with the boys that includes discussing alternative procedures should the problem arise in the future. Consequences are once again clearly described by the teacher.

Redl and Wineman (1957) list two components of life-space interviewing: emotional first aid on the spot and clinical exploitation of life events. In differentiating these two, Reinert (1976) cites the example of Dennis, a young boy who is challenged in the lunchroom for unruly behavior and who subsequently becomes "unglued," fleeing the cafeteria for his classroom. If the teacher attempts to restructure the crisis situation and enable the boy to return to lunch as quickly and painlessly as possible, this is an example of emotional first aid. If, however, the teacher elected to spend the lunch hour piecing together the precipitating events and relating them to similar events involving Dennis, this would be clinical exploitation.

Emotional first aid has five subcategories. (1) *Drainoff of frustration acidity* is an attempt to remove the "sting" from unexpected disappointment or frustration. (2) *Support for the management of panic, fury, and guilt* is a means of providing temporary support for a child who is unable to deal effectively with feelings of hate, guilt, anxiety, or anger. (3) *Communication maintenance in moments of relationship decay* is an attempt to maintain a thread of communication and to prevent the child from totally withdrawing. (4) *The regulation of behavioral and social traffic* is the consistent application of rules and/or guidelines for appropriate behavior. The final category, (5) *Umpire services*, is an attempt by an impartial adult to referee difficulties between two children or within a single child.

Redl and Wineman also identified five techniques of clinical exploitation, the in-depth analysis of situations in which problem behaviors occur. (1) *Reality rub-in* is an attempt to make the child aware of what really happened in a crisis situation. (2) *Symptom estrangement* helps the child let go of inappropriate behaviors. (3) *Massaging numb value areas* is a technique to stimulate dormant values which are appropriate to a particular situation in which the child finds himself. (4) *New tool salesmanship* is an attempt to "sell" a child on alternative forms of behavior which are more appropriate and/or socially acceptable. (5) *Manipulation of the boundaries of the self* is an attempt to make the child aware of himself as an individual so that he will not be "sucked" unawares into roles or actions defined by others.

The effectiveness of the LSI approach is dependent on the attitudes and behavior of the teacher. Consciously structuring his responses will facilitate positive outcomes. During the interview, a casual and polite atmosphere should be maintained, for this reduces the defensive and hostile feelings of the child or children. The teacher should sit close to the children and avoid towering above them. As much as possible, she should try to appear to be neutral and approachable.

If the teacher knows something about the incident, she should confront the children with this knowledge. This frequently places the problem in its proper perspective and saves time by eliminating the need for each child to give a detailed description of the event. They will readily add their own perceptions of what occurred. The teacher should avoid asking "why" questions, because many children lack the insight or verbal ability to explain their actions.

Many children feel guilty when confronted with their misbehavior; the weightiness of the problem should be minimized for them. By calmly stating that situations like this sometimes do occur, or that no real harm has been done, the teacher reassures the child that she is not such a terrible person. This enables him to more freely "open up" to his teacher. Most important, the children should be listened to, helped to plan the future incidents, and given a chance to ask questions.

The advantages of this approach have been summarized by Redl and Wattenberg (1959) as: (1) clinical exploitation of life events and (2) emotional first aid. The former demonstrates to children that they have alternative ways of dealing with their problems. At the same time, they are encouraged to see the consequences of their behavior in an actual life experience without being subjected to moralizing and punishment. Through neutral and supportive communication between child and teacher, hostilities, frustrations, and guilt are relieved. This emotional "first aid" can help to avoid explosive outbursts later that same day. Because the intervention is immediate, the desire for help and the motivation for change are greatly increased. Life-space interviewing frequently leads to as much growth in the teacher as in the pupils. This is particularly so when teachers and pupils come from different cultural backgrounds. Careful listening on the part of the teacher can lead to insights into the reasons underlying children's behavior.

There are, however, several limitations to this approach that must be described. First, in a class of perhaps twenty to thirty children, the immediate, time-consuming interview may not be feasible. However, if the teacher has confidence in the rationale of LSI, there is no reason why the teacher–pupil interaction cannot be delayed until recess or after school.

LSI requires expert emotional control and sensitivity on the part of the teacher. This sometimes presents the second limitation. If the teacher becomes involved in the emotionalism of the problem, all efforts lose their effectiveness and the technique becomes useless. The final limitation is a subtle one; by removing the child from a 30-to-1 classroom situation to a 2-to-1 personal interaction, the teacher may be reinforcing the negative behavior instead of changing it.

Projective Techniques

Projective techniques frequently utilize supportive media such as puppets, toys, art materials, and music as stimuli which will encourage children to express ("project") feelings which they might not reveal in conversation or interviews. Therapies based on projective theory have been developed largely in clinical practice and are used primarily by specially trained professionals. However, some of these techniques may be used by classroom teachers to highlight a specific problem area or to explore it in depth. In particular, role playing and puppetry are used by classroom teachers, as well as some aspects of art and music therapy. The teacher may also want to be familiar with some of the other common projective techniques because they will be used by members of the professional support team working with seriously disturbed children who are receiving help or therapy outside the classroom. The contents of this section relate to role playing, play therapy, puppetry, and art and music therapy.

Role playing. Role playing is another form of "let's pretend." The children act out situations that involve problems of getting along together. A distinctive version of role playing, called psychodrama, has been developed by Moreno (1946). Psychodrama is usually employed with a severely disturbed individual who is required to come upon a stage and express his real or fantasized feelings and problems. Psychodrama requires the use of a trained therapist because of its explosive nature; therefore, it is not recommended for use in the classroom. However, role playing as a technique for learning new behaviors and skills can be appropriately adapted to the classroom.

Interpersonal problems often find solution through acceptance of criticism or other forms of perceived punishment or rejection. Children can learn how to cope with these experiences by exploring various responses and reactions. One child can portray the role of an angry member of the class, and another child can play himself entering into a potential fight with that child. Through the use of suggestions from the teacher and class members, the child can learn to respond to anger more skillfully and without losing face. This technique can also help physically or mentally handicapped children face real or imagined social reactions without reverting to excessive emotional outbursts.

Harth (1966) applied role playing to a classroom of ten emotionally disturbed children from two public schools in a low socioeconomic area of a southern city. He studied the effects of the therapy on the children's attitudes toward school, their classroom behavior, and their reaction to frustration. During a five-week period, the experimental group engaged in two role-playing sessions weekly. During this time they portrayed school personnel in various problem situations centered around school. After the experimental period, Harth found no change in either the children's attitude toward school or their reaction to frustration. However, classroom behavior of the experimental group did change in a positive direction, while the control group showed no significant change from baseline information.

Although the results of this study indicate a cautious optimism, further studies are needed to demonstrate the effectiveness of this approach with various types and sizes of classes. This is not to imply that the teacher need wait for such substantiation before using role playing within the school setting.

Play therapy. The use of play therapy in the school differs in some ways from play as a psychotherapeutic technique. The former aims to increase the individual's understanding of himself by relating a free situation (play) in which the child is given the opportunity to self-actualize (Alexander, 1971). Axline (1964), an acknowledged authority on the technique of play therapy, states that "the child must first learn self respect and a sense of dignity that grows out of his increasing self-understanding before he can learn to respect the personalities and rights and differences of others" (p. 67). In psychotherapy the aim is to uncover unconscious motivations by interpretive techniques. Both educational and psychotherapeutic play share several common views: (1) the relationship between therapist (or teacher) and the child is the key to emotional growth, and (2) the selection and use of various play activities aids in expressing personal and social needs. The play situation is provided because it is usually the most comfortable one for the child and the most conducive to self-expression.

Play materials are provided for the child, but their use should not be contrived by the therapist. Recommended materials are:

sandbox	basin filled with water
doll house	toy dishes
toy soldiers	toy police and fire trucks
crayons	toy animals
scissors	hammer

Although there are no clear-cut procedures, Kessler (1966, pp. 376–377) restates Axline's eight basic principles of play therapy[1]:

1. The therapist must develop a warm, friendly relationship with the child.

1. From Jane W. Kessler, *Psychopathology of Childhood,* © 1966. By permission of Prentice-Hall, Inc.

2. The therapist accepts the child exactly as he is.
3. The therapist establishes a feeling of permissiveness in the relationship.
4. The therapist is alert to recognize the feelings [of the child] and to reflect the feelings back to the child so that she gains insight into his behavior.
5. The therapist maintains a deep respect for the child's ability to solve his own problems.
6. The child leads the way; the therapist follows.
7. The therapist does not attempt to hurry the therapy along.
8. The therapist establishes only those limitations that are necessary to anchor the therapy to the world of reality and to make the child aware of his responsibility in the relationship.

The effects of play therapy have been equivocal. According to Pumpfrey and Elliot (1970), the efficacy of play therapy is still doubtful. Fleming and Snyder (1947), Fisher (1953), Axline (1947), and Bills (1950) report favorable results from play therapy in relationship to personality adjustment and reading achievement with emotionally disturbed children. In a survey of 37 investigations of the efficacy of psychotherapy with children (many using play therapy), Levitt (1957) noted the absence of differences between treated children and controls. Two thirds of the children evaluated immediately after treatment and three-fourths evaluated at follow-up showed improvement. The statistics were approximately the same for control groups. Levitt concludes that this study fails to support the efficacy of this approach with children. However, the decision to use or not to use play therapy depends on more than reports of efficacy studies; the time required for the process and the size of the class are practical determinants.

Puppetry. Theories that utilize the construct of the "unconscious," as a potent motivator in human behavior recognize the need for expressing and bringing to the level of consciousness unconscious feelings. An effective way of doing this is through the use of puppetry (Woltmann, 1971). The puppets have specific meaning to each child and he is able to project his hate, anger, fears, and desires onto them in a neutral, fantasylike manner. Many of these feelings ordinarily remain suppressed because expression of them in actual life situations is often too threatening to the child. But as Woltmann states: "Puppetry carries with it the reassurance that everything on the stage is only a make-believe affair" (p. 226). To kill the bad guy is acceptable. Not only does he always come to life during the next show, but with each "killing" comes the release of suppressed rage, which often inappropriately releases itself during instructional time.

All that puppetry requires is commercially or homemade puppets and a structure than can serve as a stage. Often the children themselves can create the needed equipment. The puppet characters should combine both fantastic and realistic factors, so the child can easily enter into and identify with the characters and their problems. Woltmann suggests the use of the following types of puppet actors: (1) the hero; (2) a bad mother, often appearing as a witch; (3) a bad father, appearing as a giant; (4) a little boy or girl representing the child's idealized self; and (5) an animal. Other personalities can be added as the children begin to interact in this problem-solving world of fantasy.

Initially, it is best for an adult to act as the puppeteer who follows the commands of the audience. Some children may yell out "Kill the witch! Kill her!" while others shrink away in fear. For the fearful child, it is frequently helpful to bring him behind stage while the acting is going to assure him that it is only make-believe. During the show all pupil commands should be accepted, but afterward alternative solutions to the problems revealed in the fantasy play can be discussed. The technique can frequently dispel intense feelings and contribute to learning alternatives to stereotypic behaviors. The teacher should be careful to resolve the problem broached in the play so that the children are prepared and relaxed for the next activity.

Art and music therapy. The goals of art and music therapy parallel those previously expressed for play therapy, puppetry, and role playing, i.e., to encourage children to express themselves freely and without fear. Music and various art media such as paint and clay may elicit expressions of feelings that would not otherwise surface. Art and music therapy provide nonthreatening situations for children to share their feelings and to release inner tensions.

In art therapy, a wide variety of media should be available in the classroom or therapy room. Freestyle activities such as finger painting, clay sculpting, and drawing will provide unstructured avenues for expression. It is not unusual for teachers to detect some of the problems that children are experiencing by examining their art work. Usually, though, this will only be a confirmation of problems that have already been identified. Teachers are cautioned *not* to use art therapy as a diagnostic tool unless they have had specific training in this area.

Music is often cited as a universal language and it certainly plays an especially important role in the social life of many adolescents. Music can also have a quieting effect on unusually active children and can promote concentration, since it helps to shut out noises that might otherwise be distracting (Reinert, 1976). Aggressive behaviors can be vented through such music activities as dancing; playing drums, rhythm sticks, or sandpaper blocks; and singing action songs. Most youngsters can derive a feeling of success from art and music activities when no judgment of quality is involved.

Commercially Available Programs

Rationale. There has been a noticeable paucity of materials designed to teach affective skills, until recently when several commercial programs have become available. The purpose of most of the kits is to teach children such skills as how to cope, how to label and appropriately express feelings, and how to identify and clarify values. For instruction, they depend heavily on the use of puppetry, role playing, sociodrama, and discussion. Although most of the materials were designed with "normal" children in mind, their use need not be limited solely to this population. Teachers can use portions of the programs which seem appropriate and can integrate them with materials of their own design. To date, there are few data available on the efficacy of these materials. Several of the more popular affective materials are reviewed next.

Programs. Nine programs will be discussed briefly in this section: The Human Development Program (Palomares and Ball, 1974), Target Behavior (Kroth, 1973b), Developing Understanding of Self and Others, D-I (Dinkmeyer, 1970) and D-II (Dinkmeyer, 1973), the Adventures of the Lollipop Dragon (1970), Contact Maturity: Growing Up Strong (1972), Dimensions of Personality (Limbacher, 1969), First Things (Grannis and Schone, 1970), the Child's Series on Psychologically Relevant Themes (Fasler, 1971), and values clarification.

The Human Development Program, popularly known as Magic Circle, is one of the more widely used commercial programs for teaching affective skills. The basic premise of the program is that teacher-led discussions which take place in a structured setting (e.g., in the Magic Circle) will help students to develop richer, more meaningful interrelationships with each other. Manuals and materials are provided for students from age four to age eleven (preschool through sixth grade). Objectives of the Human Development Program include improving self-control, listening skills, and expression; learning the meaning of responsibility, fantasy, and role expectations; and developing a positive self-concept, trust, and satisfactory interpersonal relationships.

Target Behavior is a commercially packaged Q-sorting kit. It contains the formboard, behavioral items, record sheets, and instructions. The materials would be used to isolate target behaviors for change or modification. The Q-sorting technique was discussed earlier in this chapter.

The Developing Understanding of Self and Others (DUSO) kits are designed for use with kindergarteners and first graders (D-I) and for second through fourth graders (D-II). DUSO-I stresses the inquiry method of learning. Stories, puppetry, and discussion are used to promote the eight unit themes: (1) Understanding and Accepting Self; (2) Understanding Feelings; (3) Understanding Others; (4) Understanding Independence; (5) Understanding Goals and Purposeful Behavior; (6) Understanding Mastery, Competence, and Resourcefulness; (7) Understanding Emotional Maturity; and (8) Understanding Choices and Consequences. Daily lesson plans for DUSO activities are presented in the manual. Role playing, puppetry, and listening are the primary activities used to develop the eight themes in DUSO-II. Stimulus posters and situation cards are provided to assist the teacher in initiating discussion around these themes: (1) Towards Self-Identity: Developing Self-Awareness and a positive Self-Concept; (2) Towards Friendship: Understanding Peers; (3) Towards Responsible Interdependence: Understanding Growth from Self-Centeredness to Social Interest; (4) Towards Self-Reliance: Understanding Personal Responsibility; (5) Towards Resourcefulness and Purposefulness: Understanding Personal Motivation; (6) Towards Competence: Understanding Accomplishments; (7) Towards Emotional Stability: Understanding Stress; and (8) Towards Responsible Choice Making: Understanding Values.

The Adventures of the Lollipop Dragon was designed for students in the primary grades. Six filmstrips are included in the kit. They depict stories that emphasize personal relationships and interdependency (e.g., taking turns, sharing with others, and working in groups). The "hero" of the series is the Lollipop Dragon, who inhabits a small kingdom where the economy is based on the production of lollipops. The filmstrips are accompanied by records and cassettes of the stories and by a coloring book, "How the Lollipop Dragon Got His Name."

Contact Maturity: Growing Up Strong was designed for junior and senior high school students with low reading abilities. It stresses a language arts approach, and one of the major goals of the program is to encourage an interest in reading. Poetry, short stories, open-ended stories, posters, and pictures are used to stimulate discussion and values clarification. Students are also encouraged to keep diaries of their daily activities and of their feelings in specific situations.

Dimensions of Personality was written for students in the upper elementary grades (four through six). According to the manual, portions of the program may be suitable for use with low-reading junior and senior high school students as well. It purports to maintain a holistic approach to affective education through which "children will come to understand their physical, intellectual, and emotional growth better" (Reinert, 1976, p. 147).

Provocative questions, posters, pictures, and cartoons are used to stimulate discussion activities.

First Things was designed for first, second, and third graders. Five themes are developed through the use of videotapes, sociodramatics, and role playing. Group interaction and the classification and expression of feelings are stressed. The themes are: (1) Who do you think you are? (2) Guess who's in a group! (3) What happens between people? (4) You got mad: are you glad? (5) What do you expect of others?

The Child's Series on Psychologically Relevant Themes was designed for preschool and primary grade students. The themes are "relevant" within a psychoanalytic orientation. The kit contains six videotapes, each of which tells a story and promotes a major psychodynamic theme. The videotapes are (1) "The Man of the House," in which a young boy is the man of the house in his father's absence and must then relinquish the role when his father returns from a business trip; (2) "All Alone with Daddy," in which a young girl develops a close relationship with her father while her mother is away and then becomes jealous when the mother returns; (3) "Grandpa Died Today," in which a boy's reaction to the death of his grandfather is chronicled; (4) "Don't Worry Dear," in which a young girl is teased about stuttering and develops some immature habits such as bedwetting and thumbsucking; (5) "Boy with a Problem," in which a young boy develops a variety of hypochondriacal symptoms because he is keeping a problem inside himself; and (6) "One Little Girl," in which a little girl learns to compensate for her weaknesses by promoting her strengths.

Values clarification is an affective program, although it is not packaged as a kit. Several authors (such as Fine, 1973, and Weinstein and Fantini, 1970) discuss the uses of a values clarification program in the classroom. The reader is referred to an excellent book, *Values Clarification* by Simon, Howe, and Kirschenbaum (1972), which describes the technique of values clarification and provides activities for the teacher to use. In essence, values clarification is a questioning procedure which "should serve to generate thought regarding what values the student holds to, how the value was acquired, what the pragmatic implications are of the value and what complementary or competing values might exist on the part of classmates" (Fine, 1973, p. 68). Values clarification is usually most successful with older elementary students and with adolescents because the technique requires participants to be able to identify and talk about abstract concepts such as values, emotions, and feelings.

Problems in Language Development 7

Nettie R. Bartel • Diane N. Bryen[1]

This chapter deals with the comprehension and production of oral language. Primary consideration is given to (1) the nature of language; (2) the acquisition of normal language; (3) formal and informal assessment of language functioning; and (4) approaches to instruction and remediation in language.

THE NATURE OF LANGUAGE

The nature of language has been strenuously debated by psychologists, linguists, and, more recently, psycholinguists. It is generally agreed, however, that language is a symbol system which is characterized by its being *rule governed* and by its being *generative* in nature. To say that a language is rule governed means that the speaker and the hearer must agree to certain rules or conventions in order for communication to occur. These rules govern the use and understanding of the three major parts of language—semantics (meaning), syntax (grammar or structure), and phonology (speech sounds). In English, for example, speakers and listeners have agreed on the semantic convention that a certain four-legged animal found in many homes will be known as "dog," rather than say "hund," as in German. Similarly, in English syntax, one finds the convention that descriptors referring to size precede those referring to color, as in "big red ball" rather than "red big ball." While there is no intrinsic reason why one rule rather than another would be utilized in a given language, the fact is that this is the case; and observation of children's language shows that most children learn these rules

1. Dr. Bryen's contributions are the sections "Informal Approaches to Language Assessment" and "Informal Instructional Approaches."

quickly and accurately. Our concern in this chapter, of course, is with those children who experience difficulty for one reason or another.

The generative nature of language can be seen from the fact that (1) users of a language can speak and understand sentences that they have never heard or used before and (2) the rules of every known language are such that an infinite number of sentences are possible. Obviously, these aspects of language have major implications for training. For example, attempting to teach language to a child is quite different from teaching the multiplication table. In the case of the multiplication facts, all possible combinations can be presented on a matrix, and practice can occur until the child performs correctly 100 percent of the time. In teaching language, however, one can never exhaust all the possibilities. Even if one attempted to teach only one kind of simple sentence—let us say sentences of the subject–action type (e.g., "ball rolls," "dog runs," "cat jumps," "girl screams," etc.)—we would still have an infinite number of examples. Clearly, what is called for is a teaching technique that helps children discover the rules that would permit them to generate novel sentences that are appropriate for their communicative intent, and similarly to understand the intent of another speaker, even though they have never heard that particular sentence before.

Linguists call this capability for producing or understanding novel utterances *language competence*. Competence, the underlying knowledge that an individual has regarding a given language, is to be distinguished from *performance*, which is the actual expression of that competence in the understanding or producing of well-formed sentences. An individual's linguistic competence can be masked by a variety of performance variables such as poor memory, distraction, or lack of interest.

Although it would be of great educational significance to be able to measure a child's linguistic competence, competence itself can never be directly observed. One can only infer that it is or is not present in a child, on the basis of the child's understanding or production of sentences. As indicated above, a child's performance may be attenuated by a variety of factors. For this reason, the assessment of a child's language ability remains one of the most challenging tasks for educators.

The nature of linguistic competence—its rule-governed and generative aspects—indicate that language is not merely a set of conditioned responses or a series of stimulus–response bonds. It suggests that basic language structure, and the meaning given to expression through that structure, may not be trainable through rote and drill procedures. In fact, most children acquire basic linguistic competence by about four years of age without any formal instruction at all. The development of effective procedures for teaching children who have not acquired competence by that age is a critical, unresolved issue. Our position in this chapter is that the most promising possibility for effective instruction lies in an examination and adaptation of the circumstances under which most children normally acquire language competence. That is to say that it is necessary to analyze the procedures and sequence of normal language acquisition to formulate the most promising ideas about how to instruct children with language problems. It is to such an analysis that we turn next.

THE ACQUISITION OF LANGUAGE

The careful observation of very young children, or of older children who have not developed language, make it clear that a good deal of intellectual development occurs before the child begins to speak, typically at about age one. Myklebust refers to this preverbal period as the time when "inner language" is developed (Johnson and Myklebust, 1967). At this stage the child does not give overt evidence of language development, although he is beginning to organize his experiences in a systematic way.

Along the same lines, Piaget (1962) has stated:

> Language is not enough to explain thought, because the structures that characterize thought have their roots in action and in sensorimotor mechanisms that are deeper than linguistics (p. 98).

Piaget and others (e.g., Moerk, 1975; Parisi and Antinucci, 1970; Sinclair-de-Zwart, 1969; Slobin, 1970, 1971) have begun to delineate the processes engaged in by the child during this preverbal period, procedures which nonetheless have implications for the child's later verbal utterances. Using the basic functions of *assimilation* (the tendency of the organism to incorporate environmental stimuli into his system of mental structures) and *accommodation* (adjusting to the environment), the child constantly searches for *equilibrium* (i.e., balance). Even the very young child is a problem solver, attempting to reconcile events in the world around him with his present state of understanding while simultaneously changing his understanding in response to actions in his environment. As indicated in Chapter 1, such a view of the child as learner means that the child is active, not passive, and that he interacts with and transforms his conceptions of events. The child is not just a responder to acts and situations but is also an initiator—a fact that shows up in all observations of children's language acquisition. It is through the child's active and reactive manipulations of the environment that the beginnings of intelligence are revealed. Since thought precedes language, the nature of language must have its roots in the development of thought beginning sometime during the sensorimotor period.

Although Piaget emphasizes the organism's interaction with the environment, development can be explained only as the combination of maturation, social transmission, experience, and equilibration. Without the interrelationships among these factors, there can be no development, hence no learning. Language acquisition is thus based on cognitive development, as opposed solely to the accretion of linguistic items.

Observation of the interaction between an infant and its mother, even before there is any overt evidence of language capability on the part of the child, shows that the child and the mother follow each other's "line of regard," that is, they attend to the same things. It has noted that even at four months of age, the child follows the mother's line of regard, a behavior that occurs even more readily when the mother draws attention to what she is doing with statements such as "Look here!" Once the mother has the child's attention, she comments on or acts upon the object or event that has their mutual attention. From the very earliest stages of infancy then, the child learns the routine "*Attend to→Act upon*" (Bruner, 1975). The usefulness of this paradigm for teaching can scarcely be overstated. Before any significant language training can occur, steps must be taken to ensure that the child is attending to what the teacher is attending. As we have seen, this routine is basic to language instruction.

While it is a truism that children learn language from hearing others speak it, only recently have researchers begun to understand the nature of the relationship between the speaker and the child that makes this learning possible. As noted above, in the normal language learning environment, the home, the child hears comment or sees actions directed toward events to which his attention has been called. The comments and the actions that the child sees and hears are not arbitrary but serve as expressions of the mother's intent. Bruner (1975) has shown that even very young children grasp the notion that others (usually the mother) have intentions, and thus begin to make the first crucial distinctions between people and things. Soon thereafter the child himself expresses intent. A teacher can observe intent in a nonverbal child by noting the direction of the child's regard, by observing what satisfies him (does he stop whining when you let him have a certain toy?), by watching whether he substitutes one strategy for another (if he doesn't get results by looking at the closet where his coat and boots are, does he try walking to the door to convey the idea that he wants to go outdoors?), and finally, by noting the child's persistence.

We have discussed the issue of *intent* in some detail because of the significant role that it can play in language instruction. We have observed teachers spending valuable time attempting to get nonverbal children to distinguish between red and blue chips while the child sat at his desk sullenly ignoring the teacher; we have also seen teachers engaging groups of children in loud chants of "That is a pencil"; utterances that bore no relationship to the intent of the child and were never uttered spontaneously in an appropriate setting. What works so well in the informal circumstances of the preschoolers home is the commenting on and the acting upon events to which the child's attention has been directed. Bruner (1975) states that "Language is acquired as an instrument for regulating joint action and joint attention" and then again ". . . language is a specialized and conventionalized extension of cooperative action" (p. 2). Language is used to express what the child already "knows"—what he has seen acted on or what he has heard commented on. The task of language learning, from the child's point of view, has been expressed by Slobin (1973) as follows:

> In order to acquire language, the child must attend both to speech and to the contexts in which speech occurs—that is, he must be trying to understand what he hears, and be trying to express the intentions of which he is capable. This means that he must have both cognitive and linguistic discovery procedures available—in order to formulate internal structures which are capable of assimilating and relating both linguistic and nonlinguistic data, and which are capable of realizing intentions as utterances. The emergence of new communicative intentions must bring with it the means to decode those intentions in the speech the child hears, and this makes it possible for him to discover new means for expressing those intentions (p. 186).

From the very beginning, children use language in purposeful, intentional ways to comment on some event occurring in their environment or to make a request of some kind. For example, Antinucci and Parisi (1973, p. 614) recorded the following exchange between a mother and her one-and-a-half-year-old daughter, Claudia:

Mother: What do you want to eat? Noodles?
Claudia: No.
Mother. Don't you want to eat it?
Claudia: Eat Mommy.
Mother: Mommy eats it?
Claudia: Mommy noodles.

Apparently, Claudia's intent in this exchange is to request that her mother eat the noodles. However, she not yet have sufficient mastery of her language to say "Mommy eat noodles," so instead she says "Eat Mommy," and "Mommy noodles," which, taken together with her "No" in response to her mother's first question, makes her intent clear.

If Slobin (1973, p. 185) is right when he states that the appearance in a child's speech of a new formal device serves only to code a function that the child already has understood and expressed implicitly, then one would expect to soon see in Claudia's speech the emergence of "Mommy eat noodles." In a child whose language development is not proceeding normally, the presence of an exchange like that of Claudia's (above) would signal to the perceptive teacher that the time is right to teach the child "Mommy eat noodles." The rule is: *Explicit instruction of the verbal form is likely to be beneficial only when the child shows evidence of having grasped the meaning.*

It should be clear that our position is that meaning, or semantics, as it is called in linguistics, plays a primary role in language acquisition. It is to a consideration of semantics that we turn next.

The Acquisition of Semantics

According to Olson (1970), semantics involves the "categories, meanings, meaning components, and dimensions that correspond to the recurrent features of the world. [It] is closely tied to the referents, the objects, and the events in the environment, and it reflects the needs of the language community" (p. 257). Until a child understands, at least in rudimentary form, the nature of some of those objects and events in his environment, he has no referents for a semantic system or a system of meaning, and hence is incapable of learning language. MacNamara (1972) put it this way: "The infant uses meaning as a clue to language, rather than language as a clue to meaning. . . . Infants learn their language by first determining, independent of language, the meaning which a speaker intends to convey to them, and then working out the relationship between the meaning and the language" (p. 1). Meaning, according to MacNamara, refers to all that a person can express by means of a linguistic code. Sentences are names for the intentions which they express. Meanings may take the form of assertions, negations, commands, and questions. They may include aspects of a person's physical environment, his feelings, or his ideas. In order for a speaker to express an intent, he must have cognitively organized his communicative intent, whether that intent is related to the physical world or to some inner state. Similarly, in order for the hearer to comprehend the communication, he, too, must be knowledgeable about the intended referent. Semantic comprehension and production are based on cognition—the knowledge of the intended referent —not on the rules internal to language (Olson, 1970).

This point assumes great significance when one considers the nature of the semantic decisions to be made by a speaker. For purposes of illustration,

> A gold star is placed under a small, wooden block. A speaker who saw this act is then asked to tell a listener, who did not see the act, where the gold star is. In every case, the star is placed under the *same* block, a small, round, white . . . one. However, in the first case there is one alternative block present, a small, round, *black* one. In the second case there is a different alternative block present, a small, *square*, white . . . one. In a third case there are three alternative blocks present, a round

black one, a square black one, and a square white one. These three cases are shown in Figure 7–1.

In these situations, the speaker would say the following for case 1: "It's under the *white* one"; for case 2: "It's under the *round* one"; for case 3: "It's under the *round, white* one" (p. 264).

Olson summarizes his conclusions as follows:

1. Words are not simple names for things. If this were the case, each speaker would utilize the same word(s) in referring to the same thing. This clearly was not the case in the situation above.

2. Words do not name intended referents. In the example cited, the gold star is under the same block, which remains the intended referent. Yet in each case the utterances differ. "Words designate, signal, or specify an intended referent relative to the set of alternatives from which it must be differentiated" (Olson, p. 264). It is as if the speaker asks himself in this instance: "What alternatives could confuse or distract the listener; what do I need to mention so that this does not occur?" The speaker puts himself into the place of the listener, anticipates the comprehension task of the listener, and designates his response in terms that will be unambiguous for the listener. This consideration of the listener is necessary for communication to occur. The fact that it does occur is clear from the Olson paradigm, where the speaker is not varying his responses for his own personal benefit (after all, he *knows* where the gold star is, since he saw it being placed there) but for the benefit of the listener.

Figure 7–1. *Relation of an Utterance to an Intended Referent.*
[Adapted from Olson (1970).]

	Event	Alternative	Utterance
Case 1	○	●	. . . the white one
Case 2	○	□	. . . the round one
Case 3	○	□ ● ■	. . . the round, white one
Case 4	○		. . . (look under) the round, white, wooden block that is about 1 inch across . . .

3. A given utterance does not exhaust the potential features of the referent in question. Thus, in the example, any speaker could have designated the object as "wooden" or as "small" or as "inanimate," etc. Yet none did so. Rather, they utilized those aspects or features of the referent that served to distinguish it from the distractors. Consider Figure 7–2.

In each case, where the speaker is asked to identify an event (recognize a square), he does so by saying "This is a square." In case 2, however, while he says only "This is a square," the relevant meaning of "square" is its four-sidedness (to distinguish it from the alternative, triangle). In case 3, the meaning of "square" has to do with its straightedged characteristic, to distinguish it from the circle. Case 4 is an example of multiple meanings being required to distinguish it from the circle, the triangle, and the rectangle.

We have gone to considerable length on this point because of the major implications that an adequate view of semantics has for teaching children. A common problem arises when a child is taught a label for an object such as "book." The child may label it correctly as such in the instructional situation but later fail to do so when he must distinguish the book from items other than those used by the teacher. The occurrence of this problem underlines the fact that language usage must be taught in a variety of situations in which the child is required to make a variety of distinctions. Furthermore, from the earliest learning on, children need to become aware that referents do not go by only one name and that they may be referred to in many different ways, depending on what the listener is likely to be confused by. Learning the name for an object is only the first step in semantic learning; the more interesting and more functional aspects to be learned come

Figure 7–2. *Learning Word Meaning as a Function of Alternatives Differentiated.* [Adapted from Olson (1970).]

	Utterance	Event	Alternative	Meaning
Case 1	This is a square	□	——	Ambiguous
Case 2	This is a square	□	△	Four-sided
Case 3	This is a square	□	○	Straight-edged
Case 4	This is a square	□	○ △ □	Straight-edged Four-sided Symmetric

when the child uses the label appropriately in an unfamiliar context; and further, when the child learns to anticipate the problem faced by the listener and can modify his description of the referent accordingly.

Nelson (1974), in reference to concept learning, makes much the same point when she states that concept acquisition has to do with comprehending the referent in a functional or relational way rather than through the specification of a set of critical attributes. Nelson makes the further significant point that learning the meaning of a concept involves two distinct procedures. The first of these, *concept generation,* entails distinguishing reliably the referent in question in all settings and in all contexts. That is, a book is still a book, whether it is on a shelf, on a desk, or in the teacher's hand. The second part of concept learning refers to applying the new concept label to as-yet-unidentified exemplars. Thus, having learned that a given item is appropriately referred to as "book," the child must learn to refer to other similar items as "books" also. Furthermore, he must refrain from referring to noninstances of books, such as collections of loose paper, as books.

Here, again, the instructional implications are apparent. A concept is not learned (i.e., its meaning in the child's mind is not fully established) until both requirements of concept learning have been met. The child must be able to discriminate the referent in question correctly in many settings and with respect to many different alternatives. Second, he must be given experience in applying the label for the concept to other potential instances. Many games can be devised in the classroom for both these purposes.

A question that arises at this point is: What concepts or words should be taught first to the child? The question is of more than passing interest, especially when one considers the difficulty that children encounter in laboratory-type studies of acquiring such simple static concepts as those of shape or colors. Again, it is instructive to turn to observations of children's early words acquired in naturalistic settings. Nelson (1974) has made some interesting observations about children's early words. First, the words selected by the child for his first utterances tend to be words that move and change. The principle the child seems to be using in selecting words from an environment that is complex and dynamic and in which the concept domain is unlimited and undefined is: *those things are similar that can be acted upon in the same way.* The concepts selected by the child are defined in terms of logical relationships rather than in terms of common elements. Rarely, if ever, does a child select as his first word such unvarying, static concepts as "circle" which are the favorites of curriculum developers, especially those inclined to a programming approach. The child seems to go out of his way to select dynamic, changeable events that have to do with categories of agent, object, causation, time, and space.

When does the first word appear? Because of the frequently encountered difficulty in determining the precise break between babbling behavior and the emergence of the first "true" word, we suggest following Nelson's (1973) procedure of using attainment of 10 vocabulary items as definitive evidence of the beginnings of productive language, rather than looking for just the first word. The most frequently cited range for such beginnings is from 10 to 13 months of age. The typical rapidity of vocabulary growth from that point on is remarkable. McCarthy (1954) has summarized a large number of studies of vocabulary acquisition. Her data show that vocabulary growth is almost exponential, with the typical child having approximately 20 words at fifteen months of age, close to 300 words at age two, almost 1000 words at age three, and about 3000 words by the time he enters school at age six.

The number of traditional-type vocabulary studies being conducted has declined recently. It has become apparent that merely noting the presence of a word in a child's vocabulary does not tell enough about the meaning of the word to the child. Second, words are not equal in terms of what they signify for the child's language development. For example, the child who adds the words "sixty-four" and "sixty-five" to his vocabulary as he is learning to count to 100 is adding a linguistic capability that is fundamentally different in nature from the child who is adding to his active vocabulary the words "before" and "after." Yet, in studies that count vocabulary items, each new word counts the same as any other new word. Third, vocabulary studies in and of themselves do not provide a representative indication of the child's proficiency in semantics, since they do not address the crucial question of how word meanings are combined into sentence meanings. After all, children beyond the age of two rarely rely to any extent on one-word sentences.

Nelson (1973) has made some additional observations about children's first words. Based on an analysis of the first fifty words used by each of 18 children, Nelson found that the most common category (accounting for about half of the different words) used by children at this age were the general nominals (e.g., ball, doggie, snow, etc.). The next most common group were the special nominals, such as Mommy or the name of a stuffed toy. Next, accounting for somewhat over 10 percent of the different words used was a category of action words, such as bye-bye, give, or come. Less common were groups of modifiers (red, outside), and personal-social words (yes, no, please). While this breakdown reflected the distribution of different words used, some of the categories are used with great frequency, for example, some words, such as bye-bye, are used repeatedly in conjunction with general and specific nominals. Of particular interest was Nelson's finding that among the nominals representing items of clothing, children select for their usage at this age only such items that they themselves can act upon (e.g., shoes, socks). Notably absent from the children's utterances were references to such items as diaper, sweater, mittens.

In a somewhat different type of analysis, Clark (1973) has reanalyzed a number of diary studies from the point of view of looking at the child's overextensions or overgeneralizations. Clark interpreted her findings to conclude that children overextend words frequently on the basis of such perceptual attributes of features such as shape, size, sound, movement, taste, and texture. Overextensions based on color were not found. Clark's work, with its emphasis on perceptual attributes, stands in contrast to the work of Nelson (cited earlier), with its emphasis on the functions of concepts acquired by children. It is possible that different children rely on different aspects of meaning in deriving and applying conceptual learning, a fact that if true would once again exemplify the idiosyncratic nature of language development.

Bloom (1970) has given a number of examples of children using different meanings in what appear to be identical utterances. For example, the use of the utterance "Mommy sock" was found to occur in two distinct contexts: in one, to denote a genitive relationship (the sock belongs to Mommy), and in another, to show the relationship between subject and object (Mommy is putting a sock on me). Early utterances are apparently motivated by their semantic function.

Similarly, the word "no," frequently used by children, may mean, depending on context:

Negation:	"No night-night" (I don't want to go to bed.)
Rejection:	"No milk" (I don't want milk.)
Denial:	"No Teddy" (That's not a Teddy Bear.)
Lack of occurrence:	"No blanket" (No blanket in the child's bed; he had expected to see it there.)

An additional example, from Brown (1973), shows that children use the same verb form, bare and uninflected, to mean at least four different things; for example, a child's utterance "Car go" could mean:

The name of the current action or state	(The car is going.)
A reference to the immediate past	(We went for a ride in the car.)
A statement of wish or intent	(I would like to ride in the car.)
Imperative	(Car go!)

Again, an analysis of the child's meaning is necessary to determine what language instruction the child can benefit from. The child who says "Car go" to refer to the current action of the car is ready to be instructed in "The car is going," and so forth. *A prime teaching opportunity lies in the apparent lag between a child's communicative intent and his ability to manifest that intent in an appropriate form.*

To help teachers determine the meanings of a child's utterances, we cite the following suggestions from Antinucci and Parisi (1973):

1. Observe carefully and in detail the extralinguistic context in which the child's sentences and lexical items occur. (What is the child doing when he says what he does? What is he paying attention to?)
2. Carefully observe the child's intentions.
3. Observe how the child understands sentences said to him.
4. Observe how the child combines one lexical item with another.

Dale (1976) has summarized a considerable amount of research dealing with children's acquisition of labels for a number of concepts. Such concepts include "more" and "less"; the dimensions of "big," "little," "long," "short," and thick"; "before" and "after"; verbs and the expression of causation, e.g., "drop"; verbs of possession and transfer, e.g., "give"; color naming words; "left" and "right"; "I" and "you"; and words for expressing concepts of expectations. He concludes that there is no single framework that covers all patterns of development of these concepts with all children; semantic development appears to be as varied as the concepts that language encodes.

The Acquisition of Syntax

To this point, we have considered the cognitive and semantic underpinnings of all language development. While one can argue that all aspects of language derive ultimately from a communicative intent (either receptive or expressive) that is cognitive in nature, one can, for analytic purposes, deal separately with its formal, structured aspects. Accordingly, we direct our attention to that aspect of language that has to do with the arrangement of words into meaningful sequence—syntax. We also include a brief section on morphology, which deals with the smallest meaningful grammatical units of language.

During the 1960s the normal acquisition of syntactic structure was widely researched and commented on (e.g., Chomsky, 1957; McNeill, 1966, 1970; Menyuk, 1969). In addition, researchers studied extensively and longitudinally the development of sentences in three groups of children at Harvard, Berkeley, and Johns Hopkins universities. Much of what is known about the emergence of syntactic structures in normal development grew out of these studies.

At about 13–24 months of age, the child first begins to use two-word sentences. The emergence of sentences, as opposed to two-word utterances, marks the child's beginning attempts to use rules to combine linguistic units (syntax). Contrary to earlier speculation, research in the last decade has indicated that these first sentences are neither memorized imitations of adult speech or random sequences of words. Three independent investigations of this stage of language development (Braine, 1963; Brown and Bellugi, 1964; Ervin, 1964) all concluded that the first attempts at sentence production are orderly and rule-governed, as opposed to random. This is evidenced by the consistency with which children manifest the type of word combinations they use. Although there is variation from one child to the next, each individual child employs particular rules. Typical utterances of a child at this stage of development might be the following:

more horsey	Bunny allgone
more sing	truck allgone
more milk	milk allgone

While the first interpretations of these data led to the conclusions that the child utilizes a formal grammatical structure that became known as a "pivot-open" grammar, more recent interpretations have deemphasized the formal syntax presumably employed by the child when he says "more horsey." Instead, a number of investigators have attempted to show that the child utilizes a number of distinct semantic relationships to characterize these early two- and three-word utterances. Table 7–1 is adapted from Brown (1970) and summarizes the most common relationships. In addition to these common semantic relations, observation of young children also reveals use of Action–Indirect Object (give Claudia), Instrumentals (key open), Conjunction (foots flower).

By age three, the normal child's utterances show that he has mastered the basic relationships among subject, predicate, and object (Menyuk, 1969).

Table 7–1. *Semantic Relations in Two-Word Sentences*

Semantic Relation	Form	Example
1. Nomination	that + N	*that book*
2. Notice	hi + N	*hi belt*
3. Recurrence	more + N, 'nother + N	*more milk*
4. Nonexistence	allgone + N, no more + N	*allgone rattle*
5. Attributive	Arj + N	*big train*
6. Possessive	N + N	*mommy lunch*
7. Locative	N + N	*sweater chair*
8. Locative	V + N	*walk street*
9. Agent-Action	N + V	*Eve read*
10. Agent-Object	N + N	*mommy sock*
11. Action-Object	V + N	*put book*

Source: Adapted from R. Brown, *Psycholinguistics* (New York: Free Press, 1970), p. 220.

Menyuk also found that the early two-word utterances (see Table 7–1) give way to more differentiated and more complex sentences. By age three, the typical child has developed a number of sentence types in the following order:

1. Joining of elements to make sentences.
2. Development of subject + predicate sentences.
3. Expansion of the verb phrase to include an auxiliary verb and copula.
4. Embedding of an element within a sentence and attachment of the element to the verb.
5. Permutation of elements within a string (auxiliary/modal and tense markers).

Most researchers have found that sentence complexity and sentence differentiation correlates rather well with the mean length of the child's utterance (MLU). One major problem in the use of the MLU has been that each researcher used his own definition of what constitutes an utterance. Consequently, it was not possible to compare the results of one study with that of another. Recently, however, most researchers have begun to utilize the procedures for defining MLU that were developed by Brown (1973). Because of the potential usefulness of a single index of language development that correlates well with most aspects of language, we are including it here as Table 7–2.

Table 7–2. *Rules for Calculating Mean Length of Utterance (MLU)*

The following rules are reasonable for MLU up to about 4.0; by this time many of the assumptions underlying the rules are no longer valid.

1. Start with the second page of the transcription unless that page involves a recitation of some kind. In this latter case start with the first recitation-free stretch. Count the first 100 utterances satisfying the following rules. (A 50-utterance sample may be used for preliminary estimate.)
2. Only fully transcribed utterances are used. Portions of utterances, entered in parentheses to indicate doubtful transcription, are used.
3. Include all exact utterance repetitions (marked with a plus sign in records). Stuttering is marked as repeated efforts at a single word; count the word once in the most complete form produced. In the few instances in which a word is produced for emphasis or the like ("no, no, no") count each occurrence.
4. Do not count such fillers as "um" and "oh," but do count "no," "yeah," and "hi."
5. All compound words (two or more free morphemes), proper names, and ritualized reduplications count as single morphemes. Examples: "birthday," "rackety-boom," "choo-choo," "quack-quack," "night-night," "pocketbook," "see-saw."

(continued)

Table 7–2. *Rules for Calculating Mean Length of Utterance (MLU) (continued)*

6. Count as one morpheme all irregular pasts of the verb ("got," "did," "want," "saw"). Justification is that there is no evidence that the child relates these to present forms.
7. Count as one morpheme all diminutives ("doggie," "mommy") because these children at least do not seem to use the suffix productively. Diminutives are the standard forms used by the child.
8. Count as separate morphemes all auxiliaries ("is," "have," "will," "can," "must," "would"). Also all catenatives: "gonna," "wanna," "hafta." The latter are counted as single morphemes rather than as "going to" or "want to" because the evidence is that they function so for children. Count as separate morphemes all inflections, for example, possessive "s," plural "s," third person singular "s," regular past tense "d," progressive "ing."

Source: Adapted from Table 7 of R. Brown, *A First Language: The Early Stages* (Cambridge, Mass.: Harvard University Press, 1973), p. 54. © 1973 by the President and Fellows of Harvard College.

A major contribution to our knowledge of the development of semantic–syntactic usage in young children comes from the work of Bloom, Lightbown, and Hood (1975). These authors studied the language development of four children during the period in which their MLUs ranged from 1.0 to approximately 2.5. They found that verb relations were of central importance in the children's syntactical learning and that it was possible to establish a developmental sequence for a number of these categories. See Table 7–3 for a summary, in approximate developmental order, of these observed relations.

Of great instructional significance was the further finding of Bloom et al. that children vary systematically in their strategies for syntactic learning. Some children apparently search for constancies in the expression of relationships involving the semantic notions encoded by particular words. For example, they seem to base their relational learning on rules involving distributional frequency—thus the child produces many utterances, such as "allgone milk," "allgone horsey," "allgone cookie." He has the idea that words such as "allgone" can be combined with a number of other pronominal forms. Bloom (1970) called this the "pivot" strategy, after some earlier work by Braine (1963) in which he postulated that syntactical rule learning initially takes the form of combining two crude types of form classes— "pivot" and "open" classes.

Other children seem to adopt a strategy of "categorical" learning, in which they appear to formulate rules that specify how to position words performing relational functions, such as Agent–Action, Modifier–Modified, Possessor–Possessed, etc. At the present time there appears to be no way other than observation to establish which children utilize one strategy and which utilize another. Bowerman (1976) has suggested that in teaching, the teacher should group children on the basis of their preferred strategy and

Table 7–3. *Sequence of Semantic–Syntactic Relations Emerging from MLU = 1.0 to MLU = 2.5*

Type of Relation	Child's Utterance	Context
Functional relations		
Existence	there a birdie	Child picking up toy bird
Nonexistence	no more car	Child putting toy car away
Recurrence	another block	Child giving additional block
Verb relations		
Action		
Action	Gia writing	Child scribbling on paper
Locative	choo-choo fall down	Child pushing toy train down
State		
State	want more apple	Child finishes apple, whines
Notice	I see another man	Child looking out window
Locative	people on street	Child looking out window
Possession	it's mine clay	Experimenter reaches for clay child has been playing with
Attribution	red truck	Child picking up truck
Instrumentality	I write the pencil	Child holding pencil up
Dative	show you	In response to mother asking where child's sister is
Wh- questions	what engine go	Child holding up puzzle piece

Source: Adapted from L. Bloom, P. Lightbown, and L. Hood, Structure and variation in child language, *Monograph of the Society for Research in Child Development*, 1975, 40 (No. 2, Serial No. 60).

vary teaching style and content accordingly. A child who failed to make progress in one group would be switched to another where there might be a better match with his cognitive style.

An aspect of syntax not considered to this point is that of morphology. Morphemes are the smallest meaningful aspect of language. There are two types of morphemes—bound and free. Free morphemes are units that stand alone, for example, run, book, particular. Bound morphomes are always attached to other units; in English, they serve as prefixes and suffixes (e.g., -ed, -er, pre-, and un-). The order of acquisition of bound morphemes, or inflections as they are frequently called, has been studied by de Villiers and de Villiers (1973) and by Brown (1973). Their findings correspond closely in the sequence of normal development. A summary of Brown's report, with examples, is presented in Table 7–4.

Two cautions with respect to morphology are worth mentioning. The first of these is that children exhibit considerable inconsistency in their use. It is not uncommon, for example, for children to vacillate between "comed" and "came," or among "bringed," "brang," "branged," and "brought."

Table 7–4. *Acquisition of Grammatical Morphemes*

Morpheme	Example	Meaning
Present progressive	"coming" in "Daddy is coming"	Current occurrence
Preposition "on"	"on" in "Blanket on bed"	On top of, and supported by
Preposition "in"	"in" in "In the toybox"	Containment
Past irregular	"went" in "We went away"	Prior occurrence
Possessive	" 's" in "Mommy's hat"	Possession
Uncontractible copula	"was" in "He was"	Prior occurrence
Articles "the," "a"	"the" in "the house"	Specific determination
	"a" in "a dog"	Nonspecific determination
Past regular	"played" in "played ball"	Prior occurrence
Third-person singular (regular)	"comes" in "Daddy comes"	Number, prior occurrence
Third person singular (irregular)	"has" in "Mommy has candy"	number, prior occurrence
Uncontractible auxiliary	"were" in "They were coming"	Number, prior occurrence
Contractible copula	"She is" or "She's" in "She is big"	Number, prior occurrence
Contractible auxiliary	"He is" or "He's" in "He is playing"	Number, prior occurrence

Brown (1973) suggests that 90 percent correct usage be considered the criterion for mastery.

Another caution concerns the fact that inflectional usage varies enormously from one dialect of English to another. Particularly, in children using what has become known as "Black English," the teacher is likely to see evidence of a different set of rules governing morphemes. Following are a number of inflectional differences between Standard English usage and Black English usage (adapted from Bartel, Grill, and Bryen, 1973):

Feature	Standard English	Black English
Past tense		
Omission of final "ed"	passed, loaned	pass, loan
Future tense		
Omission of final "l"	you'll, he'll	you, he
Present tense		
Omission of final sound	I'm, it's	I, it
Possessive		
Deletion of final "s"	Harry's cousin	Harry cousin
Plural		
Deletion of final "s"	50 cents, 3 birds	50 cent, 3 bird
Third-person singular		
Deletion of final "s"	she works here	she work here

Clearly, when a teacher is attempting to establish whether or not a child has mastered a given morphological form, account needs to be taken of whether the child's dialect requires the use of the particular form. The situation is also the case with other syntactic structures. As a guide for helping the teacher know which are the most common dialectal syntactical differences in Black English, the following are presented (adapted once again from Bartel, Grill, and Bryen, 1973):

Feature	Standard English	Black English
Linking verb	He is going.	He goin' or he goin?
Subject expression	John lives in N.Y.	John, he live in N.Y.
Verb form	I drank the milk.	I drunk the milk.
Verb agreement	He runs home.	He run home or He be running home.
Future form	I will go home.	I'ma go home.
"If" construction	Is asked if he did it.	Is asked did he do it.
Negation	I don't have any.	I don't got none.
Indefinite article	I want an apple.	I want a apple.
Pronoun form	We have to do it.	Us got to do it.
Preposition	He is over at his friend's house.	He over to his friend house.
Copula ("be")	He is here all the time. No, he isn't.	He be here. No, he don't.

Phonological variations in Black English are presented in the subsequent section on phonology.

A number of researchers have attempted to establish whether language development in handicapped children is similar in nature and sequence to that of "normal" children. At the present time, the evidence is mixed, with some investigators concluding that the course of development is essentially similar, if somewhat slowed down (e.g., Bartel, 1970; Lackner, 1976; Lenneberg, Nichols, and Rosenberger, 1964), and others (Lee, 1966; Menyuk, 1964) reporting dissimilar development. In an attempt to resolve the issue, Morehead and Ingram (1973) made comparisons between groups of normal and linguistically deviant children where they were matched on the basis of mean length of utterance, rather than IQ or mental age. Their findings were that despite similar linguistic systems, the linguistically deficient group were less efficient in the way they used the system. For example, they would add new words to a basic acquired construction, rather than developing new and more complex combinations. This finding is of interest for it indicates that flexibility and creativity in language usage may need to be given specific and focused attention. How such flexibility and creativity develop in the natural environment of the preschoolers' homes is the question to which we turn next.

There are specific environmental variables that apparently play a major role in rapid language acquisition; several of these have been explored by

Brown and Bellugi (1964). Based upon extensive observations and recordings of mother–child interactions in the home, these researchers identified the factors of imitation and reduction, imitation with expansion, and induction of the latent structure as contributing to language mastery. Imitation and reduction refer to the fact that a great many of the early utterances of children appear to be reductions of adult speech, or "telegraphic speech," as it has been called. Thus, when the child says "See truck," it seems reasonable that he is patterning this expression on something an adult might have said, e.g., "Yes, I see the truck," or "Do you see the truck?" An analysis of these expressions led Brown and Bellugi to conclude that the child's expressions systematically retained the high-information words (usually nouns and verbs), the words that are stressed in the model sentence, and the content words, as opposed to the function words. All of this shows that the child is indeed imitating the adult model, but he is imitating in a highly selective and systematic manner.

When the child uses an expression such as "There daddy," the mother typically responds with a full sentence that both reinforces and corrects the child; "Yes, there goes daddy," or some other appropriate utterance. The cumulative effects of hundreds of bits of such feedback, day after day, may have a major impact on the efficacy of language learning.

Brown and Bellugi also found that a large number of child utterances could not readily be seen as reductions of adult sentences (e.g., "a my pencil," or "allgone lettuce"). It is highly unlikely that a child heard a sentence from which he could deduce utterances such as these. The child must be using a rule that he has deduced from hearing adults talk, and he seems to be trying the rule out. Naturally, as the child practices this rule he finds that it generates some utterances that are unacceptable. Hence, the rules must constantly be revised to incorporate new input from the linguistic environment.

In the next section, we consider the speech sound system (phonology) which provides the medium through which the child's utterances occur, and which ultimately becomes a fully developed communicative mode.

The Acquisition of Phonology

Phonemes are significant units of speech sounds: the word "significant" is used to indicate that a difference in meaning results when one phoneme is substituted for another. Thus, in English, /b/ and /p/ are phonemes because a substitution of /b/ for /p/, or vice versa, in a word such as "big" or "pig" results in a change in meaning. Phonemes may be vowels or consonants; they may be simple, /t/ or /h/, or they may be compound, /th/ or /au/. The written equivalent for a phoneme is a grapheme. The grapheme equivalent for the speech sound /k/ is either the letter "c" or "k." This example shows that the phoneme–grapheme correspondence in English is by no means perfect. Sometimes two or more graphemes represent only one phoneme, as when the letters "s" and "soft c" both have the phoneme equivalent /s/. Conversely, every teacher who has ever tried to teach phonics to a first or second grader knows that the letter "a" has several phonemic variations, as in c*a*t, *a*lways, *a*lone, br*a*vo, or s*a*id. The lack of a one-to-one correspondence in English orthography has been much lamented; several attempts have been made to overcome the problems it presents for beginning readers by using a modified phonemic–graphemic system, e.g., the International Teaching Alphabet (Mazurkiewicz, 1968). While the English spelling system is popularly believed to be an assortment of haphazard graphemic sequences, a recent book by Chomsky and Halle (1968) shows that most English spellings are highly rule-governed and constitute orderly derivations from root words.

A phoneme in any given language is not a specific, unique speech sound that is consistently used by all speakers of that language. In fact, the same speaker does not produce identical sounds when he is producing the /p/ as in p/utt as opposed to the /p/ in ha/pp/ily or in /p/it. Phonemes are really ranges of sounds; different speakers produce phonemes that are acoustically quite different from each other even when each is saying the same word. This phenomenon is most apparent when spoken speech is represented graphically on a spectrogram. The spectrogram is a visual, two-dimensional representation of acoustic cues, not entirely dissimilar to an electroencephalogram, with bands of varying frequencies and intensities portrayed on a screen or recorded on a graph. The spectogram shows that the configurations produced by an individual's speech are highly individualistic, as unique as a person's fingerprint.

Phonemes are usually described in terms of binary features (Jakobsen and Halle, 1956). Binary features are polar opposites; if a phoneme is a vowel, for example, it cannot act as a consonant. In addition to the *vowel–consonant* pair, phonemes may also be *nasal–oral*, with nasal phonemes having their primary resonance in the nasal, as opposed to the oral, cavities. This feature is not as distinctive in English as in some other languages; only the /n/, /m/, and /ng/ sounds are nasal, while all others are oral. The *voiced–unvoiced* pair describes whether a given phoneme is produced with a voiced component or not. Phonemes that are identical except in one respect (minimal pairs)—in this case voiced versus unvoiced—are /v/ and /f/, /b/ and /p/, /d/ and /t/, /g/ and /k/, /w/ and /wh/, and /th/ as in /th/at compared to /th/ as in /th/ink. The voiced–unvoiced distinction is an important one in the English language.

Consonants can be further described by noting the anatomical place of articulation. Consonants, as opposed to vowels, are produced by some part of the speech-producing anatomy (e.g., lips, tongue, teeth) that produces interference with the flow of air from the windpipe. For example, to create the /f/ sound, air is expelled without obstruction until it gets to the lip and teeth area. Here it meets upper teeth planted on lower lips. Forcing the air out through lips and teeth in this arrangement produces the characteristic /f/ sound. The point of articulation of most consonants can be determined by careful observation in front of a mirror.

The maximal utilization of all the distinctions possible from the binary features would result in a very large number of possible phonemes. Yet no existing language employs as many as sixty, or fewer than twenty-five, phonemes.

Although there has been some evidence of prenatal vocalization, the birth cry is considered to be the first speech uttered by the infant. The birth cry has no language meaning because it is merely an automatic physiological reaction. However, it can be considered as the beginning of speech and language development for the child.

During the first two or three weeks of life, the child's cries have no real significance because he simply is responding to stimuli, a reflexive act. Between two and five weeks he is still reacting reflexively, but his cries are more directly related to the stimulus. The child's cries at this time become differentiated by varying in loudness and quality. Other sounds he produces are grunts and yawns and those connected with coughing and sneezing. These verbalizations are probably related to the breathing process.

By the third and fourth weeks the infant can focus his eyes quite well and responds to the attention and voices of the adults by smiling. At this stage the child begins to use vowel sounds.

During the babbling stage (two to eight months or more) the child continues to be aware of the sounds he produces. He derives pleasure from babbling and, in turn, continues to babble. New vowel sounds are mastered and improve in articulation. Early consonant sounds are /p/, /b/, /m/, and /h/. By the time the child reaches his sixth month of life, he has used all the vowel sounds and some consonant sounds. Some observers feel that by this age the child has become proficient in the use of his sounds in influencing adults. He continues to derive satisfaction from reactions of adults to his speech sounds and smiles and laughs readily.

The child's babbling does not stop after six months but continues with a greater awareness of the speech of the people in his environment. He begins to imitate the speech sounds and other vocalizations of his companion adults.

By the end of the child's first year of life, the number of consonant sounds he produces is beginning to grow. He is learning rapidly through the attention and interaction he has with adults. The imitations that the child attempts derive from his ability to produce sounds that he hears and to respond to sounds. It is obvious that the mother who speaks frequently to the child will receive more and varied responses than the mother who does not speak frequently.

Between two and three years of age, the child begins to utilize teeth in speech production. He is better able to articulate his words, and speech sounds; the /th/ and the nasal /n/ are easier to say and understand. Since he is growing rapidly, he can maintain better control over the movement of his body, including his tongue and lips. His environment is continuing to broaden and the sounds he produces become more and more differentiated until adult phonological competence is reached.

Scope and Sequence of Language Development

To help the teacher relate the various aspects of language development, we have adapted a type of scope-and-sequence chart (Table 7–5) based on the work of Fokes (1971). This chart can be used both for assessment and intervention purposes. For example, the teacher who is working with a child who is developmentally between two and three years of age can see that such a child ordinarily has a vocabulary of about 250 words (see "Meaning" column in Table 7–5). At the same time, the child will in most cases have mastered about two thirds of the adult speech sounds (see "Sound Marking" column). During this period, the child's mean length of utterance (Table 7–2) will in most cases be developing from two words to three-and-a-half words, and some inflections and transformations will appear (see the "Grammar" column of Table 7–5). Having this information and more from Table 7–5, the teacher is able to establish whether the child in question is experiencing any major lags in the various aspects of language development. Further, more detailed probing can be undertaken through procedures described in the next section, "Language Assessment," where problems appear to exist.

Furthermore, once the child's level of functioning has been established, Table 7–5 can also be used as a guide to intervention. For example, to continue with the hypothetical case of a child who is developmentally about two years old and just beginning to use interrogative transformations (column "Grammar," part C.2), the teacher would first expect intonational questions such as "See doggie?" before attempting to teach the use of the interrogatives "who," "what," and "where." Table 7–5 can be used similarly for the assessment and remediation of other aspects of language functioning.

LANGUAGE ASSESSMENT

How does a teacher decide that a child needs to have a systematic language evaluation? The answer to this question is a relatively simple matter. We

Table 7–5. *Scope-and-Sequence Chart*

	Characteristics of the Period	*Sound Making*

Birth to Six Weeks	A. Reflexive vocalization
	1. Sounds produced from a column of air expelled from lungs and passed through tensed vocal bands (Berry and Eisenson, 1956)
	2. Primary purpose of speech mechanism for breathing and eating (McCarthy, 1954)
	3. Undifferentiated vocalization—first three weeks
	  a. No intent, awareness, meaning, or purpose
	  b. Total bodily expression in response to stimulus
	    (1) No distinguishable response to cold, hunger, pain, etc.
	    (2) Variety in intensity (Berry and Eisenson, 1956)
	    (3) Total emotional response (Anderson, 1953)
	4. Differentiated vocalization—second three weeks
	  a. Vocalization related to stimulus
	  b. Muscle pattern sets for different cries (Berry and Eisenson, 1956)
		A. Grunts, sighs, gurgles, glottal catch
		1. Similar to swallowing movements
		2. Present in whimpering rather than in crying (Van Riper, 1963)
		B. No sex difference (Irwin, 1952)
		C. Nasalization (Van Riper, 1963)
		D. Average of seven phoneme-like sounds (Irwin, 1952)
		1. Monosyllabic cries
		2. Predominantly front vowel-like sounds
		  a. Average of 4.5 distinguishable sounds (Irwin, 1952)
		  b. /ae/ most predominant sound (Berry and Eisenson, 1956)
		  c. Other sounds: / ɪ ɛ ʌ ʊ / (Irwin, 1948)
		3. Predominantly glottal and velar consonant-like sounds
		  a. Average of 2.7 sounds
		  b. Predominantly plosive and fricative /h/ sounds (Irwin, 1947a, 1947b)
		  c. Other sounds: /k g h/ (Irwin, 1947a, 1947b)

Six Weeks to Three Months	A. Beginning of babbling period (Berry and Eisenson, 1956)
	1. Sounds made "for their own sake"
	  a. Satisfaction from utterance
	  b. Different from comfort sounds
	  c. Play with sounds (Lewis, 1963)
	2. Spontaneous production of sounds
	  a. Encompass more sounds than spoken by parents
	  b. Indicate pleasurable mood (Anderson, 1953)
	  c. Self-initiated vocal play (Berry and Eisenson, 1956)
	  d. Random production of sounds
	    (1) /a/ produced at length
	    (2) Most sounds not repeated (Berry and Eisenson, 1956)
	  e. Predominantly noncrying sounds (Berry and Eisenson, 1956)
	  f. Self-enjoyment from sound making (Berry and Eisenson, 1956)
	B. Sound making still essentially reflexive (Berry and Eisenson, 1956)
		A. Coos, gurgles, squeals, sighs of contentment (Berry and Eisenson, 1956)
		B. Monosyllabic utterances (Shirley, 1933)
		1. Combination of consonant- and vowel-like sounds (McCarthy, 1954)
		2. Little repetition (Berry and Eisenson, 1956)
		3. Nasalization of sounds
		  a. Vowel-like sounds—displeasure
		  b. Consonant-like sounds—pleasure (Berry and Eisenson, 1956)
		C. Average of thirteen to fourteen different sound types (Irwin, 1952)

Three Months to Six Months	A. Continuation of the babbling period
	1. Associated with pleasure, contentment
	2. Autistic enjoyment (Mowrer, 1952)
	3. Self-imitation
	  a. Occurs when child is alone
	  b. Disappears when distracted by someone else (Templin, 1957)
	4. No longer reflexive
	  a. Source from internal stimulation
	  b. Hearing not important (Berry and Eisenson, 1956)
		A. Some control over oral region (Irwin, 1952)
		B. Disyllabic utterances (Shirley, 1933)
		1. Consonant-like plus vowel-like sounds (Irwin, 1952)
		2. Average of seventeen different sound types (Irwin, 1952)
		  a. Predominantly vowel-like sounds
		    (1) More frequent front and mid sounds
		    (2) A few back sounds
		    (3) Distinguishable sounds: /ɪ ɛ ʌ ʊ u/ (Irwin, 1948)

Intonation	Meaning	Grammar
A. Variety in intensity (Berry and Eisenson, 1956) B. Fundamental frequency of infant cry: 556 Hz (Fairbanks, 1942)	A. Beginning of crude vocabulary (Berry and Eisenson, 1956) B. Response to other's voice (Mc-Carthy, 1954) C. Response of crying when other babies cry (Lewis, 1963)	
A. Variation in pitch B. Variation in loudness (Berry and Eisenson, 1956)	A. Vocalizes for pleasure or displeasure (Berry and Eisenson, 1956) B. Reacts to sounds made (Berry and Eisenson, 1956) C. Smiles at mother's voice (Lewis, 1963)	

A. Intonation—infant cry of similar pressure waveform, much as the expiratory form of adult utterances (Lieberman, 1967)	A. Babbling—speech without content (Bullowa, 1967a, 1967b)
	  1. Dental and labial sounds expressive of contentment
	  2. Velar sounds expressive of distress (Lewis, 1963)
	B. Noises—rudiments of vocal response (Lewis, 1963)
	C. Systematic response to specific stimuli (Lewis, 1963)	

(continued)

Table 7–5. *Scope-and-Sequence Chart (continued)*

Characteristics of the Period	*Sound Making*

	b. Consonant-like sounds
	   (1) Predominantly glottal /h/ and velar sounds
	   (2) Appearance of labial sounds (Irwin, 1947b)
	   (3) Appearance of nasals, plosive, and glide types (Irwin, 1947a)

Six Months to Nine Months

Characteristics of the Period	*Sound Making*

A. Lalling stage—repetition of vocal play
  1. Expression of self
  2. Association of hearing with sound production
    a. Ear reflex—circular response involving hearing and sound production
    b. Repetition of selected heard sounds
    c. Imitation as incentive for repetition (Berry and Eisenson, 1956)
B. Accompanying motor responses to vocalizations
  1. Particular sounds accompany motor response (Berry and Eisenson, 1956)
  2. Arm movements more meaningful than mouth movements (Van Riper, 1963)
C. Language problems evident at this age through lack of lalling behavior; the deaf, retarded, aphasic, emotionally deprived (McCarthy, 1954)
	A. Frequent change in syllable repetition (Van Riper, 1963)
	B. Consonant-vowel-type combinations reduplicated (Weir, 1966)
	C. Predominantly vowel-like sounds
	  1. Front sound 92 percent of the time (Irwin, 1948)
	  2. Some back vowels: / v u o / (Weir, 1966)

Nine Months to Twelve Months

Characteristics of the Period	*Sound Making*

A. Echolalic stage
  1. Repetition of sounds made by others
    a. Sounds confined to those of native language (Berry and Eisenson, 1956)
    b. Awareness of sound patterns of native language
    c. Fixation of these sounds in vocalization (Anderson, 1953)
  2. Sounds devoid of meaning (Berry and Eisenson, 1956)
  3. Vocally fluent (Lewis, 1963)
B. Imitation
  1. Perpetuation of sounds that interest him (Weir, 1966)
  2. Rudimentary imitation—speaks on hearing someone else speak (Lewis, 1963)
  3. Regularity in response to particular sounds (Lewis, 1963)
C. Vocal play
  1. Production of vegetative sounds without demand
  2. Vocalization while playing (Weir, 1966)
	A. Consonant-like sounds beginning to exceed vowel-like sounds
	  1. Front and mid vowel-like sounds less frequent
	    a. Most frequent types: / I U ʌ /
	    b. Back sounds appearing (Irwin, 1948)
	  2. Glottal and velar sounds frequent
	    a. Appearance of postdental and labial types (Irwin, 1947b)
	    b. Additional semivowel and fricative types (Irwin, 1947a)

Characteristics of the period—true speech	*Sound making—developing of phonological system*

A. Period of silence between babbling and true speech (Jakobsen and Halle, 1956)
B. Intentional use of speech
  1. First word—accident of vocal play (Berry and Eisenson, 1956)
  2. Approximation of sound through echolalia (Lewis, 1963)
	A. Acquisition built on system of contrasts
	  1. /pa/ universal syllable (Jakobsen and Halle, 1956)
	  2. Consonants more frequent than vowels (Irwin, 1952)
	    a. Nasal/oral distinction made (Jakobsen and Halle, 1956)

Intonation	Meaning	Grammar
	D. Awareness of human speech (Shirley, 1933)	

A. Pattern of intonation heard over a number of syllables
B. Little pitch variation within a single syllable (Weir, 1966)
C. Expressive intonation
  1. Dominating factor
  2. Discrimination among different patterns of expression (Lewis, 1963)
    a. Questions or commands
    b. Elicit surprise (Van Riper, 1963)
D. Use of rhythm in vocal play (Van Riper, 1963)

A. Application of vocalization
  1. For getting attention
  2. For socialization
    a. Support rejections
    b. Express demands (Van Riper, 1963)
  3. Re-creation of sound to replace or recall a pleasurable situation or object (Mowrer, 1952)
B. Response to human speech by smiling or vocalizing
C. Distinction between angry and pleasant sounds
D. Beginning of imitation of parental utterances (Van Riper, 1963)

A. Discrimination among different patterns of expression (Lewis, 1963)
B. Development of stress/unstress pattern (Weir, 1966)
C. Fundamental frequency
  1. 340 Hz when with father
  2. 390 Hz when with mother
  3. Higher frequency when crying (Lieberman, 1967)

A. Beginning of single-word usage
  1. First word a crude approximation (McCarthy, 1954)
  2. Babblings shortened into words (Irwin, 1952)
  3. Manipulation of others through sound making (Lewis, 1963)
B. Understanding of a few words and gestures (Myklebust, 1957)
  1. Listens with selective interest (McCarthy, 1954)
  2. Responds discriminatingly to adult verbalizations (Van Riper, 1963)

A. Intonation and pitch dominating over phonetic form (Lewis, 1963)
B. Marking of sentence boundaries by intonation contours (Weir, 1966)
  1. Referential breath groups as

A. Development of vocabulary
  1. One to three words (*bye-bye, no*, etc.) (Lewis, 1963)
  2. Adaptation of child's primary experience to adult form of words (Lewis, 1963)

A. Holophrastic utterances
  1. Single-word utterances
  2. Ambiguous in meaning—broad and diffuse (McNeill, 1966)
  3. Meaning derived from the situation (Berry and Eisenson, 1956)
B. Parts of speech (adult grammar)

(continued)

Table 7–5. *Scope-and-Sequence Chart (continued)*

Characteristics of the Period	Sound Making
Twelve Months to Eighteen Months 3. Strengthening of word through repetition (Berry and Eisenson, 1956) C. Accompanying motor activity or gestures to aid in understanding and stabilizing speech (Van Riper, 1963)	b. Labial/nonlabial contrast (Leopold, 1953–1954) c. Consonant used in initial position most frequently rather than medial or final (Irwin, 1952) 3. Vowel system 1. High/low contrast 2. Front/back contrast (Weir, 1966) B. Monosyllabic or disyllabic words—some onomatopoeic in character (*bow-wow*) (Irwin, 1952) C. Girls' achievement greater than that of boys (Irwin, 1952) Intonation
Eighteen Months to Twenty-four Months A. Acquisition of new words 1. Perception of new experiences 2. Manipulation of object or activity 3. Introduction of word by adult (Van Riper, 1963) B. Use of echolalia 1. Used in private (Van Riper, 1963); monologue-type speech (Weir, 1963) 2. Prolongs sounds 3. Occurs instantly and unconsciously (Van Riper, 1963) C. Use of jargon 1. Purposeful to child 2. Provides for fluency (Van Riper, 1963) D. Beginning of primitive grammatical system (McNeill, 1966) E. Motor activity 1. Much activity with speech 2. Overflow in lips, jaw, tongue, eyes, head (Metreaux, 1950)	A. Many variants in child's system 1. Vowels most changeable (Metreaux, 1950); more front vowels than back (Irwin, 1952) 2. Instability of voicing feature (Weir, 1963) 3. Rare use of medial and final consonants (Metreaux, 1950; Irwin, 1947a) B. Articulation change under pressure of adult responses (Lewis, 1963) C. Periods of practice in perfecting sounds (Weir, 1963)
Two Years to Three Years A. Period of preoccupation with sound (Weir, 1966) B. Rapid increase in language growth 1. Use of speech for self-assertion, self-awareness, and as safety valve (Van Riper, 1963) 2. Growth in grammatical capacity C. Demand of response from others 1. Demand from adults 2. Kicks and screams with peers (Metreaux, 1950) D. Motor activity 1. Able to speak before he acts 2. Acts in relation to task at hand (Metreaux, 1950)	A. Mastery of two thirds of adult speech sounds (Irwin, 1952) 1. Vowels—90 percent correct (Irwin, 1948) 2. Specific pronunciation for most consonants a. Most correct—plosives b. Slighting of medial consonants (Irwin, 1952) c. Overpronunciation of some words—*flonwer* for *flower* (Metreaux, 1950) B. Distinctive features in production and recall 1. Voicing and nasality best maintained 2. Continuancy and stridency least maintained 3. Sounds differing in one feature (especially continuancy) most difficult (d for ð) 4. Nonperipheral sounds more difficult than peripheral (Menyuk, 1968)

Intonation	Meaning	Grammar

phonetic markers of complete sentences (Lieberman, 1967)
2. Juncture evident in utterances (Weir, 1963)
C. Stress pattern: stress/unstress (Weir, 1963)
	3. Words learned through associated actions (Lewis, 1963)
	4. Names objects (Bayley, 1935)
	5. Performative utterance—names what he is doing at the time (Bullowa, 1967a, 1967b)
	6. Begins to apply words to categories (Brown, 1965)
	B. Verbal understanding greater than production (McCarthy, 1954)
	  1. Responds to commands (McCarthy, 1954)
	  2. No understanding of questions
	    a. At times no response (Bellugi, 1965)
	    b. At times imitation or repetition of question (Bellugi, 1965)
		1. Nouns most common
		2. A few verbs and adjectives (McNeill, 1966)

A. Earliest feature acquired (Weir, 1963)
B. Indication of contrastive elements of stress (Weir, 1966)
  1. Inconsistent use
  2. Overuse of stress on syllables other than correct one (Weir, 1966)
C. Pitch rise at end of sentence (Metreaux, 1950)
D. Voice control—unstable
  1. Variation from good modulation to straining
  2. Much experimentation (Metreaux, 1950)
E. Fluency—frequent repetition of words and syllables—unforced and easily terminated (Metreaux, 1950)
	A. Twenty- to 100-word vocabulary (Irwin, 1952)
	  1. Prominence of meaningful words (McCarthy, 1954)
	  2. General referents (*cookie* refers to anything similar) (Van Riper, 1963)
	  3. One fourth of utterances understood by others (Van Riper, 1963)
	  4. Beginning of substitution of words for physical acts (Lewis, 1963)
	    a. Extension of use of words (*pay* for anything that flies)
	    b. Rudiment of generalization (*tee* for *cat* as well as *dog*) (Lewis, 1963)
	  5. Naming of objects in books (Shirley, 1933)
	B. Reportive utterances—description of things in environment without accompanying action (Bullowa, 1967a, 1967b)
	C. Lower boundary for beginning of semantic system (McNeill, 1966)
		A. Beginning of structure
		  1. Two-word sentences—words in juxtaposition (McNeill, 1966)
		  2. Telegraphic utterances
		    a. Result of limited memory span
		    b. Inclusion of informational content of message
		    c. Omission of auxiliaries, prepositions, articles, verbs, and inflections (Brown and Fraser, 1964)
		  3. Use of nouns, a few verbs, adjectives, and some pronouns of adult categories (McCarthy, 1954)
		B. Average of 1.7 words per utterance (McCarthy, 1954)

A. Intonational pattern becoming subordinated to phonetic (Lewis, 1963)
B. Voice—unstable pattern
  1. Range from high to low
  2. Presence of nasality
  3. Straining and forcing (Metreaux, 1950)
C. Fluency—broken rhythm
  1. Repetition of sounds, words, phrases
  2. Use of starters
  3. Echoic of others (Metreaux, 1950)
	A. Two-hundred-and-fifty-word vocabulary (Irwin, 1952)
	  1. Words still general in content (Metreaux, 1950)
	  2. Assignment of each referent to a category (McNeill, 1966)
	  3. Categories learned from actions rather than names of words (Brown, 1965)
	  4. Children's definitions of words in terms of action
	  5. Order of learning adverbs—locative, temporal, manner (Miller and Ervin, 1964)
	B. Period of compiling a word dictionary in building of semantic system (McNeill, 1966)
		A. Two-word utterances—primitive grammar
		  1. Selection not random
		  2. Patterned arrangements in sequential order
		  3. Missing elements
		    a. Auxiliaries, articles, determiners, pronouns, prepositions, inflections
		    b. Small-sized categorical classes
		    c. Words predictable from context
		    d. Intermediate words in adult constructions (Brown and Fraser, 1964)

(continued)

Table 7–5. *Scope-and-Sequence Chart (continued)*

	Characteristics of the Period	*Sound Making*
Two Years to Three Years		

4. Elements retained in imitation of adult
   a. Initial and final words
   b. Reference-making forms
   c. Nonpredictable forms
   d. Words with heavier stress
   e. Expandable classes (Brown, 1964)
5. Development of word classes based on privilege of occurrence (Brown, 1964)
   a. Class distinction into pivot and open word classes
      (1) Pivot—distinct category similar to function words (McNeill, 1966)
         (a) Few members
         (b) Frequent use
         (c) Heterogeneous selection on basis of adult grammar (articles, greetings, adjectives, verbs)
      (2) Open class—similar to nounlike categories
         (a) Many members
         (b) Less frequent use of each member (Brown and Fraser, 1964)
   b. Predictable structure of utterance
      (1) Pivot plus open (*pretty shoe, see mommy*)
      (2) Open plus open (*daddy shoe*)—similar to adult possessive form (McNeill, 1966)
B. Later constructions
   1. Mean word length per utterance is 3.5 words (McCarthy, 1954)
   2. Original pivot class reduced by subdivision
   3. Treatment of demonstrative pronouns and adjectives as unique classes to yield *a that horsie*
   4. Development of hierarchial structure
      a. Structure of noun phrase
      b. Structure of verb phrase
      c. Ultimate combination of noun phrase and verb phrase to form adultlike grammar (McNeill, 1966)
C. Transformations
   1. Stages of negative structure development
      a. *No* or *not* plus primitive structure (*no wash*)
      b. Addition of *can't* and *don't*

(continued)

291

Table 7–5. *Scope-and-Sequence Chart (continued)*

	Characteristics of the Period	*Sound Making*
Two Years to Three Years		

Three Years to Four Years	A. Becomes linguistic adult
	  1. Acquires adult syntax
	  2. Is versatile in use of language (McNeill, 1966)
	    a. To express emotions
	    b. To manipulate associates
	    c. To express relations
	    d. To satisfy needs
	    e. To seek verification *(What's this?)*
	    f. To express dependency
	    g. To entertain self (Templin, 1957)
	    h. Verbalizes as he acts (Lewis, 1963)
	B. Can be controlled by language (Metreaux, 1950)
	C. Learns to whisper (Metreaux, 1950)
	D. Squeals, sputters, laughs, sighs (Metreaux, 1950)
	E. Accompanies speech with tongue protrusion, lip smacking, tongue clicks (Metreaux, 1950)
	F. Continues to use echolalia
	    a. When speech becomes difficult
		A. 90 percent of vowels and diphthongs mastered (Templin, 1957)
		B. 60 percent of consonants mastered (Templin, 1957)
		  1. By manner of articulation
		    a. Nasals—92.5 percent
		    b. Plosives—79.1 percent
		    c. Fricatives—41.0 percent
		  2. By position
		    a. Initial sound—70 percent
		    b. Medial sound—68 percent
		    c. Final sound—52 percent (Templin, 1957)
		  3. By mastery of specific sounds—/ p b m w h/ (Poole, 1934)
		  4. Inconsistent production (Metreaux, 1950)
		C. Greatest change in articulatory ability
		  1. Between 3 and 3.5 years for girls
		  2. Between 3.5 and 4 years for boys (Templin, 1957)

Intonation	Meaning	Grammar

		as vocabulary items contained in primitive structure
		c. Indication of adult rule
		  (1) Use of auxiliary in affirmative (*I can see it*)
		  (2) Use of auxiliary with *n't* (*I can't see it*)
		d. Copular *be* optional (*I not big enough*)
		e. Appearance of double negative (*He never made no trip*) (Bellugi, 1964)
		2. Stages of interrogative structure development
		  a. No use of questions or comprehension of question
		    (1) No response or inappropriate response
		    (2) Imitation of question
		  b. Intonational question (*See doggie?*)
		  c. Use of interrogative words—*who, what, where*
		    (1) Initial word (*How you do it?*)
		    (2) *Why not* a single vocabulary item
		    (3) Better comprehension of adult questions
		  d. Approaching of adult form
		    (1) Use of auxiliaries
		    (2) Use of interrogative words as replacement for missing element in sentence (Bellugi, 1965)
		D. Inflections—latter part of second year
		  1. Use of present progressive
		  2. Use of present indicative (Miller and Ervin, 1964)

A. Well patterned (Van Riper, 1963)
B. Normal loudness and tone
C. Breathiness
D. Nasality with soft voice
E. Faster rate
F. Fluency
  1. Recurrence of compulsive repetitions
    a. Tonic blocks on initial syllables
    b. Grimacing, puffing
  2. Use of starters (Metreaux, 1950)
	A. 900-word vocabulary (Berry and Eisenson, 1956)
	B. Use of linguistic symbols in dealing with situations (Lewis, 1963)
	C. Use of language in imaginative play (Lewis, 1963)
	D. Self-centered explanations
	    a. Egocentric speech
	    b. No apprehension of information requirement of others (Piaget, 1960)
	E. Few semantic markers for words (McNeill, 1966)
		A. Mean word length per utterance: four words (Templin, 1957)
		B. Mean number of different words per fifty utterances
		  1. 92.5 at three years
		  2. 104.8 at three and one-half years (Templin, 1957)
		C. Acquisition of adult grammar
		  1. Well-formed utterances but not always grammatical (Brown and Fraser, 1964)
		  2. 48 percent of utterances grammatically correct (Templin, 1957)
		  3. Copular *be* optional (Brown and Fraser, 1964)
		  4. Incorporation of rules of grammar
		    a. Understand and produce sentences

(continued)

Table 7–5. *Scope-and-Sequence Chart (continued)*

	Characteristics of the Period	*Sound Making*

Three Years to Four Years

b. To assimilate associations (Myklebust, 1957)

Four Years to Five Years

A. Language a facile tool
  1. Commands giving way to spontaneous speech
  2. Questions other's activity (Metreaux, 1950)
B. Girls exceed boys in linguistic ability at four and one-half years (Templin, 1957)
C. Motor activity
  1. Tension at a minimum
  2. Overflow in gross activity
  3. Less verbalization with activity (Metreaux, 1950)

A. Consonant production 90 percent correct by four and one-half years (Templin, 1957)
  1. Percent of correct scores by manner of articulation
    a. Nasals—95 percent
    b. Plosives—90 percent
    c. Semivowels—85 percent
    d. Fricatives and combinations—60 percent (Templin, 1957)
  2. Percent of correct scores by position
    a. Initial—88 percent
    b. Medial—86 percent
    c. Final—74 percent (Templin, 1957)
  3. Substitution of /w/ for /l/ and /r/ (Metreaux, 1950); example of hierarchical development of distinctive features (Menyuk, 1968)
  4. Additional mastered sounds—/d t n g k ŋ j/ (Poole, 1934) (Templin, [tʃ] 1957)
B. Production more stable (Metreaux, 1950)

Five Years to Six Years

A. More sophisticated use of language
B. More use of language
C. More comprehensible
D. Increased speech in social interaction
E. Less repetition of adults (Brown, 1965)

A. 98 percent of vowel production correct (Templin, 1957)
B. 88 percent of consonant production correct (Templin, 1957)
  1. Percent of correct production by manner of articulation
    a. Nasals—95 percent
    b. Plosives and semivowels—85 percent
    c. Fricatives—68 percent
    d. Combinations—60 percent (Templin, 1957)
  2. Percent of correct production by position
    a. Initial—90 percent
    b. Medial—84 percent
    c. Final—80 percent (Templin, 1957)
  3. Additional sounds mastered: /f v s z/ (Poole, 1934)
C. Occasional reversals of sounds (Van Riper, 1963)

Intonation	Meaning	Grammar

		b. Has difficulty in repetition because of structure complexity and not because of sentence length (Menyuk, 1963)
		D. Inflectional rules
		  1. Use of past tense
		    a. Omission (*push* for *pushed*)
		    b. Redundancy (*pushted* for *pushed*) (Menyuk, 1963)
		  2. Use of present progressive (Bellugi, 1964)
		  3. Use of present indicative (Bellugi, 1964)

A. Imitation of parents' intonation pattern (Metreaux, 1950)
B. Voice—well modulated and firm
  1. Subdued at times (Metreaux, 1950)
  2. Whining at times (Metreaux, 1950)
C. Rate—186 words per minute (Metreaux, 1950)
D. Fewer repetitions
  1. For emphasis at times
  2. Continued blocking and grimacing (Metreaux, 1950)
	A. Rapid increase in vocabulary (Berry and Eisenson, 1956)
	B. Speech egocentric in nature (Piaget, 1960)
	C. Use of descriptive types of explanations in word definitions (Feifel and Lorge, 1950)
	D. Word association studies
	  1. Multiple-word responses
	  2. Excessive number of syntactic responses
	  3. Excessive number of noun responses (Entwisle et al., 1964)
		A. Mean number of words per utterance: 5½ (Templin, 1957)
		B. Mean number of different words per utterance: 2½ (Templin, 1957)
		C. Mean number of different words per fifty utterances:
		  1. 120.4 at 4 years
		  2. 127.0 at 4½ years (Templin, 1957)
		D. More complicated sentence structure (Anderson, 1953)
		E. Use of rules for forming simple plural, present progressive, and possession when expanded to new words never heard before
		  1. Unable to expand /ed/ to new words when final sound is /t/ or /d/ for past tense
		  2. Operate on rule: "A voiceless sibilant after a voiced consonant and a voiced sibilant after all other sounds makes a word plural." (Berko, 1958)
		  3. Use plural for counting nouns (Bellugi, 1964)
		F. No awareness of separate elements of compound words (Berko, 1958)

A. Continued improvement in fluency and phonation
B. Hesitations, pauses, and slower rate evident in speech requiring explanation rather than description (Levin et al., 1967)
	A. Vocabulary of 2000 words (McCarthy, 1954)
	B. Word-association studies
	  1. Percentage of noun responses decreases
	  2. More paradigmatic responses to verbs and adjectives (Entwisle et al., 1964)
	  3. Children less able to take advantage of semantic consistency in sentences when shadowing speech than an eight-year-old group (McNeill, 1965)
		A. Mean number of words per utterance: 5.7 (Templin, 1957)
		B. Mean number of different words per fifty utterances: 132.4 (Templin, 1957)
		C. Improved syntax (Van Riper, 1963)
		D. Perfecting of rules for forming inflections
		  a. Use of possessive
		  b. Use of third person singular (Berko, 1958)
		E. Production and recall of nongrammatical material not different from grammatical (Menyuk, 1965)

(continued)

Table 7–5. *Scope-and-Sequence Chart (continued)*

	Characteristics of the Period	*Sound Making*
Six Years to Seven and Beyond	A. Language more socially oriented (Piaget, 1960) B. Language as instrument for growth of individual personality (Lewis, 1963) C. Different languages 1. Of elders 2. Of peers 3. Of reading and writing (Lewis, 1963)	A. Boys' requirement of additional year for mastery of sounds (Poole, 1934) B. Six-year-old status 1. Correct production by manner of articulation a. Nasals and plosives—98 percent b. Semivowels—92 percent c. Fricatives—75 percent d. Combinations—65 percent 2. Correct production by position a. Initial—92 percent b. Medial—91 percent c. Final—90 percent 3. Additional sounds mastered: /v ð ʒ ʃ l/; loss of /s z/ (Poole, 1934) C. Seven-year-old status 1. Correct production by manner of articulation a. Nasals—99 percent b. Plosives—98 percent c. Semivowels—95 percent d. Fricatives—88 percent e. Combinations—70 percent (Templin, 1957) 2. Correct production by position a. Initial—100 percent b. Medial—98 percent c. Final—100 percent (Templin, 1957) 3. Additional sounds mastered: /r θ hw/ with recurrence of /s z/ (Poole, 1934); /d/ (Templin, 1957) D. Eight-year-old status 1. Correct production by manner of articulation a. Nasals—100 percent b. Plosives—98 percent c. Semivowels—98 percent d. Fricatives—98 percent e. Combinations—75 percent 2. Little difference in percentage of correct production by position with the exception of difficulty with fricatives in final position (Templin, 1957)

suggest that the teacher consider the following questions; and if she can answer any of them with a "yes," it is likely that further assessment is in order: Does language usage or lack of it call unwanted attention to the speaker? Does the speaker appear to be concerned in any way about his inadequate communication ability? Are listeners unable to readily understand the child when he speaks?

Once it is decided that the child is in need of a comprehensive assessment, there are a variety of options available, including standardized testing, speech sample analysis, and diagnostic teaching. Various tests can be administered to verify the presence of a problem or to help qualify a child for a

Intonation	Meaning	Grammar

A. Fundamental frequency for seven-year-old boys: 294 Hz; for eight-year-old boys: 297 Hz.
B. Fundamental frequency for seven-year-old girls: 281 Hz; for eight-year-old girls: 288 Hz.
C. Upward and downward voice breaks common to all groups (Fairbanks, 1950)
	A. Mean number of words per utterance
	  1. 6.4 words for six years
	  2. 7 words for seven years
	  3. 7.7 words for eight years
	B. Mean number of different words per fifty utterances
	  1. 147 at six years
	  2. 157.7 at seven years
	  3. 166.5 at eight years
	C. Grammatical system well established (Slobin, 1966)
	  1. Evaluation of passibe, negative, and negative passive sentences by six-year-olds
	  2. More time required for evaluation of complex structure (Slobin, 1966)
	  3. Percentage of correct grammatical utterances
	    a. 73.7 by six-year-olds
	    b. 76.1 by eight-year-olds (Templin, 1957)
	  4. Learning tasks and recall easier with grammatical material than with nongrammatical material Menyuk, 1965)
		A. Basic estimated vocabulary
		  1. 13,000 words (2000 spoken) at six years
		  2. 21,600 words at seven years
		  3. 28,300 words at eight years (Templin, 1957)
		B. More discriminate use of vocabulary (Lewis, 1963)
		C. Definitions of words
		  1. By use of description below six or seven years
		  2. By synonym at eight to eleven years
		  3. By categorical description or explanation above eleven years
		D. Language taking on idiosyncrasies (Lewis, 1963)
		E. Word association studies
		  1. Primarily syntagmatic responses at six years (McNeill, 1965)
		  2. Decrease in percentage of noun responses from six to eight years (Entwisle, et al., 1964)
		  3. Increase in percentage of paradigmatic responses for verbs
		F. Continuation in developing of semantic markers in child's word dictionary (McNeill, 1966)

particular school program, although the results of these are usually insufficient for planning intervention programs. Samples of a child's speech can be recorded and analyzed according to a set of criteria; or the teacher may choose to engage in diagnostic teaching activities. Each of these options is described in some detail in the following parts of this section.

Before beginning that discussion, however, we want to make a few comments about language assessment in general. It is important that the teacher be aware of a number of dimensions that are pertinent to language assessment. These involve knowledge relating to the following questions. Does the assessment procedure:

1. Yield the kinds of data about the child's language that is desired (i.e., is it valid for the purposes being contemplated?)
2. Account for dialect?
3. Measure expressive and/or receptive abilities?
   a. If expressive, does the format utilize imitation, spontaneous, or elicited speech?
   b. If receptive, does the format utilize picture identification, response to commands, etc.?
4. Inventory many aspects of language, or does it only measure specific areas (e.g., receptive vocabulary, grammar usage, articulation, etc.)?
5. Result in instructionally useful information, or is it intended for screening or research purposes only?

Standardized Testing of Language

In Table 7–6 we present a number of the most commonly used commercially available tests of language and language correlates. The teacher should be aware of the nature of these tests because of their widespread use in language evaluation. This knowledge will help teachers to interpret test results and reports, indicate where further informal assessments are necessary, and execute appropriate remediative and/or preventative strategies.

Informal Approaches to Language Assessment

In an attempt to further specify the nature of the language problem, informal assessment strategies will be necessary. The following strategies, which are adapted from Bryen (1975), are representative of informal assessment that can be conducted in the classroom.

Semantics. While semantics is probably the most critical aspect of language, it continues to be one of the least understood aspects. Since most of the language used in the classroom has the purpose of either expressing or receiving meaningful information, the informal assessment of semantics is important. In assessing a child's semantic development, one needs to tap more than the meaning of isolated words or the child's vocabulary. One needs to assess, in addition to the child's knowledge of specific words, how a child uses linguistic and situational contexts to determine the meaning of words as well as the choice of words to be used.

The word *boys* illustrates how the linguistic context determines the meaning of this word. In isolated speech this word has no one specific

Table 7–6. *Commercially Prepared Tests of Language*

Name (Author of Test)	Aspect of Language Measured	Target Population	Purported Purpose	Comments
Assessment of Children's Language Comprehension (Foster, Giddan, and Stark, 1973)	Ability of children to identify pictures containing 1, 2, 3, or 4 verbal elements	Preschool through elementary	"To define receptive language difficulty in children and to indicate guidelines for correction"	Available in group or individual form. No expressive ability in children required. Reliability and validity not reported. Not a complete test of language comprehension, as title states (no testing of syntactic comprehension), but useful for measuring number of verbal information bits child can integrate concurrently.
Carrow Elicited Language Inventory (Carrow-Woolfolk, 1974)	Expressive language in elicited situation (emphasis on syntax)	Ages 3 to 8	To assess a child's productive control of grammar	52 stimulus sentences and phrases are used to elicit responses. Child's responses are taped, require phonemic transcription. Analysis system covers 12 grammatical categories and 5 error types. Provides for in-depth analysis of child's errors on verbs.
Developmental Sentence Analysis (Lee, 1974)	Expressive syntax in spontaneous speech	Ages 2 to 7	To evaluate the grammatical structure of child's spontaneous speech	100 different intelligible spontaneous utterances are taped and analyzed according to length and type. Basic assumption: increasing length a measure of increasing grammatical complexity. Score is weighted for presence of indefinite pronoun or noun modifiers, personal pronouns, main verbs, secondary verbs, negatives, conjunctions, interrogative reversals, and wh- questions. Elements that normally occur later are given greater weight. Interjudge reliability = .94; split-half reliability = .73. Valid data supportive.

(continued)

Table 7–6. *Commercially Prepared Tests of Language (continued)*

Name (Author of Test)	Aspect of Language Measured	Target Population	Purported Purpose	Comments
Goldman–Fristoe Test of Articulation (Goldman and Fristoe, 1969)	Articulation	Above age 2	To assess child's ability to produce speech sounds	Attractively illustrated. Well standardized. Takes about 30 minutes to administer. Measures speech sound production in initial, medial, and final positions in words and sentences.
Houston Test of Language Development (Crabtree, 1963)	A variety of expressive and receptive language and language-related tasks	6 months to 6 years	To assess child's developmental language	Standardization is incomplete. Test has two parts—Part I is a checklist for parent or teacher to check items at the age they were first observed in the child. Part II measures syntactical complexity, intonation, vocabulary, comprehension, and self-identity.
Illinois Test of Psycholinguistic Abilities (Kirk, McCarthy, and Kirk, 1968)	Correlates of language such as duplicating a sequence of geometric designs, also vocabulary and expression	Ages 2 to 7	To identify the psycholinguistic abilities and disabilities of children	Based on a model that separates various skills into expressive, receptive, and organizing aspects, and into representational and automatic levels. Relationship of various subtests to language itself not well established. Overall reliability satisfactory; some subtest reliabilities too low for diagnosis of individuals. Validity issues unresolved.
Language Comprehension Tests (Bellugi-Klima, 1973)	Selected aspects of language comprehension	Preschool	To test comprehension of linguistic constructions	Child is asked to manipulate real objects in response to examiners' instructions at three levels: (1) active sentences, singular/plural nouns, possessives; (2) negative/affirmative, singular/plural verbs, inflections, adjectival modifications; (3) negative affixes, reflexivization, comparatives, passives, embedded sentences. Items are exemplary rather than comprehen-

Test	Area measured	Ages/population	Purpose	Description
Miller-Yoder Test of Grammatical Comprehension, Experimental Edition (Miller and Yoder, 1972)	Syntactic comprehension	Ages 3 to 6	To assess a child's grammatical comprehension	42 stimulus sentence pairs spoken by examiner; child points to appropriate picture on plate. Untimed. Not standardized. Internal reliability = .93. Lexical items representative of 5-year-olds. Measures active passive, prepositions, possessives, negative affixes, pronouns, singular/plural nouns and verbs, verbal inflections, adjectival modifications, reflexivizations. Test lends itself well to diagnostic teaching.
Northwestern Syntax Screening Test (Lee, 1966)	Syntactic expression and comprehension	Ages 4 to 8; standard English speakers	To screen children on the basis of receptive and expressive syntactic usage	20 receptive items are measured by child indicating which of four pictures is appropriate for sentence. 20 expressive items are similar, except child repeats stimulus sentences as he points. Age norms are presented for small standardization sample. No reliability or validity data reported.
Parsons Language Sample (Spraldin, 1963)	Expressive aspects of language, vocal and nonvocal; comprehension	Children with severe mental handicaps	To sample language behavior according to Skinnerian outline	Considerable use with very low-functioning children. Seven subtests, including vocal and nonvocal. Standardized on mentally retarded children. Overall reliability is satisfactory; subtests too highly correlated to be used diagnostically. Does not measure syntax.
Peabody Picture Vocabulary Test (Dunn, 1965)	Receptive vocabulary of standard English	Mental ages 2 to adult	To derive an IQ score	Test is untimed and well standardized. Child points to appropriate picture on plate in response to stimulus word spoken by examiner. May be given by teacher; takes 10–20 minutes.
Slingerland Screening Tests for Identifying Children with Specific Language Disability (Slingerland, 1970)	Correlates of language such as memory of geometric forms	Children in the early grades	To detect deficits in one or more areas on which receptive and	Consists of three sets of tests, each with nine subtests—eight for group administration, one for individual. Wall charts, test booklets, and cards

(continued)

Table 7–6. *Commercially Prepared Tests of Language (continued)*

Name (Author of Test)	Aspect of Language Measured	Target Population	Purported Purpose	Comments
			expressive written language is based.	are the stimulus materials. Tasks include copying from a model (both written and oral), matching, kinesthetic–motor acts, sound discrimination, sentence completion, among others. No reliability or validity data are presented.
Templin–Darley Test of Articulation (Templin and Darley, 1960)	Articulation	Ages 3 to 8	Screening or diagnosis of articulation	Sound elements tested include 25 consonant blends, 12 vowels, and 6 diphthongs. Child utters sounds in isolation, in words, and in a sentence. Short form (50 items) may be used for screening; all 176 items for diagnosis.
Test for Auditory Comprehension of Language (Carrow-Woolfolk, 1973)	Auditory comprehension of vocabulary, morphology, syntax	Ages 3 to 6	To measure receptive language in English or Spanish	Test consists of 101 pictorial stimuli plates of three drawings each. One of the drawings is the correct representation, one is the reverse of the stimulus sentence, and the other serves as a distractor. Test is individually administered, with child pointing to appropriate drawing. Provides indication of child's proficiency in vocabulary, morphology, syntax. English and Spanish versions field-tested on native speakers of each language.
Test of Language Development (TOLD) (Newcomer and Hammill, 1977)	Receptive and expressive aspects of vocabulary, syntax, and phonology	Ages 4 to 9	To give indication of child's overall strengths and weaknesses in each are tapped	Test is short and easy to administer. Five principal subtests measure receptive and expressive aspects of vocabulary and grammar. Two supplemental subtests measure articulation and speech sound discrimination. Test subtests correlate with criterion

Test	Assesses	Ages	Purpose	Description
				tests, with r's mostly in .70's. Subtests generally internally consistent and stable.
Utah Test of Language Development (UTLD) Mecham, Jex, and Jones, 1969)	Expressive and receptive language, aspects of conceptual development	Ages 1.6 to 14.5	To derive an overall picture of a child's language development as compared with his peers	Test consists of two sections—one an informant-interview section based on the Vineland Social Maturity Scale, the other a direct test requiring the child to perform such things as repeat digits, recite a story, reproduce geometric forms. Yield score in form of language age. Internal reliabilities high.
Vocabulary Comprehension Scale (Bangs, 1975)	Assesses child's ability to follow instructions involving use of various lexical and function words	Ages 2 to 6 language disabled	To provide information on comprehension of pronouns, words of position, quality, size, and quantity	Attractive kit in shape of house. Has manipulative items such as cars, balls. Instructions to child in form of games—Garage, Tea Party, Buttons, Miscellaneous. Standardized on culturally diverse middle-income population in Texas.

meaning even though in its written form the range of possible meanings can be delimited somewhat to *boys, boy's,* or *boys'*. Only in its linguistic context can the word, pronounced *boys*, begin to take on a more specified meaning. It can mean plurality, as in *The boys are running,* or singular possessive, as in *The boy's jacket fell by his chair,* or plural possessive, as in *The boys' bikes were parked by their houses.*

The situational context will also influence the meaning of words. For example, as Bloom (1970) has illustrated, the words *Mommy shoe* can indicate possessive in the situation when the young child brings the mother her shoe, or it can indicate an actor–object relationship, as when the child uses this utterance when commenting on the fact that mother is putting on her shoe.

The following procedures are examples of the kinds of tasks that can be used to informally assess semantics.

Early semantic development. Between the ages of nine and eighteen months, the normal child begins to actively experiment with language. However, during this early stage of development, the child's utterances will be tied closely to specific situational contexts for the expression and production of meaningful language.

Objective. Assess the child's early language comprehension.

Materials. None other than contexts and materials the child frequently engages with.

Procedures. Select and list the contexts of commonly occurring activities. Present simple words/phrases which are related to the context. For example, at the table where the child usually eats say "want to eat?". Or at the door, say "bye-bye?". Observe and note the child's responses.

Now, use the same procedure as above, but not in the context in which that activity usually occurs. For example, at the table say "want to go bye-bye?" or "bye-bye?". Or at a different part of the room say "want to eat?". Observe and note the child's responses.

Results. In analyzing the child's responses, note whether the child gives either behavioral or verbal indicators that he has understood the meaning of your utterance. Does the child do so only in the well-established situational context, e.g., "bye-bye" only at the door? Or has the child's early language comprehension become free from specific contexts, e.g., "bye-bye" at the table or sandbox?

Objective. Assess the child's early meaningful use of one- or two-word utterances.

Materials. Toys or objects which the child frequently uses.

Procedures. Place the familiar toys or objects in front of the child, one at a time. Engage the child in play with them. Observe the child as he manipulates the object(s) or engages in activity. Record any utterances and the context in which they occur. If no spontaneous utterances occur, try eliciting utterances by asking "What's this?" or "What's the ball doing?". Note all responses.

Results. In analyzing the child's responses, note not only the specific word(s) used but also their apparent semantic intent. This can only be assessed in relationship to the particular context in which this utterance was made. For example, is the word *cookie* used to indicate the existence of a cookie, to indicate the recurrence of a cookie, or to indicate the object of an action? This procedure should provide information not only about the words the child produces, but also the semantic function of these words.

Word association. The use of word-association tasks has provided information in regard to the semantic development of children. Specifically, it enables us to study how individuals chunk or classify words. There are two general response categories: syntagmatic or paradigmatic. A syntagmatic response to a stimulus word would be a word that would either proceed or follow the stimulus word, according to the rules of syntax. For example, the stimulus word *chair* might call forth the word *sit* or *on*, as in the phrase *Sit on the chair.* Paradigmatic responses, in contrast, are those responses of the same grammatical category as in the response *sofa* or *table* to the stimulus word *chair*. Younger children tend to respond more frequently with syntagmatic responses, with the shift to paradigmatic responses occurring between the ages of six and eight years.

Objective. Assess how the child classifies words.

Materials. Word list of familiar words.

Procedures. Supply the child with each stimulus word, telling him that this is a game and that he is to say the first word he can think of. If there is no immediate response (within 5 seconds), proceed to the next word. Vary the words using a number of nouns, adjectives, verbs, adverbs, and prepositions. Some frequently used noun words are *table, man, mountain,* and *fruit*. Words such as *sit, play, jump,* and *speak* are good verbs to use.

Frequently used adjectives are *dark, cold, deep,* and *afraid* and adverbs are *very, easily, always,* and *how.* Good prepositions to try are *up, on, with,* and *over.*

Results. Analyze the child's responses. Were there more syntagmatic or paradigmatic responses? Did the child show difficulties by reverting to many perseverative or rhyming responses? Was a particular grammatical category most difficult for the child? In other words, did the child indicate difficulty with the adverbial class of words by using syntagmatic, perseverative, or rhyming responses?

Specific and nonspecific referents. One theory touched upon in the introduction to semantics was the referential theory. According to this theory, the meaning of a word is determined by its referent. As was already discussed, there are several difficulties with this theory, for even the simple word *dog* does not refer to one specific referent but rather to a category defined by *all* four-legged animals that are frequently domesticated and utter barking sounds. Shortcomings of this theory are further evident when one examines words such as *justice* or *jealousy* or *happiness.* What is the referent here?

Objective. Analyze the various meaning the child expresses when shown a referent and when a word is given without a referent.

Materials. Several common objects the child has had some contact with: *nail, ball, scissors, pencil,* etc., and a list of words without specific referents, such as *animal, toy, hungry, arithmetic.*

Procedures. Ask the child to "tell you all about" the object presented. Probe for a variety of responses by saying "tell me more." Let the child play with and manipulate the objects. After using six referent words, ask the child to tell you about *animal* or *toy* or *hungry*—words without particular referents. Record all responses. Probe as much as possible.

Results. Analyze how the responses varied. What meanings were imposed on each word? Did the child's responses include (a) label or name of the object, (b) color, (c) shape, (d) function? Or were the child's responses restricted to one category, such as function? What difficulties, if any, were encountered with the nonreferent words? Did the child rely on specific instances of the word? For example, *ball, bat, bike,* and *truck* given in response to the word "toy" instead of a classificatory description, such as *things you can play with.*

Sentences and word meanings. As has already been mentioned, the meaning of a word is influenced by its linguistic context. Katz and Fodor (1963) have suggested that there are two aspects of semantics, that of *semantic features* and *selection restrictions*. The first aspect, semantic features, relates to the features of meaning of a particular word. For example, *father* has, among other features, the set (+ human (+ male) (+ parent). Additionally, there are semantic restrictions on the possible combinations of words in a sentence that *father* can take in a sentence in order for that sentence to be meaningful. For example, the sentence *She is my father* violates our notions of truth, because it violates these semantic restrictions. That is, the semantic features of *she* (+ human) (− male) do not include the semantic features of father. Therefore, a full assessment of semantics must include not only the child's understanding of isolated words, but how they are used in meaningful sentences.

Objective. Assess the child's semantic knowledge in particular linguistic contexts.

Materials. A list of sentences, some of which violate selection restriction and some of which are semantically correct should be used as probes. The following sentences are examples of sentences that might be used:

1. She is my brother.
2. My mother has no children.
3. The pony rides the girl.
4. She is my sister.
5. The candy eats Carol.
6. My father is a bachelor.
7. The liquid spilled.
8. The liquid clapped their hands.

Procedures. After you read each sentence, ask the child to determine if the sentences makes sense (i.e., is a "good sentence") or not (i.e., is a "bad sentence"). After the child has made a judgment ("good" or "bad sentence") about each sentence, ask him "Why is it a good (or bad) sentence?". For those sentences that the child has judged as bad, ask him to "correct it" or "make it better." Record all responses.

Results. In analyzing the child's responses, attempt to determine how the child decided which sentences were good or bad. Did he use only the semantic features of isolated words in making his judgment? Did he use *both* semantic features and linguistic context (i.e., selection restrictions) in making his judgment? Was the child able to correct semantically anomolous sentences? If not, how much did the lack of understanding of the meaning of particular words (semantic features) cause problems?

Morphology and syntax. The combining of morphemes into rule-governed sequences produces syntactically acceptable sentences. The development of these rules governing the combination of morphemes enables the child to produce and understand a potentially infinite number of sentences. Without knowledge of these rules, an individual may be restricted in both his ability to produce and comprehend the many novel sentences which are continually being used by speakers of his language. For this reason, it is important to assess the child's knowledge of morphological and syntactical structures.

Morphological production. Many languages have rules that determine the use of particular morphological markers, such as *-ed* marker for past tense, the *-s* marker for plurality, the *-ing* progressive marker, and the *-er* marker for the agentive. However, not all languages or dialects employ these morphological markers, as does Standard English. For example, it has been noted earlier that in Black English, these markers may be deleted because they are optional markers rather than obligatory as in Standard English.

Objective. To analyze the child's production of frequently used, Standard English morphological markers with familiar and unlearned words.

Materials. A series of pictures and accompanying stories that act to stimulate the child's production. For each familiar word and accompanying stimulus story there should be a comparable "nonsense" story that taps the same morphological marker. For example, the following picture stories could be used to tap the *-s* plural marker.
Picture stories can be developed for the *-ed*, *-'s*, *-ing*, and *-er* markers.

Procedures. Present each picture story (familiar first, followed by unfamiliar nonsense) to the child, saying:

"I'm going to tell you a story about some pictures. I'm going to leave out a word, so listen carefully. Your job is to fill in the missing word."

Read each story that accompanies the picture and record precisely the responses the child gives.

Familiar Story

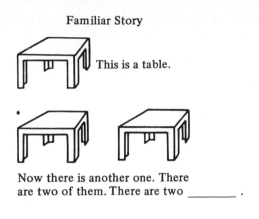

This is a table.

Now there is another one. There
are two of them. There are two _____ .

Nonsense Story

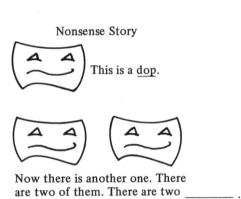

This is a <u>dop</u>.

Now there is another one. There
are two of them. There are two _____ .

Results. Analyze the child's responses to determine if he could generate
the appropriate morphological markers. Determine if he could do this with
unlearned, "nonsense" words as well as with familiar words. If errors did
occur, were they isolated to particular markers (e.g., the -*er* marker)? Develop additional picture stories to probe further these troublesome markers.
Additionally, pay closer attention to determine if the child performs similarly in his spontaneous language production. Caution again must be made
that certain English dialects may not require the obligatory -*ed*, -*s*, and -'*s*
markers. Therefore, the absence of these markers does not immediately
imply a language problem.

Word order as a conveyor of meaning. Because sentences are not
merely a random sequencing of words, change in the ordering of words may
dramatically affect the meaning conveyed by the sentence. For example, if

the ordering of *car* and *truck* were reversed in sentence (1), the resultant sentence (2) would express

> (1)   The car hit the truck.
> (2)   The truck hit the car.

an entirely different meaning. In sentence (1), the *car* is the subject of the action, the *truck* the object of the action, while in sentence (2), the opposite is the case.   In other sentences, if word order is not adhered to, the resultant sentence may be an anomaly.   Consider sentence (3),

> (3)   The girl ate the cake.

whereby a change in the word order of *girl* and *cake* would result in an anomolous sentence.   Therefore, it is important to assess the child's ability to use word order as a conveyor of meaning.

Objective. Evaluate the child's comprehension of word order.

Materials. Objects or pictures that can be used to depict various action sequences.   For example, pictures of (a) a truck hitting a car, (b) a car hitting a truck, and (c) a car and a truck driving down a road can be used to evaluate the child's comprehension of *The car hit the truck*.   Or the child can be given a toy truck and a toy car and asked to show you *The car hit the truck*.

Procedures. Identify several stimulus sentences which, if word order were violated, would result in either a different, yet meaningful sentence, or an anomolous sentence.   A few examples are provided below:

> The boy chases the dog.
> The girl drops the doll.
> The girl pushes the boy.
> The boy thinks about his dog.
> The dog chews the bone.

Present either objects or pictures which can be used to depict the meaning of each sentence and have the child identify the appropriate picture or demonstrate with the objects the meaning of each sentence.   This procedure can also be used with active/passive voice sentences, such as *The boy chases the dog* (active) versus *The boy is being chased by the dog* (passive).   Note here that if the child relies exclusively on word order, he will not have comprehended the second sentence.   Record all responses.

Results. In analyzing the child's responses, determine if the child was able to use word-order clues to obtain the intended meaning of the sentence. Note if other linguistic cues were used to obtain meaning, such as meaningful or anomolous sentence outcomes. If the child is assessed on active/passive sentences, note whether the child can use other syntactic strategies besides word order. It should be noted that the child needs to process a particular series of transformations, *not* word order, to comprehend a passive sentence.

Markers indicating the relationship among words. In addition to word order and transformational rules, function words provide important information indicating the relationship between words (He runs *and* plays) and phrases (She ran *then* fell down). A change in these function words can result in a subsequent change in the relationship between elements of a sentence, as can be seen in sentences (1), (2), and (3) below.

(1)   Give me the book *and* the crayon.
(2)   Give me the book *then* the crayon.
(3)   Give me the book *or* the crayon.

The ability to utilize these function words is important to language comprehension, especially in the classroom where children need to follow verbal instructions.

Objective. Analyze the child's comprehension of function words, such as *and, but not, or,* and *then.*

Materials. Familiar objects can be used which children can easily manipulate. In addition, stimulus sentences should be developed which tap various function words in various parts of the sentence. The following are examples of stimulus sentences which could be used or adapted.

1.   "Give me the pencil *and* the book." (*and* conjunction, coordinating two objects in the predicate)
2.   "The book *or* pencil are on the table." (*or* conjunction, relating two nouns in the subject of the sentence)
3.   "Put the book under the table, *then* hand me the pencil." (*then* conjunction, relating two independent sentences)
4.   "Stand *and* drop the book." (*and* conjunction, coordinating two verbs)
5.   "Give me the book *but not* the pencil." (*but not* conjunction, relating two objects in the predicate)

Procedures. Hand the child a book and a pencil (or any two familiar objects and say:

"Here is a pencil and a book. I'm going to tell you to do something with them. So listen carefully. You do exactly what I say."

Present each stimulus sentence to the child and record what he does with the two objects. After each sentence, return both objects to the table in front of the child before proceeding to the next sentence.

Results. In analyzing the child's correct and incorrect responses, note what linguistic features affected the child's performance (e.g., sentence length, type of function word, what elements of the sentence the function word related to, etc.). Also, try to determine whether or not the child actually understands the meaning of each function word.

Communication—language usage. In order for the child to utilize his language abilities for the purposes of giving or receiving information, he must be able to utilize accurate and precise expanded language in discourse. For the listener, this means retaining and comprehending the meaning of language as it occurs on an ongoing basis, attending to all aspects of the verbal message. This is especially true in the school situation, where the child spends a great proportion of the instructional day in the role of the listener.

Objective. To assess the child's receptive language usage without the aid of extralinguistic cues, such as gestures, contextual clues, etc.

Materials. Crayons and drawing paper or paste and cut-out construction paper of different sizes, colors, and shapes. A make-pretend script about a fantasy story which the child will draw following your dictation of the script or directions, using the cut-out shapes, which the child will follow to construct a design, mask, or scene.

Procedures. Say to the child "I'm going to tell a story and you have to make your picture just like the story I tell." Administer the directions or made-up script to the child two or three sentences at a time. Encourage the child to make his picture story (or design) exactly like the story you tell. The following is an example of different miniscripts which can be used. In this situation the child will use the cut-out shapes which are before him. Read the entire miniscript and repeat if requested.

Miniscript I:

Hi, I'm Mary Martian from Mars. As you know, I'm a little purple Martian with red, round eyes; a square head; and green pointed ears. My two little pigtails point up.

Miniscript II:

Hi, I'm Mary Martian again. Through the window of my spaceship I can see your planet earth. It has a big, round, yellow, smiling sun and blue clouds. It has green trees, flowers, and red birds flying all around.

Results. In analyzing the child's picture or cut-out design, determine if the child was able to accurately process (and produce) expanded language (i.e., shape, size, color, position, etc.). If errors in comprehension did occur, what were they—errors related to size, shape, color, or position? This error analysis should provide some insight into how the child listens and comprehends expanded language.

Objective. To assess the child's ability to engage in referential communication.

Materials. A duplicate set of blocks which vary in shape, size, color, and design (optional). A table (child-sized) and two chairs which face each other. In addition, you will need a visual barrier so that the two children engaged in the block-building task cannot see each other's blocks.

Procedures. Build a configuration of one child's blocks in two stages (i.e., arrange three blocks first and three later). Have the child whose blocks are being used for the examiner's construction give directions to the other child (the listener) with the objective being that the listener will be able to construct an identical configuration without seeing the original one. Tape-record the speaker's directions for later analysis.

Results. Analyze, from your observations and tape recording, the accuracy, precision, and specificity of language used by the speaker to give the listener necessary information. Did the speaker take into account the listener's needs and perspective? For example, did the speaker give directions slowly enough that the listener had sufficient time to complete each direction? Did the speaker use pronouns, such as *it, that one,* for which the listener had a specific referent, or did he assume that the listener "knew" what *it* or *that one* referred to? Was spatial information such as distance or left–right positioning given by the speaker?

The preceding informal assessment approaches are just a few suggested ways of obtaining information about a child's language abilities.

Needless to say, these are just a sample of the many possible ways of informally assessing language. With minimal adaptation and strategic feedback, each of these approaches can be transformed into instructional games that can act to facilitate the child's growth in language—a topic to which we now turn.

INSTRUCTIONAL APPROACHES FOR LANGUAGE DEVELOPMENT AND REMEDIATION

Upon completion of a thorough assessment, the teacher should have a composite picture of the child's language abilities and deficiencies. The selection of a specific language intervention will be based directly on what has been learned in the assessment activities. Some children will have been found to be mildly to severely delayed in most or all aspects of language functioning; others will show uneven development which may cross stage boundaries (see Table 7–5). Because language problems tend to be highly idiosyncratic in nature, we have found the informal approaches to be most successful. However, because of their widespread use, we are also including descriptions of general language stimulation materials available as kits, and descriptions of several highly structured remedially based approaches associated most frequently with an individual, such as McGinnis, Barry, and others. We turn initially to the commercially available materials.

Commercially Available "Kits"

There are many language development or stimulation "kits" on the market. Some of the more common ones are briefly described in Table 7–7. Teachers should choose among these in accordance with their particular theoretical positions regarding language and the needs of the children in question. Of course, the original sources should be consulted for more complete details concerning the various formats, rationales, and operating procedures of the particular programs that are of interest to the teacher.

Instructional Systems of Individual Professionals

For the most part, the educational systems described in this section are loose collections of sequenced activities. Some of them are constructed according to the principles of a particular "school of thought" or theoretical position; some are not. The methods are described mostly in books and usually are expositions of the authors' clinical "insights" and experiences; none of these systems are commercially available in packaged kit form. Probably because the approaches are so individualistic and the procedures are so ill-defined, researchers have as yet avoided investigating their efficacy. Regardless, many of the systems described are widely used in practice.

English Now (Feigenbaum, 1970)

Rationale. Standard English and nonstandard dialects of the English language are linguistically equal. The deciding factor for selecting one language or dialect for use in a given situation is "appropriateness." According to Feigenbaum, although standard English is deemed "appropriate" in class, it is not necessary or desirable to eradicate nonstandard English. Instead, standard English can be taught as a second dialect the same way English is taught as a second language. Feigenbaum's materials include workbooks, manuals, and cassettes. The general approach is described in Feigenbaum (1970). This method of teaching standard English as a second dialect has been called "the aural–oral approach," "the linguistic method," "the audio-lingual method," and "pattern practice." It consists of first establishing that nonstandard dialects are not indications of laziness or stupidity. The students are made aware of the social uses of both dialects. The areas of difficulty, as well as the areas of little or no difficulty, are determined by contrasting the grammatical and phonological systems of standard and nonstandard English. Standard English is taught by presentation of similarities and differences, and discrimination, identification, translation, and response drills.

Assessment. When the teacher recognizes the existence and legitimacy of nonstandard English, he can begin to understand the student who uses a nonstandard dialect and more accurately deduce his learning problems. Some students have a partial knowledge of standard English; that is, they can recognize and produce it but without accurate control. Others cannot even recognize differences between their dialect and standard English. However, all students begin with sorting out standard from nonstandard English. When they can accurately differentiate the two dialects, they move on to the other drills.

Training techniques. In the Feigenbaum program, training is initiated by the presentation of similarities and differences. Two items, one standard and the other nonstandard, show the students the structure to be learned and practiced, and indicate where mistakes may occur. For example, the following two sentences may be written on the board or projected from a transparency:

Table 7–7. *Summary of Most Widely Used Language Development Kits*

Name (Author of Kit)	Target Population	Type of Approach	Comments
DISTAR I, II, III (Engelmann and Osborn, 1970, 1973, 1975)	Preschool up	Drill and repetition; task analytic imitation and reinforcement	Highly structured and organized. Emphasis on expressive aspect of language. Moves from the familiar and simple to the more complex. Instructional groups based on performance levels. Heavy use of question–answer form of instruction—Teacher: "What's this?"—Pupils: (together) "That's a pencil!" Appears successful in teaching specific responses to specific stimuli; less adequate in generalizing to other situations.
Fokes Sentence Builder Kit (Fokes, 1975)	Learning disabled, deaf, hard of hearing, borderline to mild mentally retarded	Cognitive-psycholinguistic stimulative	Highly structured. Unique design for teaching syntactic rules and structures, but not as rote responses.
GOAL: Language Development—Games Oriented Activities for Learning. (Karnes, 1976a)	Normal to moderately handicapped	Developmental; stimulative	Highly structured. Based on Illinois Test of Psycholinguistic Abilities model. Lessons in game format. Criteria for mastery of each lesson not predetermined.
Karnes Early Language Activities (Karnes, 1976b)	All mentally handicapped	Developmental; stimulative	Downward extension of GOAL (see above). 200 model lessons. Provides instructional ideas only; actual items must be supplied by user.
Monterey Language Program (Programmed Conditioning for Language) (Gray and Ryan, 1972)	All children needing help in language	Behavioral; operant	Highly structured. User must be trained and certified by distributor. Includes pre- and posttests, placement tests, branching provisions, specific criteria. Good data showing effectiveness, including transference.
MWM Program for Developing Language Abilities (Minskoff, Wiseman, and Minskoff, 1972)	Ages 3 to 11 with evidence of language deficits	Developmental; stimulative	Rationale is based on the model of the Illinois Test of Psycholinguistic Abilities. Comprised of a teacher's guide, inventory, manual, and materials. Provisions for diagnostic screening; remediation of weak areas according to model. Activities sequenced by difficulty level.

Program	Population	Approach	Description
Peabody Language Development Kits (Dunn and Smith, 1966)	All children	General developmental; stimulative	Purpose is to stimulate oral language, heighten verbal intelligence, and enhance school progress. Overall language stressed. Attractive and motivating. Kits contain manual, lessons, manipulative materials, reinforcement chips, and picture cards. Group instruction format. Research showing effectiveness is inconclusive.
Project MEMPHIS (Quick, Little, and Campbell, 1973)	Mild to severely handicapped	Developmental	Emphasis on language for verbal and nonverbal communication. 260 lesson plans based on three steps: planning, implementing evaluation.
SYNPRO (Syntax Programmer) (Peterson, Brener, and Williams, 1974)	All ages with mild problems	Operant; drill	Can be used by professionals or aides. Provides a highly structured way of programming syntactic strings.
Visually Cued Language Cards (Foster, Giddan, and Stark, 1975)	Normal to profoundly retarded	Stimulation of functional language	Consists of five series of picture cards. Related to Assessment of Children's Language Comprehension Test. May be used at home or school.
Wilson Initial Syntax Program (Wilson, 1973)	Those with syntax problems, especially TMR	Stimulation; Chomskyian	Emphasis on improving receptive syntactic skills. Can be used by teacher aides.

He work hard.
He works hard.

The teacher would then ask how the two sentences differ and which one is standard and which nonstandard. Soliciting their observations will make the activity more interesting.

The simple activity described above takes very little time, probably not more than 15 seconds. Yet, in this short period of time, the students have sorted out and identified standard and nonstandard English, and they have indicated the particular feature that distinguishes nonstandard and standard English without an involved grammatical explanation.

Discrimination drills are then employed, giving the students practice in discriminating between standard and nonstandard English.[2] In this type of drill, pairs of sentences or words are presented to the students orally. The students indicate whether the two are the same or different (this drill is also known as "same–different drill"). The following drill is an example of this type.

Drill 1

Teacher stimulus	Student response
1. He work hard. He works hard.	1. different
2. He work hard. He work hard.	2. same
3. Paula likes leather coats. Paula likes leather coats.	3. same
4. She prefers movies. She prefer movies.	4. different
5. Robert play guard. Robert play guard.	5. same

If the students respond correctly to this type of drill, it can be assumed that their attention has been directed to the feature and that they hear it consistently.

Identification drills are attempted next; the students are required to identify a single word or sentence without the assistance of a second item.

Drill 2

Teacher stimulus	Student response
1. He work hard.	1. nonstandard
2. Paula likes leather coats.	2. standard
3. He works hard.	3. standard
4. She prefer movies.	4. nonstandard
5. She prefers movies.	5. standard
6. Paula like leather coats.	6. nonstandard

2. The drills presented here are from I. Feigenbaum, *English Now* (New York: New Century, 1970). By permission of New Century Education Corp.

If the students respond correctly, it can be assumed that they can hear the feature that distinguished standard from nonstandard English, and that they can identify the two dialects on the basis of the feature.

In a translation drill, the students translate a word or sentence from standard to nonstandard or from nonstandard to standard.

Drill 3

Teacher stimulus	Student response
1. He works hard.	1. He work hard.
2. Paula likes leather coats.	2. Paula like leather coats.
3. She prefers movies.	3. She prefer movies.

Drill 4

Teacher stimulus	Student response
1. He work hard.	1. He works hard.
2. Paula like leather coats.	2. Paula likes leather coats.
3. She prefer movies.	3. She prefers movies.

One may legitimately raise the objection that drill 3 calls for the students to practice what they already can do. This drill is useful in providing a further opportunity for the students to hear the standard forms they will be called on to produce, but, if this extra help seems unnecessary, drill 3 may be omitted.

Drill 5

Teacher stimulus	Student response
1. He works hard.	1. He work hard.
2. Paula like leather coats.	2. Paula likes leather coats.
3. She prefer movies.	3. She prefers movies.

In this drill the students make two responses: the first is to identify the sentence as standard or nonstandard, the second is to translate from one to the other.

More complex drills can be constructed. The added complexity shown below is the difference between the standard English verb forms with *he* and *they*.

Drill 6

Teacher stimulus	Student response
1. He works hard.	1. He work hard.
2. They like nylon jackets.	2. They like nylon jackets.

Drill 7

Teacher stimulus	Student response
1. He work hard.	1. He works hard.
2. They like nylon jackets.	2. They like nylon jackets.

Drill 8

Teacher stimulus	Student response
1. He works hard.	1. He work hard.
2. He work hard.	2. He works hard.
3. They work hard.	3. They work hard.

An additional complication has appeared; it is impossible to identify *They work hard* as standard or nonstandard. This point must be made clear to the students so they do not search for differentiating features.

The standard/nonstandard contrast and comparison can be carried into freer activities, in which the students have the opportunity to speak more naturally. Drill 9 is a response drill that gives the students the chance to approach generating completely natural English. (In this drill the students are to contradict the statement with an appropriate response.)

Drill 9

Teacher stimulus	Student response
1. Your best friend work.	1. No, he don't.
2. He gets good grades.	2. No, he doesn't.
3. Her boyfriend don't drive fast.	3. Yes, he do.

There can be an almost unlimited gradation within the range of activities called "response drills." In drill 10, the students are free to generate their own material:

Drill 10

Teacher stimulus
1. Do his sister go to this school?
2. Does his sister go to this school?
3. Does a boa constrictor crush its victims?

Drills 11, 12, and 13 deal with the pronunciation of the standard English final sound.

Drill 11

Teacher stimulus	Student response
1. mouth mouf	1. different
2. mouth mouth	2. same

Drill 12

Teacher stimulus	Student response
1. mouf	1. nonstandard
2. mouth	2. standard

Drill 13

Teacher stimulus	Student response
1. mouf	1. mouth
2. mouth	2. mouf

A brisk, regular rhythm of presentation mediates against the repetitiveness or drilling and the unnaturalness of the responses. Only completely natural standard English should be used and required. The drilling is best conducted for brief periods of time on a regular basis: 10 to 15 minutes of a class period.

Program evaluation. Many teachers may feel uncomfortable using nonstandard English in their classrooms. This must be overcome if the program is to work effectively. Efficacy research is lacking at the present time.

The Association Method (McGinnis, 1963)

Rationale. McGinnis was associated with the Central Institute for the Deaf (CID) for approximately forty years, beginning at about the end of World War I. Initially she worked with the deaf and with returning veterans suffering from aphasia.

Aphasia is defined by McGinnis, Kleffner, and Goldstein (1956)[3] as: ". . . an inability to express and/or to understand language symbols, and it is the result of some defect in the central nervous system rather than the result of a defect in the peripheral speech mechanism, ear or auditory nerve," or a problem of low IQ or psychosis. They qualify this definition by saying that evidence of CNS (central nervous system) pathology is not mandatory for the diagnosis of childhood aphasia; rather, diagnosis is based on observable hearing ability, language, and intelligence. While they do not believe that aphasia is the result of a hearing deficit, mental retardation, autism, emotional instability, or delayed speech, they believe the possibility of these problems existing concomitantly with aphasia does exist, thus complicating diagnosis of the major deficit considerably. Essentially, the aphasic patient does have the inner language described by Myklebust and lacks only language comprehension and expression.

McGinnis outlines three classifications of aphasia: (1) expressive or motor aphasia; (2) receptive or sensory aphasia (word deafness); and (3) repetitive patterns of vocalization with expressions, voice equality, volume, and inflection that is inappropriate to what the child is trying to express.

---

3. From M. McGinnis, F. Kleffner, and R. Goldstein, Teaching of aphasic children, *The Volta Review*, 1956, *58*, p. 239. Copyright © The Alexander Graham Bell Association for the Deaf.

Expressive aphasia is characterized by (1) partial or complete inability to imitate actions or positions of the tongue, lip, and jaw and sounds and words; (2) adequate control of muscles used in speech for other acts, such as chewing or swallowing; (3) adequate hearing; and (4) adequate intelligence.

Receptive or sensory aphasia is characterized in its clearest form by (1) a lack of understanding of speech; (2) lack of expressive speech (which can take four forms: muteness, scribble speech, echolalia, and appropriate use of limited phrases); (3) adequate control of muscles used in speech for other acts such as chewing and swallowing; (4) discrepancy between intellectual ability and the ability to understand spoken language. Hearing and intelligence may both be quite difficult to assess in the sensory aphasic (McGinnis, Kleffner, and Goldstein, 1956).

McGinnis was struck by the similarities in the language-learning problems of certain children in the Central Institute for the Deaf and of aphasic veterans. Procedures for teaching the children were modified and when significant and continued progress was made by them, the beginning of a highly structured technique for language learning was formulated. This technique is the Association Method.

The objective of the Association Method is to enable students to enter regular schools at as near the appropriate age level as possible. This goal means that although the program stresses the teaching of speech and language, academic subjects also must be an integral part of the program.

McGinnis (1963) describes in detail the three levels of language through which the child progresses. The child begins with individual sounds, then combines sounds, nouns, simple sentences, questions, and ever-increasing syntactic structures until he reaches the final stages, where much more variability in his expressive form is encouraged and should be available to him. The three units are discrete entities with a strict system for the introduction of grammatical parts. She also describes a method of color coding which is first used for syllable parts, then word parts, and finally different grammatical forms.

In addition to the language units, McGinnis describes "correlative programs." The first two, attention-getting exercises and exercises leading to writing, are reminiscent of the materials of Getman, Kephart, and Frostig. The third program involves practice of specific speech sounds and movements; the fourth and fifth programs are number and calendar work. The number work involves a great deal of new language structure, and detailed suggestions are given for its introduction.

Assessment. The Association Method is used with auditory decoding and vocal encoding problems. Once educational procedures are begun (at about four years of age), no differentiation is made between the various classifications of aphasia.

Training techniques. Classes should be composed of six to seven children and one teacher plus one assistant. The teacher handles both academic and speech and language training. Great stress is laid on the teacher's knowledge of basic speech and language elements and her skills in teaching these. The classroom assistant may be a regular employee, a student teacher, or a parent. It is suggested that parents conduct lessons with the teacher's guidance, thereby increasing their understanding of the problem and their own child. The physical arrangement of the room should be similar to a normal classroom; no amplification should be used in the early stages of speech and language development, regardless of the hearing level of the children.

Five major principles are involved in the Association Method. (1) A phonetic or elemental approach, based on individual sounds, is used. The child is taught to produce each sound and associate it with the Northampton–Yale written letter symbol. (2) Strict articulation of each sound is required before the child attempts it in a word. Initially, words are broken into their sound elements, later syllables, and finally the word is "smoothed," or spoken as a complete unit. (3) Cursive script is used because of its continuity and prevalent cultural usage. The articulatory pattern and sound are associated with the appropriate letter symbol of cursive script. (4) Expressive usage is the foundation, or starting place, of language development. In cases of receptive aphasia the child is not expected to understand any word until he has first produced it himself. (5) Systematic sensory–motor association forms the procedural base of the entire system, although it is not formally introduced until nouns are taught. An examination of the seven steps for teaching nouns reveals the emphasis of the Association Method on repetition, retention, and recall. The seven steps for teaching nouns are:

1. To produce in sequence from the written form the sounds of each word.
2. To match the picture of the object to the appropriate written form.
3. To copy the word, producing each sound as he writes the letter symbol.
4. To lip-read the word from the teacher's production, say it aloud, and match the picture to the written form.
5. To name the object from memory as pictures are presented.
6. To write the word for the object from memory, saying each sound as the letter is written.

7. To repeat the word spoken into the child's ear and then match the picture to the written form of the word (McGinnis, Kleffner, and Goldstein, 1956).

Program evaluation. The Association Method appears to be a valid multisensory approach dealing with all levels and process of language. Because of this and its systematic organization, it could prove valuable in modified form with all learning-disabled children, in addition to those with the auditory decoding and vocal encoding problems for which it was designed. It is, however, an extremely complex and detailed methodology that might fall prey to uncompromising rigidity if used by an untrained individual. No research has been done to assess its effectiveness.

Steps in Language Development for the Deaf (Pugh, 1955)

Rationale. The Fitzgerald approach was developed for the teaching of language to the deaf. It is recommended for the teaching of children with auditory misperception because they also exhibit distorted oral and written language as a result of a disorder in the primary sensory modality for the reception of oral language. Fitzgerald, in *Straight Language for the Deaf* (1949), emphasizes the structure of English, stating that coherent language depends on coherent thinking. She believes that when a model is supplied for language, correct thinking will result. The model that is supplied by Fitzgerald is a modification of and enlargement of a system that used five slates or chalkboards with separate headings for different parts of speech. The Fitzgerald Key is a very simple visual device useful for teaching the organization of language; it consists of a series of sequential headings and symbols under which words can be categorized.

The major work of Bessie Pugh is a revision and explanation of the Fitzgerald Key. *Steps in Language Development for the Deaf* is a sequential series of lessons for teaching by using the Fitzgerald Key.

Assessment. The method is recommended for instructing all children who have linguistic deficits manifested by an inability to formulate sentences. Pugh states that the Key should not be presented in its entirety to the young child; rather, the headings "Who and What" are presented first so that the child can learn to classify names of objects and people according to these headings. The child moves on in the program as he masters each level.

Training techniques. The Key is placed above the chalkboard, in most situations the appropriate area for written language activities. The use of colors with different headings facilitates mastery of them. Although specifically designed as a teaching device with a specific sequence of activities for training the deaf, the Key is now used less rigidly and more as a reference tool to aid any student who needs help in organizing his language.

Straight Language for the Deaf includes more than the Key and related activities. The first six chapters, though brief, include activities for vocabulary building, weather and calendar work, commands, and expressions. After expressing definite opinions about the mental development of the deaf, Fitzgerald introduces the Key symbols and follows with "nonlanguage" rules. The remainder of the text includes only Key activities, beginning with pronouns, adjectives, clauses, and connectives. The largest single chapter of the text includes Key activities for verbs.

The value of *Straight Language for the Deaf* is not only to be found in the Key, but also in the very great number of practical teaching techniques that are included. The activities for mental development are of particular interest: games, including pretending, absurd statements in stories to see if the children react to the absurdity, incomplete statements, true and false statements, and others.

Pugh developed levels by which the Key should be presented. The headings "Who" and "What" are presented first, so that the child can learn to classify names of objects and people according to these headings. For example, the teacher presents to the child real objects, pictures of objects and people, or the words for the objects and people, and asks him to list them under the proper heading. Names of people include not only proper names but others, such as father, mother, aunt, or sister.

After this initial classification procedure has been mastered, further headings, "How Many" and "What Color," are introduced and related to the headings "Who" and "What." The third step includes sentence building, using the pronoun "I," the verb "see," and a direct object (Pugh, 1955, pp. 5–8). Sequential development continues with emphasis on verbs and other headings. All parts of speech and their functions are eventually included.

Program evaluation. Pugh's text is based entirely on the Fitzgerald Key but is clearer and more precise in presenting examples and providing explicit directions for using the Key. The essential differences between the work of Fitzgerald and Pugh are the amount of structure provided in each and the sequence of development. Pugh provides more structure than Fitzgerald and presents a more valuable developmental sequence, because the classifying activities that are used begin the sequence of Key activities at a higher level than the rote learning of symbols, the first step in the Fitzgerald sequence.

The Key system is widely used in schools for the deaf and is successful in what it intends to accomplish. However, it has limitations. If used as the only method of teaching language, the child may develop a formal and unnatural language pattern. Second, the Key does not include all the possibilities of acceptable language. Third, when the use of complex language is attempted later, the Key may become more of a hindrance than help to understanding. Finally, emphasis is placed on using complete sentences rather than brief language. While this is necessary for training the deaf, this more lengthy form is not always necessary or appropriate for the hearing. Research is needed to determine whether this system, which has been used successfully with the deaf for fifty years, is really applicable for hearing children who have linguistic deficits in ability to formulate sentences.

A Language Approach for Young Children (Barry, 1961)

Rationale. It is Hortense Barry's premise that children who are unable to use or understand spoken language can be helped by developing their language sequentially; first learning the meaning of experience, then learning to understand what is said to them, and finally learning to express their ideas, because this is the normal process of language development that usually occurs during the first year.

Each child is first tested for awareness of sound, discrimination of voice, auditory perception, and auditory memory. Language development is then assessed to determine at which of the three levels (inner, receptive, or expressive) the child is having difficulty and should begin training. Psychomotor functioning is tested. The development of language, corrective therapy for psychomotor dysfunctions, and the physical setup are correlated and begun simultaneously. First inner, then receptive, and finally expressive language are developed.

Assessment. Barry's techniques were developed for young children of average intelligence who display aphasoid characteristics affecting the development of language. The case history, hearing tests, language evaluation, and psychomotor functioning evaluation of each child are used to determine his diagnostic training.

The case history is reviewed for developmental information from conception onward, with emphasis on illnesses, deviations from normal social development, communication, and education.

The child's hearing is then tested for his perception of sound. Awareness of sound is evaluated by response of the child to high and low instrumental frequencies that are produced while the child is playing. Speech sounds are used to determine the child's awareness of voice. Understanding and awareness of spoken language are determined by the use of simple language such as "Where are your hands?" or "Show me the ball." Satisfied that the child is aware of sounds, the examiner may probe his discrimination ability. The child is permitted to engage in exploratory play with various noisemakers. Then the child is asked to identify speech and nonspeech sounds that are produced behind his back. Auditory perception is assessed by teaching the child to imitate the teacher's actions as she beats a drum. After training, the child is asked to repeat the sound he hears. Auditory memory is evaluated by having the child repeat nonsense syllables.

The language evaluation is divided into three types: inner, receptive, and expressive. Familiar objects in the child's environment are used in language testing. When assessing inner language (i.e., communication with oneself) the child is asked to play with toy furniture or animals without verbal instruction. If the objects are arranged in a meaningful relationship, this suggests that he has integrated his experience of his environment. It also shows that his perceptual and conceptual functions are intact and that he has developed inner language (Barry, 1961). If he lacks the ability to relate objects, to classify and to group them, he has an inner language deficit. In receptive language testing, the child is asked to identify objects by responding to questions such as "Where is the car?" If the child does not respond, the language is reduced to one word. Failure reveals the need for receptive language training. Expressive language evaluation moves from the concrete to the abstract; for example, the child names objects and then describes their functions.

In testing psychomotor functioning, teacher-constructed tests are used to determine figure–ground dysfunction. Disorganization, immaturity, or confusion in the visual–motor modality are detected by the Bender Visual Motor Gestalt Test. Goodenough's "Draw-A-Man Test" assesses dysfunction in body image. A Binet-type formboard for young children and a Seguin-type formboard for older children are used to detect spatial-orientation dysfunction. Emotional and social development are based on the analysis of the case history and/or teacher evaluation. Gross motor and fine motor skills are determined by teacher observation. The Barger Mirror technique is used to evaluate speech. As the teacher and child look into the mirror, the teacher produces a sound and then observes the muscle functioning of the child's articulators as the child imitates (Barry, 1960).

Training techniques. Based on the evaluation results, review of the history, and observations, the teacher plans training and proceeds with "diagnostic training." Three areas for training children with language disorders are considered: (1) physical setup, (2) corrective therapy for psychomotor dysfunction and disturbed behavior, and (3) development of language. Training in each area is begun at the same time and is correlated because psychomotor functions are believed to develop simultaneously with language, and Barry considers physical setup and corrective therapy to be prerequisites for language training.

Language development is a complex operation that develops sequentially. During the first stage, inner language, the child develops awareness of his environment and attaches meaning to his experiences. Inner language training teaches the child to relate to his environment through the meaningful manipulation of objects. Some of the activities are: pick up the spoon and feed the doll, arrange the chairs around the table, put the utensils together, and put the daddy in the car and make it go. The child is taught to recognize his parents, everyday situations, and objects. He is taught to make-believe, to use experiences, and to integrate them. When these skills are mastered, inner language is acquired and the child moves on to the next stage, receptive language.

During the receptive language stage, which normally develops between eight to twelve months of age, the child begins to understand some words and associate the spoken word with his experiences. Receptive language is usually stimulated through a multimodality approach (auditory, visual, and kinesthetic). This allows for individualization of the program. For instance, children who have difficulty remembering auditory patterns are taught through the kinesthetic modality. Training begins with basic color words; solid, 2-inch blocks of varying colors are used. Proximity is used to maintain visual attention, and a hearing tube is used to maintain auditory attention. After the "feeding-in" process, the teacher says, "Where is red? Show me the red block." The child is trained to respond by picking up the correct block. After several colors have been taught, the teacher sits behind the child and again directs the activity. The child must now respond depending upon auditory clues alone. If the child still has difficulty remembering the auditory pattern, the printed form of the word is taught. He is taught to match the printed word form in red with the red block. Then he traces the word. When the child has mastered this approach, the words are printed in black. If the concept of color is too abstract, toy objects and figures are used. Nouns, verbs, and prepositions are taught in that order. The child is trained to respond to commands such as jump, run, and hop. Frequently used verbs and prepositional phrases are taught next, and the teacher begins to use more complex language. After the child has structured his auditory world, expressive language training is begun.

In normal children, expressive language usually develops around twelve months when a child speaks his first word. Expressive language training moves from the concrete to the abstract. Nouns, verbs, and prepositions are mastered in that order; next pronouns are introduced, then phrases and sentences. Telegraphic speech is accepted at the beginning of the training program. As the child's vocabulary increases and he is taught the parts of speech, the teacher demands complete sentences. The child is encouraged to talk about his experiences and his possessions. A Fitzgerald Key (see next section) is used to structure language. The child refers to the key as he begins to read and write. Language training is emphasized throughout all lessons, and training in speech, reading, and writing is based on individual needs. Dictionary drills, spelling rules, verb tenses, and intensive phonic work are used with older aphasic children in building functional language.

Program evaluation. Barry's language training system is developmental, concise, and explicit. It provides a wealth of information and suggestions for teaching not only language but other related functions. It was one of the first programs to recognize the need to relate assessment problems to remediation efforts.

The Psychoneurological Approach (Johnson and Myklebust, 1967)

Rationale. During his studies of children with severe language problems, Myklebust (1952; Johnson and Myklebust, 1967) became aware that the study of special children resulted in better understanding of all children. From his work with exceptional children, especially those with severe language learning disorders, he formulated his theories.

Theory. Basic to an understanding of Myklebust's "psychology of learning disabilities" is his theory of learning. He purports (Johnson and Myklebust, 1967) that learning depends not only on the provision of proper opportunities, but also on the presence of three basic types of integrities: psychodynamic factors, peripheral nervous systems (PNS) functions, and central nervous system (CNS) functions. Myklebust views learning as a hierarchy of experiences. In *The Psychology of Deafness* (1964) he outlines and explains each level of experience and its relationship to others. The levels overlap developmental periods that operate simultaneously in the normal human being. When one level of development is impaired, each of the areas above that level is presumed to be altered to some degree. The developmental levels postulated by Myklebust are:

1. *Sensation.* Sensation is a nervous-system activity resulting from activation of a given sense organ.
2. *Perception.* At this level, the individual learns to interpret sensation and to engage in anticipatory behavior.
3. *Imagery.* An image represents an object or experience. ". . . aspects of the object itself are recalled and used for the thought process; what it sounds like, looks like, and how it feels constitutes the image" (p. 227).
4. *Verbal symbolic behavior.* Symbolic behavior requires more abstraction ability than the former. Although verbal and nonverbal symbols exist, it is primarily through verbal language that we internalize experiences and are able to communicate with others. The

verbal involves: (a) relation of experience to symbols; (b) receptive language, or the comprehension of symbols; and (c) expressive language, the output of expressions using symbols. In these processes, auditory-receptive and expressive language (speaking) precede visual-receptive expressive language (writing).

5. *Conceptualization.* Conceptualization is the highest level of experience attained. It involves the classification and categorization of experiences according to common elements.

Assessment. Diagnostic study is the single most important factor in planning for learning-disabled children. Myklebust (Johnson and Myklebust, 1967) suggests that evaluation should be made by a pediatrician, neurologist, and ophthalmologist, as well as by the educator, and should include measurement of sensory acuity, intelligence, language (spoken, read, and written), motor function, educational achievement, emotional status, and social maturity. In defining problems, a multidimensional approach is used. First, the type of involvement should be defined. Next the level of involvement (according to the psychological hierachy of experiences) is determined. The effect of the disability on types of educational achievement (reading, arithmetic) is pinpointed; remedial programs then can be meaningfully prescribed.

Training techniques. Teaching is directed to the level and type of disability, as well as to the readiness and tolerance levels of the student involved. Each individual is recognized as unique; whereas perceptual training may be beneficial in one case, it may be detrimental in another. The same is true of teaching to correct deficit areas, teaching to the integrities, or using a universal multisensory approach. Clinical teaching involves maintaining the high areas of ability at their high levels while properly developing the low levels. Balance is important. It must also be emphasized that the teacher changes her method for the child, not vice versa. *Learning Disabilities*, by Johnson and Myklebust (1967), is the best available source for training activities based on the model just described.

Program evaluation. The greatest portion of Johnson and Myklebust's book is devoted to excellent, specific methods of remediation. If the teacher encounters children with moderate to severe specific problems in language, the techniques of Johnson and Myklebust will serve as an excellent source for remediation activities. The techniques are best used in a tutorial setting. As each child's problem is unique, each child's program should be individually tailored. This clinical approach is difficult to evaluate using traditional procedures, and has therefore stimulated little efficacy research.

Teaching the American Language to Kids (Dever, 1978)

Rationale. TALK addresses itself to teaching appropriate sentence patterns to children who function at a linguistically low level. The TALK program deals with problems of language acquisition rather than with the motoric aspects of speech (although speech problems may be found in children who exhibit language problems). It is hoped that by teaching language to children their overall learning rate will improve, thereby reducing negative social reactions.

Assessment. The program is based on the premise that it is of utmost importance to a teacher to understand what it is that children need to learn. For that reason, the entire program is sequenced in a hierarchical way that permits the teacher to establish precisely which prerequisite linguistic tasks a child has mastered. Assessment consists of discovering the place in the program where the child no longer can successfully master the tasks, and hence is the point at which instruction should begin.

Intervention. Four major types of sentence patterns are taught—Questions, Passives, Subordinates, and Coordinates. Each sentence type has been analyzed in terms of prerequisite required skills; these skills are taught in order before the final form of the sentence pattern is taught. The techniques used are those developed for "Teaching English as a Second Language" and involve group responses to a conversational format established by the teacher and a teacher's aide.

Program evaluation. The program has been used successfully with retarded children, learning-disabled and hearing-impaired children, and with multihandicapped children.

Informal Instructional Approaches

While it would be impossible in this format to describe the multiple options available to the teacher to informally facilitate language development or remediate a language problem, the following informal approaches are *representative* of the strategies that can be integrated into the classroom curriculum. Each activity is geared to a particular aspect of language and can be utilized with the entire class, in small groups, or in a one-to-one format. Before describing these activities, it should be noted that since assessment and instruction are essentially two sides of the same coin, the informal assessment techniques presented earlier can easily be adapted to instructional activities. One additional point needs mentioning. Since language is an interpersonal phenomenon, with communication being one of its main functions, all instructional activities *must stress* the interpersonal, communicative nature of language. This means that imitation should be kept at a minimum if it is to be used at all, and the language activities should reflect the child's ongoing activities rather than more passive activities, such as labeling pictures. Most of the following activities have been adapted from Bryen (1975).

Approaches to semantic/syntactic development. Whether your instructional approach is designed for an individual with pervasive language problems or an individual with a few specific problems, several considerations must be taken into account. First, it is crucial to determine whether the problem is primarily a *structural* (syntactical) problem or primarily related to *content* (semantics). For example, a child may have the semantic function of negation (content) yet not the appropriate syntactical structure to express it (e.g., *I not go home* instead of *I don't go home*). Second, children with language problems may have difficulty in either the reception or expression of language. Generally, instruction should begin with reception. Finally, children with language problems should begin with concrete experiences before moving on to language activities which are more abstract. Therefore, language activities should begin with the child's "here and now" long before they are encouraged to use language to describe events that are distant in time (i.e., past or future). They should be encouraged to talk about objects and events that are present before they use the same basic linguistic structures to describe objects and events that are perceptually absent. With these considerations in mind, let us explore some informal instructional activities.

Expanding noun phrases and verb phrases. One of the most common difficulties a child may encounter is the restricted usage of either the verb phrase or noun phrase of a sentence. When either phrase is restricted either in expression or reception, much potential information is lost.

Objective. Develop and expand the child's capacity to use (receptively and expressively) expanded noun phrases or verb phrases.

Materials. Familiar objects around the room can be used that would require more than a simple name or label to be identified. For example, two desks or balls or books could be used where the child could not simply refer to it by name. Children in the class could also be used.

Procedures. A "Sherlock Holmes" gamelike approach could be used whereby one child hides an object or describes a child without actually naming it. This would constitute the clue. The "mystery" would be solved when the children in the class identify on the basis of the clues the hidden object or child. Following is a list of objects or children who would have to be identified and increasingly more difficult expanded noun phrases (NP) or verb phrases (VP) needed as the clue. In using this strategy, you must first identify which phrase (noun or verb) you wish to develop. Once you have done this, it is important to determine the sequencing of structures to be developed.

Objects/People	*Expand Phrase Taught*
1. Two flowers (one green and one blue)	Color + Noun (NP)
2. Three books (one large blue book, one small blue book, and one large green book)	Size and Color and Noun (NP)
3. Two girls (one girl with a yellow skirt and one with a brown skirt)	Noun and Embedded NP
4. Two balls (one is on the box and one is in the box)	Expands VP to Verb and NP
5. Two children walking (one child walking slowly and one walking fast)	Expands VP to Verb and Adverb
6. Two children pretending (one child wanting to play a piano and one child wanting to ride a horse)	Expands VP to V and Complement

Developing transformations (e.g., negative, interrogative transformations). Many children may have developed the content or semantics of negation or interrogation but may not yet have developed the structural transformations for expressing these sentence types. For example, one child might use the sentence *I no like him* to express a negative preposition or *I go home?* (rise in intonation) to express interrogation. In both cases the child has mastered the content of each sentence type but not its structure.

Objective. Develop the appropriate transformational structures for expressing negation and interrogation.

Materials. Puppets can be used as simulated speakers and listeners.

Procedures. It is first necessary to delineate where the child is structurally in developing the appropriate transformations. The sequence of transformations for negation and yes/no questions are provided below:

Negation

Terminal structures: NP and Auxiliary Verb and Negative marker and Verb and NP (I do not (don't) like you)

Stage I: NP and Verb and NP (I like you)

Stage II: NP and Auxiliary Verb and V and NP (I do like you)

Stage III: NP and Auxiliary Verb and Negative and V and NP (I do not like you)

Stage IV: Contraction of Auxiliary Verb and Negative marker (I don't like you)

Interrogative (Yes/No Questions)

Terminal structure: Auxiliary Verb and NP and V and NP (Do you like me?)

Stage I: NP and Verb and NP? (You like me?)

Stage II: NP and Auxiliary Verb and Verb and NP? (You do like me?)

Stage III: Auxiliary Verb and NP and V and NP (Do you like me?)

Take, for example, the child who said *I no like him* or *I go home?* In using the sequences above it can be seen that in negation this child has not yet reached Stage II, where the obligatory auxiliary verb is included. Instead, this child is simply embedding the negative morpheme *no* between the NP and the verb. Similarly, this child has not yet reached Stage II in the development of interrogation, where the auxiliary verb is included. Here the child indicates a question content by using the structure of a declarative sentence with the appropriate intonation (rise in pitch at the end of the sentence). This child then should begin intervention at Stage II with the inclusion of the appropriate auxiliary verbs.

The child and teacher can begin with one puppet each. The teacher could tell the child to tell his puppet to say:

"I *do* like you"
"I *can* play ball"
"You *are* coming to my party"

In this way the teacher acts as the model and the child produces the particular structure by talking for the puppet. Once the child can generate the appropriate auxiliary verb (Stage II), he is ready for the next stage in both negation and interrogation. Similar puppet-to-puppet strategies can be used for each successive stage.

Pronominalization. An added linguistic problem that is found among many children is the difficulty in accurately comprehending or producing pronouns. The use of pronouns (both personal and impersonal) requires the ability to classify with respect to animate versus inanimate (*I, you, she* versus *it*) number—singular versus plural (*I* versus *we, he* versus *they*), gender (*he* versus *she,* as well as shifts in speaker/listener role and spatial aspects (*here* versus *there, this* versus *that,* or *I* versus *you*). For example, if a child were standing next to his female teacher and another child came by and said *She is happy* while referring to the teacher, the child must know that *she* refers to the categories animate, female, listener. Now if the teacher concurs and says *I am happy,* the child must comprehend that *I* refers to the categories animate, male or female, but now speaker. Both sentences refer to the same person, but the pronouns used have varied. This can be a very confusing linguistic concept for the child.

Objective. Develop the use of appropriate personal and impersonal pronouns.

Materials. All that is needed is a ball and some pictures of objects that can be pinned to the children's clothing.

Procedures. Select a particular set of pronouns that contrast with each other with respect to a particular category (e.g., animate versus inanimate or male versus female). In the later case (i.e., male versus female), have the children sit in a circle, girls alternating with boys. The child's task is to roll the ball to another child, but before doing so the child must determine if the recipient is a *he* or a *she* and state which.

Once the children are successful with this, an additional category such as animate/inanimate may be added. Now some children wear pictures of familiar objects, such as a car, ball, or house while the remaining children retain their animate identity. Now before a child rolls the ball, he must make two decisions (i.e., animate/inanimate and male/female) before committing himself to *he, she,* or *it.* This gamelike strategy can be used to develop the static pronominal categories just described as well as the more temporally and spatially changing pronouns such as *I/you, you/me, this/that.*

Approaches to developing language usage. Language is a means of expressing our thoughts, ideas, feelings, needs, questions, etc. The way in which we use language is dependent on many factors. First, it requires at least a minimal degree of facility with the various aspects of language (i.e., phonology, morphology, syntax, and semantics). However, competency with these aspects of language is not sufficient in and of itself to guarantee that an individual will be an effective language user or communicator. Language usage requires that the individual perceive a need to give information, express an idea, or ask a question. This reflects a desire (or lack of desire) to interact with another human being. Furthermore, effective language usage requires that the individual (both as speaker and listener) be able to take into account another person's perspective rather than only his own . Without this ability, communication will remain idiosyncratic, ambiguous, and uneffective.

Cognitive, social, emotional, and linguistic development interact to either facilitate and interfere with effective language usage. Depending on these areas of development, the functions of language will differ. Piaget has provided great insights into how the functions of language as a communicative process differ between the cognitively mature individual and the developmentally young child. For the adult, language can serve to assert, state objective facts, convey and seek information, express commands or desires, and criticize or threaten (Piaget, 1959). In other words, language is both cognitive and social. For the developmentally young child, language usage can be seen as both egocentric *and* social.

In developing instructional strategies to increase language usage, the teacher must once again take into account several cognitive and linguistic factors. For example, one must consider the child's developmental *usage* of language, regardless of how advanced his development may be in the semantic/syntactic aspects of language. For example, is the child still primarily egocentric in his use of language, in that he codes the linguistic message for himself, or is his language socialized whereby he codes the message for others? Second, when facilitating the child's development of language usage, it is crucial to start with the "here and now" and only very gradually move toward talking about past events or speculating about what will happen tomorrow or the next day. Finally, the context of the language usage strategies should as much as possible be a microcosm of the real world. Language should be used to send or receive information, ask and answer questions, and describe activities and desires. The following informal strategies provide but a small sample of the kinds of strategies that can be incorporated, developed, and expanded for use in the classroom.

Describing behavioral events. Both teachers and therapists develop stimulating activities to encourage children to talk about what occurred, to share their feelings and perspectives about the experiences, to recall and describe the sequences of events, and to share information. Trips to the zoo, the police station, the fire house, etc., are generally followed by teacher-directed questions such as "What happened?" "Where did you go?" "What did you see?" "When did you see the giraffe?" If answers are given at all, children with language and/or cognitive problems respond with minimal verbal information. For developmentally young children, the task of describing what occurred in the past, whether remote or recent, may require linguistic and cognitive abilities that are not within their psychological schemas. It is, therefore, crucial to begin a language-intervention strategy by encouraging the child to describe ongoing actions. Activities such as cooking, playing with clay, doing carpentry, and painting can generate questions by the teacher related to the ongoing actions of the child. The perceptual attributes of the objects and their relationships will aid the child in describing his ongoing actions. Questions directed by the teacher focus the child's attention on particular aspects of the events, as well as providing the structure for appropriate responses. Only after the child develops the facility to describe ongoing actions should the focus of the language program shift to describing behavioral events and activities that occurred in the past.

Objective. Strengthen the child's ability to describe behavioral events.

Procedures. In developing an approach to strengthen a child's verbal communication of behavioral events, it is important to first select several activities which include observable, discriminable events that can naturally occur in a classroom. These activities might include painting, playing with clay, building with blocks, making cookies, and eating lunch. It is also important that the child or children find the activity stimulating and enjoyable. Opportunity should be given for the children to spend as much time as needed engaging in the activities before verbal descriptions of their actions are requested. The following is one possible sequence of the various stages which could be built into the program:

Stage	Teacher Input	Child Output
1. Familiarity with activity	none	Ongoing actions with the objects
2. Following instructions	"Squeeze clay." "Roll the ball."	Appropriate motor response
3. Reporting simple ongoing actions of the child	"What are you doing?" "Where is the clay?"	* "Squeeze" or "Squeezing clay" or "I'm squeezing the clay."
4. Reporting simple ongoing actions of others	"What am I doing?" "What is Wayne doing?" "Where is Carmen's clay?"	* "Squeeze" or "Squeezing clay" or "You're squeezing the clay."
5. Following instructions involving two-component actions	"Squeeze the clay and roll the clay."	Appropriate motor response
6. Reporting two-component ongoing actions of the child	"What are you doing?" "What's happening?"	* "Squeeze clay; roll clay" or "Squeezing and rolling clay" or "I'm squeezing and rolling the clay."
7. Reporting two-component ongoing actions of others	"What am I doing?" "What is Jack doing?"	* "Squeeze clay; roll clay" or "Squeezing and rolling clay" or "You're squeezing and rolling the clay."

(continued)

Stage	Teacher Input	Child Output
8. Reporting simple actions of the child that occurred in the recent past	"What were you doing?" "Where was the clay?"	* "Squeeze clay" or "Squeezed clay" or "I squeezed the clay" or "I was squeezing clay."
9. Reporting simple actions of others that occurred in the recent past	"What was I doing?" "What was Jack doing?" "What happened?"	* "Squeeze clay" or "Squeezed clay" or "Jack was squeezing clay."
10. Reporting two-component actions of the child that occurred in the recent past	"What were you doing?" "What happened?"	* "Squeeze and roll clay" or "Squeezed and rolled clay" or "I squeezed and rolled the clay."
11. Reporting two-component actions of others that occurred in the recent past	"What was I doing?" "What was Carol doing?" "What happened?"	* "Squeeze and roll clay" or "Squeezed and rolled clay" or "Carol was squeezing and rolling the clay."

Increase the time that elapses between the activity and the verbal description.

* Several considerations should be mentioned at this point. The complexity of the language response of the child should be consonant with his structural development. For example, a child functioning at a two-word utterance level should not be required to respond with a complete sentence. You should be more concerned with the appropriateness of the content of the response than with the structure. Additionally, for linguistically delayed youngsters, the temporary use of a modeled response may be necessary. However, modeling by the teacher should be removed as a prompt as soon as possible. Finally, a gamelike atmosphere should be used for motivation. For example, one child might leave the room and if he can identify the action as described by another child, the child who described the event would be "it."

Expanding the role of the speaker. "Communication of a specific object, event or relationship to another is the simplest kind of communication . . ." (Dale, 1972, p. 226). While this may be true for many children having language problems or who are developmentally young, this form of communication poses many problems for the speaker. One reason for this difficulty is that a particular referent may be referred to by many names. Consider a block that is red in color, triangular in shape, and small in size. It may be appropriately called "a block," "a small block," "a triangular block," "it," "that one," etc. While each description may accurately refer to the particular block, only one description of the block may be used by the speaker to effectively communicate to the listener which block to select. The speaker must, therefore, consider the set of alternatives from which the listener must select the intended block (Olson, 1970). While this may seem to be a rather easy task, considering the needs of the listener, for most young children and many older ones, it is a difficult linguistic and cognitive task. As was already mentioned, much of young children's speech is egocentric. In other words, the speaker does not take into account the perspective of the listener. Therefore, the speaker may not consider the set of alternatives from which the listener must operate, so the speaker might say "move this one" without considering that the listener does not know to what referent "this one" applies.

Objective. Expand the role of the speaker, taking into account the linguistic skills required of the speaker as well as the cognitive demands of the speaker (i.e., taking into account the role of the listener).

Procedures. There are many activities that can be developed which require the speaker to communicate information about specific objects, events, or relationships. The block-building activity described on page 338 is one such activity. Others, such as building with tinkertoys or erector sets, puzzles, or making masks with various shapes cut out of colored construction paper, can be used. The range of possible activities is endless. In using these activities for the context of your language program, there are content considerations that should be explored. The cognitive demands placed on the speaker should only gradually be increased. Therefore, you might want to start with an activity that only minimally requires the speaker to consider the set of alternatives from which the listener must operate. The following illustration provides such a situation:

> Two children are seated at a table, separated by an opaque screen. Each child has a toy dog and a toy truck. The speaker's role is to verbally communicate to the listener the toy to be picked up.

In this situation, the speaker need only consider the most minimal alternatives from which the listener must operate—that of the name of the toy. The teacher and the entire audience (the rest of the class) might probe both the listener and the speaker to determine whether the information given was sufficient. By including the audience, the importance of language as a communicative process should become apparent.

As the children become "more effective communicators," the cognitive and linguistic demands made on the speaker should be increased. The following illustration provides such a setting:

> Two children separated by an opaque screen are seated at a table in front of the class. The listener is blindfolded, pretending to be blind. Each child has before him an identical collection of six blocks which vary in shape, color, and/or size. The speaker builds a construction using all of the blocks and it is his task to provide enough information to the listener so that he can replicate the construction.

This situation is cognitively much more complex than the first, in that the speaker must be aware of the visual limitations of the listener in addition to the wide set of alternative blocks and arrangements from which the listener must choose. Linguistically, the speaker must talk about shape, size, relationships, positions, etc. Once again, both the teacher and audience should participate by probing to determine if the information given by the speaker was adequate. Encourage the children to shout out: "What do you mean by 'this one'?" in reaction to nonspecific information.

Activities that gradually increase the cognitive and linguistic demands placed on the speaker can be an ongoing activity. The teacher need only consider the children's readiness for increasing these demands and a variety of activities to maintain motivation.

Using language for persuasion. While communicating about a specific object, event, or relationship is the simplest form of language usage, language may be used for other functions. One such function is that of persuasion. Language can be used not only to provide information or to instruct, but it can have the power of influencing another person's point of view or position on a particular topic. As a social tool, this function of language is well worth developing.

Objective. Expand the role of the speaker to include the cognitive/linguistic skill of persuasion.

Procedures. Although this activity is geared primarily for older children, young children *can* begin to engage in persuasion activities even though their strategies will be less sophisticated. Establish a series of situations whereby a child must persuade an adult (your aide, for example) to do something that she might not normally want to do. One such situation might be to convince the aide to give a particular child or the entire class additional time for free play. Although one child is the persuader, the audience (the rest of the class) can help the persuader develop his "argument."

The teacher should encourage the persuader to go beyond simple "pleas" and descriptions of why it is important to the child or class (e.g., "we want to play longer"). Instead, the persuader should be encouraged to take into account the attitudes or values of the listener, so that his "argument" can be viewed as valid from the perspective of the listener (e.g., "if we have additional time to play, we will be more alert for the science lesson").

The preceding informal classroom activities are by no means exhaustive or even representative of the ways an imaginative teacher can begin to facilitate the development of language. These activities were presented as examples to illustrate how language instruction can be incorporated into the classroom environment.

Assessing and Training Perceptual–Motor Skills

Donald D. Hammill

8

Today, many teachers and administrators believe that adequate perceptual abilities, especially the auditory and visual varieties, are crucial components of successful school learning. As a result of these feelings, many first graders are systematically screened with tests that include numerous perceptual–motor items; and those children who are classified as perceptual handicapped are provided with special classes or services. In some schools and clinics, children who are diagnosed as having perceptual–motor problems will not even be introduced to formal academic work until such time as they are deemed to be perceptually "ready." It is a common practice for perceptually oriented professionals to presume that the reading, spelling, written expression, spoken language, and arithmetic problems of some older children are caused by some form of disordered perception and to provide them with special perceptual exercises in addition to remedial work in academic subjects.

Personally, we very rarely recommend the use of perceptual training; and when we do, it is never for the purposes of improving children's academic skills or of making them more educable for academic work. In fact, we use perceptual training so infrequently and regret so much its present-day indiscriminant use that we considered deleting this chapter and omitting all mention of perceptual training in the second edition of this book. In the end, however, the decision was made to keep the chapter in the book so that it could serve as a vehicle for giving teachers the information that they need about this widely used and abused approach and for providing the authors with yet another opportunity to express their serious reservations about the merits of these techniques, at least as they are popularly used in educational practice today.

Before beginning, we wish to state that we have no real quarrel with the concept of "perception" per se, either as a physiological reality or as a hypothetical construct. Our concern is with the way in which the concept is being applied in the schools. For example, when the theoretical concept of perception has been "operationalized" in the forms of various tests and training programs and when these have been applied in the schools, their authors have been unable, almost without exception, to show conclusively through controlled research that their tests or programs have any educational usefulness. The tests of perception do not seem to relate to measures of academic ability to any meaningful degree; and the use of the activities with children have not been demonstrated to produce either better school performance or perceptual–motor growth itself. On the contrary, a considerable and contrary body of research is steadily accumulating that strongly suggests that this approach has little or possibly no educational value. A brief review of this research literature is provided in the final section of this chapter, and the reader should consult it carefully before deciding to use any of the procedures delimited in this chapter. Having concluded the introductory remarks, we can proceed with the discussion of perception and its role in school learning.

What is perception? How are perception and learning related? Can one actually "train" perception? How are perception and motor coordination related to academic success? These and other questions have interested educational theorists and teachers for years and have generated a wealth of research. Yet findings often appear to be contradictory, and the answers to the questions posed are far from resolution. Therefore, to aid teachers in the judicious use of perceptual–motor programs, this review will acquaint teachers with (1) basic information regarding perceptual processes; (2) an overview of formal and informal assessment procedures; (3) theories and instructional techniques that are currently widely used in the schools; (4) examples of specific methods suitable for training particular perceptual and/or motor skills; and (5) necessary considerations prior to the initiation of perceptual–motor programs.

BASIC INFORMATION REGARDING PERCEPTUAL PROCESSES

The human body is equipped with several different kinds of receptor cells that have an affinity for light (visual), sound (auditory), touch (tactile), taste (gustatory), and smell (olfactory). Each type of cell is equipped with its own nerve tracts and brain "terminals," which together constitute a specific modality or channel. In the brain a multitude of operations occur automatically and simultaneously. The incoming impulses on a particular sensory tract are related to past experience; they are also related to the incoming impulses that are associated with other channels and with their past experiences as well.

In this way, the properties of the stimulus are constructed, defined, verified, and modified. The results of these operations will range from simple awareness of color, form, and loudness, to complex interpretations of oral and graphic language, thinking, and reasoning.

In this manner the individual learns about his or her external world, and the constant interplay between new and past experience permits the refinement of his knowledge. This chain of neural occurrences permitting the individual to become aware of, interpret, associate, and store information basically represents a receiving or "taking-in" process.

Since an understanding of the receptive processes is important, the reader should resist being confused by semantic differences among writers regarding perception. To some theorists, the entire receptive process is called "perception." To others, a distinction is made between "sensation" [i.e., the passive reaction of the receptor cell (a reaction not involving memory)] and "perception" (i.e., the remainder of the process). Others write only of "sensation" and "cognition," and "perception" is subsumed under "cognition." Still other theorists distinguish between "sensation," "perception," and "cognition." The processes that involve thinking, meaningful language, or problem solving are assigned to "cognition," while those dealing with the nonsymbolic, nonabstract properties of the stimuli (e.g., size, color, shape, texture, or sequence are relegated to "perception").

The latter definition has been operationally accepted for the purposes of this reference book. To summarize that definition, perceptual processes are those brain operations that involve interpreting and organizing the *physical* elements of the stimulus rather than the *symbolic* aspects of the stimulus. Perceptual tasks, therefore, can be differentiated readily from lower- and higher-order processing tasks (e.g., visual acuity and reading comprehension, respectively). In psychometrics, almost all of the commonly used tests of perception adhere to this definition in that they include tasks which require matching of geometric or nonsense forms, fine visual–motor coordination activities, sound discrimination, memory for digits, sound blending, or the distinction of embedded figures. Actually, it is precisely these kinds of skills which most of the perception training programs attempt to develop.

An excellent review of perceptual processes is provided by Chalfant and Scheffelin (1969). The outline that follows is in part based upon their work and describes the more common kinds of perceptual–motor constructs.

1. Visual perception and/or visual–motor integration modality
   a. Spatial relationships: the orientation of one's own body in space and the perception of the positions of objects in relation to oneself and other objects.
   b. Visual discrimination: the discrimination of dominant features in different objects.

    c.   Figure–ground: the discrimination of an object from its background.

    d.   Visual closure: the identification of figures when only fragments are presented.

    e.   Visual memory: recollection of dominant features of one stimulus item or recalling the sequence of several items.

2.   Auditory–perceptual modality

    a.   Awareness of sound: discrimination of sound versus no sound.

    b.   Sound localization: awareness of source or direction of sound.

    c.   Auditory discrimination: discrimination of pitch, loudness, speech sounds, and noises.

    d.   Auditory–sequential memory: discrimination and/or reproduction of patterns involving pitch, rhythm, melody, or speech.

    e.   Auditory figure–ground: selection of relevant from irrelevant auditory stimuli.

    f.   Chalfant and Scheffelin postulated another type which they suggested was similar to "auditory agnosia." Because of the similarity of auditory agnosia and aphasia, this particular auditory problem is discussed in Chapter 7.

3.   Haptic modality

    a.   Tactile: perceptions of the environment, including geometric information (size, shape, lines, and angles), texture, consistency (hard, soft, resilient, viscous), pain, and pressure.

    b.   Kinesthetic: perceptions derived from bodily movement concerning the body itself, including dynamic movement patterns, static limb positions, and sensitivity to direction.

4.   Motoric modality (only those motor skills which are related to perception are presented here; motor abilities associated with writing and speech are discussed in Chapters 5 and 7).

    a.   Vocal: fine motor acts usually associated with auditory inputs. They involve the speech mechanism (e.g., movements of the tongue, teeth, diaphragm, or jaw for the purposes of sound production).

    b.   Graphic: fine motor acts usually associated with visual inputs. They involve the hand muscles in the use of writing implements for the purposes of drawing, scribbling, coloring, or printing.

    c.   Motor: gross and fine motor acts associated with all input systems. They involve the large and small muscular structures for the purpose of executing bodily movement necessary for locomotion and manipulation skills.

Identifiable perceptual–motor deficits can derive from many sources, including brain dysfunction (both injuries and inherited disorders), peripheral nerve damage, and mental retardation. Some writers would add to these inadequate sensory experience, emotional disturbance, and lack of attention. It is extremely difficult to determine the exact cause for a problem in an individual child. Some children will make full recovery; other will exhibit improvement only after considerable effort by the teacher; still others will register very minimal gains. However, all children are probably capable of making some improvement.

ASSESSING PERCEPTUAL–MOTOR PROBLEMS

The teacher can profit from both formal and informal assessments of children, although the latter will likely be the more useful. The formal approach is based primarily upon the interpretation of standardized tests; the informal assessment is dependent upon the interpretation of the child's actual performance in teacher-directed activities.

Review of Formal
Perceptual–Motor Tests

While a number of perception tests have been devised, this discussion is limited to those that are widely used in educational settings (a review of the educational literature determined the most commonly used tests). They are discussed briefly along with some recently developed test instruments that show promise. Tests of visual perception predominate in this discussion, as they predominate the literature. The tests are grouped under three headings: (1) visual perception and visual–motor integration tests, (2) auditory–perception tests, and (3) gross-motor tests.

Devices used for measuring haptic abilities are not dealt with because of their infrequent use in education. For the vast majority of school children, knowledge of tactile and/or kinesthetic skill is not believed to be germane to their educational problems. Teachers who wish to probe this area, however, are referred to the tests prepared by Crandell, Hammill, Witkowski, and Barkovich (1968), Newland (1961), Nolan and Morris (1965), and Ayres (1966b), among others.

Most tests of perception require the child to demonstrate his competence by executing complicated motor or vocal operations such as drawing geometric forms from memory, tracing, copying, or speaking. Such devices, which equally tap perception and motor–vocal processes, are viewed as perceptual–motor integration tasks, while other measures that reduce the response requirements to pointing or simple "yes–no" responses are viewed as perception tasks.

For the most part, the teacher should use the tests about to be described when he is engaged in research and needs an objective measure of a perceptual trait, or when he is screening a large number of pupils for perceptual difficulties and does not have the time to study the children individually. If his purpose is to assemble an inventory of a child's perceptual status and prepare a remedial program, he would find the use of informal procedures more efficient.

When perception is to be studied in the schools, responsible persons must direct attention to the following questions:

1. Do I wish to assess perception, perceptual–motor integration, or both?
2. Am I interested in a particular perceptual skill (e.g., discrimination, figure–ground, or closure, or in overall perceptual ability)?
3. Is the measure appropriate for the prospective sample (i.e., are the children physically able to respond, and is the test too easy or too difficult)?
4. Is the measure reliable enough to be used for educational purposes (i.e., as the basis for diagnosing the problem of an individual child, or for research purposes)?
5. Is the formation to be derived worth the time to administer the test?

Visual perception and visual–motor integration tests. There are many tests of visual and visual–motor performance available today. Several of the more commonly used ones are discussed below.

The *Marianne Frostig Developmental Test of Visual Perception* (DTVP) (Frostig, Maslow, Lefever, and Whittlesey, 1964) is the most popular measure of visual perception used in the schools today. The DTVP has five subtests: (1) Eye–Hand Coordination, (2) Figure–Ground, (3) Form Constancy, (4) Position in Space, and (5) Spatial Relations. They are presumed to be relatively distinct perceptual abilities which are related to school success.

The DTVP takes approximately 45 minutes to administer to individuals and at least 1 hour to administer to groups. Three of the subtests (1, 2, and 5) require the child to make precise motoric responses (e.g., drawing straight, curved, and angled lines between boundaries of various widths, or copying forms and patterns). In these instances scoring is weighted heavily on the accuracy of the motor performance. In the Form Constancy subtest, the motor response is scored more leniently, and in the Position in Space subtest the child merely marks his choice.

If the teacher's purpose is to identify specific patterns of perceptual–motor inadequacy, he must consider the reliability and independence of these subtests. The reliability studies accomplished to date (Frostig et al., 1964; Hammill, Goodman, and Wiederholt, 1971) provide ample data to indicate that the subtests simply lack sufficient reliability to be used with confidence for any purposes other than in research projects using large numbers of subjects.

The independence of the subjects have been investigated in many studies, including those by Corah and Powell (1963), Sprague (1965), Ohnmacht and Rosen (1967), Ohnmacht and Olson (1968), Olson (1968), Hammill, Colarusso, and Wiederholt (1971), Cawley, Burrow, and Goldstein (1968), and Boyd and Randle (1970). All of these researchers have failed to identify five separate perceptual factors. In fact, in all the studies but two, the researchers concluded that the subtests of the DTVP tapped a single perceptual factor rather than the five hypothesized by Frostig.

Although the subtests may have little value to teachers, Corah and Powell (1963), Boyd and Randle (1970), and Hammill, Goodman, and Wiederholt (1971), among others, have respect for the total scores to be derived from the DTVP. Where knowledge of the child's visual–motor performance is required and where the DTVP is used, the Perceptual Quotient or Total Raw Score should be considered. The DTVP test has been thoroughly researched. Syntheses of work done to date may be obtained from Mann (1972) and/or Hammill and Wiederholt (1972b).

The *Purdue Perceptual Survey Rating Scale* (Roach and Kephart, 1966) assesses the child's ability in jumping, identification of body parts, stepping stones, and ocular pursuits, and his performance on the walking board, chalkboard tasks, visual achievement forms, among other activities. A respectable reliability coefficient is reported for the total score, but it is based on a sample of only thirty children of varying ages. Reliability of the subscales, an important factor in making specific evaluations, and test reliability for differing age groups is unknown. It is likely that the Purdue was never intended for use as a standardized instrument and that it is better employed as a structured informal device.

The *Bender Visual–Motor Gestalt Test* (Bender, 1938) is another well-known assessment device. The test consists of nine designs which the child copies on a sheet of paper. In addition to its use as a measure of visual perception, the Bender has been employed to diagnose emotional disturbance and brain injury, and to predict school achievement. The most extensive work in adapting the test for use with emotionally disturbed or brain-damaged children has been done by Koppitz (1963); those who wish to use the test for these children should become familiar with her work. The information in this book relating to the Bender test is based solely on Koppitz's findings. The reader should note the weak reliability of this measure before adopting it for either diagnostic or screening purposes.

The *Perceptual Achievement Forms Test* (Lowder, 1956; sometimes called the "Winter Haven" test) is similar to the Bender measure in that it requires the child to copy seven geometric forms. The reproductions are scored qualitatively according to four categories: shape, rotation, size, and integration. In a later study, DiMeo (1967) concluded that the lack of objectivity in scoring the test presented a major problem and lowered its reliability.

Many other Bender types of devices exist. They all involve copying geometric forms or drawing such forms from memory. Because they are not widely used in the schools, only mention of them is made here. They include:

1. The Chicago Test of Visual Discrimination (Weiner, Wepman, and Morency, 1965; Weiner, 1968)
2. The Revised Visual Retention Test (Benton, 1955)
3. The Memory for Designs Test (Graham and Kendall, 1960)
4. The Primary Visual Motor Test (Haworth, 1970)
5. The Slosson Drawing Coordination Test (Slosson, 1967)
6. The Developmental Test of Visual–Motor Integration (Beery and Buktenica, 1967)

The *Motor-free Test of Visual Perception* (Colarusso and Hammill, 1972) was developed so that teachers could have a quick, reliable, and motor-free test of overall visual perception. It contains thirty-six multiple-choice items; the child points to his choice. A variety of different perceptual items, such as visual discrimination, closure, memory, figure–ground, and position in space are included. The test is standardized on a national sample and is sufficiently reliable for ages five through eight. In addition, its usefulness for the physically handicapped (Newcomer and Hammill, 1973a; 1973b) and mentally retarded (Johnson, Brekke, and Follman, 1976) has been demonstrated. Because of the strong opinions expressed in the opening paragraphs of this chapter concerning the role of perception, as measured in academic success, the reader will not be surprised to learn that Colarusso and myself (1972) implicitly state that the MVPT

is offered to those who wish to estimate visual perceptual ability in children. No claims are made regarding the relationship of the ability tapped to reading or to any other school skills; actually, our validity findings suggest that little commonality exists between the MVPT and measures of school achievement or intelligence. This finding is not unique to the MVPT but may be generalized to other tests of visual perception (p. 21).

Subtests of other familiar assessment devices are often employed to assess visual-perceptual skills. Some of these include the Visual Closure and Visual Sequential Memory subtests from the Illinois Test of Psycholinguistic Abilities (Kirk, McCarthy, and Kirk, 1968). Matching and copying from the Metropolitan Readiness Tests (Hildreth, Griffiths, and McGauvran,

1969); and all subtests of the Wechsler Intelligence Scale for Children (Wechsler, 1949), with the exception of Picture Arrangements, which requires the symbolic interpretation of picture stories.

Although seldom mentioned in the educational literature, the work of Ayres (1962; 1964; 1966a; 1968) is a good source for teachers who desire standardized tests of highly specific perceptual skills, such as figure–ground, motor accuracy, and space perception.

Auditory perception tests. Compared with the number of tests of visual perception, few tests of auditory perception are available. This section will focus upon those tests that most clearly estimate auditory perception as defined earlier. Abilities such as "sound blending," "sound–letter association," and other phonics skills are discussed in Chapter 2; auditory–vocal skills associated with speech production (e.g., articulation) are described in Chapter 7.

By far the two most commonly assessed auditory abilities in schools are "auditory discrimination" and "auditory–sequential memory." Attempts to estimate auditory discrimination involve asking the child to differentiate between spoken pairs of words or nonsense words which differ only in a single phoneme (e.g., "pass–path" or "pig–big"). Auditory–sequential memory is generally measured by having the child listen to and then repeat a series of words, digits, or nonsense syllables.

While these abilities, as tested, probably do measure some type of auditory processing ability, their significance in terms of school performance has not been clearly established to date. In fact, there is some evidence which suggests that some auditory-perceptual abilities, as measured, have little to do with one basic skill—reading. Hammill and Larsen (1974) have reviewed over 280 different correlation coefficients depicting the relationship between tests of auditory perception and reading. The median coefficient was not statistically significant at the 5 percent level of confidence; no practical relationship was found between sound blending, discrimination, memory, or auditory–visual integration and either word recognition or reading comprehension. The median correlation was no higher for beginning readers than for high-school-aged readers.

Tests of auditory abilities are probably most efficiently used when the teacher is interested in a child's performance on a highly specialized auditory skill. Their use as devices to identify children as potential school failures, as readiness for school measures, or as predictors of reading is not recommended.

The *Wepman Auditory Discrimination Test* (1958), a test of sound discrimination, is quick to administer and easy to score, reliability is good, and validity information is available in the manual. The word-pair principle is used and a "same–different" response is required.

The Goldman-Fristoe-Woodcock Test of Auditory Discrimination (Goldman, Fristoe, and Woodcock, 1976) was developed to measure speech-sound discrimination abilities under two conditions, with and without background noise. The two tape-recorded subtests are individually administered using a recorder and headset. The student is instructed to point to one of four pictures which corresponds to a spoken word (e.g., chair). Each of the four pictures, displayed on an easel, represents similar speech sounds (e.g., chair, fair, pear, hair). The first subtest was recorded without background noise while the second was recorded over various cafeteria noises.

The instrument was standardized on 745 subjects from ages 3 to 84. Percentile norms are given for 32 age levels ranging from 3.8 to 70+. A procedure for conducting error analysis according to distinctive sound features is given; however, reliability of this measure was found to be poor. The two overall subtest reliabilities (test–retest) are adequate (.81–87).

Content, construct, and concurrent validity are supported by correlations with clinical judgment (.68), by reporting mean scores for various ages, and by comparisons of the test performance of normal and nine clinical groups. Correlations with measures of letter recognition, sound blending, and memory for related symbols were reported; however, in no case did the coefficients exceed .35. Some effort was made to show that the G-F-W TAD results were independent of intelligence by reporting normal scores made by 19 retarded subjects. The authors made no attempt to correlate scores with other auditory discrimination instruments, because in their opinion the other tests lacked validity and appear to involve factors other than auditory discrimination. No evidence, however, is offered in support of these presumptions. The authors make no claim as to specific clinical application of test information or predictive usefulness; presumably they offer the test as a measure of a specific perceptual ability only. Information reported by Goldman, Fristoe, and Woodcock (1976) suggest that the G-F-W TAD can be useful in screening those students in need of more in-depth assessment of specific auditory perceptual skills.

School personnel who wish to investigate auditory memory are referred to the ITPA subtest, Auditory Sequential Memory, the WISC subtest, Digit Span, or to the Detroit subtests pertaining to attention of related and non-related syllables. Other auditory–perceptual skills for which suitable tests exist include auditory closure (ITPA), auditory–visual integration (Birch and Belmont, 1965), and nonphonemic sound discrimination (Seashore, Lewis, and Saetveit, 1939).

In addition to the tests of specific auditory functions, there are a few test batteries available that are comprised exclusively or mostly of auditory subtests. These include the Auditory Skills Test Battery (Goldman, Fristoe, and Woodcock, 1976), The Kindergarten Auditory Screening Test (Katz, 1971), The Detroit Tests of Learning Aptitude (Baker and Leland, 1967), and the batteries by Sabatino (1969) and Kimmell and Wahl (1969). Since these batteries follow similar formats and measure similar abilities, we thought that it would be unnecessary to describe them all in detail and have decided to review only one.

The Goldman–Fristoe–Woodcock Auditory Skills Test Battery (Goldman, Fristoe, and Woodcock, 1976) was designed as a comprehensive, diagnostic test battery to measure selected areas of auditory perceptual "processing" that are purported to exist between acuity and comprehension. The areas are Auditory Selective Attention (one test, four parts), Diagnostic Auditory Discrimination (one test, three parts), Auditory Memory (three tests), and Sound–Symbol Correspondence (seven tests). The tests are administered from recorded tapes and subjects are first trained to identify the pictures utilized throughout the test in order to minimize factors other than those directly related to auditory skills (i.e., vocabulary, memory, etc.). A brief discussion of each area tested follows.

1. The Auditory Selective Attention Test attempts to measure the ability to listen in the presence of noise distractions which are varied in both types and intensity. In administering the test, the examiner names a word (e.g., chair) and the subject is asked to point to one of four easel-displayed pictures (e.g., chair, tear, pat, patch). The items on this test are divided into four sections representing responses without background noise or with background distractions such as an electric-fan-like noise, cafeteria noise, and a voice telling a story.

2. The Diagnostic Auditory Discrimination Test is reported to measure the general ability to discriminate speech sounds; no extraneous noises are involved. The subject is again asked to point to the appropriate picture; in this case, the pictures represent very similar speech sounds. Students who experience difficulty with Part I of the test are administered Parts II and III, which are designed to yield specific diagnostic information regarding the sounds that constitute the problem.

3. The Auditory Memory Test consists of three separate tests: Recognition Memory, Memory for Content, and Memory for Sequence. In administering Recognition Memory, five recorded lists, each of 22 words, are spoken to the child. The student responds "yes" or "no" after each word is given, depending on whether or not the word has occurred previously in the list. Memory for Content involves listening to a list of words, immediately followed by presentation of a set of pictures to which the subject is to point to two which were not named in the preceding list. Memory for

Sequence requires the subject to listen to a list of words and afterward arrange the corresponding pictures in the sequence heard.

4. The Sound–Symbol Tests are seven in number: (a) Sound Mimicry—to which the subject must imitate a nonsense word given on tape; (b) Sound Recognition—where the subject must point to the word given as a series of isolated sounds; (c) Sound Analysis—in which the subject must repeat the first, middle, or last sound in a given syllable; (d) Sound Blending—where the subject responds with the correct word when given its phonemes in isolation; (e) Sound–Symbol Association—in which the subject is presented novel visual symbols paired with oral nonsense syllables and then selects the correct figure from several when presented one of the nonsense syllables; (f) Reading of Symbols—requires the subject to utilize phoneme to grapheme translation by reading 70 nonsense words one to three syllables in length which contain all the major English spellings; and (g) Spelling of Sounds—where the subject must record given nonsense words after saying it to her/himself.

Apparently, the test was aimed primarily for use with school-aged populations, since more than half of the 7199 children used in the four-state standardization sample ranged from 3 to 10 years of age. Norms are reported for ages 3 to "better than 19" in the form of age equivalents and percentile ranks of age groups. Internal consistency reliability data are reported for three age ranges: 3–8, 9–18, and 19 and over. After partialing for age, reliability coefficients for the subtests ranged from .46 to .97, with only 28 of the 39 subtest coefficients reaching the adequate criteria of .80. The age range of 9–18 was the least reliable. The test performance of two clinical populations (i.e., a group of children with mild speech and learning difficulties) being served in the regular classroom and a group of educable and trainable mentally retarded students attending special classes were studied. The reliability coefficients reported with these clinical groups ranged from .74 to .99. In support of the test's content validity, the authors asserted, without empiric demonstration, that the items on each of the subtests are much like those "auditory skills" required in real-life situations. Construct validity was dealt with in several ways, e.g., by noting an increase in scores with age followed by a decline after puberty, by reporting the intercorrelations of the subtests indicating that each measured a different construct, and by reporting analysis-of-variance ratios comparing normal group scores with the scores of students who have mild and severe learning problems. Caution should be made in utilizing these results, for there was little significance other than age found between the normal and mild groups and no evidence given that an attempt was made to control the variable of intelligence. Although the test manual makes several references to these skills as they are related to speech, language, reading, writing, spelling, and learning disorders, no attempt was made to correlate the test scores with measures of these skills or constructs. Even though the statistical data associated with this test exceed those of many measures of "perceptual skills," the practical value of the test or the constructs on which it is based remains to be demonstrated through carefully designed research.

Gross-motor tests. For the most part, when the gross-motor ability of a child is assessed, informal techniques are employed. Few standardized, or even remotely standardized, tests are readily available. Therefore, teachers often resort to checklists of numerous skills, such as jumping, catching, or grasping. Like all informal procedures, these are useful, but occasionally the situation will require that a child's motor performance be reduced to percentiles, quotients, or age equivalents. For those occasions the following devices seem suitable.

The *Lincoln–Oseretsky Motor Development Scale* (Sloan, 1954) is the most popular device for assessing gross-motor skills. Although the Purdue Perceptual Survey Rating Scale, described in the section dealing with visual–perception tests, includes several gross-motor subscales, as a whole it is considered to be geared more toward perceptual than motor abilities. The Lincoln–Oseretsky consists of thirty-six items arranged in order of difficulty and suitable for children between six and fourteen years of age. The skills involved include speed, dexterity, coordination, rhythm, balancing, and jumping. Although often used in school research, little information regarding validity and reliability is available.

The *Preschool Attainment Record* (Doll, 1966) is comprised of eight subscales, of which two pertain to gross-motor activity—Ambulation and Manipulation. The Record is completed by teachers, parents, or any person who knows the child well enough to respond. Currently only the research edition is available and consequently reliability and validity information are unknown. This should not inhibit the use of this instrument, however, as it has been carefully constructed. The device is suitable for children from less than a year to seven years of age.

Review of Informal Perceptual–Motor Assessment Techniques

Informal assessment of perceptual–motor abilities is based on the interpretation of the child's actual performance in teacher-directed activities. The utility of these procedures are completely dependent upon the teacher's knowledge, experience, and talent. The teacher who has taught the first grade for four years has observed the growth of approximately 120 different youngsters over a one-year interval. After such an experience, it is entirely possible that he can identify with confidence those children who cannot catch balls, who are awkward and poorly coordinated, who cannot hold a pencil correctly, or who evidence more than expected difficulty in learning to print.

It is rare that a child with a severely debilitating auditory–perceptual problem could go undetected for more than a few weeks in the classroom of a diagnostically oriented teacher. Such a child would constantly be asking the teacher to repeat commands or instructions, failing in his phonics lessons, or evidencing misarticulations. The teacher should recognize such behavior as diagnostically important.

Because these kinds of behaviors may also result from sensory impairments (blindness, partial sight, deafness, hearing damage) or motor impairment (mild paralysis, cerebral palsy, postpolio conditions), all children identified by the teacher as exhibiting a possible perceptual–motor difficulty should be referred to the school nurse and a detailed description of the precise behaviors that motivated the referral should be submitted.

Once the teacher is satisfied that a child does have a significant perceptual problem, he should probe the problem informally to prepare an inventory of precise skills which the child lacks. The purpose of the informal examination is not to label the pupil as a "visual memory" case, or an "auditory-sequencing" problem, or even a "perceptually handicapped" pupil. The purpose is to prepare an instructional program for the pupil based upon his performance and needs.

Informal assessment incorporates both teaching and evaluation. Therefore, training activities themselves are suitable assessment tasks. The performance of a child on any of the specific techniques presented at the end of this chapter may be interpreted diagnostically (see the section "Specific Techniques for Perceptual–Motor Training" later in this chapter). Readers who are interested in additional teacher diagnostic procedures relating to perception are referred to Hammill (1971), R. M. Smith (1968, 1969), Reger et al. (1968), and Valett (1967).

Informal visual–motor assessment techniques. It is not uncommon for a child in the first grade to write his name in the following manner:

(GEORGE)

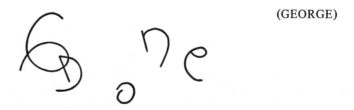

If this performance does not improve measurably with regular training, the teacher might refer the child for a formal evaluation. During this evaluation, he will likely be administered the Wechsler Intelligence Scale for Children, the Developmental Test of Visual Perception, and the Bender Visual–Motor Gestalt Test. Just as likely, he will do poorly on the Performance subtests of the WISC, the DTVP, and the Bender, leading eventually to a diagnosis of visual–perceptual–motor disorder. Yet, the teacher should have been able to reach that conclusion with much less expenditure of time and money. The example of George's written name is in and of itself evidence of perceptual–motor disorder and actually indicates possible problems in visual memory, perseveration, spatial relations, form constancy, and figure–ground. Informal procedures should be undertaken by the teacher at once to answer the following questions.

1. Does the child require glasses?
2. Is he attempting to write with his dominant hand?
3. Can he copy his name?
4. Can he trace his name?
5. Does he hold a pencil with a correct three-finger grip?
6. Are his drawing and coloring acceptable?
7. Can he use scissors adequately?

If he is unable to do several of these activities satisfactorily, lower-level gross-motor skills should be evaluated, especially those involving the upper part of the body.

1. Can he catch a ball?
2. Does he grasp objects properly?
3. Can he throw accurately?
4. Can he complete simple puzzles and parquetry exercises?

The informal perceptual–motor evaluation is accomplished by giving the child specific tasks or by interpreting his playground and classroom performance. There are, of course, many bits of information that can eventually be collected out of which can evolve a specific teacher-designed program for the child.

Informal auditory–perception assessment techniques. The teacher who suspects, either from her own observations or from test information, that her pupil has an auditory–perceptual problem can proceed in the following manner. Let us take a specific example, a child who has failed Digit Span (WISC) and who has not been too responsive to auditory cues in class. The fundamental questions now emerge and form the basis of the informal assessment.

1. Is the suspicion valid? Test the child on memory for digits once again. This time use reinforcers. If his performance is now within acceptable ranges, terminate probing the auditory problem and either forget the whole thing or begin assessing motivational factors.

2. Can he hear? Drop a coin behind him and see what happens. Or cover your mouth with a piece of paper and ask him, "Are you a girl?" In either instance, if he hears, he will let you know in a very noticeable fashion. If his response is equivocal, seek the help of other professionals (usually the speech therapist, school nurse, or whoever administers the audiometric examinations in the school).

3. Is his problem associated with sequential, symbolic auditory memory tasks (i.e., tasks that convey linguistic meaning)? For example, can he proficiently recall a series of words, phrases, or sentences or carry out a series of simple spoken commands? If he can do these to the teacher's satisfaction, terminate this whole line of assessment, for he would have demonstrated auditory competence at a higher level than that under suspicion. If, however, he still does poorly, try to teach him some of the tasks he failed. The rate at which he learns will give insight as to what to expect when an instructional program for this child is implemented.

4. Is his problem associated with other sequential nonsymbolic auditory memory tasks? For example, can he recall a series of nonsense syllables, a vocal pattern such as "dum-de-dum-dum?" If the child failed Digit Span and several activities described above, it is very likely he will do poorly here as well.

By this time, the teacher should be thinking that the pupil may evidence a general auditory–vocal problem and should branch out to investigate his phonics and speech-related skills. His performance on comparable visual–motor activities might also prove interesting.

BASIC APPROACHES TO TRAINING PERCEPTUAL–MOTOR PROCESSES

The individuals who are discussed here have contributed perceptual–motor theories, techniques, or programs which are used extensively in the schools. The brief discussions are provided merely to acquaint the teacher with these basic approaches and are not considered as substitutes for studying the original sources. After reading a particular summary, the reader may wish to read in detail the author's work in order to prepare instructional units for use in his or her own classroom.

It should be mentioned that some basic differences exist between the authors of this book and the authors about to be discussed, especially regarding perceptual learning and the effectiveness of many of the training activities. This should not be interpreted to mean that we never recommend perceptual–motor training or the techniques associated with Frostig, Kephart, Barsch, or Getman. We choose activities selectively and cautiously from these sources and use them with individual children on a remedial basis rather than with all children in the name of readiness training. Any improvement in perception which is a result of training is its own reward; activities should never be recommended in the hope that somehow the improvement will generalize to reading, speech, or other activities. It is necessary to point out that even though these teaching systems are widely used in the schools, we view them as still experimental, nonvalidated techniques rather than as programs which have been demonstrated to be effective. We do use parts of these programs but in the spirit just expressed. In reading this section, the reader should keep in mind that we are discussing the positions of others; our opinions are expressed in other sections of this chapter.

Newell C. Kephart

Rationale. Kephart contends that concept formation depends upon the manipulation of perceptual data and that solid concepts rest on solid precepts, which, in turn, rest on solid, basic motor patterns. Subsequently, inadequate development of perceptual–motor skills prevents children from effectively participating in the educational program. Of the basic motor patterns that emerge from the early motor responses of children, Kephart (1971) maintains that *posture* is primary and that all subsequent motor patterns develop from it. An important motor pattern is *laterality* (i.e., the initial awareness of the two sides of the body and their difference), which later becomes the basis for concepts of direction in space. *Directionality*, a projection of laterality into external space, is comprised of awareness of the up–down axis and laterality of the body. These three operate to produce a unity of impressions about one's body called *body image*. Body image provides the point of origin against which all spatial relations outside the body are compared.

Concomitant with the development of motor patterns, but beginning later, is the development of perceptual organization. Tactual, kinesthetic, visual, and auditory data received from the developing perceptual system are compared with existing motor information. The result is a synthesis of data, called the *perceptual–motor match,* which serves to provide the child with consistent information about his environment. *Form perception, spatial discrimination,* and *ocular control* are three perceptual skills closely associated with the perceptual–motor match.

Training techniques. Kephart does not have a training program as such, i.e., there is no special kit containing apparatus and materials which might be purchased. Instead, he offers a collection of activities each of which can be related to his theory. These activities are presented in their clearest form in *The Slow Learner in the Classroom* (1971); they may be supplemented by consulting Ebersole, Kephart, and Ebersole (1968). Exercises are presented under the categories of Perceptual–Motor Training, Perceptual–Motor Match, Training Ocular Control, Chalkboard Training, and Training Form Perception. An example of an exercise appropriate for each category follows.

1. Perceptual–Motor Training. The child is taught to walk the Walking Board, an 8- to 12-foot long, 2-inch by 4-inch board resting on a brace which provides a 2-inch elevation and support. The child learns to perform forward, backward, sidewise, and to turn and bounce as well. Such exercises are purported to aid the child in developing balance, posture, laterality, and directionality. Kephart (1968) provides a list of 62 different Walking Board exercises.
2. Perceptual–Motor Match. Any exercise that requires the child to integrate perception with movement is appropriate; for example, scribbling and other eye–hand activities.
3. Training Ocular Control. Any activity in which the child has to follow a moving object with his eyes is suitable (e.g., most ball games).
4. Chalkboard Training. These activities are designed to help the child establish directionality. Dots are drawn on the chalkboard for the child to connect. If he is unable to do this, the teacher guides his hand through the appropriate motions.
5. Training Form Perception. Any activity based on the matching principle would be satisfactory (e.g., the matching of objects, pictures, geometric forms, or visual patterns).

Assessment procedure. Kephart (1971) recommends the use of the Purdue Perceptual Survey Rating Scale for evaluating the child's motor and perceptual–motor abilities, and suggests that additional information can be obtained from the Wepman Auditory Discrimination Test, the Marianne

Frostig Developmental Test of Visual Perception, and the Illinois Test of Psycholinguistic Abilities.

Program evaluation. Kephart (1971), Ball (1971), and others have attempted, quite justifiably, to demonstrate the validity of his theory by pointing out its compatability with other theories, notably those of Piaget, Hebb, and Montessori, and by explaining the neurological bases underlying the theory. Much deductive support exists for Kephart's rationale, but hard data are missing. For example, Kephart maintains that if certain perceptual–motor skills are lacking, the development of academic skills will likely be affected. This is not necessarily the case. Bateman (1967) states ". . . there are children who manifest severe spatial orientation, body image, perceptual, coordination, etc., problems and who are not dyslexic" (p. 11). Similarly, Dunn (1967) reminds us that "efficacy studies in the area of motor development and perceptual learning with Strauss-type children are nonexistent" (p. 130). Relative to the effectiveness of the activities, Goodman and Hammill (1973) have reviewed forty-two studies which attempted to develop perceptual–motor skills using the Kephart–Getman techniques. The overall conclusion of this review raises serious questions about the value of such training. Neither the relationship between the suggested activities and Kephart's theory nor the usefulness of the activities themselves have been demonstrated sufficiently through carefully designed research.

Gerald N. Getman

Rationale. To Getman, perception is learned and developmental, and plays a significant role in the educational process; and of all the perceptions, vision is the most important. Although Getman (1962) does not articulate his theory in such detail or in such sophisticated style as Kephart does, the type and sequence of perceptual–motor generalizations postulated by the two are quite similar. In Getman's terminology, the child progresses through six sequential and interrelated developmental stages, including (1) General Movement Patterns, (2) Special Movement Patterns, (3) Eye Movement Patterns, (4) Visual Language Patterns, (5) Visualization Patterns, and (6) Visual–Perceptual Organization.

Training techniques. Getman has provided a collection of training activities for each of his postulated stages. The primary sources for these techniques are Getman (1962), Getman and Hendrickson (1966), and Getman, Kane, Halgren, and McKee (1968). A sample training activity for each stage follows.

1. General Movement Patterns. In addition to the use of the Walking Board, work on the trampoline or basic physical education exercises (sit-ups, toe touches) are recommended.
2. Special Movement Patterns. Suggested activities include hammer and nail sets, jacks, or Lincoln Logs, as well as any activity involving bilateral and eye–hand operations.
3. Eye Movement Patterns. As with Kephart, chalkboard activities are strongly recommended.
4. Visual Language Patterns. Activities offered for this stage are not, strictly speaking, perception activities at all. The emphasis is on language and concept formation, and the activities include story telling, imitation of sounds, naming and classifying, and verb games.
5. Visualization Patterns. Exercises here are concerned with form, shape, and recall (e.g., simple jigsaw puzzles or matching activities).
6. Visual Perception Organization. No activities are suggested specifically for this stage because Getman is convinced that these patterns emerge when adequate perceptual organization exists at the other stages.

Assessment procedures. No particular evaluation tests are suggested. Presumably Getman, a clinically oriented professional, feels comfortable with informal procedures. Readers who have need of standardized tests are referred to Kephart's recommendations regarding assessment devices.

Program evaluation. Most of the criticism leveled at Kephart has also been directed at Getman's theories and training program. In fact, it would be difficult to separate these two critiques. Results of studies pertaining to the Kephart techniques can probably be generalized to the techniques of Getman. As with Kephart, Getman's theories and techniques lack research-established validity at the present time.

Ray H. Barsch

Rationale. Barsch is concerned with the child's movement in space in his spatially oriented approach to learning disabilities. Since Barsch believes that space is the most vital domain in which children exist, nonacademically oriented curricula should be designed to create spatial proficiency. The theory behind Barsch's (1967) orientation is "movigenics" (i.e., the study of the child's movement in space and the ramifications of this movement). Twelve dimensions are hypothesized by him to explain this development. The first four, *muscular strength*, *dynamic balance*, *body awareness*, and *spatial awareness*, aid the individual in maintaining body control and movement through space. The second four, *tactual dynamics, kinesthesia, auditory dynamics,* and *visual dynamics,* are necessary for processing information. *Bilaterality, rhythm, flexibility,* and *motor planning* enhance the efficiency of the other dimensions.

Training techniques. The movigenics curriculum (Barsch, 1965) is based specifically on his twelve dimensions. As with Kephart and Getman, specific activities are selected to correspond to the postulated categories. The reader will note that for the most part, the activities suggested by Kephart, Getman, and Barsch are remarkably similar. An example of a training exercise for each dimension follows.

1. Muscular Strength, Forceful exercise, such as jumping, pushing, lifting.
2. Dynamic Balance. Walking board.
3. Spatial Awareness. Children turn in a direction commanded (e.g., "turn left, turn right").
4. Body Awareness. Learning to label body parts.
5. Visual Dynamics. Any visual steering, tracking, or memory exercise.
6. Auditory Dynamics. Imitation of sounds or sound discrimination activities, among others.
7. Kinesthesia. Working with pegboards, scissor cutting, etc.
8. Tactual Dynamics. Child is taught to identify objects by touch alone.
9. Bilaterality. Imitation of bilateral movements made by the teacher.
10. Rhythm. Movement associated with metronomes, tom-toms, clapping.
11. Flexibility. No specific activities are described.
12. Motor Planning. No specific activities are described.

Assessment procedures. No particular tests are recommended (see the Assessment Device section in the Kephart discussion and consult the review of perceptual and/or motor tests presented earlier in this chapter for suitable evaluation measures).

Program evaluation. Review of the literature indicates that virtually no research has investigated the movigenics curriculum. One study that did (Painter, 1966) reported positive findings, however. Once again, the comments concerning Kephart are probably applicable here. Awaiting the accumulation of more data, Barsch's theory and training program must be classified as nonvalidated, at least for the present.

Marianne Frostig

Rationale. Frostig, consistent with other individuals discussed in this section, emphasizes the visual–motor processing system, but not to the same degree. She also maintains that adequate perceptual functioning in young children is an important foundation upon which later school success is built. She asserts that visual perception is comprised of definable subskills and that these are measurable and trainable.

Frostig credits the work of Guilford, Wedell, Cruickshank, and others as influencing the development of her theories and instructional techniques. Together with her own experience, their work led to the identification of five primary perceptual–motor abilities which would in time form the structure of both the Developmental Test of Visual Perception and the Developmental Program in Visual Perception. These five skills—eye–hand coordination, figure–ground, form constancy, position in space, and spatial relations—were to be critical for the acquisition of school learning (Frostig et al., 1961).

Training techniques. Frostig and Horne (1964) have developed a structured, sequential, visual–perception training program that corresponds roughly to the subtests of the Developmental Test of Visual Perception (see the sections on visual–perception and visual–motor tests earlier in this chapter). This program is geared for kindergarten and first-grade children. Modifications of the program provide for individual or classroom use and for exceptional children. The program can be used as a supplement to a traditional kindergarten readiness curriculum or as a remedial program for children who evidence perceptual–motor difficulties.

The program itself consists primarily of programmed worksheets divided into five sections corresponding to the five DTVP subtests. The sheets in each section are arranged in an easy-to-difficult order. It is recommended that training in sensory–motor and language functions be integrated with the program and that the worksheets not be used in isolation. A variety of sensory–motor and movement exercises that can be used to supplement the program is also provided by Frostig (1970).

Assessment procedures. Four basic tests are used by Frostig (1967) in the psychoeducational evaluation: the Developmental Test of Visual Perception, the Illinois Test of Psycholinguistic Abilities, the Wepman Test of Auditory Discrimination, and the Wechsler Intelligence Scale for Children. A survey of motor abilities, the Lincoln–Oseretsky Tests of Motor Proficiency, may also be used. Observation, interviews, case studies, and projective tests may also be useful for evaluating the child with learning difficulties.

Program evaluation. The Frostig–Horne procedures have prompted more research than any other perception training program. In part, this is probably due to its popularity in the schools and, in part, to its highly structured nature that facilitates its implementation, thereby making it more attractive to many researchers than the comparatively less structured Kephart–Barsch–Getman approaches.

At least forty to fifty studies have been undertaken using the Frostig–Horne materials with various groups of children. These have been concerned with the effects of such training on reading, reading readiness, and perception itself. The consensus of these investigations is that the Frostig–Horne approaches (1) will not affect the reading ability of children in any way; (2) may produce some benefits regarding readiness; and (3) may be of no or limited value in improving perception in children. Readers interested in a more complete discussion of these studies are referred to Wiederholt and Hammill (1971) and Hammill and Wiederholt (1972b), who have reviewed most of the research which has attempted to assess training visual perception with the Frostig–Horne materials.

SPECIFIC TECHNIQUES FOR PERCEPTUAL–MOTOR TRAINING

No serious attempt is made to provide an exhaustive list of all the possible corrective or remedial methods available for teaching specific perceptual–motor skills. Rather, a few representative activities are included to demonstrate various kinds of techniques that advocates of perceptual–motor training might develop and sequence for a particular child. These can form a nucleus which the process-oriented teacher can augment from the work of the persons reviewed earlier and from the work of those who are referred to in this section. In general, the techniques may be divided into those designed to develop auditory–vocal skills and those designed for visual–motor skills.

Developing Auditory–Vocal Skills

The specific techniques associated with auditory–vocal skills, outlined below, are arbitrarily grouped under the headings of auditory awareness, discrimination, and memory sequencing. These activities are assembled from the works of Betts (1956), Karnes (1968), Van Witsen (1968), Russell and Russell (1959), and Valett (1967), and provide an adequate resource for teachers interested in the auditory areas. The comprehensive work of Oakland and Williams (1971) is replete with exercises and techniques for developing and assessing auditory–perceptual skills.

Readers interested in deficiencies in articulation, syntax, or other speech skills are referred to the standard texts in speech correction (Berry and

Eisenson, 1956; Van Riper, 1972). Barry and Myklebust also have much to contribute to the understanding of auditory–vocal instruction; but as they actually focus on language abilities, they are discussed elsewhere.

A. Auditory awareness
   1. Present a wristwatch to each ear and train the child to listen and to raise his hand when he no longer hears the tick.
   2. Whisper commands to the child from varying directions for each ear. Click coins by each ear.
   3. Present commands in a normal voice in front of the room and note response.
   4. Present pictures and recordings of common noises.
   5. Imitation.
   6. Whisper games with cardboard tube.

B. Auditory discrimination
   1. Hide a ticking clock in the classroom. Ask the children to point in the direction of the clock.
   2. Respond bodily to varying rhythms.
   3. Reproduce rhythmic patterns with a variety of simple instruments.
   4. Resonator bells.
   5. Piano scales. "My fingers can walk up the piano." (Play the scale.) "Now what happened?" (Slide down the scale.) Play scale slowly. "Am I walking or running?" "Am I going up or down?"
   6. Identify everyday sounds using tapes.
   7. Rhyming word drills.
   8. A blindfolded child identifies a peer from his voice.
   9. Tap on the desk several times. Children listen, count mentally, and then tell the number of taps.
  10. All close eyes. One child recites a jingle. Others try to guess who spoke by recognizing his voice.
  11. Musical glasses presented in varying tones.
  12. Identify sound sources by pointing to a picture that goes with the sound.
  13. Imitate intensity, rhythm, inflection, and mood of speaker in repeating a sentence.
  14. "Tell me a word that begins like mother."
  15. "Tell me which of these words begin with the same sound: "Mat, Oh, Me."
  16. "Clap when you hear a word that begins like mild."
  17. Create sounds that are suggested by pictures.
  18. Child listens with eyes closed and then tries to determine

which of the following was done while he listened: skipping, running, jumping, hopping, walking, bouncing a ball.

19. Imitate the instrument heard by using gestures when listening to a recording.
20. Distinguish between sounds made by wooden beads, glass beads, pebbles, coins.
21. Present paired words. Respond "same" or "different."
22. "Speecho" and other discrimination games.
23. Discriminate near and far, high and low, loud and soft.

C. Auditory memory and sequencing
   1. One child gives his telephone number and asks someone to repeat it.
   2. Clap out a simple pattern and ask them to repeat it.
   3. Jingles—children join in on rhyming words.
   4. Grocery list. Use props: an egg carton, a butter box, a soap container, empty tin cans. Place each item on the table as it is added to the grocery list. Repeat the list as it grows.
   5. Suitcase packing. Use a small suitcase and actual items. "I am going on a trip. I will put shoes in my suitcase." "I am going on a trip. I will put shoes and socks in my suitcase." Each child repeats the previous list and adds a new item.
   6. Elevator boy. After several children name the floor at which they want to get off, the elevator boy repeats these numbers and ends by saying "Everybody off."
   7. The giant's garden. Each time a child walks past the giant's house, he must repeat three or four nonsense syllables correctly or else help the giant hoe weeds.
   8. Sequence of numbers. "Ten Little Indians."
   9. Sequence of items or objects. "Old MacDonald."
   10. "The Farmer in the Dell."
   11. Recall directions given by teacher.
   12. Game rules. "Tell me how you play tag."
   13. Daily activities. "What do we do at 8 o'clock?"
   14. Dot, dash. Use chalkboard and write pattern ./-./-./-.
   15. Spelling. Teacher spells out various words, then the pupil writes them on chalkboard or paper.
   16. Tell simple jokes and have pupil repeat them.

Developing Visual–Motor Skills

In Table 8–1 the visual–motor skills have been arranged in developmental order from simple skills, essentially motor in nature, to complex activities that require considerable visual memory and fine digital manipulation.

Table 8–1. *Examples of Activities Designed to Develop Selected Visual–Motor Skills*

Type	Definition	Training Activities
Walking	The ability to walk erect in a coordinated fashion without support. Walking is a neuromuscular act requiring balance and coordination. Children should be presented with opportunities to develop increasing skill in more difficult tasks.	1. First have child walk to the right one step at a time. Next, cross left over right foot. Repeat, moving to the left. 2. Elephant walk. Have the pupil bend forward at the waist, allowing his arms to hang limp. Ask the child to take big lumbering steps, swaying from side to side. 3. Walking beam. Move forward, backward, and sideways. 4. Stepping stones.
Running	The ability to run a track or obstacle course without a change of pace. Proficient running requires muscular strength, coordination, and endurance, and contributes to total psychomotor learning.	1. Running in place. 2. Dog run. Pupil gallops by running forward with both hands on the floor and the knees slightly bent. 3. Sprinting and marching to music.
Throwing	The ability to accurately throw an object.	1. Beanbag toss and pitching horseshoes. 2. Distance throws using a softball. 3. One-legged throws: stand on one leg and throw various balls at target.
Jumping	The ability to jump simple obstacles without falling.	1. Instruct the children to lie on the floor on their stomachs and get up quickly by putting their hands on the floor and jumping on their feet. 2. Mattress jump. Use an air mattress three-quarters filled. Jump forward and backward without falling. 3. Running broad jump.
Body–spatial organization	The ability to move one's body in an integrated way around and through objects in the spatial environment. Body awareness and control of movement in space should be taught through imitative and exploratory exercises.	1. Obstacle races involving climbing on a chair, jumping over a block, crawling under a table, etc. 2. Twister game. 3. "Simon Says." 4. Pupil first imitates teacher's body movement, watching the back of the instructor; teacher then turns and faces pupil, who imitates body movements with correct right and left orientation.
Directionality	The ability to know right from left, up from down, forward from backward, and directional orientation. Since	1. Pegboards. 2. Chalkboard activities.

	many learning and problem-solving situations require directional orientation, it is important that these skills be taught.	3. Have children sort and identify right and left gloves, shoes, paper hand and foot outlines. 4. Whole-body movements. Give directions: Move over to the left of John. Sit in the chair to the right of my desk. Crawl under the first table to the left of the door. 5. After children learn the points of the compass, have a student stand in the center of a circle while another youngster instructs "it" to face east, north, etc.
Skipping	The ability to skip in normal play. Skipping is a difficult task of coordination and timing that also requires strength and endurance.	1. Hop on one foot and on both feet, with eyes open and eyes closed. 2. Child should imitate the teacher in consecutively alternating right and left foot in skipping around the room.
Body concepts	The awareness of one's own body in relation to orientation, movement, and other behavior. Children should be taught to locate body parts and describe them by name and function.	1. Encourage children to touch various parts of their bodies as they are named and then to raise or move that part. 2. Functional description of body parts.
Muscular strength	The ability to use one's muscles to perform physical tasks. Muscular strength is best developed through a systematic physical fitness program adapted to individual growth patterns.	1. Crouch and jump: crouch low and jump high. 2. Use weights on arms and legs while performing various physical exercises. 3. Trunk-ups. Lie on stomach with feet together and hands behind head. Lift trunk and head up from floor while being timed.
Balance and rhythm	The ability to maintain gross and fine motor balance and to move rhythmically. The maintenance of body balance and the perception and expression of rhythmic patterns are fundamental to readiness for more advanced perceptual motor experiences.	1. One foot stand. With arms out to side, pupil stands on one foot and counts to five; stands on other foot and gradually extends time. 2. Jump on board or trampoline to music. 3. Indian walk on balance beam. 4. Teach rhythm to contemporary dances.
Ocular pursuits	The goal of ocular pursuit training is the control of eye movements. Such control is reported by several sources to be important to the achievement of reading and copying skills.	1. Child is instructed to watch the lateral, vertical, diagonal, and rotary movement of a pencil. 2. Child is asked to move his eyes between points within his visual field. 3. Electric train light. Pupil sits in a corner of a dark room and tracks an electric train by following the headlight of the engine. 4. Word and sentence tracking. Pupil tracks reading

(continued)

Table 8–1. *Examples of Activities Designed to Develop Selected Visual–Motor Skills (continued)*

Type	Definition	Training Activities
Visual form discrimination	The ability to differentiate among forms and symbols. The seeing of likenesses and differences is viewed by many educators as a prerequisite to symbolic differentiation and interpretation required in reading.	material on large chart and in books following penlight or pointer as directed by teacher. 1. Templates. 2. Puzzles and parquetry sets. 3. Geometric forms. Present three wooden blocks and one cylinder; pupil points out the one that is different. Repeat with triangles, spheres, and rectangles. 4. Form completion exercises. 5. Have the children locate all the various shapes in the classroom. 6. On the floor of the classroom, tape all the shapes and use them for follow-the-leader, hopping, and tag games. 7. Have children trace their own shapes from templates and then cut them out. With the shapes they can design their own collages.
Visual–motor fine muscle coordination	The coordination of visual perception with fine motor responses.	1. Provide open stencils of forms for precise tracing followed by coloring and cutting. 2. Teacher prepares gadget board with extensive series of locks, latches, plugs, zippers, levers, snaps, and buttons. Pupils manipulate objects with increasing skill. 3. Have pupil write name both in cursive and manuscript style, trace, enlarge, color over, cut out, and paste.
Visual–motor integration	The ability to integrate total visual–motor skills in complex problem solving.	1. Request pupils to draw pictures of themselves and one another; next, have them draw pictures of families. 2. Block and advanced pegboard designs. 3. Have each pupil draw a map of his neighborhood and construct a paper mosaic of it. 4. Write simple words and sentences in both manuscript and cursive on the chalkboard and have pupils copy them in crayon on art paper; have pupils cut up paper into a puzzle and reassemble it.

Visual figure–ground differentiation	The discrimination of objects in foreground and background.	1. Ask children to point out various categories of objects in the classroom, such as round things, red things, or specific objects. 2. Ask children to find a square button in a box of round ones, a large block among smaller ones, a piece of rough paper among smooth pieces. 3. Verbal description: Use picture books, nature walks, slides, etc., and have child point to "the bug on the leaf," "the bird in the sky," etc. 4. Gestalt completion. Put up black silhouetted pictures of animals and objects and paste on white paper with each piece separated by space. Use for visual identification exercises.
Visual memory	The ability to recall accurately prior visual experience.	1. Immediate verbal recall. Pupil closes eyes and describes his clothes, bulletin board, etc. 2. Concentration games. 3. Prepare visual-memory cards with various geometric designs drawn on them. After a brief exposure of the cards, have the children replicate the designs on their own papers. 4. Tachistoscopic training.
Visual–motor memory	The ability to motorically reproduce prior visual experiences.	1. Arrange bead patterns on string, expose to pupil for 10 seconds, remove, and have child rebuild pattern from memory. 2. Display simple items such as airplane, dog, doll, book, pencil, shoestring, and block. Have pupil study objects for 1 minute. Cover objects and remove one, placing it in box with other assorted objects. Remove cover and have pupil find and present removed object.

Source: R. E. Valett, *The Remediation of Learning Disabilities* (Belmont, Calif.: Lear Siegler, Inc., Fearon Publishers, 1967). Used by permission of author and publisher.

369

The contributions of Frostig and Horne (1964), Getman et al. (1968), Kephart (1971), and Valett (1967) are primary sources for specific techniques in this area. For supplemental materials, teachers are referred to those developed by Applegate (1969), Arena (1969), and Belgau (1966). The skills and training activities presented here were selected from Valett (1967) to serve as examples of those which are available to teachers.

THOUGHTS TO CONSIDER BEFORE BEGINNING A PERCEPTUAL–MOTOR PROGRAM

Before implementing a systematic perceptual–motor training program, the teacher should have a clear understanding of what can and cannot be accomplished by such a program. In particular, the teacher should be cognizant of research on the effects of perceptual–motor training on reading, readiness, and perceptual–motor ability. Familiarity with these findings should enable the teacher to formulate more realistic, effective goals regarding perceptual–motor activities.

Most, if not all, of the perception programs and tests are based on the assumption that perception is an important factor, if not the most important factor, in the educational process. Justification for such a belief rests upon a score or more of correlative studies; upon possible misinterpretations of developmental theories espoused by Piaget and Inhelder (1967), among others; upon the work of Gesell (1940) and Ilg and Ames (1965); and upon advocacy by such contributors to the pedagogical literature as Frostig, Getman, Kephart, Delacato, and Barsch. Although many educators believe that the mastery of perceptual skills is a fundamental prerequisite to achievement in reading, writing, and other school subjects, the teacher should be aware of different points of view.

Cohen (1969) believes that instruction in reading is preferable to training in perception, if improvement in reading is the goal. In apparent agreement with this, Bibace (1969) questions the assumption that perceptual–motor ability is a prerequisite for scholastic achievement, while Mann (1970, 1971) challenges the theoretical and empirical foundations upon which perceptual training programs rest. The recent research literature lends support to their positions and is now briefly reviewed.

The correlational studies that focused upon the relationship of visual perception and academic performance have been thoroughly analyzed by Larsen and Hammill (1975), who reviewed more than 60 studies and 700 coefficients depicting the relationship of tests of visual perception to tests of reading, arithmetic, and spelling. They reported that the consensus of the research suggests that the relationship is not significant enough to be of use to teachers. Hammill and Larsen (1974) have also reviewed a considerable part of the correlational research dealing with the relationship of *auditory* perception to reading ability. In this review, the results of 33 separate studies yielding 297 different coefficients were investigated. The authors of the studies that were analyzed had all correlated children's performance on tests of auditory–visual integration, memory, discrimination, and blending with measures of reading comprehension or word recognition. The conclusion based on the interpretation of this literature was that particular auditory perceptual skills, as measured, do not appear to be essential to the reading process; a large percentage of children who perform well on tests of auditory perception experience difficulty in learning to read, and an equally sizable percentage who do poorly on these same tests have no problem in reading.

But what success have teachers and researchers had in training children in perception? The comments that follow pertain only to visual perception. Because of the current interest in this area and the availability of numerous treatment programs, visual perception has been studied more thoroughly than auditory perception. Only a few systematic programs for developing auditory perception, analogous to those in vision, are available [e.g., Semel's *Sound-Order-Sense: A Developmental Program in Auditory Perception* (1970)], although more such programs will probably be forthcoming. Most people who do attempt to train audition incorporate their efforts into a general or specific oral language development program and, therefore, were more appropriately discussed in Chapter 7.

Since the results of the correlation research strongly suggests that perception and academic abilities are not related to any practical degree, one should not be surprised to learn that the research also indicates that concomitant improvement in school subjects cannot be expected as a result of perceptual–motor training.

In *Methods for Learning Disorders*, Myers and Hammill (1976) report the findings of an extensive review of the research literature dealing with attempts to train or to develop visual perceptual–motor abilities in children. In all, 81 studies were reviewed and 500 different statistical comparisons were analyzed. Only studies that employed ten or more experimental subjects, used control groups, and implemented the techniques of Frostig, Barsch, Kephart, Getman, or Delacato were included. The results of the review indicated that none of the treatments was particularly effective in stimulating cognitive, linguistic, academic, or school readiness abilities and that there was a serious question as to whether the training activities even have value for enhancing visual perception and/or motor skills in children.

The conclusions of this review confirmed or extended those of three earlier efforts to synthesize the perception training literature [i.e., the reviews of Robbins and Glass (1968), Hammill, Goodman, and Wiederholt (1974), and Hallahan and Cruickshank (1973)]. The review by Hallahan and

Cruickshank is particularly noteworthy. They analyzed the results of 42 perceptual–motor training studies and noted (1) the methodological short-comings of each study and (2) whether its findings were positive or negative regarding the effects of perceptual training. Hammill and Myers utilized this information to prepare a 2-by-2 chi-square matrix to see if there was a relationship between the positive–negativeness of a study's results and the adequacy–inadequacy of its design. The resulting analysis yielded a highly significant chi-square, which means that the better designed research, as defined by Hallahan and Cruickshank, is more likely to produce negative findings than the poorly designed research.

Because perceptual–motor programs are currently much in vogue, thousands of elementary, special education, and preschool teachers base their readiness, preventive, and corrective activities exclusively or in part on such programs. Entire classes are being issued materials from various nonvalidated programs to stimulate perceptual growth in the belief that the programs will make children more educable. These materials cost local schools millions of hard-to-get dollars each year and are diverting an unaccountable number of teacher hours into these projects. If, however, the decision is made to provide perceptual–motor training, teachers should be urged to implement the programs on a remedial basis only in those few cases where improvement in perception is the goal and to consider even these efforts as being highly experimental. The efficacy of providing such training to children has not been sufficiently demonstrated to warrant the expenditure of the school's funds or the teacher's time. In general, perceptual–motor training is viewed as more acceptable for preschool than for kindergarten or school-aged children, and is never recommended as a substitute for teaching language, reading, or arithmetic skills.

Selecting Educational Materials and Resources 9

Judy Wilson

In any teaching situation, much time is usually devoted to selecting the content of the curriculum that will be used, to assessing the individual needs of the students involved, and to choosing the specific teaching methods that will be employed. Comparatively little time is spent on the selection or alteration of the instructional materials that will be used. This is indeed surprising when one realizes that at least 75 percent, and as much as 99 percent, of the students' instructional time is arranged around the materials used in the classroom. If teaching is viewed as the interaction among the curriculum, the student, and the teacher, then the choice of materials must be made carefully to assure that those which are selected are compatible with all three elements in the traid and in fact serve to draw them together.

It has long been known that instructional materials are designed to meet the needs of groups of students, not one specific student. Therefore, teachers have always had to make certain accommodations in the materials used in order to meet individual differences (e.g., having a child use chapters out of sequence or complete only the even-numbered questions). This need for accommodation becomes greater the further the student's needs and abilities deviate from those of the group for whom the material was designed.

For the student with learning and/or behavior problems, the variance may necessitate the use of completely different materials, a need that is often overlooked or inappropriately met by many teachers, owing to their training and orientation. Most teachers have been trained to teach a prescribed curriculum which is usually dictated by the school, to use the materials that have been selected for them by the textbook committee, and to move all students through the same set of learning experiences. To satisfy the special, and often unique, requirements of the student with problems, the teacher must exchange this group orientation for one that identifies the curricular requirements in terms of the exact skills to be taught to a particular child and which selects instructional materials on the basis of curricular, student, and teacher variables.

To aid in the process of appropriate selection of materials, this chapter includes: a discussion of the variables related to the curricula–student–teacher triad; an application of this information to the retrieval of materials; a system for the analysis of materials; and a representative listing of materials by skill areas. It is not the author's purpose to provide a comprehensive listing of items to be used with learning and/or behavior problem students, but rather to provide teachers with a frame of reference for selecting those materials that are appropriate to their own curricula, student, and self.

VARIABLES RELATED TO THE CURRICULAR–STUDENT–TEACHER TRIAD

The curricular–student–teacher triad and its effect upon selection of material is analogous to the building–occupant–builder triad. The specifications for the building most certainly influence the materials to be used; but the selection of materials is also affected by the needs of the occupants, the desires of the builder, and what he knows to be effective and available.

Curricular Variables

In elementary and secondary schools, teachers often are forced to use a curriculum in which educational goals are vague, global, and/or much too general. Sometimes the curriculum is dictated by a specific text. Thus, it is difficult for a teacher to specify what precise skills the student must learn at any given point. Yet, for the student with problems, it is this precise identification of targeted skills that may be most conducive to proper instruction. To aid the teacher in this identification, much of the content in preceding chapters has been devoted to presenting the skill sequences and needs related to successful performance in learning. Such information must be used by teachers to determine exactly what it is that they will include in aa curriculum for the student with problems and still keep the teaching as nearly as possible related to the components of the regular curriculum. The information that is to be taught should be stated in terms of the expected learning outcomes. If this is done, the teacher will be better able to articulate precisely the instructional materials that are required for carrying out the teaching of the curricula.

In the delineation of curricular variables the teacher should consider such items as the following:

1. Content area.
2. Specific skills.
3. Theories and techniques associated with the concepts.
4. Methodology.
5. Modification.

Content area. Is the information usually associated more closely with one area or does it cut across several content areas, for example, initial consonants in reading or in reading, oral language, spelling, etc.?

Specific skills. Are there specific skills that can be identified as components of the concepts, for example, addition with sums greater than nine vs. the broad concept of addition?

Theories and techniques associated with the concepts. Are there specific theories of curriculum development for the concepts or area, for example, the spiral curriculum of social sciences?

Methodology. Does the curriculum require certain types of methods, for example, oral language development would require materials that allowed for dialogue, discussion, etc.?

Modification. Is the curricula capable of being modified or is it developmental, for example, in mathematics, skills are developmental and multiplication builds upon concepts developed in addition?

Knowledge about these items may serve to assist the teacher in the evaluation of an existing curriculum and the alteration and/or development of one suited to meeting the needs of an individual student.

Student Variables

The two variables that are most critical from the standpoint of the student are those of current level of functioning and the most immediate educational needs. In considering the variables of individuals, the list would obviously be influenced by the specific nature of each student; however, there are some common areas that should be examined. These areas include:

1. Needs of the student.
2. Current level of functioning.
3. Grouping.
4. Programming.
5. Methods.
6. Physical, social, and psychological characteristics.

Needs of the student. What skills and concepts are required of the student for immediate success?

Current level of functioning. What is the student's level of performance within the sequence of skills? What is the student's current reading level for instructional purposes?

Grouping. How well does the student work in groups of varying size (e.g., small, large, individually)?

Programming. What is the best arrangement for presentation to the student: for example, can the student work independently; is the student self-directed and motivated; does the student require direct teaching and/or frequent reinforcement?

Methods. Is there a history of success or failure with any particular methods? Does the student react positively or negatively to particular modes of instruction (e.g., multimedia vs. print only)?

Physical, social, and psychological characteristics. Are there characteristics that imply unique needs (e.g., orthopedic restrictions, family problems, ethnic or cultural diversity, etc.)?

This list could also include such concerns as ability to follow directions, both written and oral; ability to deal with material on a grade level different from the child's placement; and others.

Teacher Variables

The authors of most of the literature that relates to materials state that teachers need only know what and who is to be taught in order to select materials. This simplicity neglects one third of the triad, the teachers. The fact is that it is the teacher who must act as the catalyst to assure interaction between the other two components. Since the teacher must make decisions about curricular and student variables, her desires, knowledge, and competence must be considered. These items like those for the student will no doubt be affected by the nature of the individual but, again, certain common areas exist:

1. Method.
2. Approach.
3. Time.
4. Training.
5. Education.

Method. What method does the teacher want to employ; what is the philosophy toward the teaching of the particular content?

Approach. What approach does the teacher and the teacher's organization require (e.g., group instruction vs. students on a one-to-one basis or a phonic approach)?

Time. Does the teacher have specific and required time constraints for delivery of instruction or does the teacher have someone else who can deliver the instruction?

Training. Has the teacher been trained to use certain materials without additional training?

Education. Has the teacher been trained to be competent in the content area, or will the teacher require that the material be all inclusive?

None of these lists of variables is intended to be exhaustive in nature. Rather, they are intended to serve as guidelines for identification of relevant variables that will aid in the selection and use of materials and to assure that the materials indeed meet the specified needs of the curricula, student, and teacher.

RETRIEVAL OF MATERIALS

Once the critical variables involved with selecting materials have been identified, the teacher is ready to secure information on the specific materials that are being considered for use. Regardless of the method used to retrieve materials, a set of descriptors must be selected that best represent the type of materials desired. These descriptors should include the skill to be taught, the content area, the grade or reading level, and the format or type of material. These four choices are made based upon the triad variables. For example, the selection of a game or kit for format might reflect that it requires interaction with others; it might reflect the student's need to work in a certain size group; and/or it might reflect the teacher's philosophical approach to a particular area of instruction. Once the teacher has defined the desired materials in terms of specific variables, the number of available materials designed to meet those needs is pared to a more manageable number and thus aids the teacher in getting to the final selection process. It is essential to select only a few materials for in-depth examination, since a teacher's time does not allow for careful scrutiny of all available materials. If a teacher is looking for reading materials, it is not necessary to examine all reading materials, only those that utilize the specified approach, the target skill, appropriate format, and the correct reading level. If this is done, all materials that do not meet the specific criteria are eliminated.

To utilize this approach a teacher must have either a high degree of knowledge of many materials or depend upon other resources. Instructional media/materials retrieval systems provide such a resource. Commercial systems for the retrieval of educational materials information are becoming more and more prevalent. These systems are available for purchase and installation in school buildings, districts, curriculum centers, and regions. The following descriptions of four systems are included to give an overview of the different types and range of services provided by such systems.

The *Prescriptive Materials Retrieval System* (1973), commonly known as PMRS, is one of the oldest special education retrieval systems on the market. It was originally designed to allow for the retrieval of information specific to the needs of the learning-disabled population. The system contains items of instructional media/materials that have been analyzed and coded according to grade level, reading level, input–output process, and format. The system uses a punched card/illuminated card reader method of retrieval. The user selects the terms that best describe the child's educational problem. By using the cards that correspond to those terms, the numbers of the materials fitting all descriptors can be located. Utilizing manual manipulation of cards, the effect of each descriptor on the ultimate retrieval can readily be seen. Once satisfied with the number of items in the retrieval, the user is referred to the corresponding Descriptive Analysis Sheets (DAS). Each of these sheets contains a detailed analysis of each of the specific pieces of media/material included in the retrieval. The DAS includes format, reading level, cost, title, author, publisher, copyright, a descriptive narrative, and titles within the series. The cost of the total system is $2950. It contains approximately 7000 items from 200 publishers, is manually manipulated to allow for change in the choice of descriptive characteristics, is advertized to be updated each eighteen months, and may be purchased for installation at any location. The available set includes materials in approximately ten curriculum areas and a list of all publishers.

The *Educational Patterns Incorporated (EPI) Retrieval System* (1974) is another commercially available retrieval system that uses a rod-sorted marginal punch system. The EPI system consists of two sets, the Base System and the Custom Designed System. The Base System and teacher-made package includes, according to the publisher, 10,000 items in three curriculum areas. Of those items, 500 are teacher-made materials. The Custom Designed System is individually compiled based upon materials information supplied by the purchaser. Materials are coded according to general skills, subcomponents of general skills, format, grade or interest level, stimulus/response aspects, and teacher/learner interaction (e.g., a teacher-directed small group). Users select appropriate descriptors to describe the needed materials. Terms have been punched on the cards so that when the rod is placed through a set of marginal holes, materials described by a particular term will be released from the deck. That group of cards may then be used in the addition of successive descriptors. Cards remaining at the completion of the retrieval process contain the data analysis for materials fitting all descriptors used. Since the EPI is a manual manipulation system, it allows the user to relate the effect of each additional descriptor to the total retrieval. Data analysis on each card includes the following: bibliographic data, general skill, subdescriptors, grade or interest level, format, contents, additional equipment, stimulus/response, teacher/learner interaction, time, objective, entering skills, summary. The cost of the total EPI program is $2950. Updates of the Custom Design System depend upon the purchaser. It may be purchased for installation at any location.

Systems FORE (1972–1973), an acronym for Fundamentals/Operations/Resources/Environment, is an approach to individualized instruction which includes a component of instructional materials and resources. This program is designed to be a total approach to individualized instruction. The resource component lists approximately 500 materials. The materials are keyed directly to the measured skill levels and are organized as follows: by strand, which may be considered as a set of subcomponents of a skill area; by level, which correspond to approximate ages; and by item, which may be considered as an objective. Since this resource listing is a part of a total instructional system, the materials are neither retrieved nor analyzed in the same manner as those systems previously described. In this system, once needs are specified, materials may be identified to address those needs. The citations of materials are by title, publisher, and format. The system does not provide an analysis of materials nor information on how materials were identified as being appropriate to specific skills or areas. *Systems FORE* retails at $25 per set. No manipulation of the resource items is called for. Update information is not noted in the literature. The system may be purchased for use in any classroom.

These represent three commercially available retrieval systems. Other retrieval systems are being used by special educators in various locations across the country. Some of the other programs are not presently available outside their immediate location or are not fully developed. Most of the systems have a common component since all are designed to help teachers narrow the search for materials identified as meeting specific educational needs. Thus, regardless of the system used, the process is one of trying to identify those materials that best meet the needs of the child, teacher, and curriculum.

In addition to these commercial systems, a federally funded computerized retrieval system is now available throughout the country. The *National Instructional Materials Information System,* known as NIMIS, is a service that has been provided since 1975 through the NCEMMH/ALRC/SO network. This system provides information in instructional media/materials appropriate to the needs of nine areas of learning handicaps. The system clearinghouse is located at the National Center for Educational Media/ Materials for the Handicapped, NCEMMH, Columbus, Ohio. It has on-line telecommunications hook-ups with all regional Area Learning Resource Centers (ALRC) and the Specialized Offices: CO 1, Specialized Office for the Blind; SO 2, Specialized Office for the Deaf; SO 3, Specialized Office for Other Handicaps; and SO 4, Specialized Office for Materials Distribution. The system may be used by making appropriate contact with the ALRC serving a particular geographic area or directly with NCEMMH. Responses to requests result from a computer search at the clearinghouse. Since the NIMIS System has only recently become operational, a full range of services has yet to be explored. However, the NCEMMH publications and information indicate plans for the availability of searches by categories of curricular need, by handicapping conditions, and by specific publisher. The system has a thesaurus of terms acceptable to the computerized information base. Plans are under way to develop topical bibliographies and/or responses to high-frequency requests. It is anticipated that after fiscal 1977, this system will contain abstracts of approximately 45,000 pieces of media/materials appropriate to the needs of handicapped learners. These abstracts were prepared by the Specialized Offices with input to NCEMMH. Abstracts contain all bibliographic data on the items, the descriptors assigned to the item, and a brief description of the item. This system is not commercially available for installation at the local level but does provide the service through a national network of centers.

When possible, a retrieval system should be used in the materials-selection process. This allows the teacher to systematically search collections of materials and retrieve those most applicable to the current needs.

ANALYSIS OF MATERIALS

Once the teacher has located certain available materials, these materials should be carefully examined prior to making a final selection. This step is usually considered to be one of analysis. It may best be described as a static evaluation, since it is based on the physical characteristics of the material rather than on the experimental data derived from the use of the material. This physical examination should be carried out in a systematic manner to assure that the materials are all evaluated on an equal basis.

Many articles (Armstrong, 1971; McIntyre, 1970; Junkala, 1970) have addressed the issues involved in materials analysis and have suggested various ways to conduct such evaluations. For a more comprehensive discussion of materials analysis and experimental evaluation, the reader is referred to Watson and Van Etten (1976), Bleil (1975), and V. Brown (1975). Each of these articles provides suggested approaches and criteria for the examination of materials. In reviewing most of the articles, it may be noted that although the priority of the criteria may change with changing needs, certain relevant variables are included. These variables may be grouped into such categories as:

1. Bibliographic information and price.
2. Instructional area and skills scope/sequence.
3. Component parts of the material.
4. Level of material (readability, vocabulary control, interest).
5. Quality (packaging, print, illustration, paper durability).
6. Format (form, layout, receptive and expressive requirements, and special equipment needs).
7. Support materials (teacher's manuals and resources, student evaluations, objective clusters, etc.).
8. Time requirements (length of tasks, flexibility, scheduling).
9. Field test and research data.
10. Method, approach, or theoretical bases.

Each of these categories may have subcomponents and be expanded to the extent the teacher feels is necessary. The process should, however, be kept short and simple enough to be a help and not a hindrance. Closer examination of the categories may help clarify the type of information that can be useful.

Bibliographic information. In this section the purpose should be, first, to record all the information necessary for future reference or purchase. Second, this section should be used to make determinations and answer questions that may assist in analysis. Consider such items as:

Author—Is it someone known for their work in a specific area or someone associated with a particular approach?
Copyright—Is it current? Will it reflect new trends and facts?
Price—Is it within the budget limitations? Is it in keeping with other materials prices and does it appear reasonable?
Publisher—Does the company have a reputation for producing a certain kind or quality of material? Does the company support its products through fair practices, staff development, and service for purchasers?

Instructional area and skills scope and sequence. Does the material cover the content area or specific components of the area? Does it address the specific skills needed? Does the material present initial instruction, remediation, practice, and/or reinforcement activities for the skills? Are the skills presented in the appropriate sequence? Is each skill given an equal amount of coverage?

Component parts of the material. Are there multiple pieces to the material? Can the pieces be used independently? Can the pieces be used for other purposes? Are there consumable pieces? Can the pieces be purchased independently? Will it be a problem to keep track of all components?

Level of the material. Does the publisher state the readability level of the material? Is it consistent throughout the material? Is there more than one book for each level? Is there an attempt to control the use of content-specific vocabulary? Is the interest level appropriate to the content, pictures, and publisher's statements?

Quality of the material. Is the packaging adequate? Is it durable? Is the print clear and of appropriate size and contrast with the background color? Are the illustrations clear, relevant to content, and do they add to rather than detract from the instruction? Is the material (e.g., paper, tape, acetate, film, etc.) of good and durable quality?

Format of the material. Is the form appropriate (e.g., workbook, slide–tape, etc.)? Does it utilize the appropriate receptive and expressive modes for the content? Is the material clear and easy to follow? Are there special needs required (e.g., projector, recorder, etc.)?

Support materials. Are there additional components beyond the child-use instructional items (e.g., placement tests, check-tests, resource files, objective clusters)? Are there teacher's guides, teacher's editions, and/or teacher's manuals? Are there teacher-training materials?

Time requirements. Are the tasks of an appropriate length? Does the material allow flexibility for scheduling? Does it allow flexibility in instructional procedures?

Field test and research data. Does the publisher offer any research that would support the validity or reliability of the material? Are there any data to support either process or product studies? In essence, do the data support the contention that the material will do what the publisher says it will do for the type of student indicated?

Method, approach, theoretical bases. Does the material utilize a specific approach or method; or is it based upon a specific theoretical concept? Is it one that meets the needs of the triad? Is it compatible with other on-going instruction? Is the method, approach, or basic theory substantiated by any published research?

As in the case of the curricular–student–teacher triad, these variables may change with needs; however, they should serve as at least basic criteria for the selection process. Selection of materials cannot be viewed as a simple process but rather as one that requires a great deal of effort and knowledge on the part of the trained professional responsible for the design and delivery of instruction for students with learning and behavior problems.

REPRESENTATIVE MATERIALS

The following section of this chapter provides a sample listing of instructional materials that may be appropriate for use with students who have learning and/or behavior problems. The list is not intended to be comprehensive, but rather to serve as a guide to teachers for the selection of educational materials and resources. The section is concluded with a list of publishers and their current addresses.

Reading

Title	Function			Grade Level	Publisher
	Developmental	Skill/Remediation	Supplemental		
A.B.C. Dictation Skills Program		X		Primary	Educators Publishing Service
Alpha One: Breaking the Code		X		Primary	New Dimensions in Education
Alphabet Mastery Program		X	X	K–Primary	Bell & Howell
Basic Reading	X			Elementary	J. B. Lippincott Co.
Basic Reading Series		X		Elementary	Science Research Associates
BFA Comprehension Skills Lab		X		Elementary/Jr./Sr. High	BFA Educational Media
Code 78 Reading Program	X			Intermediate/Jr./Sr. High	Melton Book Co.
Corrective Reading Program	X			Intermediate/Jr./Sr. High	Science Research Associates
Directional Phonics		X		Elementary/Jr./Sr. High	Teaching Technology Corp.
Distar Reading I, II, III	X			Primary	Science Research Associates
Dolch Basic Sight Word Cards			X	Elementary	Garrard Publishing Co.
Dolch Sight Phrase Cards			X	Elementary	Garrard Publishing Co.
First Talking Alphabet		X		Primary	Scott, Foresman and Co.
Getting to Read		X		Primary	Houghton Mifflin Co.
Landon Phonics		X		Elementary	Chandler Publishing Co.
Language Experiences in Reading	X			K–6	Encyclopaedia Britannica Educational Corp.
Let's Read	X			Elementary	C. L. Barnhart
Mastering Decoding Skills		X		Elementary	Bell & Howell
Merrill Linguistic Readers	X			Elementary	Charles E. Merrill Publishing Co.

(continued)

Title	Publisher	Grade Level			
A Multi-Sensory Approach to Language Arts for Specific Language Disability Children	Educators Publishing Service	Intermediate–Adult			X
New Phonics We Use	Lyons & Carnahan	Elementary		X	
New Practice Readers	McGraw-Hill Book Co.	Elementary/Jr. High		X	
New Streamlined English Series—Laubach Method	New Readers Press	Elementary–Adult			X
Newslab I and II	Science Research Associates	Intermediate/Jr. Sr. High		X	
Open Court Correlated Language Arts Program	Open Court Publishing Co.	Elementary		X	X
Peabody Rebus Reading Program	American Guidance Service	Elementary			X
Phoenix Reading Series	Prentice-Hall Educational Books Division	Elementary			X
Phonics Is Fun	Modern Curriculum Press	Elementary			X
Phonovisual	Phonovisual Products	Primary			X
Programmed Reading	Webster/McGraw-Hill Book Co.	Elementary		X	X
REACH (Reading Extravaganza of American Cycling and Hydraplane Show)	Economy Co.	Intermediate/Jr. Sr. High		X	
+ 4 Reading Booster Kit	Webster/McGraw-Hill Book Co.	Intermediate/Jr. Sr. High			
Reading for Understanding	Science Research Associates	Intermediate/Jr. High		X	
Reading Laboratory Series	Science Research Associates	Elementary–Adult		X	
Reading Mastery Program	Mastery Programs	Elementary–Jr. High	X	X	
Real People at Work—Supplemental Reading Skills	Changing Times Education Service	Grade 2–Adult		X	

Reading

Title	Function			Grade Level	Publisher
	Developmental	Skill/Remediation	Supplemental		
Remedial Techniques in Basic School Subjects (Fernald Technique)	X			Intermediate–Adult	McGraw-Hill Book Co.
Remedial Training for Children with Specific Disability in Reading, Spelling, and Penmanship	X			Elementary–Adult	Educators Publishing Service
Royal Road Readers	X			Elementary	Chatto & Windus
Schmerler Reading Program		X		Secondary	EMC Corp.
Schoolhouse Comprehension		X	X	Intermediate	Science Research Associates
Schoolhouse Word Attack		X	X	Primary	Science Research Associates
Sounder		X		Elementary–Jr. High	Edmark Associates
Specific Skills Series		X		Elementary–Jr. High	Barnell Loft
Starting Line Series		X		K–6	Bowmar Publishing Corp.
Structural Reading	X			Elementary	Random House/Singer School Division
Systems 80: Learning Letter Sounds; Reading Words in Context		X		Elementary	Borg-Warner Educational Systems
Tempo Series		X		Secondary	Macmillan Publishing Co.
Try Experiences for Young Children		X	X	Primary	Noble and Noble Publishers
What's Happening? Newspaper Reading Skills		X	X	Intermediate/Jr./Sr. High	Associated Press

High Interest/Low Vocabulary

Title	Interest Level	Reading Level	Publisher
Action Kit	Adolescent	2.0–4.0	Scholastic Book Services
Behind the Bright Lights	4–12	5.0	EMC Corp.
Breakthrough!	Jr./Sr. High	2.0–6.0	Allyn and Bacon
Checkered Flag Series	Intermediate/Jr. High	2.4–4.5	Addison-Wesley Publishing Co.
City Limits Series, I and II	Adolescent	5.0–6.0	Webster/McGraw-Hill Book Co.
Contact Series I, II, III	Adolescent	4.0–6.0	Scholastic Book Services
Contemporary Problems Reading Series	7–12	4.0–5.0	Educational Activities
Curriculum Enrichment Series	Elementary	2.0–6.0	Rand McNally/Lyons & Carnahan
Curriculum Motivation Series	Elementary	1.0–6.0	Rand McNally/Lyons & Carnahan
Dan Frontier Series	Intermediate	2.0–4.0	Benefic Press
Deep Sea Adventure Series	Intermediate	1.8–5.0	Addison-Wesley Publishing Co.
Dimensions Series: Our Story, Women of To-day and Yesterday	Intermediate/Adult	3.0–8.9	Science Research Associates
Double Action	Adolescent	3.0–5.0	Scholastic Book Services
Everyreaders	5–12	4.0	Webster/McGraw-Hill Book Co.
Face-Off	4–10	5.0	EMC Corp.
Fantasy Reading Activity Program	5–up	5.0–7.0	Sunburst Communications
FLIER Library (Fearon Lively Interest Read-ing)	Jr./Sr. High	1.9–4.6	Fearon Publishers
Getting It Together	Adolescent	2.0–6.0	Science Research Associates
Hip-Pocket Stories	Adolescent	2.8–3.3	Random House/Singer School Division
Hockey Heroes	4–12	4.0	EMC Corp.
Incredible Series	Intermediate/Sr. High	4.0–6.0	Barnell Loft
Inner City Series	2–7	2.0–4.0	Benefic Press
Kaleidoscope Readers	Intermediate/Adolescent	2.5–9.5	Addison-Wesley Publishing Co.
Tom Logan Series	2–6	2.0–3.0	Benefic Press
Mystery Adventure Series	4–9	2.0–5.0	Benefic Press
Open Door Books	Adolescent	5.0	Children's Press
Pal Paperback Program, Kits A and B	4–12	2.5–5.5	Xerox Education Publications
Personal Reading Modules	Jr./Sr. High	4.2–5.1	Relevant Publications/Melton Book Co.
Pilot Library Series	3–9	2.0–12.0	Science Research Associates

(continued)

High Interest/Low Vocabulary

Title	Interest Level	Reading Level	Publisher
Racing Wheels Series	4–12	2.0–4.0	Benefic Press
Reader's Digest Adult Readers	Adolescent–Adult	1.0–4.0	Reader's Digest Services
Reading Incentive Series	Intermediate–Jr. High	3.0	Bowmar Publishing Corp.
Really Me!	4–10	3.0	EMC Corp.
Red Line/Blue Line	4–10	5.0	EMC Corp.
Reluctant Reader Libraries	Jr./Sr. High	3.0–8.0	Scholastic Book Services
Saddle Up!	4–9	2.0–4.0	EMC Corp.
Scope Activity Kits	8–12	4.0–6.0	Scholastic Book Services
Space Science Fiction Series	4–12	2.0–6.0	Benefic Press
Sports Action Skills Kit	4–12	4.0	Melton Book Co.
Sports Close-Ups	4–12	5.0	EMC Corp.
Sports Mystery Series	5–Adult	2.0–4.0	Benefic Press
Sports Reading Activity Program	5–9	4.0–6.0	Sunburst Communications
Target Today Series	4–12	2.0–6.0	Benefic Press
Teen-Age Tales	Jr./Sr. High	3.0–6.0	D. C. Heath and Co.
Tromp It	4–10	5.0	EMC Corp.
Venture	7–12	4.0–6.5	Follett Publishing Co.
Winners All	4–10	5.0	EMC Corp.
Women Who Win	4–12	5.0	EMC Corp.
World Adventure Stories	4–12	5.0	Benefic Press
Young Adventure Series	Adolescent	4.0–6.0	Bowmar Publishing Corp.

Spoken and Written Language

Title	Function			Grade Level	Publisher
	Developmental	Skill/Remediation	Supplemental		
Activity-Concept English (ACE)	X			Secondary	Scott, Foresman and Co.
Adventure Guide for Practical Language Understanding		X		Primary	Learning Resource Center
Association Picture Cards		X		Elementary	Developmental Learning Materials

Title				Level	Publisher
A Behavioral–Psycholinguistic Approach to Language Training			X	Elementary	American Speech and Hearing Association
Big Book of Language Through Sounds	X			Elementary	Interstate Printers and Publishers
Building Language Skills Program	X		X	Intermediate/Secondary	Educators Publishing Service
Building Your Language Power	X		X	Secondary	New Readers Press
Category Cards	X			Elementary	Developmental Learning Materials
Classification Game	X		X	Elementary	Instructo Corp.
Communications 1, 2, 3				Secondary	Follett Publishing Co.
Developmental Syntax Program	X			Elementary/Secondary	Learning Concepts
Discovering Opposites	X			Elementary	Instructo Corp.
Distar Language, Levels 1 and 2			X	Elementary	American Guidance Service
Dolch Word Cards	X			Elementary	Garrard Publishing Co.
Duso Kits	X	X		Elementary	American Guidance Service
English in Action	X		X	Intermediate/Jr.	Regents Publishing Co.
Everyday Reading and Writing	X			Intermediate	New Readers Press
Fun with Rhymes	X		X	Elementary	Instructo Corp.
Goal Program	X		X	Elementary	Milton Bradley Co.
Goldman–Lynch Sound Symbol Developmental Kit				Elementary	American Guidance Service
Guide Book to Better English	X			Intermediate/Secondary	Economy Co.
Individualized English/Programmed Instruction, Sets J and H	X			Secondary	Follett Publishing Co.
Interactive Language Development Teaching	X		X	Elementary	Research Press

(continued)

Spoken and Written Language

Title	Function			Grade Level	Publisher
	Developmental	Skill/Remediation	Supplemental		
Keys to English Mastery	X			Secondary	Economy Co.
Keys to Good Language	X			Elementary	Economy Co.
Keys to Language	X			Elementary	Economy Co.
Kindergarten Short Books		X		Primary	Modern Curriculum Press
Language Activities for Fun			X	Elementary	Frank Schaffer Co.
Language Concepts		X		Elementary	Developmental Learning Materials
Language Exercises		X		Elementary	Steck-Vaughn Co.
Language Exercises in Reading	X			Elementary	American Guidance Service
Language Instruction Activities Books 1 and 2		X		Elementary	Love Publishing Co.
Language Lotto: Relationships, Prepositions, Objects		X		Elementary	Appleton-Century-Crofts
Language Master, Language Stimulation Program		X		Elementary/Jr. High	Bell & Howell
Language Master, Reinforcement Program		X		Elementary/Jr. High	Bell & Howell
Language Master, Word-Picture Program		X		Elementary/Jr. High	Bell & Howell
Language Patterns		X		Elementary	Milton Bradley Co.
Language Program for the Non-Language Child	X	X		Elementary	Research Press
Language Training for Adolescents		X		Jr./Sr. High	Educators Publishing Service
Lessons for Self-Instruction: Mechanics of English	X			Elementary/Secondary	CTB/McGraw-Hill Book Co.
Lessons in Syntax	X	X		Elementary/Secondary	Educational Activities
Let's Learn Sequence		X		Elementary	Instructo Corp.
Living Your English	X			Secondary	D. C. Heath and Co.
Magic Circle Program		X	X	Elementary	Human Development Training Institute

Title				Grade Level	Source
Many Faces of Youth Posters	X			Jr./Sr. High	Developmental Learning Materials
Organizing and Reporting Skills		X		Intermediate/Jr.	Science Research Associates Corp.
Parts of Speech		X		Elementary/Jr.	Teaching Resources Corp.
Peabody Articulation Cards		X		Elementary	American Guidance Service
Peabody Language Development Kits, Levels P, 1, 2, 3			X	Elementary	American Guidance Service
Photo Sequential Cards		X		Elementary/Secondary	Developmental Learning Materials
Playing in Playstreet		X		Primary	Macmillan Publishing Co.
Preschool Language			X	Primary	University of Hawaii Press
Reading with a Purpose: Study Skills for Information		X		Intermediate/Jr.	Coronet Instructional Media
Report Writing Skills		X		Intermediate/Jr.	Coronet Instructional Media
Retrieval Series		X		Intermediate/Jr.	Allyn and Bacon
Solving Language Difficulties		X		Intermediate/Jr.	Educators Publishing Service
Story Boards		X		Elementary	Childcraft Education Corp.
Story Builders	X			Elementary/Jr.	Childcraft Education Corp.
Talking Time Filmstrips		X		Elementary	Interstate Printers and Publishers
Target on Language			X	Elementary	Christ Church Child Center
Troubleshooter 1 and 2		X		Secondary	Houghton Mifflin Co.
Wilson Initial Syntax Program		X	X	Elementary	Educators Publishing Service
The Writing Bug		X		Intermediate/Jr.	Random House/Singer School Division
Verbal Communication Picture, Story Sets 1, 2, 3		X		Elementary	Bowmar Publishing Corp.

(continued)

Written Language

Title	Function			Grade Level	Publisher
	Developmental	Skill/Remediation	Supplemental		
Alphabet Cards and Alphabet Sheets		X		Elementary	Zaner-Blosser Co.
Basic Goals in Spelling	X			Elementary/Jr.	McGraw-Hill Book Co.
Continuous Progress in Spelling	X			Elementary	Economy Co.
Dr. Spello (2nd Edition)		X		Intermediate/Jr.	McGraw-Hill Book Co.
Gateway to Correct Spelling	X	X		Secondary	Steck-Vaughn Co.
Ginn Individualized Spelling Program	X	X		Elementary/Jr.	Ginn and Company
Harbrace Spelling Program	X			Elementary/Jr.	Harcourt Brace Jovanovich
Petersen Handwriting	X			Elementary	Macmillan Publishing Co.
Power to Spell	X			Elementary	Houghton Mifflin Co.
Reading Road to Spelling	X			Elementary/Jr.	Harper & Row, Publishers
Spell and Write	X			Elementary/Jr.	Noble and Noble, Publishers
Spelling Word Power Lab		X		Intermediate/Jr.	Science Research Associates
Spelling Workbook Series		X		Elementary/Secondary	Educators Publishing Service
Swing into Letters	X			Elementary	Educators Publishing Service
Systematic Spelling		X		Intermediate/Jr.	Educators Publishing Service
Word Book Spelling Series		X		Elementary/Jr.	Lyons & Carnahan
The Writing Center		X		Intermediate/Jr.	Holt, Rinehart and Winston
Writing Our Language	X			Elementary	Scott, Foresman and Co.

Title	Developmental	Skill/Remediation	Supplemental	Grade Level	Publisher
Writing Our Language	X			Secondary	Scott, Foresman and Co.
Written Language Cards	X		X	Elementary/Jr.	Developmental Learning Materials

Math

Title	Developmental	Skill/Remediation	Supplemental	Grade Level	Publisher
		Function			
	Developmental	*Skill/Remediation*	*Supplemental*	*Grade Level*	*Publisher*
Abacus, Large			X	K–2	Developmental Learning Materials
Abacus, Modern School			X	1–3	Ideal School Supply Co.
Abacus, Small			X	K–2	Developmental Learning Materials
Agencies That Protect the Consumer: Food and Drug Administration Federal Trade Commission Post Office Department Department of Agriculture State, County, City and Independent Services		X		7–12	Universal Education and Visual Arts
AOT (Arithmetic Operational Tools) Series Addition Subtraction Multiplication Division Multiples and Remainders		X		3–8	Developmental Learning Materials
Applying for Credit		X		9–12	Interpretive Education/ Melton Book Co.
Arithmetic Exercises Grade 4 (1st part)		X		4	Milliken Publishing Co.
Arithmetic Exercises Grade 4 (2nd part)		X		4	Milliken Publishing Co.
Arithmetic Fact Kit		X		3–Adult	Science Research Associates
Arithmetic Instructional Activities Books 1 and 2		X		Elementary	Love Publishing Co.

(continued)

Math

Title	Function			Grade Level	Publisher
	Developmental	Skill/Remediation	Supplemental		
Arithmetic Quizmo		X		1–4	Milton Bradley Co.
Arithmetic Step-by-Step		X		1–6	Continental Press
Arithmetic That We Need	X			1–6	Frank E. Richards Co.
Arrow Math		X		K–4	Teaching Resources Corp.
Basic Concepts in Economics: Producers and Consumers: Why Do People Work?		X		7–9	BFA Educational Media
Factors of Production: What Do We Need to Get Work Done?					
Specialization: How Do We Organize to Get Things Done?					
Economic Interdependence: Can We Live by Ourselves?					
Saving and Lending: What Do Banks Do with Our Money?					
Our Market Economy: Who Tells People What to Make and Do?					
Basic Essentials of Mathematics: Parts 1 and 2	X			5–9	Steck-Vaughn Co.
Basic Mathematics c. 1974: Spirit Duplicating Mathematics Program Kit A, B, C		X		7–9	Charles E. Merrill Co.
Basic Mathematics, Set 1:					Educational Activities
Easier Facts	X			2–4, remedial –5	
Harder Facts	X			3–6, rem. sec.	
Combination Number Facts	X			4–6, rem. sec.	
Measurement	X			2–4, rem. 5–6	
Writing Numerals	X			2–4, rem. 4–6	
Multiplying by Tens and Hundreds	X			3–4, rem. 5–6	
Rounding Numbers	X			3–5, rem. 6	
Estimating	X			3–5, rem. 6	
Problem Solving	X			3–5, rem. 6	
Harder Problem Solving	X			3–5, rem. 6	

Material	Grade Level		Publisher
Basic Mathematics, Set II:	6–8, rem. 9	X	Educational Activities
Writing Decimals			
Rounding Decimals			
Renaming Fractions and Decimals			
Renaming Decimals and Percents			
Renaming Percents and Fractions			
Renaming Percents, Fractions, and Decimals			
Adding Positive and Negative Numbers			
Subtracting Positive and Negative Numbers			
Multiplying Positive and Negative Numbers			
Dividing Positive and Negative Numbers			
Basic Mathematics, Set III:		X	Educational Activities
Easier Missing Facts	2–4, rem. 5		
Harder Missing Facts	3–6, rem. sec.		
Combination Missing Facts	4–6, rem. sec.		
Basic Operations: Using Math Vocabulary	2–4, rem. 5		
Finding Multiples	3–5, rem. 6		
Finding Factors	3–6, rem. sec.		
Prime and Composite Numbers	4–6, rem. sec.		
More Problem Solving	3–5, rem. 6		
Roman Numerals	3–6, rem. sec.		
Dividing by Tens and Hundreds	4–6, rem. sec.		
Basic Practice in Addition, Subtraction, Multiplication, Division	K–Jr. High	X	Love Publishing Co.
Basic Skills Filmstrips Series:	4–12	X	Silver Burdett Co.
Decimal/Metric Package: Using Decimals			
Part 1: Addition and Subtraction			
Part 2: Multiplication and Division			
Graphing Package:			
Part 1: What Is a Graph?			
Part 2: Locating Points			
Part 3: Showing Relationships			
Part 4: Inferring Relationships			
Part 5: Other Kinds of Graphs			
Bead Frame	Elementary	X	Educational Teaching Aids/Daigger & Co.

(continued)

Math

Title	Function			Grade Level	Publisher
	Developmental	Skill/Remediation	Supplemental		
Before You Buy: People in Trouble with Credit Credit Decision Lending Institutions Bankruptcy		X		9–12	Universal Education and Visual Arts
Beginner's Metric Cards			X	1–3	Constructive Playthings
Beginner's Metric Kit		X		4–6	Educational Teaching Aids/Daigger & Co.
Beginning Metric Measurement		X		K–3	Society for Visual Education
BFA Computation Skills Labs		X		Elementary	BFA Educational Media
Budgeting Series: What Is a Budget? Why Budget? What Are Expenses? How to Budget Budget Help		X		9–12	Interpretive Education/Melton Book Co.
Business Systems Series: Simplified Computer Arithmetic Simplified Computer Logic Bicom 255 (Binary Counter Computer Model 225) Simplified Computer Input		X		9–12	Fearon Publishers
Calcumate		X		4–6	H & H Enterprises
Celsius Student Thermometer		X		Nongraded	Constructive Playthings
Celsius Thermometer		X		Nongraded	Cole Supply Co.
Centerimeter Decimal Set			X	4–8	Invicta/Baker and Taylor
Centimeter Grid Paper			X	Nongraded	Houghton Mifflin Co.
Centimeter Rod Activity Card Kit		X		K–3	Houghton Mifflin Co.
Centimeter Rods		X		1–6	Houghton Mifflin Co.
Change Maker Kit		X		Elementary/Jr. High	Tech-Um Co.
Clock, Dial (2 faces)		X		K–Primary	Ideal School Supply Co.

Clock, Plastic	X		Primary	Developmental Learning Materials
Clock Arithmetic: Addition Subtraction Multiplication Problems	X		5–7	Wollensak
Clock Stamp	X		Primary	Developmental Learning Materials
Coin Stamps (Heads and Tails)	X		Elementary	Developmental Learning Materials
Coins and Bills	X		Elementary	Developmental Learning Materials
Comprehensive Metric Kit	X		Nongraded	Educational Teaching Aids/Daigger & Co.
Computapes, Modules 1–6	X		1–6	Science Research Associates
Computapes, Modules 7–11	X		5–9	Science Research Associates
Consumer Education Series: Understanding Tags and Labels How to Judge Shopping Values Shopping Tips Bargain Hunting How to Read Ads	X		9–12	Interpretive Education/Melton Book Co.
Consumerism	X		4–12	Relevant Publications/Melton Book Co.
Consumerism Unit/Scholastic Dimension	X		4–6	Scholastic Book Services
Counting Tiles	X		Elementary	Creative Playthings
Cross Number Puzzles: Multiplication—Beginners Multiplication—Advanced Fractions—Addition Decimals—Addition Addition—Beginners Addition—Advanced			4–9	Ideal School Supply Co.
Cubes, Colored		X	Primary	Ideal School Supply Co.

(continued)

Math

Title	Function			Grade Level	Publisher
	Developmental	Skill/ Remediation	Supplemental		
Cubic Foot Dissectible		X		Elementary	Ideal School Supply Co.
Cuisenaire Rods, Classroom Kit		X		K–9	Cuisenaire Company of America
Date Wheel		X		Primary	Developmental Learning Materials
Decimal Lines			X	4–8	
Developing Math Skills, Decimals: Kit L:		X		3–12	Borg-Warner Educational Systems
Lesson 1, Place Value					
Lesson 2, Tenths					
Lesson 3, Hundredths					
Lesson 4, Review of Lessons 1, 2, 3					
Lesson 5, Thousands, Decimal Understanding					
Lesson 6, Addition and Subtraction of Decimals on a Number Line					
Lesson 7, Addition and Subtraction of Decimals in Column Form					
Lesson 8, Review of Lessons 5, 6, 7					
Test Lesson					
Developing Math Skills, Fractions: Kit I:		X		3–12	Borg-Warner Educational Systems
Lesson, Congruence					
Lesson 2, $\frac{1}{2}$, $\frac{1}{3}$					
Lesson 3, $\frac{1}{4}$, $\frac{1}{8}$					
Lesson 4, Review of Lessons 1, 2, 3					
Lesson 5, $\frac{1}{5}$, $\frac{1}{6}$					
Lesson 6, $\frac{2}{3}$, $\frac{3}{4}$					
Lesson 7, Numerator, Denominator, Fraction Knowledge					
Lesson 8, Review of Lessons 5, 6, 7					
Test Lesson					
Distar Arithmetic I and II	X			Elementary	Science Research Associates

Title	Publisher	Grade			
Dollars and Sense:	Troll Associates	4–6		X	
How Money Goes Round and Round					
Different Kinds of Money					
How Money Is Made					
How We Borrow Money					
How Budgets Work					
How Taxes Work					
Dominoes	Ideal School Supply Co.	Elementary	X		
Duplicating Workbook (Metric Measure)	Educational Teaching Aids/Daigger	4+		X	
Economics for Primaries	Singer/SVE (order from SVE)	1–3		X	
EDL Math Path:	Educational Developmental Lab/McGraw-Hill (SPECO)				
Math Path C		3			X
Math Path D		4			X
Math Path E		5			X
Elements of Mathematics	Silver Burdett Co.	7–9		X	
Environmental Mathematics Series:	BFA Educational Media	7–9		X	
Term and Sets: Waste Disposal					
Addition and Subtraction: Taxes					
Multiplication and Division: Environmental Planning					
Graphing: Governmental Processes					
Mean, Median, and Mode: Determining Public Opinion					
Problem Solving Techniques: Population Control					
Everyday Business:	Lawson Book Co.	7–12		X	
Banking					
Buying					
Budgeting					
Federal Income Tax					
Insurance					
Explora Tapes: Mathematics Program 100	Educational Progress Corp.	3–5		X	
Figure It Out, Book 2	Follett Publishing Co.	7–12/Adult Education		X	
Financing a Car	Relevant Publications/Melton Book Co.	9–12/SPED		X	

(continued)

Math

Title	Function			Grade Level	Publisher
	Developmental	Skill/Remediation	Supplemental		
Flash Cards:					
Addition		X		1–3	Ideal School Supply Co.
Subtraction				1–3	
New Math Addition				1–3	
New Math Subtraction				1–3	
Relationship Cards				1–3	
Multiplication				3–4	
Division				3–4	
Fraction Squares			X	2–6	Ideal School Supply Co.
Fractions and Fractional Numbers		X		4–8	Milton Bradley Co.
Fractions as Easy as Pie		X		2–6	Fisher-Price Toys
Fun and Games with Mathematics			X	4–9	Prentice-Hall Educational Books Division
Fundamentals of Modern Mathematics:					
Sets and Set Operations		X		4–9	Scott Education
The Whole Numbers					
The Integers					
The Rational Numbers					
Relations					
Functions					
Finite Mathematical Systems					
Numeration Systems					
Shapes					
Areas					
General Mathematics	X			7–12/Adult Education	National Book Co.
Geoboards:					
Introducing Geoboards		X	X	K–6	Cuisenaire Company of America
Activity Cards					
Geoboards (Classroom Kits): Primary and Intermediate					
Geometric Models Construction Kit		X		4–9	Milton Bradley Co.
Geometry (Constructional)	X			7–12/Adult Education	National Book Co.

(continued)

Title					Grade Level	Source
Getting a Line on Mathematics	X				6-12	Cuisenaire Company of America
Getting Acquainted with the Metric System		X			4-Adult	Outdoor Pictures, Inc.
Going Metric		X			4-6	Scholastic Book Services
Good Time Mathematics (by the Amazing Life Games Company)		X			4-7	Holt, Rinehart and Winston
Good Times *Again* with Math		X			4-9	Prentice-Hall Educational Books Division
Graded Difficulty Arithmetic, Sets I and II		X			1-8	Bell & Howell
Graphs, Reading and Constructing:		X	X			Wollensak
Developing a Picture Graph					2-4	
Graphing Around in a Circle					2-4	
Swagger Up to the Bar Graph					3-5	
Pick a Dandy Line Graph					4-6	
How to Tell a Graph					5-7	
Guidebook to Mathematics		X			3-5/Adult	Economy Co.
Hard Spots in Modern Math: Grade 4		X			4	Milliken Publishing Co.
Grade 5		X			5	
Grade 6		X			6	
Here-To-There	X				4-9	Scott, Foresman and Co.
History of the Measurement of Length (from Measurement)		X			7-12	Visual Education Consultants
How to Handle Money		X			9-12/SPED	Relevant Publications/Melton Book Co.
How to Read a Ruler (from Metric System)		X			7-12	Creative Visuals
How to Use a Metric Ruler		X			1-6	Visual Education Consultants
I.D.E.A.S (Individually Diagnosed Error Analysis System) 1975				X	3-12	Holt, Rinehart and Winston
Imma Whiz—Arithmetic Games: Add., Sub., Mult., Div.		X			2-6	Kenworthy Educational Service
Improving Your Ability in Mathematics to Add, Subtract, Multiply, Divide					4+	Harcourt Brace Jovanovich
Individualized Mathematics Improvement Series:				X	3-12	Holt, Rinehart and Winston
Set 1, Operations with Whole Numbers						
Set 2, Operations with Fractions						

Math

Title	Function			Grade Level	Publisher
	Developmental	Skill Remediation	Supplemental		
Set 3: Operations with Decimals and Percent					
Individualized Mathematics Improvement Series: 400, 500, 600		X		4–6	Bobbs-Merrill Co.
International System of Units (Metric Units)		X		7–12	Society for Visual Education
Introducing Graphs: Why Graphs? Bar and Pictographs Single-Bar and Circle Graphs Coordinate System		X		4–8	BFA Educational Media
Introducing the Metric System: Let's Take Measures for Good Measure		X		K–3	Educational Communication Association
Kaleidoscope of Skills: Arithmetic, Grades 5, 6, 7		X		5–7	Science Research Associates
Learn Metrics by Doing Metrics		X		K–12	Academic Therapy Publications
Learning Skills Series: Arithmetic Acquiring Arithmetic Skills Building Arithmetic Skills Continuing Arithmetic Skills Directing Arithmetic Skills		X		4–12	Webster/McGraw-Hill Book Co.
Let's Go Metric		X		K–4	Teaching Resources Corp.
Let's Learn About the Metric System		X		1–4	Stallman Susser
Let's Talk Metric		X		3–6	Multi-Media Productions
Linear Measures			X	3–6	Developmental Learning Materials
Liter Volume (from Volume Concepts)		X		4–8	Science Related Materials
Macmillan School Mathematics Program Developing Mathematics Series	X			K–8	Macmillan Publishing Co.
Magic Squares: Levels A–E		X		2–6	Charles E. Merrill Co.

Title				Grade	Publisher
Math Applications Kit		X		4–8	Science Research Associates
Math Balance		X	X	K–3	Educational Teaching Aids/Daigger & Co.
Math Games Box		X		2–6	Educational Insights
Math Readiness Addition and Subtraction		X	X	1–3	Educational Activities
Math Wheels: Market Math Dial Kitchen Math Dial Auto Math Dial Freeway Math Dial		X		4–6	Ideal School Supply Co.
Mathematics Around Us	X	X		Elementary	Scott, Foresman and Co.
Mathematics for Career Education		X		9–12	Charles E. Merrill Co.
Mathematics for Individual Achievement		X		K–8	Houghton Mifflin Co.
Mathematics: Modern Concepts and Skills	X	X		Jr. High	D. C. Heath and Co.
Mathematics Structure and Skills		X		7–9	Science Research Associates
Mathematics Teaching Tape Program, Intermediate Level		X		4–7	Houghton Mifflin Co.
Mathlab		X		5–8	Benefic Press
Measure Dry and Liquid		X	X	1–4	Ideal School Supply Co.
Merrill Mathematics Skilltapes Series: Base 10 System of Counting Addition of Whole Numbers Subtraction of Whole Numbers Multiplication of Whole Numbers Division of Whole Numbers Understanding Fractions Fractions: Addition and Subtraction Fractions: Multiplication and Division Decimals: Understanding and Operations		X		3–9	Charles E. Merrill Co.
Meter Reader—A Metric Workbook		X		**7–12**	Fearon Publishers
Metric Activity Cards		X		4+	Educational Teaching Aids/Daigger & Co.
Metric America		X		6–Adult	Aims Instructional Media Services

(continued)

Math

Title	Function			Grade Level	Publisher
	Developmental	Skill/Remediation	Supplemental		
Metric Future (from Measurement)		X		7–12	Visual Educational Consultants
Metric Length Construction Kit		X		4–6	Educational Teaching Aids/Daigger & Co.
Metric Measurement		X		3–8	Imperial International Learning Co.
Metric Multimedia Kits		X		4+	Educational Teaching Aids/Daigger & Co.
Metric System (from General Math)		X		7–12	McGraw-Hill Book Co.
Metric System: Elementary Program		X		4–6	National Education Corp.
Metric System: Selected Materials for Special Education		X		SPED	National Education Corp.
Metric System Mini-Module		X		1–3	Society for Visual Education
Metric Tasks: Skill Development Activities		X		3–6	Love Publishing Co.
Metrication of America		X		4–8	Westinghouse Learning Corp.
Metrikit		X		3–8	Charles E. Merrill Co.
Michigan Arithmetic Program: Numbers and Numerals Addition 0–10 Addition 10–20 Multiplication Subtraction 10–0 Subtraction 20–10 Division	X			3–12/SPED	Ann Arbor Publishers
Michigan Prescriptive Program		X		9–12/Adult	Ann Arbor Publishers
Modern Arithmetic Through Discovery	X			K–2	Silver Burdett Co.
Modern Mathematics Through Discovery	X			3–6	Silver Burdett Co.
Modern School Mathematics: Structure and Use	X			Elementary	Houghton Mifflin Co.
Money Book		X		7–12/Reading Level 4.0	Xerox Education Publications

Title				Grade	Source
Money Dominos	X			2–4	Developmental Learning Materials
Money Handling		X		7–9/SPED	Melton Book Co.
Mr. Windbag in Metric Land		X		K–3/Remedial	Educational Products
Multiplication Rock Series	X			1–8	Xerox Films
My Number Book, Parts 1, 2, 3		X		2	Continental Press
Number Equalizer Balance	X			K–2	Developmental Learning Materials
Number Learner	X	X		K–1	Creative Playthings
Number Rods	X			K–2	Ideal School Supply Co.
Number Wheels, Self-Instructional		X		1–4	Ideal School Supply Co.
Pacemaker Practical Arithmetic Series		X		Elementary/Jr. High	Fearon Publishing Co.
Pegboard Pegs	X			K–4	Developmental Learning Materials
Percent: Operations		X		7–9	Wollensak
Richard Petty Pit Stop Math	X			1–6	Classroom World Productions
PhotoNumber Group Card Game	X			K–2	Developmental Learning Materials
Preparing to Live on Your Own Series	X	X		7–9	Singer/SVE (order from SVE)
Primary Economics Series	X	X		K–3	BFA Educational Media
Primary Math Lotto	X			K–1	Creative Playthings
Primary Math Lotto	X			K–3	Childcraft Education Corp.
Programmed Math			X	Elementary	Webster/McGraw-Hill Book Co.
Progressional Number Concepts		X		K–2	Ideal School Supply Co.
Project Math			X	Elementary	Educational Progress Corp.
Project Mathematics		X		K–6	Winston Press Productions
Rods and Counters	X			K–3	Childcraft Education

(continued)

Math

Title	Function			Grade Level	Publisher
	Developmental	Skill/ Remediation	Supplemental		
Rounding Off: Whole Numbers Fractions to Whole Numbers Fractions to Fractions Decimals		X		5–7	Wollensak
Same or Different Size Cards		X		K–2	Developmental Learning Materials
School House Mathematics		X		1–2	Science Research Associates
Sequential Mathematics		X		1–8	Harcourt Brace Jovanovich
Shopping Bag		X		3–8	Creative Teaching Associates
Shopping Lists Game		X		1–4	Developmental Learning Materials
Shopping Lists Game II		X		4–6	Developmental Learning Materials
Silver Burdett Mathematics System: Grades 7, 8	X			7–8	Silver Burdett Co.
Situational Math, Level II		X		5–6	United Learning Co.
Size Concept Posters			X	1–3	Developmental Learning Materials
Skill Building Counting Rods			X	K–2	Teaching Resources Corp.
Skill Modes in Mathematics, Levels 1, 2, 3		X		4–Adult	Science Research Corp.
Spatial Relation Picture Cards			X	K–3	Developmental Learning Materials
SRA Mathematics Learning System	X			Elementary/Jr. High	Science Research Associates
SRA Mathematics Learning Systems Resource Boxes			X	2–8	Science Research Associates
Structural Arithmetic (Stearns)	X			K–Elementary	Houghton Mifflin Co.

Title		Grade Level	Publisher
Sum Fun	×	K–3	Ideal School Supply Co.
Synchromath/Experiences	×	7–12	Rand McNally
Tell Time Quizmo	×	4–9	Cole Supply Co.
Thermometer	×	1–3	Ideal School Supply Co.
Time and Telling Time	×	2.9 Reading Level	Fearon Publishers
Time Tracks	×	1–3	Developmental Learning Materials
Useful Arithmetic, Volumes I and II	×	7–12	Frank E. Richards Co.
Using Dollars and Cents	×	4–9	Fearon Publishers
Using Money Series, Books 1–4	×	4–12	Frank E. Richards Co.
Wollensak Teaching Tape Series: Consumer and Saving Wise Consumer Spending	×	10–12	Wollensak
World of Whole Numbers, Filmstrips: Missing Addend Bowler's Mathematics Sporting Mathematics Missing Factor Doughnut Stand	×	7–9	BFA Educational Media
You and Your Money	×	Adult Education	Steck-Vaughn Co.

Perceptual–Motor

Title	Function			Grade Level	Publisher
	Motor	Motor-Perceptual	Perceptual		
Alike/Unalike Strip Books			×	Preschool/Primary	Teaching Resources Corp.
Animal Puzzles with Knobs		×		Preschool/Primary	Childcraft
Auditory Discrimination in Depth			×	Elementary	Teaching Resources Corp.
Auditory Perception Training (APT)			×	Primary	Developmental Learning Materials
Balance Beam Activities	×			Preschool/Primary	Educational Activities
Balance Board	×			Preschool/Primary	Childcraft Education Corp.
Balls of various sizes, jacks, marbles, and jump ropes	×			Preschool/Elementary	Toys that may be found in local department stores

(continued)

Perceptual–Motor

Title	Function			Grade Level	Publisher
	Motor	Motor-Perceptual	Perceptual		
Beads of various sizes and shapes for stringing, workbenches for pounding, color stacking, discs and nesting boxes		X		Preschool/Kindergarten	Toys that may be found in local department stores
Best Vests and Dressing Frames		X		Preschool/Primary	Educational Teaching Aids/Daigger & Co.
Blocks—wooden, cardboard, foam, plastic, interconnecting, stacking		X		Preschool/Kindergarten	Toys that may be found in local department stores
Body Position Cards	X			Primary	Teaching Resources Corp.
Buzzer Board			X	Preschool/Kindergarten	Developmental Learning Materials
Ruth Cheves Program/1		X	X	Preschool/Primary	Teaching Resources Corp.
Clothespin Circle		X		Preschool/Primary	Educational Teaching Aids/Daigger & Co.
Clown Bean Bag Game	X			Preschool/Primary	Constructive Playthings
Congo Board			X	Elementary	Teaching Resources Corp.
Crawl Thru	X			Preschool/Primary	Constructive Playthings
Double-Layer Surprise Puzzles		X		Preschool/Primary	Childcraft Education Corp.
Dubnoff School Program/1, Levels 1 and 2		X		Preschool/Primary	Teaching Resources Corp.
Dubnoff School Program/2		X	X	Primary	Teaching Resources Corp.
Dynamic Balancing Activities	X			Preschool/Primary	Educational Activities
Erie Program/1		X	X	Preschool/Primary	Teaching Resources Corp.
Fairbanks–Robinson Program/1, Level 1		X	X	Preschool/Primary	Teaching Resources Corp.
Fairbanks–Robinson Program/1, Level 2		X	X	Primary	Teaching Resources Corp.
Figure–Ground Activity Cards			X	Primary	Developmental Learning Materials
Form Puzzles			X	Primary	Developmental Learning Materials
Frostig MGL Move-Grow-Learn		X		Primary	Follett Publishing Co.

Material				Level	Source
Giant Tic-Tac-Toe			X	Preschool/Primary	Constructive Playthings
House Lotto	X			Primary	Childcraft Education Corp.
Illustrated Dominoes	X			Preschool/Primary	Childcraft Education Corp.
Individual Motor Achievement Guided Education			X	Preschool/Intermediate	Devereux Foundation Press
Look Alikes	X			Elementary	Teaching Resources Corp.
Matching Cards	X			Preschool/Primary	Teaching Resources Corp.
Match-Up Wheel	X			Elementary	Teaching Resources Corp.
Missing Match-Ups	X			Primary	Developmental Learning Materials
Movement Fun	X		X	Preschool/Primary	Educational Activities
The Parkinson Program for Special Children				Primary	Follett Publishing Co.
Parquetry Design Blocks	X			Elementary	Milton Bradley Co.
Pathway School Program/1		X	X	Preschool/Primary	Teaching Resources Corp.
Peg Board		X		Preschool/Primary	Milton Bradley Co.
Peg Sorting Board		X		Preschool/Kindergarten	Childcraft Education Corp.
Perception Puzzles	X			Preschool/Kindergarten	Developmental Learning Materials
Perceptual Bingo	X			Primary	Teaching Resources Corp.
Perceptual Development through Paper Folding		X		Elementary	Educational Activities
Petals	X			Preschool/Primary	Childcraft Education Corp.
Pre-Kindergarten Puzzle Series		X		Preschool/Kindergarten	Judy Co.
Puzzles		X		Preschool/Primary	Playschool (order from Milton Bradley Co.)
Puzzles—Beginner's Wood Inlays		X		Preschool/Primary	Childcraft Education Corp.
Puzzles with Small Knobs		X		Preschool/Primary	Childcraft Education Corp.
Rhythmic Eye-Hand and Patterned Movement Activities			X	Elementary	Educational Activities
Ring Toss Game	X		X	Primary	Milton Bradley Co.
Same or Different Size Cards	X			Preschool/Primary	Developmental Learning Materials
See It—Do It	X			Primary	Developmental Learning Materials

(continued)

Perceptual–Motor

Title	Function			Grade Level	Publisher
	Motor	Motor–Perceptual	Perceptual		
Sequential Sorting Box		X		Preschool/Kindergarten	Childcraft Education Corp.
Shake-and-Match Sounds			X	Preschool/Primary	Teaching Resources Corp.
Shape Match			X	Elementary	Childcraft Education Corp.
Size and Shape Puzzle			X	Preschool/Primary	Developmental Learning Materials
Size Sequencing Cards			X	Preschool/Primary	Developmental Learning Materials
Sound/Order/Sense			X	Primary	Follett Publishing Co.
Square Peg Board		X		Preschool/Kindergarten	Educational Teaching Aids/Daigger & Co.
Strip Books			X	Primary	Teaching Resources Corp.
Tactile Sensory Training Bridges		X		Preschool/Primary	Educational Teaching Aids/Daigger & Co.
Tactilmat Pegboard with Easygrip Pegs		X		Preschool/Primary	Constructive Playthings
Threading Block		X		Preschool/Kindergarten	Childcraft Education Corp.
Visual Discrimination Flip Books		X		Primary	Developmental Learning Materials
Visual-Discrimination Matching Cards			X	Preschool/Primary	Developmental Learning Materials
Visual Memory Cards			X	Primary	Developmental Learning Materials
Visual–Perceptual Games			X	Elementary	Teaching Resources Corp.
Visual Sequential Memory Exercises			X	Primary	Developmental Learning Materials
What's Missing Puzzles			X	Primary	Childcraft Education Corp.

PUBLISHERS

Academic Therapy Publications
1539 Fourth Street
San Rafael, CA 94901

Addison-Wesley Publishing Co.
2725 Sand Hill Road
Menlo Park, CA 94025

Aims Instructional Media Services
P.O. Box 1010
Hollywood, CA 90028

Allyn and Bacon, Inc.
470 Atlantic Avenue
Boston, MA 02210

American Guidance Service
Publishers' Building
Circle Pines, MN 55014

American Speech and Hearing
  Association
9030 Old Georgetown Road
Washington, DC 20014

Ann Arbor Publishers
611 Church Street
Ann Arbor, MI 48104

Appleton-Century-Crofts
292 Madison Avenue
New York, NY 10017

Associated Press
50 Rockefeller Plaza
New York NY 10020

Barnell Loft Ltd.
958 Church Street
Baldwin, NY 11510

C. L. Barnhart, Inc.
P.O. Box 250
Bronxville, NY 10708

Bell & Howell
Audio Visual Products Division
7100 McCormick Road
Chicago, IL 60645

Benefic Press
10300 West Roosevelt Road
Westchester, IL 60153

BFA Educational Media
P.O. Box 1795
Santa Monica, CA 90406

The Bobbs-Merrill Company, Inc.
4300 West 62nd Street
Indianapolis, IN 46206

Borg-Warner Educational Systems
600 West University Drive
Arlington Heights, IL 60004

Bowmar Publishing Corp.
622 Rodier Drive
Glendale, CA 91201

Milton Bradley Company
Springfield, MA 01101

Chandler Publishing Company
  See Garrett Book Company
    130 East 13th Street
    P.O. Box 1588
    Ada, OK 74820

Changing Times Education Service
1729 H Street, N.W.
Washington, DC 20006

Chatto & Windus Ltd.
40–42 William IV Street
London WC 2, England

Childcraft Education Corp.
20 Kilmer Road
Edison, NJ 08817

Children's Press
1224 West Van Buren Street
Chicago, IL 60607

Christ Church Child Center
8011 Old Georgetown Road
Bethesda, MD 20014

Classroom World Productions
22 Glenwood Avenue
Raleigh, NC 27602

Cole Supply Co.
103 East Bud Street
Pasadena, TX 77502

Constructive Playthings
1040 East 85th Street
Kansas City, MO 64131

Continental Press
Elizabethtown, PA 17022

Coronet Instructional Media
65 South Water Street East
Chicago, IL 60601

Creative Playthings
Princeton, NJ 08540

Creative Teaching Associates
P.O. Box 7714
Fresno, CA 93727

Creative Visuals
Box 1911
Big Springs, TX 79720

CTB/McGraw-Hill Division
Del Monte Research Park
Monterey, California 93940

Cuisenaire Company of America
12 Church Street
New Rochelle, NY 10805

Developmental Learning Materials
7440 Natchez Avenue
Niles, IL 60648

Devereux Foundation Press
Devon, PA 19333

The Economy Company
P.O. Box 25308
Oklahoma City, OK 73125

Edmark Associates
13249 Northup Way
Bellevue, WA 98005

Educational Activities, Inc.
P.O. Box 392
Freeport, NY 11520

Educational Communication Association
960 National Press Building
Washington, DC 20004

Educational Development Labs, Inc.
Division of McGraw-Hill (SPECO)
1221 Avenue of the Americas
New York, NY 10020

Educational Insights, Inc.
20435 South Tillman Avenue
Carson, CA 90746

Educational Products, Inc.
Oaklawn, ILL 60453

Educational Progress Corporation
P.O. Box 45663
Tulsa, OK 74145

Educational Teaching Aids/A. Daigger
  & Company
159 West Kinzie Street
Chicago, IL 60610

Educators Publishing Service, Inc.
75 Moulton Street
Cambridge, MA 02138

EMC Corporation
180 East 6th Street
St. Paul, MN 55101

Encyclopaedia Britannica Educational
Corporation
425 North Michigan Avenue
Chicago, IL 60611

Fearon Publishers,
  Lear Siegler, Inc.
6 Davis Drive
Belmont, CA 94002

Fisher-Price Toys
East Aurora, NY 14052

Follett Publishing Company
1010 West Washington Blvd.
Chicago, IL 60607

Garrard Publishing Co.
1607 North Market Street
Champaign, IL 61820

Ginn and Company
191 Spring Street
Lexington, MA 02173

H & H Enterprises, Inc.
P.O. Box 3342
Lawrence, KS 66044

Harcourt Brace Jovanovich, Inc.
757 Third Avenue
New York, NY 10017

Harper & Row, Publishers
10 East 53rd Street
New York, NY 10022

D. C. Heath and Company
125 Spring Street
Lexington, MA 02173

Holt, Rinehart and Winston, Inc.
P.O. Box 3323, Grand Central Station
New York, NY 10017

Houghton Mifflin Company
1 Beacon Street
Boston, MA 02107

Human Development Training Institute
1081 East Main Street
El Cajon, CA 92021

Ideal School Supply Co.
Oak Lawn, IL 60453

Imperial International Learning Co.
Box 548
Kankakee, IL 60901

Instructo/McGraw-Hill Division
Paoli, PA 19301

Interpretive Education
c/o Melton Book Co.
111 Leslie Street
Dallas, TX 75207

The Interstate Printers and Publishers,
Inc.
19–27 North Jackson Street
Danville, IL 61832

Invicta
from:
Baker and Taylor
Audio Visual Services Div.
P.O. Box 230
Momence, IL 60954

Judy Company
310 North 2nd Street
Minneapolis, MN 55401

Kenworthy Educational Service
P.O. Box 3031
Buffalo, NY 14205

Lawson Book Company
9488 Sara Street
Elk Grove, CA 95624

Learning Concepts
2501 North Lamar Blvd.
Austin, TX 78705

Learning Resource Center, Inc.
10655 S.W. Greenburg Road
Portland, OR 97223

J. B. Lippincott Company
Educational Publishing Division
East Washington Square
Philadelphia, PA 19105

Love Publishing Company
6635 East Villanova Place
Denver, CO 80222

Lyons & Carnahan
407 East 25th Street
Chicago, IL 60616

McGraw-Hill Book Company
1221 Avenue of the Americas
New York, NY 10020

Macmillan Publishing Co., Inc.
866 Third Avenue
New York, NY 10022

Mastery Programs, Ltd.
P.O. Box 90
Logan, UT 84321

Melton Book Company
111 Leslie Street
Dallas, TX 75207

Charles E. Merrill Publishing Company
1300 Alum Creek Drive
Columbus, OH 43216

Milliken Publishing Co.
1100 Research Blvd.
St. Louis, MO 63132

Modern Curriculum Press, Inc.
13900 Prospect Road
Cleveland, OH 44136

Multi-Media Productions
P.O. Box 5097
Stanford, CA 94305

National Book Co.
1019 S.W. 10th Avenue
Portland, OR 97205

National Education Corp.
  from:
    Baker and Taylor
    Audio Visual Services Div.
    P.O. Box 230
    Momence, IL 60954

New Dimensions in Education
160 Dupont Street
Plainview, New York 11803

New Readers Press
P.O. Box 131
Syracuse, NY 13210

Noble and Noble Publishers, Inc.
1 Dag Hammarskjold Plaza
New York, NY 10017

Open Court Publishing Company
P.O. Box 599
LaSalle, IL 61301

Outdoor Pictures, Inc.
Box 277
Anacortes, WA 98221

Phonovisual Products
12216 Parklawn Drive
Rockville, MD 20852

Prentice-Hall Educational Books
Division
Englewood Cliffs, NJ 07632

Rand McNally/Lyons & Carnahan
P.O. Box 7600
Chicago, IL 60680

Random House/Singer School
  Division
201 East 50th Street
New York, NY 10022

Reader's Digest Services, Inc.
Pleasantville, NY 10570

Regents Publishing Co., Inc.
2 Park Avenue
New York, NY 10016

Relevant Publications
c/o Melton Book Company
111 Leslie Street
Dallas, TX 75207

Research Press
P.O. Box 31775
Champaign, IL 61820

Frank E. Richards Co.
324 First Street
Liverpool, NY 13088

Frank Schaffer
26616 Indian Peak Road
Palos Verdes Peninsula, CA 90275

Scholastic Book Services
904 Sylvan Avenue
Englewood Cliffs, NJ 07632

Science Related Materials
Box 1422
Janesville, WI 53545

Science Research Associates, Inc.
259 East Erie Street
Chicago, IL 60611

Scott Education Division
Holyoke, MA 01040

Scott, Foresman and Company
200 East Lake Avenue
Glenview, IL 60025

Silver Burdett Company
250 James Street
Morristown, NJ 07960

(SVE) Society for Visual Education
1345 Diversey Parkway
Chicago, IL 60614

Stallman Susser
P.O. Box AL
Roslyn Heights, NY 11577

Steck-Vaughn Company
P.O. Box 2028
Austin, TX 78768

Sunburst Communications
39 Washington Avenue, Room 335
Pleasantville, NY 10570

Teaching Resources Corporation
100 Boylston Street
Boston, MA 02116

Teaching Technology Corporation
11680 Rendleton Avenue
Sun Valley, CA 91352

Teech-Um Company
P.O. Box 4232
Overland Park, KS 66204

Troll Associates
320 Route 17
Mahwah, NJ 07430

United Learning Company
3455 Olive Street
Eugene, OR 97405

Universal Education and Visual Arts
100 Universal City Plaza
Universal City, CA 91608

University of Hawaii Press
535 Ward Avenue
Honolulu, HI 96814

Visual Education Consultants
P.O. Box 52
Madison, WI 53701

Webster Division/McGraw-Hill
   Book Company
1221 Avenue of the Americas
New York, NY 10020

Westinghouse Learning Corp.
100 Park Avenue
New York, NY 10017

Winston Press
25 Groveland Terrace
Minneapolis, MN 55403

Wollensak/3M Company
Building 224-6E, 3M Center
St. Paul, MN 55101

Xerox Education Publications
Education Center
1250 Fairwood Avenue
Columbus, OH 43216

Zaner-Bloser Company
612 North Park Street
Columbus, OH 43215

References

Adventures of the Lollipop Dragon. Chicago: Society for Visual Education, 1970.

Alexander, E. D. School centered play-therapy program. In N. J. Long, W. C. Morse, and R. G. Newman (Eds.), *Conflict in the classroom.* Belmont, Calif.: Wadsworth, 1971. Pp. 251–257.

Allen, K. E., Turner, K. D., and Everett, P. M. A behavior modification classroom for Head Start children with problem behaviors. *Exceptional Children,* 1970, *37,* 119–127.

Allen, R., and Allen, C. *Language experiences in reading.* Chicago: Encyclopaedia Britannica, Inc., 1970.

Anastasi, A. *Psychological testing,* 3rd ed. New York: Macmillan, 1968.

Anderson, D. W. *Teaching handwriting.* Washington, D. C.: National Educational Association, 1968.

Anderson, V. *Improving the child's speech.* New York: Oxford University Press, 1953.

Antinucci, F., and Parisi, D. Early language acquisition: A model and some data. In C. A. Ferguson and D. I. Slobin (Eds.), *Studies of child language development.* New York: Holt Rinehart and Winston, 1973. Pp. 607–619.

Applegate, E. *Perceptual aids in the classroom.* San Rafael, Calif.: Academic Therapy Publications, 1969.

Archer, C. P. Transfer of training in spelling. In *University of Iowa studies in education.* Iowa City, Iowa: University of Iowa Press, 1930.

Arena, J. I. (Ed.). *Teaching through sensory-motor experiences.* San Rafael, Calif.: Academic Therapy Publications, 1969.

Armstrong, C., and Clark, W. *Los Angeles Diagnostic Tests.* Los Angeles: California Test Bureau, 1947.

Armstrong, J. R. A model for materials development and evaluation. *Exceptional Children,* 1971, *38,* 327–334.

Ashlock, R. B. *Current research in elementary school mathematics.* New York: Macmillan, 1970.

Ashlock, R. B. *Error patterns in computation: A semi-programmed approach.* Columbus, Ohio: Charles E. Merrill, 1972.

Axelrod, S. *Behavior modification for the classroom teacher.* New York: McGraw-Hill, 1977.

Axline, V. M. Non-directive therapy for poor readers. *Journal of Consulting Psychology,* 1947, *11,* 61–69.

Axline, V. M. *Dibs: In search of self.* New York: Ballantine Books, 1964.

Ayers, L. P. *A scale for measuring the quality of handwriting of school children.* New York: Russell Sage Foundation, 1920.

Ayllon, T. Intensive treatment of psychotic behavior by stimulus satiation and food reinforcement. In L. Krasner and L. P. Ullmann (Eds.), *Case studies in behavior modification.* New York: Holt, Rinehart and Winston, 1965.

Ayres, J. *Ayres Space Test.* Los Angeles: Western Psychological Services, 1962.

Ayres, J. *Southern California Motor Accuracy Test.* Los Angeles: Western Psychological Services, 1964.

Ayres, J. *Southern California Figure–Ground Visual Perception Test.* Los Angeles: Western Psychological Services, 1966. (a)

Ayres, J. *Southern California Kinesthesia and Tactile Perception Tests.* Los Angeles: Western Psychological Services, 1966. (b)

Ayres, J. *Southern California Perceptual–Motor Tests.* Los Angeles: Western Psychological Services, 1968.

Baker, H. J., and Leland, B. *The Detroit Tests of Learning Aptitude.* Indianapolis, Ind.: Bobbs-Merrill, 1967.

Ball, T. S. *Itard, Sequin, and Kephart: Sensory education—a learning interpretation.* Columbus, Ohio: Charles E. Merrill, 1971.

Bangs, T. *Vocabulary Comprehension Scale.* Austin, Tex.: Learning Concepts, 1975.

Bannatyne, A. D. *Psycholinguistic color system.* Urbana, Ill.: Learning Systems Press, 1966.

Barksdale, M. W., and Atkinson, A. P. A resource room approach to instruction for the educable mentally retarded. *Focus on Exceptional Children,* 1971, *3,* 12–15.

Barrett, T. C. The relationship between measures of pre-reading visual discrimination and first-grade reading achievement. *Reading Research Quarterly,* 1965, *1,* 51, 76.

Barry, H. Training the young aphasic child. *The Volta Review,* 1960, *7,* 326–328.

Barry, H. *The young aphasic child.* Washington, D.C.: Alexander Graham Bell Association for the Deaf, 1961.

Barsch, R. *A movigenics curriculum.* Madison, Wis.: State Department of Public Instruction, 1965.

Barsch, R. *Achieving perceptual–motor efficiency.* Seattle, Wash.: Special Child Publications, 1967.

Bartel, N. R. The development of morphology in moderately retarded childern. *Education and Training of the Mentally Retarded,* 1970, *5,* 164–168.

Bartel, N. R., Grill, J. J., and Bryen, D. N. Language characteristics of black children: Implications for assessment. *Journal of School Psychology,* 1973, *11,* 351–364.

Basic Educational Skills Inventory in Math. Olathe, Kans.: Select-Ed, 1972.

Bateman, B. Learning disabilities—yesterday, today, and tomorrow. In E. C. Frierson and W. B. Barbe (Eds.), *Educating children with learning disabilities.* New York: Appleton-Century-Crofts, 1967. Pp. 10–23.

Bayley, N. The development of motor abilities during the first three years. *Monograph Society for Research in Child Development,* 1935, *1,* 1–26.

Beery, K., and Buktenica, N. A. *Developmental Test of Visual–Motor Integration.* Chicago: Follett, 1967.

Belgau, F. A. *A motor perceptual developmental handbook of activities for schools, parents and preschool programs.* La Porte, Tex.: Perception Development Research Associates, 1966.

Bell, S. *Bell Adjustment Inventory.* Monterey, Calif.: Consulting Psychologists Press, 1961.

Bellak, L., and Bellak, S. S. *Children's Apperception Test.* Monterey, Calif.: Consulting Psychologists Press, 1961.

Bellugi, U. The Emergence of Inflections and Negation Systems in the Speech of Two Children. Paper presented at The New England Psychological Association Conference. Chicopee, Mass., November 1964.

Bellugi, U. The Development of Interrogative Structures in Children's Speech. Paper presented at the First Symposium on the Development of Language Functions. Ann Arbor, Mich., October 1965.

Bellugi-Klima, U. Language comprehension tests. In C. Lavatelli (Ed.), *Language training in early childhood education.* Champaign-Urbana, Ill.: University of Illinois Press, 1973.

Bender, L. *The Bender Visual–Motor Gestalt Test for Children.* New York: American Orthopsychiatric Association, 1938.

Benthul, H. F., Anderson, E. A., Utech, A. M., Biggy, M. V., and Bailey, B. L. *Spell correctly.* Morristown, N.J.: Silver Burdett, 1974.

Benton, A. L. *Revised Visual Retention Test: Clinical and experimental application.* New York: Psychological Corporation, 1955.

Berko, J. The child's learning of morphology. *Word,* 1958, *14,* 150–177.

Berry, M. F., and Eisenson, J. *Speech disorders.* New York: Appleton-Century-Crofts, 1956.

Betts, E. A. *Foundations of reading instruction.* New York: American Book, 1956.

Bialer, I. Conceptualization of success and failure in mentally retarded and normal children. *Journal of Personality,* 1961, *29,* 303–320.

Bibace, R. Relationships between perceptual and conceptual cognitive processes. *Journal of Learning Disabilities,* 1969, *2,* 17–29.

Bills, R. E. Non-directive play-therapy with retarded readers. *Journal of Psychology,* 1950, *14,* 246–249.

Birch, H. G., and Belmont, L. Auditory-visual integration, intelligence and reading ability in school children. *Perceptual and Motor Skills,* 1965, *20,* 295–305.

Bleil, G. Evaluating educational materials. *Journal of Learning Disabilities,* 1975, *8,* 19–26.

Bloom, B. S., Englehart, M. D., Furst, E. J., Hill, W. H., and Krathwohl, D. R. *Taxonomy of educational objectives, Handbook I: Cognitive domain.* New York: David McKay, 1956.

Bloom, L. *Language development: Form and function in emerging grammars.* Cambridge, Mass.: MIT Press, 1970.

Bloom, L., Lightbown, P., and Hood, L. Structure and variation in child language. *Monograph of the Society for Research in Child Development,* 1975, *40* (No. 2, Serial No. 60).

Boning, R. A. *Specific skill series.* Rockville Centre, N.Y.: Barnell Loft, 1970.

Bower, E. M., and Lambert, N. M. In-school screening of children with emotional handicaps. In N. J. Long, W. C. Morse, and R. G. Newman (Eds.), *Conflict in the classroom.* Belmont, Calif.: Wadsworth, 1971.

Bowerman, M. Semantic factors in the acquisition of rules for word use and sentence construction. In D. M. Morehead and A. E. Morehead (Eds.), *Normal and deficient child language.* Baltimore: University Park Press, 1976. Pp. 99–180.

Boyd, L., and Randle, K. Factor analysis of the Frostig Developmental Test of Visual Perception. *Journal of Learning Disabilities,* 1970, *3,* 253–255.

Braine, M. The ontogeny of English phrase structure: The first phase. *Language,* 1963, *39,* 1–13.

Brophy, J., and Good, T. *Teacher–child dyadic interaction: A manual for coding classroom behavior.* Austin, Tex.: Research and Development Center, University of Texas, 1969.

Brown, R. *Social psychology.* New York: Free Press, 1965.

Brown, R. *Psycholinguistics.* New York: Free Press, 1970.

Brown, R. *A first language: The early stages.* Cambridge, Mass.: Harvard University Press, 1973.

Brown, R., and Bellugi, U. Three processes in the child's acquisition of syntax. *Harvard Educational Review,* 1964, *34,* 133–151.

Brown, R., and Fraser, C. The acquisition of syntax. *Monograph of the Society for Research in Child Development,* 1964, *29,* 43–79.

Brown, V. L. A basic Q-sheet for analyzing and comparing curriculum materials and proposals. *Journal of Learning Disabilities,* 1975, *8,* 409–416.

Brownell, W. A. Arithmetic readiness as a practical classroom concept. *The Elementary School Journal,* 1951, *52,* 15–22.

Brueckner, L. J. *Diagnostic tests and self-helps in arithmetic.* Los Angeles: California Test Bureau, 1955.

Brueckner, L. J., and Bond, G. L. The diagnosis and treatment of learning difficulties. In E. C. Frierson and W. B. Barbe (Eds.), *Educating children with learning disabilities.* New York: Appleton-Century-Crofts, 1967. Pp. 442–447.

Bruner, J. The ontogenesis of speech acts. *Journal of Child Languages,* 1975, *2,* 1–19.

Bryen, D. N. Issues and activities in language. Unpublished manuscript, Temple University, Philadelphia, 1975.

Buchanan, C. D. *Programmed reading book 4.* New York: McGraw-Hill/Webster Division, 1968.

Buck, N. J. The House–Tree–Person (H-T-P) Test. *Journal of Clinical Psychology,* 1948, *4,* 151–159.

Buffie, E. G., Welch, R. C., and Paige, D. D. *Mathematics: Strategies of teaching.* Englewood Cliffs, N.J.: Prentice-Hall, 1968.

Bullowa, M. The Onset of Speech. Paper presented at Society for Research in Child Development, March 1967. (a)

Bullowa, M. The Start of the Language Process. Paper presented at the Tenth International Congress of Linguists. Bucharest, September 1967. (b)

Burns, P. C. Arithmetic fundamentals for the educable mentally retarded. *American Journal of Mental Deficiency,* 1962, *66,* 57–61.

Burns, P. C. Analytical testing and follow-up exercises in elementary school mathematics. *School Science and Mathematics,* 1965, *65,* 34–38.

Burns, P. C., Broman, B. L., and Wantling, A. L. L. *The language arts in childhood education.* Chicago: Rand McNally, 1971.

Buros, O. K. *The seventh mental measurements yearbook.* Highland Park, N.J.: Gryphon, 1972.

Burton, W. H., Kemp, G. K., Baker, C. B., Craig, I., and Moore, V. *The developmental reading text workbook series.* Indianapolis, Ind.: Bobbs-Merrill, 1975.

Carlson, R. K. *Sparkling words: Two hundred practical and creative writing ideas.* Berkeley, Calif.: Wagner, 1965. (Distributed through the National Council of Teachers of English, Urbana, Ill.)

Carrow, M. A. The development of auditory comprehension of language structure in children. *Journal of Speech and Hearing Disorders,* 1968, *33,* 99–111.

Carrow-Woolfolk, E. *Test for Auditory Comprehension of Language.* Austin, Tex.: Learning Concepts, 1973.

Carrow-Woolfolk, E. *Carrow Elicited Language Inventory.* Austin, Tex.: Learning Concepts, 1974.

Cawley, J. F. Extrapolating the usefulness of instructional materials. Unpublished manuscript, University of Connecticut, Storrs, Conn., 1971.

Cawley, J. F. Learning disabilities in mathematics: A curriculum design for upper grades. Unpublished manuscript, University of Connecticut, Storrs, Conn., 1976.

Cawley, J. F. An instructional design in secondary school mathematics for learning-disabled students. In L. Mann, L. Goodman, and J. L. Wiederholt, *Learning disabilities in the secondary school.* Boston: Houghton Mifflin, 1978.

Cawley, J. F., Burrow, W. H., and Goldstein, H. A. An appraisal of Head Start participants and nonparticipants. Research Report, Contract OEO 4177. Storrs, Conn.: Department of Special Education, University of Connecticut, 1968.

Chalfant, J. C., and Scheffelin, M. A. Central processing dysfunctions in children. Bethesda, Md.: National Institutes of Health, 1969.

Chomsky, N. *Syntactic structures.* The Hague: Mouton, 1957.

Chomsky, N. A review of B. F. Skinner's *Verbal behavior. Language,* 1959, *35,* 26–58.

Chomsky, N., and Halle, M. *The sound pattern of English.* New York: Harper & Row, 1968.

Christopolos, F., and Renz, P. A critical examination of special education programs. *Journal of Special Education,* 1969, *3,* 371–379.

Clark, E. What's in a word? On the child's acquisition of semantics in his first language. In T. E. Moore (Ed.), *Cognitive development and the acquisition of language*. New York: Academic Press, 1973.

Clary, L. M. Tips for testing reading informally in the content areas. *Journal of Reading*, 1976, *20*, 156–157.

Clay, M. M. A syntactic analysis of reading errors. *Journal of Verbal Learning and Verbal Behavior*, 1968, *1*, 434–438.

Cloward, R. D. Studies in tutoring. *Journal of Experimental Education*, 1967, *36*, 25.

Clymer, T. What is "reading"? Some current concepts. In H. M. Robison (Ed.), *The sixty-seventh yearbook of the National Society for the Study of Education*. Chicago: University of Chicago Press, 1968.

Cohen, A. S. Oral reading errors of first grade children taught by a code emphasis approach. *Reading Research Quarterly*, 1974–1975, *10*, 616–650.

Cohen, S. A. Studies in visual perception and reading in disadvantaged children. *Journal of Learning Disabilities*, 1969, *2*, 498–507.

Colarusso, R., and Hammill, D. D. *The Motor-Free Test of Visual Perception*. San Rafael, Calif.: Academic Therapy Publications, 1972.

Coleman, J. C., Berres, F., Hewett, F. M., and Briscoe, W. S. *The deep sea adventure series*. Palo Alto, Calif.: Field Educational Publications, 1962.

Coleman, J. H., and Jungeblut, A. *Reading for meaning*. Philadelphia: Lippincott, 1965.

Connolly, A., Nachtman, W., and Pritchett, E. M. *Key Math Diagnostic Arithmetic Test*. Circle Pines, Minn.: American Guidance Services, Inc., 1976.

Contact maturity: Growing up strong. Englewood Cliffs, N.J.: Scholastic Book Service, 1972.

Coopersmith, R. *The antecedents of self-esteem*. San Francisco: W. H. Freeman, 1968.

Corah, N. L., and Powell, B. J. A factor analytic study of the Frostig Developmental Test of Visual Perception. *Perceptual and Motor Skills*, 1963, *16*, 59–63.

Crabtree, M. *Houston Test of Language Development*. Houston: Houston Press, 1963.

Crandall, V. C., Kathovsky, W., and Crandall, V. J. Children's beliefs in their own control of reinforcement in intellectual–academic achievement situations. *Child Development*, 1965, *36*, 91–109.

Crandell, J. M., Hammill, D. D., Witkowski, C., and Barkovich, F. *The International Journal for the Education of the Blind*, 1968, *18*, 65–68.

Cronbach, L. J. *Educational psychology*. New York: Harcourt, Brace & World, 1970.

Cruickshank, W. M., Bentzen, F. A., Ratzeburg, F. H., and Tannhauser, M. *A teaching method for brain-injured and hyperactive children*. Syracuse, N.Y.: Syracuse University Press, 1961.

Cunningham, P. M. Investigating a synthesized theory of mediated word identification. *Reading Research Quarterly*, 1975–1976, *11*, 127–143.

Cushenberry, D. C. *Reading improvement in the elementary school*. Englewood Cliffs, N.J.: Parker, 1971.

Dale, P. S. *Language development: Structure and function.* New York: Holt, Rinehart and Winston, 1972.

Dale, P. S. *Language development: Structure and function,* 2nd ed. New York: Holt, Rinehart and Winston, 1976.

Darby, G. *The time machine series.* Palo Alto, Calif.: Field Educational Publications, 1966.

Davidson, J. *Using the Cuisenaire rods.* New Rochelle, N.Y.: Cuisenaire, 1969.

Dechant, E. V. *Improving the teaching of reading.* Englewood Cliffs, N.J.: Prentice-Hall, 1964.

Dever, R. B. *TALK (Teaching the American Language to Kids).* Columbus, Ohio: Charles E. Merrill, 1978.

de Villiers, P., and de Villiers, J. A cross-sectional study of the acquisition of grammatical morphemes in child speech. *Journal of Psycholinguistic Research,* 1973, *2,* 267–278.

DiMeo, K. P. *Visual–motor skills: Response characteristic and pre-reading behavior.* Winter Haven, Fla.: Winter Haven Lions Research Foundation, 1967.

Dinkmeyer, D. *Developing understanding of self and others, D-I.* Circle Pines, Minn.: American Guidance Services, Inc., 1970.

Dinkmeyer, D. *Developing understanding of self and others, D-II.* Circle Pines, Minn.: American Guidance Services, Inc., 1973.

Dolce, C. J. The inner city—a superintendent's view. *The Saturday Review,* January 1969, p. 36.

Doll, E. A. *The Preschool Attainment Record.* Circle Pines, Minn.: American Guidance Services, Inc., 1966.

Drew, C. J., Freston, C. W., and Logan, D. R. Criteria and reference in evaluation. *Focus on Exceptional Children,* 1972, *4,* 1–10.

Dubrow, H. C. *Learning to write.* Cambridge, Mass.: Educators Publishing Service, 1968.

Duncan, E. R., Capps, L. R., Dolciani, M. P., Quast, W. G., and Zweng, M. J. *Modern school mathematics: Structure and use K-6.* Boston: Houghton Mifflin, 1970.

Dunn, L. M. *Peabody Picture Vocabulary Test.* Circle Pines, Minn.: American Guidance Services, Inc., 1965.

Dunn, L. M. Minimal brain dysfunction: A dilemma for educators. In E. C. Frierson and W. B. Barbe (Eds.), *Educating children with learning disabilities.* New York: Appleton-Century-Crofts, 1967.

Dunn, L. M. Special education for the mildly retarded—is much of it justifiable? *Exceptional Children,* 1968, *35,* 5–22.

Dunn, L., and Smith, J. O. *Peabody language development kits.* Circle Pines, Minn.: American Guidance Services, Inc., 1966.

Durost, W. Bixler, H. H., Wrightstone, J. W., Prescott, G. A., and Balow, I. W. *Metropolitan Achievement Tests.* New York: Harcourt, Brace & World, 1971.

Durr, W., and Hillerich, R. *Reading skills lab.* Boston: Houghton Mifflin, 1968.

Durrell, D. D. *Improvement of basic reading abilities.* Yonkers, N.Y.: World Book, 1940.

Durrell, D. D. *Durrell Analysis of Reading Difficulty.* New York: Harcourt, Brace & World, 1955.

Dutton, W. H., and Adams, L. J. *Arithmetic for teachers,* Englewood Cliffs, N.J.: Prentice-Hall, 1961.

Ebersole, M., Kephart, N. C., and Ebersole, J. B. *Steps to achievement for the slow learner.* Columbus, Ohio: Charles E. Merrill, 1968.

Edgington, R. But he spelled them right this morning. *Academic Therapy Quarterly,* 1967, *3,* 58–59.

Educational Patterns, Inc. (EPI). *Retrieval system.* Rego Park, N.Y.: 62–83 Woodhaven, 1974.

Engelmann, S., and Bruner, E. C. *Distar: An instructional system.* Chicago: Science Research Associates, 1969. For reading instruction.

Engelmann, S., and Carnine, D. *Distar: An instructional system.* Arithmetic I, II, and III. Chicago: Science Research Associates, 1976.

Engelmann, S., and Osborn, J. *Distar: An instructional system.* Chicago: Science Research Associates, 1970. For language instruction.

Entwisle, D., Forsyth, D., and Muuss, R. The syntactic–paradigmatic shift in children's word association. *Journal of Verbal Learning and Verbal Behavior,* 1964, *3,* 19–29.

Erickson, M. R. A study of a tutoring program to benefit tutors and tutees. Ann Arbor, Mich.: University of Michigan, University Microfilm, 1971. No. 71–16914.

Ervin, S. Imitation and structural change in children's language. In E. Lenneberg (Ed.), *New directions in the study of language.* Cambridge, Mass.: The MIT Press, 1964. Pp. 163–189.

Fairbanks, G. An acoustical study of the pitch of infant hunger wails. *Child Development,* 1942, *13,* 227–232.

Fairbanks, G. An acoustical comparison of vocal pitch in seven- and eight-year-old children. *Child Development,* 1950, *21,* 121–129.

Farr, R., and Anastasiow, N. *Tests of reading readiness and achievement: A review and evaluation.* Newark, Del.: International Reading Association, 1969.

Fasler, J. *Child's series on psychologically relevant themes.* Westport, Conn.: Videorecord Corporation of America, 1971.

Feigenbaum, I. *English now.* New York: New Century, 1970.

Feifel, H., and Lorge, I. Qualitative differences in the vocabulary responses of children. *Journal of Educational Psychology,* 1950, *41,* 1–18.

Fernald, G. *Remedial techniques in basic school subjects.* New York: McGraw-Hill, 1943.

Ferster, C. B., and Skinner, B. F. *Schedules of reinforcement.* New York: Appleton-Century-Crofts, 1957.

Fine, M. J. *The teacher's role in classroom management.* Lawrence, Kans.: Psych-Ed, 1973.

Fisher, B. Group therapy and retarded readers. *Journal of Educational Psychology,* 1953, *44,* 354–360.

Fiske, D. W., and Cox, J. A., Jr. The consistency of ratings by peers. *Journal of Applied Psychology,* 1960, *44,* 11–17.

Fitzgerald, E. *Straight language for the deaf.* Washington, D.C.: Volta Bureau, 1949.

Flanders, N. *Analyzing teacher behavior*. Menlo Park, Calif.: Addison-Wesley, 1970.

Fleming, L., and Snyder, W. U. Social and personal changes following non-directive group therapy. *American Journal of Orthopsychiatry*, 1947, *17*, 101–106.

Fletcher, H. L. Suggestions on correcting left-to-right reversals in reading and writing. In J. Arean (Ed.), *Teaching educationally handicapped children*. San Rafael, Calif.: Academic Therapy Publications, 1967. Pp. 41–48.

Fokes, J. Developmental scale of language acquisition. In B. Stephens (Ed.), *Training the developmentally young*. New York: John Day, 1971.

Fokes, J. *Fokes sentence builder kit*. Boston: Teaching Resources, 1975.

Foster, R., Giddan, J. J., and Stark, J. *Assessment of Children's Language Comprehension Test*. Palo Alto, Calif.: Consulting Psychologists Press, 1973.

Foster, R., Giddan, J. J., and Stark, J. *Visually cued language cards*. Palo Alto, Calif.: Consulting Psychologists Press, 1975.

Fountain Valley Teachers Support System in Mathematics. Huntington Beach, Calif.: R. A. Zweig Associates, 1976.

Freeman, F. W. A new handwriting scale. *Elementary School Journal*, 1959, *59*, 218–221.

Freeman, F. W. *Reference manual for teachers. Grades one through four*. Columbus, Ohio: Zaner-Bloser, 1965.

Frostig, M. Testing as a basis for educational therapy. *Journal of Special Education*, 1967, *2*, 15–34.

Frostig, M. *Movement education: Theory and practice*. Chicago: Follett, 1970.

Frostig, M., and Horne, D. *The Frostig program for the development of visual perception*. Chicago: Follett, 1964.

Frostig, M., Lefever, D. W., and Whittlesey, J. R. B. A developmental test of visual perception for evaluating normal and neurologically handicapped children. *Perceptual and Motor Skills*, 1961, *12*, 383–394.

Frostig, M., and Maslow, P. *Learning problems in the classroom*. New York: Grune & Stratton, 1973.

Frostig, M., Maslow, P., Lefever, D. W., and Whittlesey, J. R. B. *The Marianne Frostig Developmental Test of Visual Perception*. Palo Alto, Calif.: Consulting Psychologists Press, 1964.

Fry, D. The development of the phonological system in the normal and the deaf child. In F. Smith and G. Miller (Eds.), *The genesis of speech*. Cambridge, Mass.: MIT Press, 1966. Pp. 187–206.

Garrett, H. E. *Statistics in psychology and education*. New York: Longmans Green, 1954.

Garrett, H. E. *Testing for teachers*. New York: American Book, 1965.

Gates, A. I. *The Improvement of reading*. New York: Macmillan, 1947.

Gates, A., and Peardon, C. C. *Reading exercises*. New York: Teachers College Press, 1963.

Gattegno, C. *Words in color*. Chicago: Learning Materials, 1962.

Gesell, A. *The first five years of life*. New York: Harper & Row, 1940.

Getman, G. N. *How to develop your child's intelligence*. Leverne, Minn.: G. N. Getman, 1962.

Getman, G. N., and Hendrickson, H. H. The needs of teachers for specialized information on the development of visual–motor skills in relation to academic performance. In W. M. Cruickshank (Ed.), *The teacher of brain injured children*. Syracuse, N.Y.: Syracuse University Press, 1966. Pp. 153–168.

Getman, G. N., Kane, E. R., Halgren, M. R., and McKee, G. W. *Developing learning readiness*. Manchester, Mo.: McGraw-Hill Webster Division, 1968.

Gibson, E. J. Learning to read. *Science*, 1965, *148*, 1066–1072.

Gibson, E. J. The ontogeny of reading. *American Psychologist*, 1970, *25*, 136–143.

Gillingham, A. Correspondance. *Elementary English*, 1958, *35*, 118–122.

Gillingham, A., and Stillman, B. *Remedial training for children with specific disability in reading, spelling, and penmanship*. Cambridge, Mass.: Educators Publishing Service, 1970.

Glavin, J. P., Quay, H. C., Annesley, F. R., and Werry, J. S. An experimental resource room for behavior problem children. *Exceptional Children*, 1971, *38*, 131–137.

Glavin, J. J., Quay, H. C., and Werry, J. S. Behavioral and academic gains of conduct problem children in different classroom settings. *Exceptional Children*, 1971, *37*, 441–446.

Goldman, R., and Fristoe, M. *Goldman–Fristoe Test of Articulation*. Circle Pines, Minn.: American Guidance Services, Inc., 1969.

Goldman, R., Fristoe, M., and Woodcock, R. W. *The Goldman–Fristoe–Woodcock Test of Auditory Discrimination*. Circle Pines, Minn.: American Guidance Services, Inc., 1970.

Goldman, R., Fristoe, M., and Woodcock, R. W. *The Goldman–Fristoe–Woodcock Auditory Skills Test Battery*. Circle Pines, Minn.: American Guidance Services, Inc., 1976.

Goodman, K. S. A linguistic study of cues and miscues in reading. *Elementary English*, 1965, *42*, 639–642.

Goodman, K. S. (Ed.). *The psycholinguistic nature of the reading process*. Detroit: Wayne State University Press, 1968.

Goodman, K. S. Analysis of oral reading miscues: Applied psycholinguistics. *Reading Research Quarterly*, 1969, *5*, 9–30.

Goodman, L. Montessori education for the handicapped. The methods—the research. In L. Mann and D. Sabatino (Eds.), *The second review of special education*. Philadelphia: JSE Press, 1974. Pp. 153–192.

Goodman, L., and Hammill, D. D. The effectiveness of the Kephart–Getman activities in developing perceptual–motor and cognitive skills. *Focus on Exceptional Children*, 1973, *4*, 1–9.

Goodman, L., and Hammill, D. D. *The Basic School Skills Inventory*. Chicago: Follett, 1975.

Goodman, Y. M., Using children's miscues for teaching reading strategies. *The Reading Teacher*, 1970, *23*, 455–459.

Goodman, Y. M. Reading diagnosis—qualitative or quantitative. *The Reading Teacher*, 1972, *26*, 32–37.

Graham, F. K., and Kendall, B. S. Memory-for-Designs Test. *Perceptual and Motor Skills*, 1960, *11*, 147–190.

Grannis, J. C., and Schone, V. *First things*. Pleasantville, N.Y.: Guidance Associates, 1970.

Gray, B. B., and Ryan, B. P. *Monterey language program (Programmed conditioning for language)*. Palo Alto, Calif.: Monterey Learning Systems, 1972.

Greene, H., and Petty, W. *Developing language skills in the elementary school*. Boston: Allyn and Bacon, 1967.

Guilford, J. P. *Fundamental statistics in psychology and education*. New York: McGraw-Hill, 1956. (a)

Guilford, J. P. The structure of intellect. *Psychological Bulletin*, 1956, *53*, 267–293. (b)

Hall, R. V. *Behavior modification: Applications in home and school*. Lawrence, Kans.: H & H Enterprises, 1971. (a)

Hall, R. V. *Behavior modification: Basic principles*. Lawrence, Kans.: H & H Enterprises, 1971. (b)

Hall, R. V. *Behavior modification: The measurement of behavior*. Lawrence, Kans.: H & H Enterprises, 1971. (c)

Hallahan, D. P., and Cruickshank, W. M. *Psychoeducational foundations of learning disabilities*. Englewood Cliffs, N.J.: Prentice-Hall, 1973.

Hammill, D. D. Evaluating children for instructional purposes. *Academic Therapy*, 1971, *4*, 341–353.

Hammill, D. D., Colarusso, R. P., and Wiederholt, J. L. Diagnostic value of the Frostig test: A factor analytic approach. *Journal of Special Education*, 1971, *3*, 279–282.

Hammill, D. D., Goodman, L., and Wiederholt, J. L. Use of the Frostig DTVP with economically disadvantaged children. *Journal of School Psychology*, 1971, *9*, 430–435.

Hammill, D. D., Goodman, L., and Wiederholt, J. L. Visual–motor processes: What success have we had in training them? *The Reading Teacher*, 1974, *27*, 469–478.

Hammill, D. D., and Larsen, S. The relationship of selected auditory perceptual skills and reading ability. *Journal of Learning Disabilities*, 1974, *7*, 429–435. (a)

Hammill, D. D., and Larsen, S. The effectiveness of psycholinguistic training. *Exceptional Children*, 1974, *41*, 5–15. (b)

Hammill, D. D., Larsen S., and McNutt, G. The effects of spelling instruction: A preliminary study. *The elementary school journal*, 1977, *78*, 67–72.

Hammill, D. D., and Wiederholt, J. L. *The resource room: Rationale and implementation*. Philadelphia: Journal of Special Education Press, 1972. (a)

Hammill, D. D., and Wiederholt, J. L. Review of the Frostig Visual Perception Test and the related training program. In L. Mann and D. Sabatino (Eds.), *First review of special education*, Vol. 1. New York: Grune & Stratton, 1972. (b)

Hanna, P. R., Hanna, J. S., Hodges, R. E., and Rudorf, E. H. Phoneme–grapheme correspondences as cues to spelling improvement. Washington, D.C.: Department of Health, Education, and Welfare, 1966.

Hanna, P. R., Hodges, R. E., and Hanna, J. S. *Spelling: Structure and strategies*. Boston: Houghton Mifflin, 1971.

Hanna, R., and Moore, J. T. Spelling—from spoken word to written symbol. _Elementary School Journal_, 1953, _53_, 329–337.

Harris, A. J. Diagnosis and remedial instruction. In H. M. Robinson (Ed.), _The sixty-seventh yearbook of the National Society for the Study of Education_. Chicago: University of Chicago Press, 1968.

Harris, A. J. _How to increase reading ability_, 5th ed. New York: David McKay, 1970.

Harris, T. L., and Herrick, V. E. Children's perception of the handwriting task. In V. E. Herrick (Ed.), _New horizons for research in handwriting_. Madison, Wis.: University of Wisconsin Press, 1963. Pp. 159–184.

Harth, R. Changing attitudes toward school, classroom behavior, and reaction to frustration of emotionally disturbed children through role-playing. _Exceptional Children_, 1966, _33_, 119–120.

Hathaway, S. R., and McKinley, J. L. _Minnesota Multiphasic Personality Inventory_. New York: Psychological Corporation, 1951.

Hawisher, P. _The resource room: Access to excellence_. Lancaster, S.C.: S.C. Region V Educational Service Center, 1975.

Haworth, M. R. _The Primary Visual Motor Test_. New York: Grune & Stratton, 1970.

Heddens, J. W., and Smith, K. J. The readability of elementary mathematics textbooks. _The Arithmetic Teacher_, 1964, _11_, 466–468.

Heilman, A. W. Phonics emphasis approaches. _Perspectives in reading_. Newark, Del.: International Reading Association, 1965.

Herrick, V. E., and Erlebacher, A. The evaluation of legibility in handwriting. In V. E. Herrick (Ed.), _New horizons for research in handwriting_. Madison, Wis.: University of Wisconsin Press, 1963. Pp. 207–237.

Hildreth, G. H., Griffiths, M. L., and McGauvran, M. E. _The Metropolitan Readiness Tests_. New York: Harcourt, Brace & World, 1969.

Hill, F. G. A comparison of Words in Color with the basic readiness program used in the Washington Elementary School District. _Dissertation Abstracts_, 1967, _27_, 3619-A.

Hodges, R. E., and Rudorf, E. H. Searching linguistics for cues for the teaching of spelling. _Elementary English_, 1965, _42_, 529–533.

Hoepfner, R., Strickland, G., Stangel, G., Jansen, P., and Patalino, M. _Elementary school test evaluations_. Los Angeles: Center for the Study of Evaluation, UCLA Graduate School of Education, 1970.

Hollander, E. P. Validity of peer nominations in predicting a distant performance criterion. _Journal of Applied Psychology_, 1965, _49_, 434–438.

Horn, E. Phonetics and spelling. _Elementary School Journal_, 1957, _57_, 424–432.

Hunter, W., and LaFollette, P. _Learning skills series: Arithmetic_. New York: McGraw-Hill, 1976.

Iano, R. P. Shall we disband our special classes? _Journal of Special Education_, 1972, _6_, 167–178.

Ilg, F. L., and Ames, L. B. _School readiness_. New York: Harper & Row, 1965.

Irwin, O. Infant speech: Consonant sounds according to manner of articulation. _Journal of Speech Disorders_, 1947, _12_, 402–404. (a)

Irwin, O. Infant speech: Consonant sounds according to place of articulation. *Journal of Speech Disorders,* 1947, *12,* 397–401. (b)

Irwin, O. Infant speech: Development of vowel sounds. *Journal of Speech and Hearing Disorders,* 1948, *13,* 31–34.

Irwin, O. Speech development in the young child: II. Some factors related to speech development of the infant and young child. *Journal of Speech and Hearing Disorders,* 1952, *17,* 269–279.

Jakobsen, R., and Halle, M. *Fundamentals of language.* The Hague: Mouton, 1956.

Jastak, J. F., and Jastak, S. R. *Wide Range Achievement Test.* Wilmington, Del.: Guidance Associates, 1965.

Johnson, D. J. Educational principles for children with learning disabilities. *Rehabilitation Literature,* 1967, *28,* 317–322.

Johnson, D. J., and Myklebust, H. R. *Learning diabilities: Educational principles and practices.* New York: Grune & Stratton, 1967.

Johnson, D. L., Brekke, B., and Follman, D. Appropriateness of the Motor-Free Visual Perception Test when used with the trainable mentally retarded. *Perceptual and Motor Skills,* 1976, *43,* 1346.

Johnson, M. S., and Kress, R. A. *Informal reading inventories.* Newark, Del.: International Reading Association, 1969.

Junkala, J. Teacher evaluation of instructional materials. *Teaching Exceptional Children,* 1970, *2,* 73–76.

Kaluger, G., and Kolson, C. J. *Reading and learning disabilities.* Columbus, Ohio: Charles E. Merrill, 1969.

Karnes, M. B. *Helping young children develop language skills: A book of activities.* Arlington, Va.: The Council for Exceptional Children, 1968.

Karnes, M. B. *GOAL: Language development—Games oriented activities for learning.* Springfield, Mass.: Milton Bradley, 1976. (a)

Karnes, M. B. *Karnes early language activities.* Champaign, Ill.: GEM, P. O. Box 2339, Station A, 1976. (b)

Katz, J. *The Kindergarten Auditory Screening Test.* Chicago: Follett, 1971.

Katz, J. T., and Fodor, A. The structure of semantic theory. *Language,* 1963, *39,* 170–120.

Kelley, T., Madden, R., Gardner, E., and Rudman, H. *Stanford Achievement Tests.* New York: Harcourt, Brace & World, 1964.

Kephart, N. C. Teaching the child with a perceptual-motor handicap. In M. Bortner (Ed.), *Evaluation and education of children with brain damage.* Springfield, Ill.: Charles C Thomas, 1968. Pp. 147–192.

Kephart, N. C. *The slow learner in the classroom,* 2nd ed. Columbus, Ohio: Charles E. Merrill, 1971.

Kersh, B. Y. Learning by discovery: Instructional strategies. *The Arithmetic Teacher,* 1965, *12,* 414–417.

Kessler, J. W. *Psychopathology of childhood.* Englewood Cliffs, N.J.: Prentice-Hall, 1966.

Kimmell, G. M., and Wahl, J. *The Screening Test for Auditory Perception.* San Rafael, Calif.: Academic Therapy Publications, 1969.

Kirk, S. A. From labels to actions. Selected papers on learning disabilities. Third annual conference of American Association for Children with Learning Disabilities. Tulsa, Okla., 1966. Also in D. Hammill and N. Bartel (Eds.), *Educational perspectives in learning disabilities*. New York: John Wiley, 1971. Pp. 304–313.

Kirk, S. A. *Educating exceptional children*. Boston: Houghton Mifflin, 1972.

Kirk, S. A., McCarthy, J. J., and Kirk, W. *Illinois Test of Psycholinguistic Abilities*. Urbana, Ill.: University of Illinois Press, 1968.

Kliebhan, M. C. *An experimental study of arithmetic problem-solving ability of sixth grade boys*. Washington, D.C.: The Catholic University Press, 1955.

Kohfeldt, J. *Contracts*. Wayne, N.J.: Innovative Educational Support Systems, 1974.

Kopp, F. S. Evaluation of the youth tutoring youth program. Atlanta, Ga.: Atlanta Public Schools, 1972 (ED 075560).

Koppitz, E. M. *The Bender Gestalt Test for Young Children*. New York: Grune & Stratton, 1963.

Kottmeyer, W. *The classroom reading clinic*. St. Louis: McGraw-Hill Webster Division, 1962.

Kottmeyer, W. *Teacher's guide for remedial reading*. New York: McGraw-Hill, 1970.'

Kottmeyer, W., and Claus, A. *Basic goals in spelling*. New York: McGraw-Hill, 1968, 1972.

Kramer, K. *The teaching of elementary school mathematics*. Boston: Allyn and Bacon, 1970.

Kroth, R. The behavioral Q-sort as a diagnostic tool. *Academic Therapy*, 1973, 8, 317–330. (a)

Kroth, R. *Target behavior*. Olathe, Kans.: Select-Ed, 1973. (b)

Lackner, J. R. A developmental study of language behavior in retarded children. In D. M. Morehead and A. E. Morehead (Eds.), *Normal and deficient child language*. Baltimore: University Park Press, 1976. Pp. 181–208.

Lane, P., Pollack, C., and Sher, N. Remotivation of disruptive adolescents. *Journal of Reading*, 1972, 15, 351–354.

Lankford, F. S. What can a teacher learn about a pupil's thinking through oral interviews? *Arithmetic Teacher*, 1974, 21, 26–32.

LaPray, M., and Ross, R. The graded word list: A quick gauge of reading ability. *Journal of Reading*, 1969, 12.

Larsen, S., and Hammill, D. D. The relationship of selected visual perceptual skills to academic abilities. *Journal of Special Education*, 1975, 9, 281–291.

Larsen, S., and Hammill, D. D. *The Test of Written Spelling*. Austin, Tex.: Pro-Ed, 1976.

Laten, S., and Katz, G. *A theoretical model for assessment of adolescents: The ecological/behavioral approach*. Madison, Wis.: Madison Public Schools, Special Educational Services, 1975.

Lazar, M. Individualized reading: A dynamic approach. *Reading Teacher*, 1957, 11, 75–83.

Learning Research and Development Center. *Individually prescribed instruction (IPI)—Mathematics*. Pittsburgh, Pa.: University of Pittsburgh, 1969, rev. 1972.

Lee, L. Developmental sentence types: A method for comparing normal and deviant syntactic development. *Journal of Speech and Hearing Disorders*, 1966, *31*, 311–330.

Lee, L. *Developmental sentence analysis.* Evanston, Ill.: Northwestern University Press, 1974.

Lenneberg, E. H. Language disorders in childhood. *Harvard Educational Review*, 1964, *34*, 152–177.

Lenneberg, E. H. *Biological foundations of language.* New York: John Wiley, 1967.

Lenneberg, E. H., Nichols, I. A., and Rosenberger, E. F. Primitive stages of language development in mongolism. In *Proceedings of the Association for Research in Nervous and Mental Disease*, 1964, *42*, 119–137.

Leonard, R., and Briscoe, W. *The wildlife adventure series.* Palo Alto, Calif.: Field Educational Publications, 1966.

Leopold, W. Patterning in children's language learning. *Language Learning*, 1953–1954, *5*, 1–14.

Lepore, A. A comparison of computational errors between educable mentally handicapped and learning disability children. Unpublished manuscript, University of Connecticut, Storrs, Conn., 1974.

Lerch, H. H., and Hamilton, H. A comparison of a structured-equation approach to problem solving with a traditional approach. *School Science and Mathematics*, 1966, *66*, 241–246.

Lerner, J. W. *Children with learning disabilities.* Boston: Houghton Mifflin, 1976.

Levin, H., Silverman, I., and Ford, B. Hesitations in children's speech during explanation and description. *Journal of Verbal Learning and Verbal Behavior*, 1967, *6*, 560–564.

Levitt, E. E. Results of psychotherapy with children: An evaluation. *Journal of Counseling Psychology*, 1957, *25*, 189–196.

Lewis, M. *Language, thought, and personality in infancy and childhood.* London: G. G. Harrap, 1963.

Lieberman, P. *Intonation, perception, and language.* Research Monograph 38. Cambridge, Mass.: MIT Press, 1967.

Lilly, S. M. Special education: A teapot in a tempest. *Exceptional Children*, 1970, *37*, 43–48.

Limbacher, W. *Dimensions of personality.* New York: Pflaum, 1969.

Lindquist, E., and Hieronymous, A. *Iowa Test of Basic Skills.* New York: Harcourt, Brace & World, 1956.

Lindzey, G., and Borgatta, E. F. Sociometric measurement. In G. Lindzey (Ed.), *Handbook of social psychology.* Reading, Mass.: Addison-Wesley, 1954.

Linn, S. H. Spelling problems: Diagnosis and remediation. *Academic Therapy Quarterly*, 1967, *3*, 62–63.

Lockmiller, P., and Di Nello, M. Words in Color vs. a basal reading program with retarded readers in grade two. *Journal of Educational Research*, 1970, *63*, 330–334.

Long, N. J., and Newman, R. G. Managing surface behavior of children in schools. In N. J. Long, W. C. Morse, and R. G. Newman (Eds.), *Conflict in the classroom.* Belmont, Calif.: Wadsworth, 1971.

Lovitt, T. C. Applied behavior analysis and learning disabilities. Part I. Characteristics of ABA, general recommendations, and methodological limitations. *Journal of Learning Disabilities,* 1975, *8,* 432–443. (a)

Lovitt, T. C. Applied behavior analysis and learning disabilities. Part II: Specific research recommendations and suggestions for practitioners. *Journal of Learning Disabilities,* 1975, *8,* 504–518. (b)

Lowder, R. G. *Perceptual ability and school achievement.* Winter Haven, Fla.: Winter Haven Lions Research Foundation, 1956.

MacNamara, J. Cognitive basis of language learning in infants. *Psychological Review,* 1972, *79,* 1–13.

Maier, H. W. *Three theories of child development.* New York: Harper & Row, 1969.

Mann, L. Perceptual training: Misdirections and redirections. *American Journal of Orthopsychiatry,* 1970, *40,* 30–38.

Mann, L. Psychometric phrenology and the new faculty psychology: The case against ability assessment and training. *The Journal of Special Education,* 1971, *5,* 3–14.

Mann, L. Marianne Frostig Developmental Test of Visual Perception. In O. K. Buros (Ed.), *The seventh mental measurements yearbook.* Highland Park, N.J.: Gryphon, 1972.

Mazurkiewicz, A. J. *New perspectives in reading structure.* New York: Pittman, 1968.

Mazurkiewicz, A. J., and Tanyzer, H. J. *The i/t/a handbook for writing and spelling: Early-to-read i/t/program.* New York: Initial Teaching Alphabet Publications, 1966.

McCall, W. A., and Crabbs, L. M. *Standard lessons in reading.* New York: Teachers College Press, 1961.

McCarthy, D. Language development in children. In L. Carmichael (Ed.), *Manual of child psychology.* New York: John Wiley, 1954. Pp. 492–630.

McGinnis, M. A. *Aphasic children.* Washington, D.C.: Alexander Graham Bell Association for the Deaf, 1963.

McGinnis, M., Kleffner, F., and Goldstein, R. Teaching of asphasic children. *The Volta Review,* 1956, *58,* 239–244.

McIntyre, R. B. Evaluation of instructional materials and programs: Application of a systems approach. *Exceptional Children,* 1970, *37,* 213–220.

McNeill, D. Development of the Semantic System. Paper prepared at the Center for Cognitive Studies, Harvard University, 1965.

McNeill, D. Developmental psycholinguistics. In F. Smith and G. A. Miller (Eds.), *The genesis of language.* Cambridge, Mass.: MIT Press, 1966, Pp. 15–84.

McNeill, D. The development of language. In P. H. Mussen (Ed.), *Carmichael's manual of child psychology,* 3rd ed. New York: John Wiley, 1970. Pp. 1061–1161.

Mecham, M. J., Jex, J. L., and Jones, J. D. *Utah Test of Language Development.* Salt Lake City, Utah: Communication Research Associates, 1967.

Meighen, M., and Pratt, M. *Phonics we use.* Chicago: Lyons & Carnahan, 1964.

Menyuk, P. A preliminary evaluation of grammatical capacity in children. *Journal of Verbal Learning and Verbal Behavior,* 1963, *2,* 429–439.

Menyuk, P. Comparison of grammar of children with functionally deviant and normal speech. *Journal of Speech and Hearing Research,* 1964, *7,* 109–121.

Menyuk, P. Children's learning and recall of grammatical and non-grammatical nonsense syllables. *MIT Quarterly Progress Report,* 1965, *80.*

Menyuk, P. The role of distinctive features in children's acquisition of phonology. *Journal of Speech and Hearing Research,* 1968, *11,* 138–146.

Menyuk, P. *Sentences children use.* Cambridge, Mass.: MIT Press, 1969.

Metreaux, R. Speech profiles of the preschool child—18 to 54 months. *Journal of Speech and Hearing Disorders,* 1950, *15,* 35–53.

Miller, J., and Yoder, D. *Miller-Yoder Test of Grammatical Competence, Experimental Edition.* Madison, Wis.: University of Wisconsin Bookstore, 1972.

Miller, L. K. *Principles of everyday behavior analysis.* Monterey, Calif.: Brooks/ Cole, 1975.

Miller, W., and Ervin, S. The development of grammar in child language. *Monograph of the Society for Research in Child Development,* 1964, *29,* 9–34.

Minskoff, E., Wiseman, D. E., and Minskoff, G. *The MWM program for developing language abilities.* Ridgefield, N.J.: Educational Performance Associates, 1972.

Moerk, E. L. Piaget's research as applied to the explanation of language development. *Merrill-Palmer Quarterly,* 1975, *21,* 151–169.

Montessori, M. *The Montessori method.* New York: Schocken Books, 1964.

Montessori, M. *Dr. Montessori's own handbooks.* New York: Schocken Books, 1965. (a)

Montessori, M. *The Montessori elementary material.* Cambridge, Mass.: Robert Bentley, Inc., 1965. (b)

Morehead, D., and Ingram, D. The development of base syntax in normal and linguistically deviant children. *Journal of Speech and Hearing Research,* 1973, *16,* 330–353.

Moreno, J. L. *Psychodrama.* New York: Beacon House, 1946.

Moreno, J. L. *Who shall survive? Foundations of sociometry, group psychotherapy, and sociodrama,* 2nd ed. New York: Beacon House, 1953.

Mowrer, H. Speech Development in the young child: I. The autism theory of speech development and some clinical applications. *Journal of Speech and Hearing Disorders,* 1952, *17,* 263–268.

Murray, H. A. *Thematic Apperception Test.* Cambridge, Mass.: Harvard University Press, 1943.

Myers, P. I., and Hammill, D. D. *Methods for learning disorders.* New York: John Wiley, 1976.

Myklebust, H. R. Aphasia in childhood. *Journal of Exceptional Children,* 1952, *19,* 9–14.

Myklebust, H. Babbling and echolalia in language theory. *Journal of Speech and Hearing Disorders,* 1957, *22,* 356–360.

Myklebust, H. R. *The psychology of deafness: Sensory deprivation, learning, and adjustments.* New York: Grune & Stratton, 1964.

Myklebust, H. R. *Development and disorders of written language.* New York: Grune & Stratton, 1965.

National Center on Educational Media/Materials for the Handicapped. *National instructional materials information system.* Columbus, Ohio: Ohio State University, 1975.

Nelson, K. Structure and strategy in learning to talk. *Monograph of the Society for Research in Child Development,* 1973, *38* (1–2, Serial No. 149).

Nelson, K. Concept, word, and sentence: Inter-relations in acquisition and development. *Psychological Review,* 1974, *81,* 276–285.

Newcomer, P., and Hammill, D. D. Visual perception of motor impaired children. *Exceptional Children,* 1973, *39,* 335–337. (a)

Newcomer, P., and Hammill, D. D. A visual perception test for motorically handicapped children. *Rehabilitation Literature,* 1973, *34,* 45–56. (b)

Newcomer, P., and Hammill, D. D. *Psycholinguistics in the schools.* Columbus, Ohio: Charles E. Merrill, 1976.

Newcomer, P., and Hammill, D. D. *Test of Language Development (TOLD).* Austin, Tex.: Empiric Press, 1977.

Newland, T. E. An analytical study of the development of illegibilities in handwriting from the lower grades to adulthood. *Journal of Educational Research,* 1932, *26,* 249–258.

Newland, T. E. *The Blind Aptitude Test.* New York: American Foundation for the Blind, Conference on Research on Braille, 1961.

Nihira, K., Foster, R., Shellhaas, M., and Leland, H. *Adaptive behavior scales manual.* Washington, D.C.: American Association on Mental Deficiency, 1969.

Noble, J. K. *Better handwriting for you.* New York: Noble & Noble, 1966.

Nolan, C., and Morris, J. Development and validation of the Roughness Discrimination Test. *International Journal for the Education of the Blind,* 1965, *15,* 1–6.

Norton, J. K., and Norton, M. *Foundation of curriculum building.* New York: Ginn, 1936.

Oakland, T., and Williams, F. *Auditory perception.* Seattle, Wash.: Special Child Publications, 1971.

Ohnmacht, F., and Olson, A. V. Canonical analysis of reading readiness measures and the Frostig DTVP. *Educational and Psychological Measurement,* 1968, *28,* 470–484.

Ohnmacht, F., and Rosen, C. L. Perception, readiness and reading achievement. Paper presented at the International Reading Association. Seattle, Wash., April 1967.

O'Leary, K. D., and Becker, W. C. Behavior modification of an adjustment class: A token reinforcement program. *Exceptional Children,* 1967, *33,* 637–642.

Olson, A. V. Factor analytic studies of the Frostig Developmental Test of Visual Perception. *Journal of Special Education,* 1968, *2,* 429–433.

Olson, D. On a theory of instruction: Why different forms of instruction result in similar knowledge. *Interchange,* 1972, *3,* 9–24.

Olson, D. R. Language acquisition and cognitive development. In H. C. Haywood (Ed.), *Social-cultural aspects of mental retardation.* New York: Appleton-Century-Crofts, 1970. Pp. 113–202.

Otto, W., and McMenemy, R. A. *Corrective and remedial teaching.* Boston: Houghton Mifflin, 1966.

Otto, W., McMenemy, R. A., and Smith, R. J. *Corrective and remedial teaching,* 2nd ed. Boston: Houghton Mifflin, 1973.

Pace, A. Understanding and the ability to solve problems. *The Arithmetic Teacher*, 1961, *8*, 226–233.

Painter, G. The effect of a rhythmic and sensory motor activity program on perceptual motor spatial abilities of kindergarten children. *Exceptional Children*, 1966, *33*, 113–119.

Palomares, V. H., and Ball, G. *Human development program*. La Mesa, Calif.: Human Development Training Institute, 1974.

Parisi, D., and Antinucci, F. Lexical competence. In G. B. Flores d'Arcais and W. J. M. Levelt (Eds.), *Advances in psycholinguistics*. Amsterdam: North-Holland, 1970. Pp. 197–210.

Parker, D., and Scannell, G. *SRA reading laboratories*. Chicago: Science Research Associates, 1961.

Perline, I. H., and Levinsky, D. Controlling behavior in the severely retarded. *American Journal of Mental Deficiency*, 1968, *73*, 74–78.

Personke, C., and Yee, A. A model for the analysis of spelling behavior. *Elementary English*, 1966, *43*, 278–284.

Personke, C., and Yee, A. The situational choice and the spelling program. *Elementary English*, 1968, *45*, 32–37.

Peters, L. J. *Prescriptive teaching*. New York: McGraw-Hill, 1965.

Peterson, H. A., Brener, R., and Williams, L. L. *SYNPRO (Syntax Programmer)*. St. Louis: Mercury Co./Division of EMT Labs, 1974.

Piaget, J. *The language and thought of the child*. London: Routledge & Kegan Paul, 1959.

Piaget, J. *Language and thought in the child*. New York: Meridian Books, New American Library, 1960.

Piaget, J. *The language and thought of the child*. New York: World Publishing, 1962.

Piaget, J. *The child's conception of number*. New York: W. W. Norton, 1965.

Piaget, J. *Six psychological studies*. New York: Vintage Books, Random House, 1967.

Piaget, J., and Inhelder, B. *The child's conception of space*. London: Routledge & Kegan Paul, 1963.

Piaget, J., and Inhelder, B. *La Psychologie de l'enfant*. Paris: Presses Universitaires de France, 1967.

Pitman, J. The future of the teaching of reading. Paper presented at the Educational Conference of the Educational Records Bureau, New York City, October 30–November 1, 1963.

Poole, I. Genetic development of articulation of consonant sounds in speech. *Elementary English Review*, 1934, *2*, 159–161.

Pooley, R. C. Dare schools set a standard in English usage? *English Journal*, 1960, *49*, 179–180.

Prescriptive materials retrieval system. Torrance, Calif.: B. L. Winch & Associates, P.O. Box 1185, 1973.

Pugh, B. *Steps in language development for the deaf*. Washington, D.C.: Volta Bureau, 1955.

Pumpfrey, D., and Elliot, C. D. Play therapy, social adjustment and reading attainment. *Journal of Educational Research*, 1970, *12*, 183–193.

Quay, H. C., and Peterson, D. R. Manual for the Behavior Problem Checklist. Champaign, Ill.: Children's Research Center, 1967. Mimeographed.

Quick, A. D., Little, T., and Campbell, A. *Project MEMPHIS*. Belmont, Calif.: Fearon Publishers, 1973.

Rambeau, J., and Rambeau, N. *The Morgan Bay mysteries*. Palo Alto, Calif.: Field Educational Publications, 1962.

Rambeau, J., Rambeau, N., and Gullett, J. *The Jim Forest readers*. Palo Alto, Calif.: Field Educational Publications, 1959.

Ramming, J. Using the chalkboard to overcome handwriting difficulties. *Academic Therapy*, 1968, *4*, 49–51.

Raths, L. E., Wasserman, S., Jonas, A., and Tothstein, A. M. *Reader's Digest science reader*. Pleasantville, N.Y.: Reader's Digest Services, 1963.

Raths, L. E., Wasserman, S., Jonas, A., and Tothstein, A. M. *Teaching for thinking: Theory and application*. Columbus, Ohio: Charles E. Merrill, 1967.

Raths, L. E., Wasserman, S., Jonas, A., and Tothstein, A. M. *Reading skill builders*. Pleasantville, N.Y.: Reader's Digest Services, 1968.

Redl, F. The concept of a therapeutic milieu. *American Journal of Orthopsychiatry*, 1959, *29*, 721–734.

Redl, F., and Wattenberg, W. *Mental hygiene in teaching*. New York: Harcourt, Brace & World, 1959.

Redl, F., and Wineman, D. *The aggressive child*. New York: Free Press, 1957.

Reger, R., Schroeder, W., and Uschold, K. *Special education: Children with learning problems*. New York: Oxford University Press, 1968.

Reinert, H. J. *Children in conflict*. St. Louis: Mosby, 1976.

Reisman, F. K. *A guide to the diagnostic teaching of arithmetic*. Columbus, Ohio: Charles E. Merrill, 1972.

Reynolds, H. H. Efficacy of sociometric rating in predicting leadership success. *Psychological Reports*, 1966, *19*, 35–40.

Roach, E. G., and Kephart, N. C. *Purdue Perceptual Motor Survey*. Columbus, Ohio: Charles E. Merrill, 1966.

Robbins, M. P., and Glass, G. V. The Doman–Delacato rationale: A critical analysis. In J. Hellmuth (Ed.), *Educational therapy*. Seattle, Wash.: Special Child Publications 1968.

Roberts, G. H. The failure strategies of third grade arithmetic pupils. *Arithmetic Teacher*, 1962, *15*, 442–446.

Rogers, D. C., Ort, L. L., and Serra, M. C. *Word book*. Chicago: Lyons & Carnahan, 1970.

Rorschach, H. *The Rorschach Psychodiagnostic Plates*. New York: Grune & Stratton, 1954.

Rotter, J. B. *Social learning and clinical psychology*. Englewood Cliffs, N.J.: Prentice-Hall, 1954.

Russell, D., Clymer, T., Gates, D., and McCullough, C. *Wings to adventure*. Lexington, Mass.: Ginn, 1956.

Russell, D. H., and Russell, E. F. *Listening aids through the grades*. New York: Teachers College Press, 1959.

Sabatino, D. A. The construction and assessment of an experimental test of auditory perception. *Exceptional Children*, 1969, *36*, 729–737.

Sabatino, D. A. An evaluation of resource rooms for children with learning disabilities. *Journal of Learning Disabilities*, 1971, *4*, 84–93.

Samuels, J., Begy, G., and Chen, C. C. Comparison of word recognition speed and strategies of less skilled and more highly skilled readers. *Reading Research Quarterly*, 1975–1976, *11*, 72–86.

Schoolfield, L., and Timberlake, J. *The phonovisual method*. Washington, D.C.: Phonovisual Products, 1960.

Scott, L., Immerzeel, G., and Wiederanders, D. *Ginn elementary mathematics series*. Lexington, Mass.: Ginn, 1972.

Seashore, C. E., Lewis, D., and Saetveit, J. *Seashore Test of Musical Talents*. Camden, N.J.: Educational Department, Radio Corporation of America, 1939.

Semel, E. M. *Sound-order-sense: A developmental program in auditory perception*. Chicago: Follett, 1970.

Serio, M. Cursive writing. *Academic Therapy*, 1968, *4*, 67–70.

Shirley, M. The first two years: A study of 25 babies. *Institute of Child Welfare Monographs*, Series 7, Vol. 2, 1933, pp. 139–141.

Shulman, L. S. Perspectives on the psychology of learning and the teaching of mathematics. In W. R. Houston (Ed.), *Improving mathematics education for elementary school teachers*, A Conference Report, 1967. Pp. 23–37.

Simon, L. *Individualized computation skills series*. New York: Holt, Rinehart and Winston, 1975.

Simon, S. B., Howe, L. W., and Kirschenbaum, H. *Values clarification*. New York: Hart, 1972.

Sinclair-de-Zwart, H. Developmental psycholinguistics. In D. Elkind and J. H. Flavell (Eds.), *Studies in cognitive development: Essays in honor of Jean Piaget*. New York: Oxford University Press, 1969. Pp. 315–336.

Skinner, B. F., and Krakower, S. *Handwriting with writing and see*. Chicago: Lyons & Carnahan, 1968.

Slingerland, B. H. *Slingerland Screening Tests for Identifying Children with Specific Language Disability*, 2nd ed. Cambridge, Mass.: Educators Publishing Service, 1970.

Sloan, W. *The Lincoln–Oseretsky Motor Development Scale*. Chicago: Stoelting, 1954.

Slobin, D. Grammatical transformations and sentence comprehension in childhood and adulthood. *Journal of Verbal Learning and Verbal Behavior*, 1966, *5*, 219–227.

Slobin, D. I. Universals of grammatical development in children. In G. B. Flores d'Arcais and W. J. M. Levelt (Eds.), *Advances in psycholinguistics*. Amsterdam: North-Holland, 1970. Pp. 174–186.

Slobin, D. I. *Psycholinguistics*. Glenview, Ill.: Scott, Foresman, 1971.

Slobin, D. I. Cognitive prerequisites for the development of grammar. In C. A. Ferguson and D. I. Slobin (Eds.), *Studies of child language development*. New York: Holt, Rinehart and Winston, 1973. Pp. 175–208.

Slosson, R. I. *Slosson Drawing Coordination Test*. East Aurora, N.Y.: Slosson Educational Publications, 1967.

Smith, F. *Understanding reading*. New York: Holt, Rinehart and Winston, 1971.

Smith, J. *Creative teaching of the language arts in the elementary school.* Boston: Allyn and Bacon, 1967.

Smith, J. O. Group language development for educable mental retardates. *Exceptional Children,* 1962, *29,* 95–101.

Smith, N. B. *Reading instruction for today's children.* Englewood Cliffs, N.J.: Prentice-Hall, 1963.

Smith, N. B. *Be a better reader.* Englewood Cliffs, N.J.: Prentice-Hall, 1968.

Smith, R. M. *Clinical teaching: Methods of instruction for the retarded.* New York: McGraw-Hill, 1968.

Smith, R. M. (Ed.). *Teacher diagnosis of educational difficulties.* Columbus, Ohio: Charles E. Merrill, 1969.

Soar, R., Soar, R., and Ragosta, M. *The Florida climate and control system.* Gainesville, Fla: Insitiue for the Development of Human Resources, College of Education, University of Florida, 1971.

Spache, G. D. *Investigating the issues of reading disabilities.* Boston: Allyn and Bacon, 1976.

Spalding, R. B., and Spalding, W. T. *The writing road to reading.* New York: William Morrow, 1962.

Special Education Instructional Materials Center. *Instructional materials and resource material available to teachers of exceptional children and youth.* Austin, Tex: Special Education Instructional Materials Center, University of Texas, 1972.

Spivak, G., and Spotts, J. *The Devereux Child Behavior Rating Scale.* Devon, Pa.: Devereux Foundation, 1966.

Spivak, G., Spotts, J., and Haimes, P. E. *The Devereux Adolescent Behavior Rating Scale.* Devon, Pa.: Devereux Foundation, 1967.

Spivak, G., and Swift, M. *The Elementary School Behavior Rating Scale.* Devon, Pa.: Devereux Foundation, 1967.

Sprague, R. Learning difficulties of first grade children diagnosed by the Frostig visual perception tests: A factor analytic study. *Dissertation Abstracts,* 1965, *25,* 4006–A.

Spraldin, J. E. Assessment of speech and language of retarded children: The Parsons Language Scales. *Journal of Speech and Hearing Disorders.* Monograph Supplement 10, 1963, 8–31.

SRA Educational Assessment Laboratory. *Mastery: An evaluation tool.* Chicago: Science Research Associates, 1975.

Starkel, J. P. Demonstration of reliability and validity of the Criterion Test of Cursive Penmanship. Unpublished Master's thesis in special education. The University of Kansas, Lawrence, Kans., 1975.

Steffe, L. P. The relationship of conservation of numerousness to problem-solving abilities of first-grade children. *The Arithmetic Teacher,* 1968, *15,* 47–52.

Stephens, T. M. *Directive teaching of children with learning and behavioral handicaps.* Columbus, Ohio: Charles E. Merrill, 1970.

Stephens, W. B. Piaget and Inhelder: Application of theory and diagnostic techniques to the area of mental retardation. *Education and Training of the Mentally Retarded,* 1966, *1,* 75–86.

Stephens, W. B. A Piagetian approach to arithmetic for the mentally retarded. Paper presented at the International Meeting of the Council for Exceptional Children. Miami, April 1971.

Stern, C. *The structural reading series.* Syracuse, N.Y.: Singer, 1963.

Stern, C. *Structural arithmetic.* Boston: Houghton Mifflin, 1965.

Sternberg, L. *Patterns Recognition Skills Inventory.* Northbrook, Ill.: Hubbard Scientific Co., 1976.

Stone, C. R. *Progress in primary reading.* St. Louis: Webster, 1950.

Sulzbacker, S. I., and Hauser, J. E. A tactic for eliminating disruptive behavior in the classroom: Group contingent consequences. *American Journal of Mental Deficiency,* 1968, *73*, 88–90.

Systems FORE. Tucson, Ariz.: J. K. E. Enterprises, P.O. Box 802, 1972–1973.

Templin, M. C. *Certain language skills in children: Their development and interrelationships.* Minneapolis, Minn.: University of Minnesota Press, 1957.

Templin, M. C., and Darley, F. L. *The Templin–Darley Tests of Articulation.* Iowa City, Iowa: Bureau of Educational Research and Service, State University of Iowa, 1960.

Thomas, J. L. Tutoring strategies and effectiveness: A comparison of elementary age tutors and college age tutors. *Dissertation Abstracts,* 1972, *32,* 3580–A.

Thorndike, E. L. Handwriting. *Teachers College Record,* 1910, *11,* 83–175.

Thorndike, E. L. Reading as reasoning: A study of mistakes in paragraph reading. *Journal of Educational Research,* 1917, *8,* 323–332.

Thorndike, E. L., and Lorge, I. *A teacher's workbook of 30,000 words.* New York: Bureau of Publications, Teacher's College, Columbia University, 1944.

Thorndike, R. L., and Hagen, E. Measurement and evaluation in psychology and education. New York: John Wiley, 1969.

Thorpe, L. P., Clark, W. W., and Tiegs, E. W. *California Test of Personality Manual.* Los Angeles: California Test Bureau, 1942.

Thorpe, L. P., Lefever, D. W., and Naslund, R. A. *SRA achievement series in arithmetic.* Chicago: Science Research Associates, 1969.

Tiegs, E. W., and Clark, W. W. *California Arithmetic Test.* Los Angeles: California Test Bureau, 1970.

Treacy, J. P. The relationship of reading skills to the ability to solve arithmetic problems. *Journal of Educational Research,* 1944, *38,* 86–96.

Trieschman, A. E. Understanding the stages of a typical temper tantrum. In A. E. Trieschman, J. K. Whittaker, and L. K. Brendtro (Eds.), *The other 23 hours.* Chicago: Aldine, 1969.

Ullmann, L. P., and Krasner, L. *A psychological approach to abnormal behavior.* Englewood Cliffs, N.J.: Prentice-Hall, 1969.

Urban, W. H. *The Draw-A-Person Test.* Los Angeles: Western Psychological Corporation, 1963.

Valett, R. E. *The remediation of learning disabilities: A handbook of psycho-educational resource programs.* Belmont, Calif.: Fearon Publishers, 1967.

Van Riper, C. *Speech correction: Principles and practices.* Englewood Cliffs, N.J.: Prentice-Hall, 1963.

Van Riper, C. *Speech correction: Principles and methods.* Englewood Cliffs, N.J.: Prentice-Hall, 1972.

Van Witsen, B. *Perceptual training activities handbook.* New York: Teachers College Press, 1968.

Venezky, R. L., and Calfee, R. C. The reading competency model. In H. Singer and R. B. Ruddell (Eds.), *Theoretical model and processes of reading.* Newark, Del.: International Reading Association, 1970, 273–291.

Wadsworth, H. O. A motivational approach toward the remediation of learning-disabled boys. *Exceptional Children,* 1971, *38,* 33–42.

Walker, H. M. *Walker Problem Behavior Checklist.* Los Angeles: Western Psychological Corporation, 1970.

Watson, B., and Van Etten, C. Materials analysis. *Journal of Learning Disabilities,* 1976, *9,* 408–416.

Weber, R. M. The study of oral reading errors: A survey of the literature. *Reading Research Quarterly,* 1968, *4,* 96–119.

Weber, R. M. A linguistic analysis of first-grade reading errors. *Reading Research Quarterly,* 1970, *5,* 427–451.

Wechsler, D. *Wechsler Intelligence Scale for Children.* New York: Psychological Corporation, 1949.

Weener, P., Barritt, L. S., and Semmel, M. I. A critical evaluation of the ITPA. *Exceptional Children,* 1967, *33,* 373–380.

Weinberg, J. S., Deighton, L. C., and Sanford, A. B. *The Macmillan reading spectrum.* New York: Macmillan, 1964.

Weiner, P. S. A revision of the Chicago Test of Visual Discrimination. *Elementary School Journal,* 1968, *65,* 330–337.

Weiner, P. S., Wepman, J. M., and Morency, A. S. A test of visual discrimination. *Elementary School Journal,* 1965, *65,* 330–337.

Weinstein, G., and Fantini, M. D. *Toward humanistic education: A curriculum of affect.* New York: Praeger, 1970.

Weir, R. *Language in the crib.* The Hague: Mouton, 1962.

Weir, R. *Language in the crib.* The Hague: Mouton, 1963.

Weir, R. Some questions on the child's learning of phonology. In F. Smith and G. Miller (Eds.), *The genesis of language.* Cambridge, Mass.: MIT Press, 1966. Pp. 153–168.

Wepman, J. M. *Auditory Discrimination Test.* Chicago: Language Research Associates, 1958.

West, P. V. *Manual for the American Handwriting Scale.* New York: Palmer, 1957.

West, W. W. *Developing writing skills.* Englewood Cliffs, N.J.: Prentice-Hall, 1966.

Westerman, G. *Spelling and writing.* San Rafael, Calif.: Dimensions, 1971.

Wiederholt, J. L. Predictive validity of Frostig's constructs as measured by the Developmental Test of Visual Perception. *Dissertation Abstracts,* 1971, *33,* 1556–A.

Wiederholt, J. L., and Hammill, D. D. Use of the Frostig–Horne perception program in the urban school. *Psychology in the Schools,* 1971, *8,* 268–274.

Wiederholt, J. L., Hammill, D. D., and Brown, V. *The resource teacher: A guide to effective practices.* Boston: Allyn and Bacon, 1978.

Williams, J. P. Learning to read: A review of theories and models. *Reading Research Quarterly*, 1973, *8*, 121–146.

Wilson, J. W. The role of structure in verbal problem solving. *The Arithmetic Teacher*, 1967, *14*, 486–497.

Wilson, M. S. *Wilson initial syntax program.* Cambridge, Mass.: Educators Publishing Service, 1973.

Woltmann, A. G. The use of puppetry in therapy. In N. J. Long, W. C. Morse, and R. G. Newman (Eds.), *Conflict in the classroom.* Belmont, Calif.: Wadsworth, 1971. Pp. 223–227.

Woodcock, R. W. *Peabody rebus reading program.* Circle Pines, Minn.: American Guidance Services, Inc., 1967.

Worthen, B. R. A comparison of discovery and expository sequencing in elementary mathematics instruction. *Research in Mathematics Education.* Washington, D.C.: The National Council of Teachers of Mathematics, 1967. Pp. 44–59.

Yee, A. The generalization controversy on spelling instruction. *Elementary English*, 1966, *43*, 154–161.

Zaner-Bloser staff. *Evaluation scale.* Columbus, Ohio: Zaner-Bloser, 1968.

Author Index

Subject Index